Workers and Employers

Documents on Trade Unions and Industrial Relations in Britain
Since the Eighteenth Century

Edited by

J. T. WARD

and

W. HAMISH FRASER

M

Introduction, selection and editorial matter © J. T. Ward and
W. Hamish Fraser 1980

First published 1980 by
THE MACMILLAN PRESS LTD
London and Basingstoke
Associated companies in Delhi Dublin
Hong Kong Johannesburg Lagos Melbourne
New York Singapore and Tokyo

Printed in Great Britain by
LOWE AND BRYDONE PRINTERS LIMITED
Thetford, Norfolk

British Library Cataloguing in Publication Data

Workers and employers.
  1. Industrial relations–Great Britain–
History–Sources
  I. Ward, John Towers   II. Fraser, William
Hamish
  331'.0941   HD8390

ISBN 0–333–15412–6
ISBN 0–333–15413–4 Pbk

Workers and Employers

Contents

To

KAY and HELEN

Acknowledgements

The authors and publishers wish to thank the following who have kindly given permission for the use of copyright material:

Amalgamated Union of Engineering Workers for extracts from their Union Journals, 1966 and 1974; Birmingham City Libraries for the extract from the letter from Wall to Rennie from the Boulton and Watt Collection; British Institute of Management for extracts from *The Making of Scientific Management*, II (1949), by L. F. Urwick and E. F. L. Brech; The British Library of Political and Economic Science for the extract from the *Minutes of the Conference of Almagamated Trades*; Cambridge University Press Ltd for extracts from *Wages and Income in U.K. Since 1860* by A. L. Rowley (1937) and *Industrial Relations in a British Car Factory* by G. Clack (University of Cambridge, Dept of Applied Economics, Occasional Paper, No. 9); The Controller of H.M. Stationery Office for the letter from George Salmond to D. Cleghorn and the letter from John Greig to the Lord Advocate; The Council of the Scottish History Society for the extract from the *Minutes of the Edinburgh Trades Council 1859–1873* (1968) ed. Ian MacDougall; Aidan Crawley and Times Newspapers Ltd for an extract from *Signpost to Success* (1957) reprinted in the *Sunday Times* (6–27 January 1957); The Daily Telegraph Ltd for an extract from an article in the *Daily Telegraph* (27 May 1952); Faber and Faber Ltd for an extract from *Sir James Sexton, Agitator. The Life of the Dockers' M. P.* by Sir James Sexton; Fabian Society for an extract from *Industrial Relations: Sweden Shows the Way* by J. Cooper, Fabian Research Series 235; The Financial Times Ltd for an extract from an article in the *Financial Times* (27 November 1974); Furniture, Timber and Allied Trades Union for extracts from the Trades Union Congress 1940 Award 'Relations Between Unions' Statement; General and Municipal Workers' Union for extracts from *NUGMW Journal 1955*, *Evidence to Royal Commission on Trade Unions 1966* and *Why an Incomes Policy?*; Guardian Newspapers Ltd for an extract from *Trades Union Congress 1965* by P. Jenkins; William Heinemann Ltd for an extract from *Winston S. Churchill II* Companion Part II (1969), by R. S. Churchill; Lawrence & Wishart Ltd for extracts from *Revolt on the Clyde* by W. Gallacher and *Serving My Time* and *Trade Unionists –*

What Next? by H. Pollitt; Liverpool City Libraries and Liverpool Trades Council for the extract from the letter from Robert Applegarth to Charles Williams; National Union of Mineworkers for extracts from their published reports of 1936, 1943, 1944 and 1945; National Union of Public Employees for extracts from *Five Years Review 1939; Public Employees Journal March/April 1951; The Challenge of New Unionism, 1963* and *Public Employee, October 1970*; Policy Studies Institute for an extract from *The Structure and Organisation of British Trade Unions*; Sheffield University Library for extracts from *The Mundella–Leader Correspondence in the Mundella Papers*; Society of Graphical and Allied Trades for an extract from the General Rules; Times Newspapers Ltd for an extract from a Law Report in *The Times* (22 January 1964), and a news report on the Electrical Trades Union from the *Sunday Times* (10 May 1953); Trades Union Congress for extracts from TUC Statements and Reports; Transport and General Workers Union for extracts from *TGWU The Union, Its Work and Problems* (1939).

Every effort has been made to trace all the copyright holders but if any have been inadvertently overlooked the publishers will be pleased to make the necessary arrangement at the first opportunity.

Abbreviations

AEU	Amalgamated Engineering Union
ASCJ	Amalgamated Society of Carpenters and Joiners
ASE	Amalgamated Society of Engineers
ASLEF	Associated Society of Locomotive Engineers and Firemen
ASRS	Amalgamated Society of Railway Servants
ASCJ	Amalgamated Society of Carpenters and Joiners
ASW	Amalgamated Society of Woodworkers
AUEFW	Amalgamated Union of Engineering and Foundry Workers
AUEW	Amalgamated Union of Engineering Workers
CBI	Confederation of British Industries
DATA	Draughtsmen and Allied Trades' Association
ETU	Electrical Trades' Union
FBI	Federation of British Industries
GRWU	General Railway Workers' Union
ICI	Imperial Chemical Industries
IRLR	Industrial Relations Law Reports
IRSF	Inland Revenue Staff Federation
ISKTC	Iron, Steel and Kindred Trades' Confederation
LTC	London Trades Council
MFGB	Miners' Federation of Great Britain
NAFTA	National Amalgamated Furnishing Trades' Association
NALGO	National Association of Local Government Officers
NAPSS	National Association for the Promotion of Social Science
NASDS	National Amalgamated Stevedores and Dockers' Society
NATSOPA	National Society of Operative Printers and Assistants
NEDC	National Economic Development Council
NIRC	National Industrial Relations Court
NUGMW	National Union of General and Municipal Workers
NUJ	National Union of Journalists
NUM	National Union of Mineworkers
NUPE	National Union of Public Employees
NUR	National Union of Railwaymen

Parl. Debs	Hansard Parliamentary Debates
PP	British Parliamentary Papers
RC	Royal Commission
RCA	Railway Clerks' Association
SC	Select Committee
TA	Typographical Association
TUC	Trades Union Congress
TGWU	Transport and General Workers' Union
WEA	Workers' Educational Association

Introduction

The study of labour history has developed rapidly in recent years. Learned societies debate the subject; learned journals are devoted to it; University and other classes attempt to study it. A plethora of studies, ranging from the superb to the trivial and from the academically argued to the polemically contrived, has been published. A serious and important branch of Clio's craft has come of age.

However, despite the development of wide interest in the history of labour and industrial relations, teachers and students alike have long complained about the dearth of accessible documentary tools for their trade. Certainly, some collections of material have appeared from time to time. But we believe that a comprehensive collection may now be of value.

In selecting extracts from a wide range of published and other material we have observed some self-imposed rules. From the start, we determined that we would not present an annotated general history of British industrial relations; instead, editorial comment has been kept to a minimum, to allow the documents to 'speak for themselves'. Secondly, we have intentionally avoided broadening our theme to comprehend what some writers have called 'the working-class movement'. We have generally eschewed politics, except where it inevitably impinged on our central theme.

Of course, any selection rests upon personal choice. In preparing this book, we have reluctantly (and sometimes even sadly) decided to delete or abbreviate long-cherished and carefully transcribed documents. Our aim has been to produce a fair and balanced collection of material which may be useful as a source book to everyone interested in a theme which fascinates us.

While the editorial decisions inevitably remain our responsibility, we have to thank very many people, too numerous to mention individually by name, who have given us generous help over the years. To some of our colleagues in the University of Strathclyde, to many officials and members of trade unions and trades councils, to many managers, industrialists, teachers and lecturers, to many other friends and not least to our students we owe sincere thanks for helpful advice and suggestions which have helped to contour our approach to the subject. We hope that they may understand our inability to acknowledge the kindness of each and every one of them.

We are deeply indebted to Mr Derick Mirfin of Macmillan for his long-sustained encouragement and tolerant forbearance as our labours were elongated, and to Sarah Mahaffy who finally saw the book to press. We also owe our deep gratitude to our typists, Miss Catherine Summerhill and Mrs Elizabeth Thrippleton, who patiently deciphered an often difficult manuscript. Finally, we are grateful for the understanding patience of our wives and children during the long gestation of this book.

J. T. W.
W. H. F.

Table of Contents

1. Roots and Origins

2. *The Turbulent Years, 1825–42*

3. *Towards Acceptance, 1843–67*

4. *Investigation and Vindication, 1867–75*

5. *The Unskilled*

6. *The Growth of Collective Bargaining*

7. The Militant Years

8. *The First World War and After*

9. *The Years of Crises*

12. *The Fifties*

13. *The Sixties*

14. *The Search for a Solution*

1. *Roots and Origins*

As Sidney and Beatrice Webb declared in their great *History of Trade Unionism* (1894), 'Strikes are as old as history itself', and wherever a situation existed in which an employer employed more than one worker there was the possibility of these workers combining to exert pressure on their employer. Such early organisations had but a brief existence, and it is not until the eighteenth century that substantial evidence of the existence of permanent organisations of journeymen is to be found. However, even ephemeral unions were a cause of concern to the authorities, and as early as 1381 the corporation of the City of London decreed 'that no person should make congregations, alliances, or covins of the people, privily or openly', particularly 'those belonging to the trades'. Action was taken against journeymen's organisations, but evidence of continued activity is plentiful in court records. In 1387 a group of journeymen cordwainers was charged with making 'congregations, or unions, or sects', and in 1396 a group of saddlers was accused of using its semi-religious fraternity for trade purposes (1).

(1) H.T. Riley, *Memorials of London and London Life in the XIIIth, XIVth and XVth Centuries* (1868) [20 Rich. II, AD 1396. Letter-book H, fo. ccix]

Whereas there had arisen no small dissension and strife between the masters of the trade of Saddlers, of London, and the serving-men, called *yomen*, in that trade; because that the serving-men aforesaid, against the consent, and without leave, of their masters, were wont to array themselves all in a new and like suit once in the year, and oftentimes held divers meetings, at Stratford and elsewhere without the liberty of the said city, as well as in divers places within the City; whereby many inconveniences and perils ensued to the trade aforesaid; and also, very many losses might happen thereto in future times, unless some quick and speedy remedy should by the rulers of the said city be found for the same:—therefore the masters of the said trade, on the 10th day of the month of July, in the 20th year etc., made grievous complaint thereon to the excellent men, William More, Mayor, and the Aldermen of the City aforesaid, urgently entreating that, for the reasons before mentioned they would deign to send for Gilbert Dustone, William Gylowe, John Clay, John Hiltone, William Berigge, and Nicholas Mason, the then governors of the serving-men aforesaid; to appear before them on the 12th day of July then next ensuing.

1

And thereupon, on the same 10th day of July, precept was given to John Parker, serjeant of the Chamber, to give notice to the same persons to be here on the said 12th day of July etc. Which governors of the serving-men appeared, and, being interrogated as to the matters aforesaid, they said that time out of mind the serving-men of the said trade had had a certain Fraternity among themselves, and had been wont to array themselves all in like suit once in the year, and, after, meeting together at Stratford, on the Feast of the Assumption of the Blessed Virgin Mary [15 August], to come from thence to the Church of St. Vedast, in London, there to hear mass on the same day, in honour of the said glorious virgin.

But the said masters of the trade asserted to the contrary of all this, and said that the fraternity, and the being so arrayed in like suit, among the serving-men, dated from only thirteen years back, and even then had been discontinued of late years; and that under a certain feigned colour of sanctity, many of the serving-men in the trade had influenced the journeymen among them, and had formed covins thereon, with the object of raising their wages greatly in excess; to such an extent, namely, that whereas a master in the said trade could before have had a serving-man or journey-man for 40 shillings or 5 marks yearly, and his board, now such a man would not agree with his master for less than 10 or 12 marks, or even 10 pounds, yearly; to the great deterioration of the trade.

During Tudor and Stuart times, as industry expanded, the State began to play an increasing role in regulating conditions of work and wages. With the decline in the influence and importance of craft guilds, the State, to a large extent, took over their role. Legislation in the 1550s restricted the number of looms a person could own and forbade the use of the gig-mill. In 1563, under the Statute of Artificers, the regulation of conditions of work in the major part of existing industry was made the responsibility of the crucial figure in Elizabethan administration, the justice of the peace (2), and seventeenth-century legislation built on this measure (3).

(2) An Act Touching Divers Orders for Artificers, Labourers, Servants in Husbandry and Apprentices, 1563, 5 Eliz. c. iv, *Statutes of the Realm*, IV

II No person after the aforesaid last day in September . . . shall be retained, hired or taken into service to work for any less time than for one whole year in any of the sciences . . . or arts of clothiers, woollen cloth weavers, tuchers, fullers, cloth workers, shearmen, dyers, brewers, hosiers, tailors, shoemakers, tanners, pewterers, bakers, brewers, glovers, cutlers, smiths, furriers, curriers, saddliers, spurriers, turners, cappers, hat-makers, or feltmakers, bowyers, fletchers, arrowhead-makers, butchers, cooks, or millers.

III Every person being unmarried and every other person being under the age of thirty years that after the feast of Easter next shall marry, and having been brought up in any of the said arts . . . or that hath exercised any of them by the space of three years or more, and not having lands . . . copyhold or freehold of an estate or inheritance or for term of lives of the clear yearly value of 40s nor being worth of his own goods the clear value of £10 . . . nor being retained with any person in husbandry or in any of the aforesaid arts . . . nor in any other art, nor in household or in any office with any nobleman, gentleman or others . . . nor having a convenient farm or other holding in tillage whereupon he may employ his labour, shall (during the time that he shall so be unmarried or under the age of 30 years), upon request made by any person using the art or mystery wherein the said person so required hath been exercised as is aforesaid, be retained and shall not refuse to serve according to the tenor of this Statute upon the pain and penalty hereafter mentioned.

iv No person which shall retain any servant shall put away his said servant, and no person retained according to this Statute shall depart from his master, mistress or dame before the end of his term, upon the pain hereafter mentioned, unless it be for some reasonable cause to be allowed before two Justices of Peace, or one at least. . . .

xi And for the declaration what wages servants, labourers and artificers, either by the year or day or otherwise, shall receive, be it enacted, that the justices of the peace of every shire . . . and the sheriff of that county if he conveniently may, and every mayor, bailiff or other head officer within any city . . . shall before the 10th day of June next coming, and afterwards yearly at ever general sessions first to be holden after Easter, calling unto them such discreet and grave persons of the said county or city as they shall think meet, and conferring together respecting the plenty or scarcity of the time and other circumstances necessary to be considered, having authority within the limits of their several commissions to rate and appoint the wages as well of such of the said artificers . . . or any other labourer, servant or workman. . . .

(3) An Act Empowering Justices to Fix Minimum Rates of Payment, 1603, 1 Jas I, c. 6 *Statutes of the Realm*, iv

And whereas the said act [(2) *supra*] hath not, according to the true meaning thereof, been duly put in execution, whereby the rates of wages for poor artificers, labourers and other persons whose wages were meant to be rated by the said act, have not been rated and proportioned according to the plenty, scarcity, necessity, and respect of the time, which was politicly intended by the said act, by reason that ambiguity and question have arisen and been made whether the rating of all manner artificers, workmen and workwomen, his and their wages, other than such as by some statute and law have been rated, or else such as did work about husbandry, should or might be rated by the said law; Forasmuch as the said law hath been found beneficial for the commonwealth, be it enacted by authority of this present parliament, that the said statute, and the authority by the same statute given to any person or persons for assessing and rating of wages, and the authority to them in the said act committed, shall be expounded and construed, and shall by force of this act give authority to all persons having any such authority to rate wages of any labourers, weavers, spinsters, and workmen or workwomen whatsoever, either working by the day, week, month, year, or taking any work at any person or persons' hands whatsoever, to be done in great or otherwise. . . .

And furthermore be it enacted by the authority aforesaid, that if any clothier or other shall refuse to obey the said order, rate or assessment of wages as aforesaid, and shall not pay so much or so great wages to their weavers, spinsters, workmen or workwomen as shall be so set down rated and appointed, according to the true meaning of this act, that then every clothier and other person or persons so offending shall forfeit and lose for every such offence, to the party aggrieved, ten shillings. . . .

Similar legislation was passed in Scotland. Whereas in England it very largely fell into disuse during the eighteenth century, in Scotland it seems to have been applied, at least in some areas, throughout the century.

(4) C. A. Malcolm, *The Minutes of the Justices of the Peace for Lanarkshire 1707-1723* (Edinburgh: Scottish History Society, 1931)

Lanark, Tuesday, seventh August one thousand seven hundred and sixteen, being a General Meeting and Quarter Session of the said Justices.

The said Commissioners and Justices of the Peace for the said shire of Lanark, assembled for the time in pursuance of their instructions concerning the time and manner of hiring domestick servants, and concerning the ordinary hire, wages, and fees of workmen, labourers and servants, and the pryces of craftsmens work – haveing seriously advised and considered the same, do therefore order and appoint the said time and manner of hireing domestick servants; the said hire, wages and prices in manner following, viz.:– . . .

(xxvi) Item, A mason is not to have above a mark Scots, without meat or drink, and half a mark, with meat and drink, for a days service. Young boys and prentises are to be paied according as their work shall deserve.

(xxvii) Item, A wright is not to have above twelve shillings, without meat and drink, and six shillings, with meat and drink, for a days service.

(xxviii) Item, A barrowman is not to have above twelve shillings, without meat and drink, and three shillings, without [*sic*] meat and drink, for a days work.

(xxix) Item, A thacher of houses, who is so designed for his constant trade in that service, is not to have above ten shilling Scots, without meat and drink, for a days service.

(xxx) Item, A taylour, getting his meat in the house, is not to have above fourty pennies for a days work.

(xxxi) Item, The daily wages to be appointed for craftsmen and labourers in the Articles above written, are understood to be due only from the first of March to the last of September, but betwixt the first of October and the last of Febriwary the said daily wages are to be diminished, respective, in the sixth part, because of the winter season and shortness of the day – except such as work with candle light, in which case they are to have the full wages above exprest.

(xxxii) Item, A plough wright, for makeing of a plough, is not to have above a mark Scots.

(xxxiii) Item, It is ordained that the respective pryces aforesaid, both for craftsmen and servants, shall be in full satisfaction of all bounties, rewards, morning and four hours drinks, sowing of corns, beer lintseed, or any other thing which formerly has been given to servants or to craftsmen.

(xxxiv) Item, That no master give, nor servant, workmen, harvest shearer or craftsmen shall receive, any greater fees, pryces or wages than is above exprest, with certification if they shall faill herein, they shall incur the penalty of the equivalent of the fee, pryce or wages so given and received, contrair to the tenor of the several articles above written, *toties quoties*, both master, servant harvest shearer and craftsmen, and a fourth part thereof to be disposed upon by the said Justices of the Peace as they shall think fitt and expedient, attour imprisonment at the discretion of the Justices.

(xxxv) Item, that all masters take notice that if they shall not, from time to time, satisfy and pay their tennants fees and wages, as the same shall become due as they are respectively and particularly above mentioned, upon complaint thereof the said master shall be compelled to pay the said fees, by and attour the damnages (to be modified by two of the Justices of the Peace) sustained by the said servants for the want of their fees and wages, and that summarly without any tedious or long proces of law.

From the early decades of the eighteenth century there was an increasing number of complaints by employers that their journeymen were combining against them. Frequently such combinations were merely for the purpose of strike action, but the social gathering of workmen from the same trade at particular public houses readily provided a nucleus for continuous organisation. As in the case of the London tailors such meeting places had by 1720 developed into 'houses of call' where tailors went to hear of vacant situations (5). In the case of the printers the organisational unit was the 'chapel', and since at least the seventeenth century printers' chapels had been laying down working rules for their printing houses. As Benjamin Franklin was to discover when he came to work in London in the 1720s, the 'chapel' had ways of ensuring its rules were obeyed (6). In such an old craft as Norwich worsted weaving, a sympathetic divine considered a more traditional form of organisation appropriate (7).

(5) F. W. Galton, *Select Documents Illustrating the History of Trade Unionism: The Tailoring Trade* (1896): 'The Case of the Master Taylors Residing within the Cities of London and Westminster. . . . Humbly offer'd to the consideration of Parliament (1720)'. [The result was the Act for Regulating the Journeymen Taylors within the Weekly Bills of Mortality (1722), 7 Geo. I, c. 13]

The Journeymen Taylors in and about the cities of London and Westminster, to the number of seven thousand and upwards, have lately entered into a combination to raise their wages, and leave off working an hour sooner than they used to do; and for the better carrying on their design, have subscribed their respective names in books prepared for that purpose, at the several houses of call or resort, (being publick houses in and about London and Westminster) when they use, and collect considerable sums of money to defend any prosecution against them.

At this time, there are but few of them come to work at all, and most of those that do, insist upon, and have, twelve shillings and ninepence per week (instead of ten shillings and ninepence per week, the usual wages), and leave off work at eight of the clock at night (instead of nine, their usual hour, time out of mind), and very great numbers of them go loitering about the town, and seduce and corrupt all they can meet: to the great hindrance and prejudice of trade. . . .

This combination of the Journeymen Taylors is and may be attended with many very ill consequences: inasmuch as the publick is deprived of the benefit of the labour of a considerable number of the subjects of this kingdom, and the families of several of these journeymen thereby impoverished, and likely to become a charge and burthen to the publick: And the very persons themselves who are under this unlawful combination, choosing rather to live in idleness, than to work at their usual rates and hours, will not only become useless and burthensome, but also very dangerous to the publick; and are of very ill example to journeymen in all other trades; as is sufficiently seen in the Journeymen Curriers, Smiths, Farriers, Sail-makers, Coach-makers, and artificers of divers other arts and mysteries, who have actually entered into confederacies of the like nature; and the Journeymen Carpenters, Bricklayers, and Joyners have taken some steps for that purpose, and only wait to see the event of others. . . .

As to the said houses of call, or publick-houses, there a great number of them in London and the suburbs, where these journeymen taylors frequently meet and use, and spend all or the greatest part of the moneys they receive for their wages; and the masters of these houses of call support, incourage and abet these journeymen in their unlawful combinations for raising their wages, and lessening their hours.

The hours now in being for regulating of artificers, labourers, and servants, were made in the fifth of Queen Elizabeth, and might be well adapted for those times; but not altogether so proper for the trade of London and Westminster, etc., as it is now carry'd on.

Therefore, the masters humbly hope this honourable house will take such measures, by passing of a law for redress of the publick grievances aforesaid, or grant such other relief as in their great wisdoms shall seem meet.

(6) *Works of the late Celebrated B. Franklin: Consisting of His Life, by Himself, and Essays* (Edinburgh, 1808)

On my entrance I worked at first as a pressman, conceiving that I had need of bodily exercise, to which I had been accustomed in America, where the printers work alternately as compositors and at the press. I drank nothing but water. The other workmen, to the number of about fifty, were great drinkers of beer. . . .

My fellow pressman drank every day a pint of beer before breakfast, a pint with bread and cheese for breakfast, one between breakfast and dinner, one at dinner, one again about six o' clock in the afternoon, and another after he had finished his day's work. This custom appeared to me abominable: but he had need, he said, of all his beer, in order to aquire strength to work.

At the end of a few weeks, Watts having occasion for me above stairs as a compositor, I quited the press. The compositors demanded of me garnish money afresh. This I considered as an imposition, having already paid below. The master was of the same opinion, and desired me not to comply. I thus remained two or three weeks out of the fraternity. I was consequently looked upon as excommunicated; and whenever I was absent, no little trick that malice could suggest was left unpractised upon me. I found my letters mixed, my pages transposed, my matter broken, etc. etc. all of which was attributed to the spirit that haunted the chapel, and tormented those who were not regularly admitted. I was at last obliged to submit to pay, notwithstanding the protection of the master; convinced of the folly of not keeping up a good understanding with those among whom we are destined to live.

(7) J. C., DD, *The Weaver's Pocket Book: or Weaving Spiritualized* (Dundee, 1766)

Lastly, I observe, That hardly any trades will maintain their glory, without some government; every particular tradesman having neither wit nor honesty enough to be a law to himself. In all considerable trades, therefore, prudent statesmen thought fit to make corporations, where the multitude are under the inspection, rule, and government of the most experienced, wise, and discreet men of that occupation. And most trades, which to any considerable degree multiply tradesmen, either have such governors, or in all short time come to nothing for want of them. . . .

Lastly, I observe, that in all trades, when tradesmen multiply to any great number, the trade never thrives long without a prudent regulation and government, all men having not (as I said before) either wit or honesty enough to be a law to themselves, nor doth the trade, unless the governours be discreetly chosen. 2, Unless they justly discharge their trust. To this purpose, ordinarily such tradesmen are left to chuse their own governours, as being best acquainted with the trade, and the persons that have most skill in it, and have best approved their honesty in the managery of it.

By the eighteenth century legislation on wages was not offering the protection to workers which had been originally intended, and the process of getting adjustment of rates obtaining was slow if, as in the case of the tailors, it required petition to the House of Commons (8). In addition, by the second half of the century the position of the craftsmen in many trades was being eroded as new workers or half-trained workers from the country moved into the urban crafts. Employers sought to take advantage of that explosion of demand which was such an important trigger of the Industrial Revolution, and combinations of workmen seemed a hindrance to growth. In old trades such as tailoring or in new ones such as steam-engine making, employers, seeing new and expanding markets, sought to reduce costs (9).

(8) Galton, *Select Documents* . . . , 'The Case of the Journeymen Taylors and Journeymen Staymakers, Residing within the Cities of London and Westminster, and Weekly Bills of Mortality', presented to the House of Commons 28 Jan. 1752.

Since the making the said Act [see (5) *supra*], the price of labour, and wages, in most trades and businesses, are much increased, occasioned by the dearness of provisions and other accidents; whereof the Master Taylors were so sensible, that the greatest part and most eminent among them for several years last past, have paid their journeymen two shillings and sixpence a day all the year.

The Justices of the Peace in London and Middlesex, at their respective general Quarter-Sessions of the Peace, have, upon the application as well of the said Master Taylors, as of their journeymen, made several alterations as to the said journeymen's wages, and their hours of work.

From Midsummer, until some time after Michaelmas, in every year, the journeymen taylors in general have little or no work, and are not employed in the whole, above thirty-two weeks in the year; which, at 2/6 a day, doth not exceed, one week with another, 9/– a week: which any taylors who employ at some times in the year twenty or thirty men, at other times but eight or ten, and sometimes none: And as for the number of men in the said business, any gentleman may be satisfied thereof, who will but consider that the mourning occasioned by the melancholy death of His Royal Highness the late Prince of Wales was completed, both as to town and country orders, in three weeks' time; and even tradesmen were served in one month.

Many Master Taylors, in order to have their work done cheap, get a great number of young, raw, and unexperienced lads out of the country, who, for better instructions, are glad to work at low prices; and, by such means, great numbers of the best and most experienced journeymen taylors are forced to go into all parts of the kingdom, to the great prejudice of themselves, their wives and children; whereby the business is not so well done as formerly in London and Westminster; and the trade every year declines through the avarice of some Master Taylors, who, the more effectually to facilitate their encroachments on the journeymen's labour, most fallaciously insinuate that they only want to be relieved from being obliged to pay 2/6 a day to every journeyman, if ever so bad workman; a necessity they never laboured under: And the journeymen humbly submit it to the consideration of every impartial person, whether (considering the great variety in the Genius of men) it is not practicable, or at least very inequitable, by any positive law to put an equal value on every man's labour;

and more especially to put such a restriction on one particular business only. But, even supposing a necessity for it, the rate must be proportioned according to the merits of that part of the trade called workmen; otherwise there will be no room for improvement, no encouragement for emulation, no need for endeavours to excel; under which disadvantage the trade must unavoidably droop and decay, to its utter ruin. Indeed, it may be said, what must they do that are not workmen? To that we may justly answer, that there is no law to hinder such from agreeing with masters according to their merit: And it would be a great danger and injury to the trade, to cramp it by depriving workmen of their deserts.

(9) James Watt to John Rennie, Birmingham, 2 July 1786, Boulton and Watt Collection, Birmingham Reference Library

Dear sir,

I would have answered yours of the 28th sooner but having been obliged to attend as a Commissioner in the valuation of some lands to be occupied by the Canal had it not in my power to do it sooner.

I am very sorry to learn the rebellion of the Journeymen at such a critical time, however it should on no account be given way to – I recommend to you as I have done before to employ carpenters for every thing they can do and when you meet with a tractable hand to engage him and to make it an article of Agreement with all your men that they shall not under a heavy penalty become members of the Millwright Club nor attend the meetings of the same while they are your servants. The Masters should prosecute the journeymen for an unlawful combination and take advice of some good Lawyer on that head.

There are many young Scotch Cabinet Makers and joiners come up to London who have not completely learnt their trade and would be willing to engage with you on moderate terms and the more moderate the better servants they will prove for they will have less to spend in idleness. . . .

Combination persisted among many groups. A typical example of a cotton spinners' society was the Friendly Associated Cotton Spinners founded at Oldham in 1796, the rules of which were approved by Salford Quarter Sessions in 1797.

(10) W. A. Appleton, *Trade Unions. Their Past, Present and Future* (1925), Rules of the Friendly Associated Cotton Spinners

> We'll friendly join
> As Rose and Vine
> We'll spin our Threads with equal Twine,
> Which showeth plain we good design.

. . . We humbly conceive that every unprejudiced mind admires and applauds those actions which flow from a desire to promote the good of others; and the highest and most exquisite pleasures arise from a consciousness of having acted in conformity to the dictates of kind and good affections. Therefore, to sweeten the disposition, restrain vice, allay discord, promote virtue, establish social and domestic happiness, to relieve the sick and infirm, we have agreed to the following Articles and Regulations, to which we subscribe our names. . . .

17. That no member of this society shall instruct any person in the art of cotton spinning (except his own children, and paupers who receive relief from overseers of the poor) until such person has paid the sum of one guinea thereto, exclusive of entrance money and weekly subscription. . . .

28. That any member cursing, swearing, or using bad language tending thereto, or rasing disputes about religion or politics, or speaking disrespectfully of the State and the laws of the nation, His Majesty, or either House of Parliament, any officer or magistrate, or anything to disturb the order of the nation, or the society at any meeting, for every offence shall be excluded.

In 1799 London master millwrights petitioned the Commons against the 'dangerous combination of journeymen millwrights'. They could probably have had redress in the courts against what, in common law, were conspiracies 'in restraint of trade', but, like other groups of employers during the century, they preferred to have the backing of a statute forbidding combination in their particular trade. A Select Committee recommended legislation 'to prevent Unlawful Combinations of workmen employed in the Millwright Business'. However, at the suggestion of William Wilberforce, this was abandoned in favour of a more all-embracing measure, which prohibited all combinations. The Combination Act of 1799, amended in 1800, remained in force until 1824 and allowed summary proceedings to be taken against combining workmen before two magistrates.

(11) Combination Act, 1800, 39 and 40 Geo. III, c. 106

II . . . No journeyman, workman or other person shall at any time after the passing of this Act make or enter into, or be concerned in the making or entering into any such contract, covenant or agreement, in writing or not in writing . . . and every . . . workman . . . who after the passing of this Act, shall be guilty of any of the said offences, being thereof lawfully convicted upon his own confession, or oath or oaths of one or more credible witness or witnesses, before any two Justices of the Peace . . . shall, by order of such Justices, be committed to and confined in the common gaol, within his or their jurisdiction, for any time not exceeding 3 calendar months, or at the discretion of such Justices shall be committed to some House of Correction within the same jurisdiction, there to remain and to be kept to hard labour for any time not exceeding 2 calendar months.

III . . . Every . . . workman . . . who shall at any time after the passing of this Act enter into any combination to obtain an advance of wages, or to lessen or alter the hours and duration of the time of working, or to decrease the quantity of work, or for any other purpose contrary to this Act, or who shall, by giving money, or by persuasion, solicitation or intimidation, or by any other means, wilfully and maliciously endeavour to prevent any unhired or unemployed journeyman or workman, or other person wanting employment in such manufacture, trade or business, from hiring himself to any manufacturer or tradesman, or person conducting any manufacture, trade or business, or who shall for the purpose of obtaining an advance of wages, or for any other purpose contrary to the provisions of this Act, wilfully and maliciously decoy, persuade, solicit, intimidate, influence or prevail, or attempt or endeavour to prevail, on any journeyman or workman, or other person hired or employed in any such manufacture, trade or business, to quit or leave his work, service or employment, or who shall wilfully and maliciously hinder or prevent any manufacturer or tradesman, or other person, from employing in his or her manufacture, trade or business, such journeyman, workman or other persons as he or she shall think proper, or who, being hired or employed, shall, without any just or reasonable cause, refuse to work with any other journeyman or workman employed or hired to work therein, and who shall be lawfully convicted of the said offences, upon his own confession, or the oath or oaths of one or more credible witness or witnesses, before any two Justices of the Peace for the county . . . shall, by order of such Justices, be committed to . . . gaol for . . . any time not exceeding 3 calendar months; or otherwise be committed to some House of Correction . . . for any time not exceeding 2 calendar months.

No more than common-law and eighteenth-century statutes did the Combination Acts prevent workmen from continuing to combine. Some sought to maintain an organisation under cover of a friendly society (12), since friendly societies were deliberately encouraged by Parliament. Others used their legal right of combining to petition Parliament for redress of grievances and the enforcement of legislation to prevent the encroachments on the traditional customs and wages of their trade which industrialisation brought (13, 14). Yet other societies of workmen seem to have existed quite openly as social clubs that could readily be adapted to trade purposes (15). Such groups regularly attempted to maintain an image of respectability (16, 17, 18).

(12) 'Articles of Agreement. Made, concluded and agreed upon by the Amicable and Brotherly Society of Journeymen Millwrights, held at the *Red Lion, Clements Lane* [crossed out in original] Swan in Fish St. Hill, City of London, this twelfth day of October, 1801, in pursuance of Act of Parliament, passed in the thirty second year of his present Majesty, intituled "An Act for the Encouragement and Relief of Friendly Societies".'

Whereas, we whose names are hereunto subscribed have formed and united ourselves into an Amicable and Brotherly Society for the mutual good and benefit of each other, and considering the many Uncertainties of life and fortune by means of which we may by lingering illness be afflicted with any bodily disease or by the Infirmities of Age be rendered incapable of providing for ourselves and families, we do hereby agree to the several Articles, Rules, Orders and

Restrictions hereafter mentioned, and also to be subject to such Orders, Alterations and Amendments therein as shall or may be made at any Time or Times, hereafter pursuant to the Act of Parliament made for the Relief and Encouragement of Friendly Societies.

First. It is agreed that this Society shall be called the Amicable and Brotherly Society of Journeymen Millwrights, that it shall not be confined to any Limited Number of Members, but that no one shall be admitted a Member who is not a Journeyman Millwright *who has served a legal apprenticeship to the said Trade or Business and at the time of his Admission shall work for some Master or Masters who is or are entitled to use exercise and carry on the said Trade and Business of a Millwright* [crossed out in the original with the marginal note 'This has the appearance of an improper combination'].

(13) *Commons Journals* (17 July 1806) Report on Calico Printers' Petition

Your committee have naturally endeavoured to ascertain the causes of those discontents, and, as far as they have been able to collect from the minutes of evidence referred to them, they find it has arisen principally from the multiplication of apprentices. That this has gone to an extent, and that the disproportion of apprentices to journeymen exists to a degree, far beyond that understood to prevail in any other mechanical profession whatever, appears to your committee in several instances. In one instance, that of the shop of Berry and Co. of Lancashire, they find that 55 apprentices were employed, and only two journeymen; in another, that of the shop of Tod and Co. of Dumbarton, there were 60 apprentices, and only two journeymen. Such a disproportion, your committee conceive, must strike as extraordinary any one in the least degree acquainted with the custom of the trade.

The practice of introducing such an increased number of apprentices, which commenced about the year 1790, does not appear from the minutes of evidence to have proceeded from any scarcity of hands to supply the demands of the masters, or make up the work required; on the contrary, it appears that in the course of the period when this excessive multiplication of apprentices went on, a number of journeymen were seeking in vain for employment.

With regard to the multiplication of apprentices, while your committee declare that they are not friendly to the idea of imposing any restrictions upon trade, they are ready to state that the inclination of their minds is this, that either all restrictions ought to be abolished, and the masters and journeymen left to settle matters between themselves, or an additional restriction ought to be introduced to counteract the evils obviously resulting from the restrictions which already exist. This restriction your committee mean of course to apply to apprentices; and if a precedent were wanted to justify such a measure, they would refer to the case of the silk weavers, and that of other trades, which are to be found on the Statute Book. In the instance of the silk weavers, no more than two apprentices can be legally taken by any master, whatever may be the number of his journeymen; and yet, since the enactment of this law, no scarcity of hands has ever been complained of in that flourishing branch of trade. Indeed, throughout all the mechanical professions, it is, as far as has come to the knowledge of any of the members of your committee, the general rule, that no master shall have more than two or three apprentices at the most. This general rule is conceived to be established through an understanding between the masters and the journeymen.

(14) *Commons Journals* (26 Feb 1807): Petition of Journeymen Cotton Weavers

A petition of the several Journeymen Cotton Weavers resident in the counties of Lancaster, Chester, York, and Derby, was presented and read; setting forth, that the petitioners suffer great hardships by the reduction of their wages, and that whenever the demand for goods becomes slack, many master manufacturers adopt the expedient of reducing wages, thereby compelling the petitioners, in order to obtain a livelihood, to manufacture greater quantities of goods at times when they are absolutely not wanted, and that great quantities of goods so manufactured are sacrificed in the market at low prices, to the manifest injury of the fair dealer, and the great oppression of the petitioners, who are reduced one half of the wages they are justly entitled to, and in many cases, are not able to earn more than nine shillings per week: And therefore praying, That leave may be given to bring in a bill to regulate from time to time, the wages of the petitioners.

(15) W. Taylor, *An Answer to Mr. Carlile's Sketches of Paisley* (Paisley, 1809)

The Paisley operatives are of a free communicative disposition. They are fond to inform one another in anything respecting trade; and in order to receive information in a collective capacity they have, for a long course of years, associated in a friendly manner in societies denominated clubs. These in general consist of from thirty to fifty members; though often not above half of those attend regularly. They meet once in a week; a few on Thursday; but mostly on the Saturday evening. They are to be found in every decent public house. Their laws are few. The chairman and collector include all their office bearers. These continue in office only one month. Every candidate before admission must be recommended by two or more of the members. When met the first hour is devoted to promiscuous conversation. At eight the newspapers of the day are produced. They are read aloud by one of the company. This occupies nearly an hour. At nine o'clock the chairman calls for silence; then the report of trade is heard. The chairman reports first what he knows or what he has heard of such a manufacturing house or houses, as wishing to engage operatives for such fabric or fabrics; likewise the price. Then each reports as he is seated; so in the period of an hour not only the state of trade is known, but any difference that has taken place between manufacturers and operatives. In one word anything respecting trade, even mountings &c. After the labour of the week, here are three hours devoted to useful information for the trifling sum of 6d. each. These clubs are academies of the fancy work, and the tribunals to which imposition trambles to appeal. What the merchant of manufacturer is on the 'change, so the operative is in his club.

(16) Society of (London) Journeymen Brushmakers, *Articles* (1806)

No person shall be admitted a member who is not well affected to his present Majesty and the Protestant Succession, and in good health and of a respectable character.

(17) Keighley Royal Benefit Society, *Rules and Regulations* (Leeds, 1812)

That each member shall, when he enters into this society, be under the age of forty-five years; and should any member of this society die and leave a family, and the overlookers of the poor think the relief allowed from this society to be a sufficient maintenance for such family, that the steward shall have power to withhold the payment of such relief granted by their society, till some other mode of payment can be established to prevent the overseers of the poor from having any benefit of this society, but that the family of the deceased member may receive every benefit arising therefrom.

(18) R. M. Lancaster, *Leeds Typographical Society . . . Centenary, 1810–1910: A Souvenir* (Leeds, 1910) Rules and Regulations of the Leeds Typographical Society (1815)

1.—That no person be admitted a member of the Society unless he produce satisfactory proof of a legal servitude, or unless some member shall vouch for the same. . . .

6.—When any member, who has been six months in this Society, shall be rendered incapable of working, by sickness or lameness, he shall receive, during such incapacity five shillings per week; and if more than one member be sick at the same time, an extra subscription shall be levied (if necessary) to make a proper allowance to each. No member shall receive the sick allowance until he has been ill a week, but it shall be reckoned from the beginning of his sickness. No member shall receive benefit for any hurt or illness occasioned by fighting, or diseases contracted by improper conduct. If any member continue sick for Four Months, and his sickness is likely to be of longer duration, then he shall receive such sum as the society shall determine. No member shall be entitled to relief, unless he give proper notice.

Among some groups of workers, faced, in many cases, with a threat to their position from the introduction of machinery, moderate methods gave way to violence, and from 1811, disturbances occurred in the Midlands, Yorkshire and Lancashire. In some cases, the disturbances were no more than what Professor E. J. Hobsbawm has called 'collective bargaining by riot', a traditional pre-trade-union method of exerting pressure on recalcitrant employers. However, in other cases, the mobbing and destruction of property was aimed at those machines which threatened the livelihood of numbers of workers (19, 20).

(19) *Annual Register for 1811* (1812)

The public tranquillity had been little disturbed in England, notwithstanding the pressure of the times, during the greatest part of the year; but before it terminated, a series of disorders broke out which soon put on a serious aspect, and have been the prelude of a riotous and mischievous disposition in a large tract of the manufacturing districts, the effects of which still continue to be the occasion of much trouble and alarm. Their commencement was in the neighbourhood of Nottingham, the hosiers of which town having been obliged, from the decrease of demand for their manufactures, to discharge many of their workmen, much distress necessarily ensued for want of employment. This was enhanced by the new application of a certain wide frame in the weaving of stockings, whereby a considerable saving of manual labour was produced, and a consequent further diminution of hands. On November the 10th, a number of weavers, assembling near Nottingham, began forcibly to enter houses in which were frames of this kind, and destroy them. On the 11th they appeared before the house of a manufacturer at Bullwell, which was barricaded by the owner, who had also armed his men in its defence. On attempting to break in the mob was fired at, and one person killed. This roused them to fury and in increased numbers they renewed their attack, made an entry, the family having escaped to save their lives, and burnt everything in the house. This act seemed a signal for more extensive outrages, which spread over the circumjacent towns and villages. Though the obnoxious frames were the chief object of their hostility, they began to declare enmity with millers, corn-dealers, and all who they supposed instrumental in raising the price of provisions. The magistrates at length found it necessary to call in the aid of the military, but before any number of them could be collected, much further mischief was done. And after a sufficient force was stationed at Nottingham to suppress any open violations of the peace in that vicinity, the destruction of frames still continued, as it could be easily effected by small parties, which finished their business, and dispersed before notice was given of their assembling. Their proceedings appeared to be directed by a spirit of system that rendered them the more dangerous. The rioters assumed the name of *Luddites,* and acted under the authority of an imaginary *Captain Ludd,* which name seems to have signified not one individual, but a secret committee of management. The spirit of tumult spread into the neighbouring counties of Derby and Leicester, in the manufacturing parts of which many frames were destroyed during the month of December, though Nottinghamshire still continued the principal scene of mischief, and an advance of pay to the workmen had not the desired effect of restoring order. Through the course of this year, however, the evil was confined to the districts of the hosiery manufacture.

(20) Dr Robert Taylor, *Letters on the Subject of the Lancashire Riots in the Year 1812* (Bolton, 1813)

There was in reality . . . a violent prejudice against machinery – there was no denying that potatoes were above doubled in price – and our eyesight was sufficient to tell us, that many of the poor manufacturers were more than half starved.

The Combination Acts did not apply to Scotland, but the same hostility to combination existed, and workers found that even redress through legal means came up against the disapproval of the courts (21); judges reflected contemporary views in disapproving restrictions of any kind on the free development of industry and trade (22).

(21) *Scots Magazine*, LXXV (April, 1813)

On the 12th of March, came on the trial of William McKimmie, Thomas Smith, James Johnstone, Charles Christie, and James Granger, all weavers in Glasgow, accused of illegal combination or conspiracy. The pannels, who had been on bail, all appeared at the bar, except Smith, who was consequently outlawed for not appearing – The indictment states:–

> That whereas, by the laws of this and every other well-governed realm, illegal combination or conspiracy, and particularly illegal combination or con-spiracy, among many thousands of workmen or artificers, to compel their masters or employers to raise their wages, or the prices of their work or labour – by striking work in a body, or in great numbers, and in different parts of the country, at one, or nearly at one and the same time; – by supporting those workmen who so strike work, and stand out against their masters or employers, with money subscribed, collected, or borrowed for that purpose, and by the interposition of the joint credit of the persons so combining or conspiring, or of some of their number; – by preventing workmen willing to work at wages or prices different from, or lower than those demanded by the workmen or artificers so combining or conspiring from so working, by either masterfully depriving them of the possession of machinery or implements necessary for carrying on their work, or by improperly excluding them, or denying them the use of the same, is a crime of an heinous nature, and severely punishable, more especially when committed by intimidating, by means of threats, abuse, or violence, workmen so willing to work, from so working, and by extorting money for the aforesaid purpose; Yet true it is and of verity, &c . . . .

A great number of witnesses were examined for the prosecution, from whose testimony it appeared that in the year 1809, a combination commenced among the operative weavers in Glasgow and its vicinity, which afterwards extended to Lanark, Rutherglen, Hamilton, Douglas, Airdrie, Strathaven, Pollockshaws, Paisley, Kilbarchan, &c., &c. in all which places district associations were formed, to the number of nearly 70; in some of these associations there were often 500 members and upwards, and they elected delegates, who held their meetings in Campbell-street, Glasgow. The general association raised money, and issued directions to the district associations, and also corresponded with similar associations of operative weavers in different places in England and Ireland. It also appeared that the operative weavers raised a process before the Justices of peace for Lanark praying for a rise in the rate of their wages, which, after various proceedings before them, was decided in favour of the operative weavers, in the month of November 1812. The masters, however, alledging that they were unable to afford higher wages, would not comply with this decision.

In consequence of this refusal on the part of the masters, a meeting was held of the general association of Glasgow, on the 10th of November, when it was agreed to strike work, unless the masters agreed to give the wages decerned by the Justices. At this, and other meetings, it was also agreed to raise funds, in order to support such operative weavers as should require or ask support in consequence of striking work. It was also agreed that the operative weavers should possess themselves of all revels and beaming machines, in order to prevent weavers from working at the low rate of wages. Similar resolutions were entered into in most of the other places in the west country who had joined in the association, and considerable sums of money were raised in order to support those who stood out. These sums of money were generally applied to establish credits with grocers, &c. to furnish different articles of provisions to such as stood in need of assistance. In consequence of the resolution of the weavers to seize the revels and beaming machines, the whole of these implements were seized, not only in Glasgow, but in general wherever the association extended, and, where not voluntarily surrendered, they were, in several cases taken by force. This was proved in the case of William Rankine, weaver in Wester Carntyne, from whom a revel was taken by force near Drygate toll, and also in the case of George Dunn, weaver at Parkhead, from who two revels were taken.

(22) Lord Meadowbank's judgement on the Glasgow weavers, *Glasgow Herald* (19 March 1813)

What right had the operative weavers of Glasgow, or any other place, to form themselves into associations, and say, we will not permit a person to take but a limited number of apprentices – that these apprentices would serve seven years – that women and girls should not be employed; and that no one shall carry on his business, or get a loom, without holding a ticket from this illegal association? – suppose the persons employed in agricultural pursuits, ploughmen for instance, were to enter into such a combination, could it be tolerated for an instance? and still where was the difference between them and the operative weavers?

A number of attempts by different groups of workers to revitalise the legislation that gave justices of the peace the responsibility for regulation of wages and conditions of work, such as apprenticeship requirements, threatened to halt the breakdown of traditional work methods which industrialisation was bringing. Such a restraint on growth was unacceptable, and in 1813 the Government repealed the legislation on wages (23), and in the following year the restrictions on apprenticeship were removed.

(23) *Parl. Debs*, 1st ser., xxv (6 April 1813)

Artificer's Wages Bill. Viscount *Sidmouth* adverted to a Bill on the table brought from the Commons, for repealing so much of certain acts in England and Scotland as directed magistrates at the quarter sessions to fix the wages of artificers, artizans, handicraftsmen, and labourers, and observed, that the existence of these Acts had, until lately, been unknown, particularly an Act of Queen Elizabeth, which had fallen into desuetude, and the existence of which was unknown to the magistrates, and even to high authorities in the law, as well as to the committee of the House of Commons, which had the subject of wages under their consideration last session. By that Act, magistrates were directed to assemble in every county at the Easter quarter sessions (any one being absent without sufficient cause being liable to a penalty), to fix the rate of wages of artizans, &c. and any person of that description receiving less or more wages than the rate thus fixed, was liable to imprisonment for 14 days, and any master paying less or more wages to imprisonment for seven days. Had this Act remained in desuetude, there would perhaps have been no necessity to repeal it; but as it had in some instances recently been vexatiously attempted to carry the Act into effect, it became necessary to repeal it. He was satisfied there was no necessity for him to point out to the enlightened minds of their lordships the pernicious consequences which must result from the operation of Acts of this description, he should therefore merely now move that the Bill be read a second time.

With the end of Government intervention, workers sought to use their trade societies to maintain restrictions on entry to their trade and to defend their craft. By the end of the second decade of the nineteenth century there existed in most traditional crafts an 'honourable' section, which sought to maintain the methods of work, the standards and the wages of the craft; and a 'dishonourable' section, where demand was the arbiter of wages, division of labour among unskilled workers replaced the fully-qualified craftsmen, and cheapness was of greater importance than quality (24).

(24) *The Gorgon* (3 Oct. 1818)

The system of combination of the journeymen Tailors, is by far the most perfect of any; and whatever may be said to the contrary it is by no means pernicious in its consequences, under the existing laws against combinations of workmen; but it is actually necessary and highly useful. Shut out as these men in common with all other workmen are, from all legal remedy, no other means than those of combination, in order to prevent the utmost degradation remain, and the more perfect the combination, the less the degradation; this we intend to prove in any essay on the laws respecting combinations in which it will also be made manifest, that those tradesmen among whom combination is the least perfect, are the most degraded and most wretched.

The organization of the Tailors is nearly as follows:– they are divided into two classes, called Flints and Dungs, – the Flints have upwards of thirty houses of call, and the Dungs about nine or ten; the Flints work by the day, the Dungs by the day or piece. Great animosity formerly existed between them, the Dungs generally working for less wages, but of late years there has not been much difference in wages, the material difference being the working by the piece or day, instead of the day only; and at some of the latest strikes both parties have usually made common cause.

There was more than one attempt to link together different trade societies in a defensive organisation and, from about 1815, there were meetings of delegates from trades in the metropolis whenever a major crisis arose. The Deptford shipwright John Gast was a leading advocate of united action and was probably the force behind both the Philanthropic Hercules of 1819 and the pioneer workers' paper, *The Gorgon* (25). Almost simultaneously a similar 'Philanthropic Society' was established at Manchester (26).

(25) 'Philanthropic Hercules' *The Gorgon* (23 Jan. 1819)

A society under this appellation [Philanthropic Hercules] has recently been established in London; and from the judicious principles on which it is founded, promises to be of immense utility to journeymen and mechanics. The object of this association is to provide a fund by *weekly penny* subscriptions; which fund is, to preserve the workmen of every trade from degradation, by enabling them to resist the encroachments of avarice and oppression. Every trade which joins the Union, appoints a deputy to a general committee; these deputies are appointed for six months, and go out in rotation. When the number of efficient deputies in any trade belonging to the Union exceeds one hundred, an extra deputy is appointed for every additional two hundred and fifty members. Besides the general committee, sub-committees are appointed by each trade for the management of its particular concerns. Each trade retains possession of its own funds; but returns of its amount are regularly made to the general committee, who have the power to direct its application to any purpose they deem expedient.

(26) Home Office Papers, 42/181: Philanthropic Society

The following Address and Resolutions were unanimously agreed to.

At a GENERAL MEETING of TRADES convened to take into consideration the Distressed State and Privations to which the Working Class of Society are reduced, by their avaricious Employers reducing wages to less than sufficient to support nature or purchase the bare necessities for our existence with great economy and hard labour; therefore, to render redress in such cases of distress to any Body or Party reduced as aforesaid.

RESOLUTIONS.

FIRST.   That there be a Union of All Trades called the PHILANTHROPIC SOCIETY, to be held in Manchester on the second Monday in every month, when all TRADES shall send a Delegate with proper credential for admission.

SECOND.   That every Trade be recommended to raise a Fund amongst themselves, for the general Benefit of all TRADES joined in this Union; and in particular any Trade that may be engaged in resisting Oppression or to alleviate distress, and to enable the labouring part of the Community to live in comfort and decency. . . .

The manifest failure of both legislation and stern admonitions (27) to prevent the formation and spread of trade societies, together with a carefully managed campaign against the Combination Acts by Francis Place and others, backed by the intellectual might of the philosophical radicals, encouraged Parliament to take a fresh look at the problem of industrial relations. With the reaction of Sidmouth having given way to the liberal Toryism of Robert Peel and William Huskisson the time was ripe for change. Joseph Hume, radical member for Montrose, raised the matter in the Commons early in 1824 and by June all anti-combination legislation had been swept away (28, 29).

(27) *Address to the Labouring Classes in the Manufacturing Districts* (Halifax, 1823)

With respect to your employers, who risk their capitals in finding you work, you must be sensible, if you will reflect at all, that should you be justly chargeable with neglecting to fulfil your engagements to them and consequently prevent the execution of orders, you not only put them to great inconvenience, which may be remembered to your disadvantage hereafter, but eventually cut the sinews of commercial enterprise and national prosperity, and thus bring the greatest scourge upon yourselves.

(28) *Parl. Debs* 2nd ser., x (12 Feb. 1824)

Joseph Hume: On the next branch of the subject which related to what were usually termed the Combination Laws, he intended to be very brief. For many years past, the country has been burthened by a system of laws preventing the labouring classes of the community from combining together against their employers. Their employers, who, though few in number, were powerful in wealth, might combine against them, and might determine not to give them more than a certain sum for their labour. The workmen could not, however, consult together about the rate they ought to fix on that labour, without rendering themselves liable to fine and imprisonment, and a thousand other inconveniences which the law had reserved for them. The masters, on the other hand, could combine against the men; they were comparatively few in number, possessed every advantage of power and station, and could, at any time, agree among themselves, what rate of wages they would allow. The master shoemakers, the master saddlers, and many others, had adopted resolutions for this purpose; so that, in fact, the operators were completely at the mercy of their employers. Of course, this gross inequality in law had been a source of perpetual dissatisfaction. Some of those persons, who were well satisfied with the state of things, without knowing exactly what the state was, professed to feel pride that, in the eye of the British law, all were equal – that high and low, rich and poor, were alike protected. It might be so theoretically; but, practically, and, in many instances, the case was directly otherwise. In this instance, the men were not protected against the injustice of their masters, while the masters were protected from the combinations of the men. It was said, that if these laws were repealed, there would be nothing but rioting and quarrelling between the masters and the men; but this he denied, on the authority of persons conversant in trade, who informed him, that a strike for wages never took place, except in cases where the men found their wages insufficient for their support, or under other circum-stances of severe extremity. They were compelled to strike; so that the masters brought the evil upon themselves. It was also very important, in relation to this point, to mention, that it was the decided opinion of the hon. and learned member for Peterborough (Mr. Scarlett) that if all the penal laws against combinations by workmen for increase of wages were struck out of the Statute-book, the common law of the land would still be amply sufficient to prevent the mischievous effects of such combinations (hear, hear!) . . . .

Mr *Huskisson* rose, not for the purpose of opposing, but of concurring in the present motion.

(29) *Parl. Debs.*, 2nd ser., XII (29 March 1825)

William Huskisson: He would briefly review the course and effect of that proceeding. It commenced by a motion introduced by an hon. gentleman on the opposite side of the House, who pointed out the hardships to which, under the then subsisting laws, journeymen and others were liable; and there could be no doubt that, in too many cases, those laws were, in a great degree unjust and prejudicial in their operation. A committee was accordingly granted to the motion of the hon. gentleman; in which it was proposed to go largely into evidence and inquiries on those topics. It was a very full committee, consisting of about fifty members, and it undoubtedly examined a vast variety of evidence, upon all questions connected with main intention of its labours. The result of those labours was – not that a report was made to that House (which, as he thought, would have been the most desirable course), stating the grounds upon which the committee had come to the determination of recommending the introduction of their bill, and thereby affording to the public, and in a more especial manner to parliament, the necessary information, as to the motives which induced them to recommend such a change of the existing law; but that the committee adopted, finally, a string of resolutions which involved no such statement whatever . . . .

The consequence of all this had been that some of the provisions of the bill which afterwards passed into an act were of a very extraordinary nature. Not only did the bill repeal all former statutes relative to combinations and conspiracies of workmen, but it even provided, that no proceedings should be had at common law, on account of any such combination, meeting, conspiracy, or uniting together of journeymen, &c.; for, in fact, almost any purpose: and thus, by one clause, it went to preclude the possibility of applying any legal remedy to a state of things which might become and which had since become, a great public evil. . . . The bill itself, however, repealing thirty or forty acts of parliament, and in this singular manner putting aside the common law altogether, was brought into the House at a late period of the session, passed through its first stage, subsequent to the first reading, on Wednesday, the 2nd of June; and, on Saturday the 5th of June, only four days after the second reading, and in the same week, was read a third time and passed, without any discussion. The measure was therefore hurried on with as much expedition, as was usually applied to the most pressing bills.

2. *The Turbulent Years, 1825–42*

The repeal of the Combination Acts brought into the open many of the trade societies which had quietly persisted through the years of illegality. New societies burgeoned, and strikes were widespread. Some observers, such as the leaders of the Glasgow Mechanics' Institute, hoped that repeal would usher in an era of industrial peace (1), while to Thomas Hodgskin (1783–1869) and other anti-capitalist economists at the London Mechanics' Institute it offered the possibility of a war against capital (2). There was a strong assertion of new-found power on the part of some unions (3), and the Government was undoubtedly taken aback by the extent of unionism. As a result, the Combination Laws Repeal Act of 1824 was amended, and the Combination of Workmen Act of 1825 more narrowly defined the right to combine (4). Protection from common-law charges of criminal conspiracy which the 1824 Act had granted were removed and for nearly half a century the position of unions was legally circumscribed in fairly narrow terms.

(1) *The Glasgow Mechanics' Magazine* (1824): 'Address on the Repeal of the Combination Laws to the Mechanics of Scotland',

By the Repeal of the Combination Laws, a wise and upright measure of the present very popular administration of our country, you have been favoured with a degree of liberty unknown for many years, and we would therefore seriously recommend to you to avoid an error into which you are liable to fall, namely, an abuse of the privileges which have been granted to you in common with your masters. Haters, as we are, of oppression in every form, we cannot but rejoice that you have at last obtained a power of preserving yourselves in future from any unjust or harsh measures that might be attempted against you, or that might prevent you from gaining a decent and respectable livelihood. On the other hand, however, as we are equally haters of licentiousness in every form, we would sincerely regret any appearance of a spirit of insubordination, or of improper retaliation, among those who may have suffered, perhaps severely, from the effects of those laws, which, by their repeal, are acknowledged to have been injurious to the interests of the country, and unjust to a class of men who are both its pride and support.

It is of the greatest importance to observe, that while your liberties have been increased, your responsibility has not been diminished; and that, while fond as you may be of making use of your privileges, you ought to beware of the opposite extreme, namely, that of abridging those of others. . . . No one, we are sure, who carefully reads the Act, or hears it read over, from beginning to end, will ever imagine that he may combine to leave his work, which he has agreed to perform, or to cause others to do the same, or to prevent them from taking work when they are willing to do it, without infringing the express terms of the statute. . . .

Combination, in itself, is evidently no crime, unless it be for illegal purposes. Now, will any one pretend to say, that a combination to put an individual out of trade, is not an unjust and illegal purpose? Combination to raise wages, is not illegal; . . . combination to lessen or alter the hours of working, is not illegal . . . combinations to effect any of these or similar purposes, by fair and open agreement amongst each other, without force, compulsion, or intimidation, against those who are unwilling to join, is not illegal. . . .

Combination, however, for effecting any of the above purposes, by violence to person or property, by threats or intimidation, either in word or deed, is not only illegal and contrary to the express terms of the Act, but is evidently contrary to the first principles of natural liberty, which allows [sic] every man to do what he will with his own, and to serve or not serve any master he chooses, for whatever wages he thinks proper; or, if he should take a fancy for it, for no wages at all. . . .

(2) Thomas Hodgskin, *Labour Defended against the Claims of Capital* (1825)

In truth, also, however the matter may be disguised, the combinations among workmen to obtain higher wages which are now so general and so much complained of, are practical attacks on the claims of capital. The weight of its chains are felt, though the hand may not yet be clearly seen which imposes them. Gradually as the resistance increases, as laws are multiplied for the protection of capital, as claims for higher wages shall be more strenuously and more violently repressed, the cause of this oppression will be more distinctly seen. The contest now appears to be between masters and journeymen, or between one species of labour and another, but it will soon be displayed in its proper characters; and will stand confessed a war of honest industry against the idle profligacy which has so long ruled the affairs of the political world with undisputed authority – which has for its own security, added honour and political power to wealth, and has conjoined exclusion and disgrace with the poverty it has inflicted on the labourer. On the side of the labourers there is physical strength, for they are more numerous than their opponents. They are also fast losing that reverence for their opponents which was and is the source of their power, and they are daily acquiring a moral strength which results from a common interest and a close and intimate union.

The capitalists and labourers form the great majority of the nation, so that there is no third power to intervene betwixt them. They must and will decide the dispute of themselves. Final sucess, I would fain hope, must be on the side of justice. I am certain, however, that till the triumph of labour be complete; till productive industry alone be opulent, and till idleness alone be poor, till the admirable maxim that 'he who sows shall reap' be solidly established; till the right of property shall be founded on principles of justice, and not those of slavery; till *man* shall be held more in honour than the clod he treads on, or the machine he guides, there cannot, and there ought not to be either peace on earth or goodwill amongst men. . . .

In the system of Nature, mouths are united with hands and with intelligence; they and not capital are the agents of production . . . it must be plain that all these numerous advantages, those benefits to civilisation, those vast improvements in the condition of the human race, which have been in general attributed to capital, are caused in fact by labour . . . and that the best means of securing the progressive improvement both of individuals and of nations, is to do justice and allow labour to possess and enjoy the whole of its produce.

(3) SC on Combination Laws, *PP* 1825 IV, appendix no. 13

At a General Meeting of Shipwrights, held at St. Helena Tavern, Rotherhithe, on Monday, October the 4th, 1824, Mr. N. G. Clark in the chair, the following resolutions were unanimously agreed to:–

1. That whenever an individual or a company of people is offered a job in any yard, and the parties to whom the job is offered, do give a fair price, according to the custom of the river, that job is exclusively the right of the party who first had the offer; and as it is too much the practice of builders to vent their spleen on the first parties, by not agreeing to their proposals, by way of punishment they will, in some instances, offer more to others than what they were first asked, on purpose of dividing and governing the people, therefore it is requested that no persons will be induced by any fallacious promises to interfere between the first parties and the builders.
2. That it is too generally the practice in yards, where there is a job of running work, to offer the same as a lump job, with a view of baffling the judgment of the workmen, and deprive them of the advantage of such running work. Therefore, we do agree, that in future, all running work shall be done in the old river price, until the new regulations come out.
3. That the mode of apprenticeship, as now adopted on the river Thames, is very injurious to the journeymen, and equally injurious to the apprentice, inasmuch, that being left without that necessary check, and having considerable pecuniary means in his power, he forgets the relative duty he has to perform towards the people as well as his master, he is thereby made the instrument to rob the men of their rights, which is the only party by whom he learns his trade, and which he will feel the effects of when out of his time.
4. That if any master forms into a company a number of apprentices and employ them in taking to pieces any old ship come into dock for repair, at the exclusion of the journeymen, that no journeyman upon any condition whatever go to work on that part of the work where apprentices have been so

employed; but as it is the wish of every man to be in union with all, it is requested that all companies of people will willingly take with them a proper proportion of apprentices, so that they may have every advantage of learning their trade.

5. That should any builder, by forming a number of apprentices into a company, let to the said apprentices any new ship to build, that all members of the Union desist from doing any part of the said ship.

6. That any member of the Union who has a son, who is desirous of being brought up to the trade, shall bind his son to himself; and at all times, when the father cannot employ for his son, that an application be made to the large company of people, who are requested to employ such apprentice, by which act the Union will become consolidated.

(4) The Combination of Workmen Act, 1825, 4 Geo. IV, c. 34

III And be it further enacted, that from and after the passing of this act, if any person shall by violence to the person or property or by threats or intimidation, or by molesting or in any way obstructing another, force or endeavour to force any journeyman, manufacturer, workman or other person hired or employed in any manufacture, trade or business, to depart from his hiring, employment or work, or to return his work before the same shall be finished, or prevent, or endeavour to prevent, any journeyman, manufacturer, workman or other person, not being hired or employed, from hiring himself to, or from accepting work or employment from any person or persons; or if any person shall use or employ violence to the person or property of another, or threats or intimidation, or shall molest or in any way obstruct another for the purpose of forcing or inducing such person to belong to any club or association, or to contribute to any common fund, or to pay any fine or penalty, or on account of his not belonging to any club or association, or not having contributed or having refused to contribute to any common fund, or to pay any fine or penalty, or on account of his not having complied or of his refusing to comply with any rules, orders, resolutions or regulations made to obtain an advance or to reduce the rate of wages, or to lessen or alter the hours of working, or to decrease or alter the quantity of work, or to regulate the mode of carrying on any manufacture, trade or business, or the management thereof; or if any person shall by violence to the person or property of another, or by threats or intimidation, or by molesting or in any way obstructing another, force or endeavour to force any manufacturer or person carrying on any trade or business, to make any alteration in his mode of regulating, managing, conducting or carrying on such manufacture, trade or business, to limit the number of his apprentices, or the number or description of his journeymen, workmen or servants; every person so offending or aiding, abetting or assisting therein, being convicted thereof in the manner hereinafter mentioned, shall be imprisoned only, or shall and may be imprisoned and kept for hard labour, for any time not exceeding three calendar months.

IV Provided always, and be it enacted, that this act shall not extend to subject any persons to punishment, who shall meet together for the sole purpose of consulting upon and determining the rate of wages or prices, which the persons present at such meeting or any of them, shall require or demand for his or their work, or the hours or time for which he or they shall work in any manufacture, trade or business, or who shall enter into any agreement, verbal or written, among themselves, for the purpose of fixing the rate of wages or prices which the parties entering into such agreement, or any of them, shall require or demand for his or their work, or the hours of time for which he or they shall work in any manufacture, trade or business, or who shall enter into any agreement, verbal or written, among themselves, for the purpose of fixing the rate of wages or prices which the parties entering such agreement, or any of them, shall require or demand for his work, or the hours of time for which he or they will work, in any manufacture, trade or business; and that persons so meeting for the purpose aforesaid, or entering into any such agreement as aforesaid, shall not be liable to any prosecution or penalty for so doing; any law or statute to the contrary notwithstanding.

Despite the limitations imposed by the 1825 Act, unions spread and grew. Local societies began to form links with societies in other towns and the need for organisations to cope with the artisan tramping in search of work and for larger strike funds encouraged the development of regional and national unions (5, 6). Some of the most active unions existed among the cotton spinners in Lancashire with John Doherty (1798–1854) as leader (7). Other spinners' organisations operated in Scotland (8) and Ireland. In December 1829, the principal bodies of spinners, meeting at a delegate conference in the Isle of Man established the Grand General Union of All the Operative Spinners of the United Kingdom (9).

(5) *Rules of the Mechanics' Friendly Institution, as Agreed upon by the Deputies from the Different Branches, Convened at Leeds, Aug. 16th, 1824* (Bolton, 1824)

Rule First: The different orders of Mechanics to be admitted members of this Institution are to be Model Makers, Smiths, Filers, Joiners, and Wood and Iron Turners, engaged in the making of Steam Engines only, and Machinery for the preparing and spinning of Flax, Tow, Hemp, Cotton, Woollen, Worsted, or Silk; and every person who has not worked five years at one or more of the Branches above stated, by the time he is twenty-one years of age, must be considered ineligible, except one son of any of the members of this Society, who shall be admitted on the same terms as those who may have served five years. Every one who is a member of this Institution at the time of the general distribution of these Rules shall remain a member. . . .

x A box with three locks and keys shall be provided and lodged in the house where the meetings of this branch of the Institution are held, in which are deposited the money, books, and papers belonging to the Institution. One key of the said box to be kept by the foreman of the committee, one key by one of the stewards, and the remaining key by the landlord of the house where the business of the branch is transacted.

XI The landlord of the house where the box is kept, and who has the custody of the box, shall be approved of as a proper person by the committee of trustees, and shall give security of them for the safe custody of the box and its contents.

XII Any person who shall become a member of this Institution to be relieved in distress and death, shall pay three half-pence per week; and any person wishing to be relieved in sickness, shall pay threepence per week. . . .

XVII Any member compelled to travel in order to obtain employ (having his certificate) shall, on application to the Stewards, receive one penny per mile to the place where he is going; which place shall be inserted in his certificate. But he shall not be entitled to any more relief if work can be obtained, unless in cases of extreme emergency. All officers shall direct such persons on travel to the most likely place where they think employment may be found, and observe the same conduct towards him as the above mentioned officers have done.

XVIII Every member of this Insitution shall contribute towards the support of it, as above stated, to be paid every meeting night to the stewards; and when that sum is found insufficient, the same shall be made known to the Institution, and the contributions advanced to meet the demand.

XIX Any member, having travelled all day and found no employment, shall, by applying to the officer of the place he is near, be furnished with a supper, two pints of beer, a bed and breakfast next morning, together with one penny per mile to the next place. . . .

XXV Every member when visited with sickness or lameness which renders him incapable of following his employment, and which is not occasioned by drunkenness, fighting, or anything contrary to the true intent and meaning of these Rules, shall be relieved by the stewards with one and sixpence per day, during the time of his sickness or lameness, for the space of six calendar months; at the end of which time he shall receive one shilling per day for the term of two years. Should he still continue sick, his case shall be referred to a committee.

   (6) Steam Engine Makers' Society, *Annual Report*, 1919

At a Meeting of Delegates from the different branches of the Steam Engine Makers' Society, held at Manchester, 18 December, 1826, the following rules and regulations were agreed upon:–

ARTICLE I. That this society shall consist only of persons who have been employed two years previous to the commencement of this Society (2nd November, 1824) in the manufacturing of steam engines – viz., Filers, turners, and erectors of steam engines, or persons who may hereafter serve a legal apprenticeship by indenture or to his father. . . .

ARTICLE II. That every person who shall have been bound an apprentice for the space of five years previous to the commencement of this society. . . shall be admitted a member upon paying, exclusive of his entrance money, the sum of 10s. 6d. for each year he may be deficient of seven years. . . .

ARTICLE VII. That each member shall pay a monthly contribution of one shilling each into the box, out of which fourpence shall be spent in refreshment, according to the custom of the society. . . .

ARTICLE XII. That if any member comes into the clubroom disguised in liquor, or shall curse, swear, or make use of any abusive or indecent language to any other member during club hours, he shall be ordered to withdraw, and on his refusal be fined sixpence. . . .

ARTICLE XIV. That if any member of this society should leave his employ for want of work, or any other just cause, he shall upon proof thereof, apply to the secretary for his certificate (for which certificate he shall pay sixpence) acknowledging him to belong to this society, and that he has paid all contribution, fines, etc. entitling him to the benefits arising thereof; he shall on producing the same to the secretary of the next box, be provided with his supper, one pint of beer, one night's lodging, his breakfast in the morning, and one penny for every mile he may have travelled since last relieved; every member to be relieved from the nearest box on the way he may have to come, and no member to be relieved from the same box twice in six months, nor shall any member receive any tramp money before he has been in the society one year.

(7) 'Abstract of the Evidence of Combinations of Workmen taken before a Select Committee of the House of Commons in 1838', NAPSS, *Trades' Societies and Strikes* (1860)

Between 1824 and 1829 there were ten or twelve partial strikes against individual masters, for the most part not very successful.

In March, 1829, began the general strike of the fine spinners, which continued for six months, and ended in the submission of the men to the masters' demands. The cause of the strike was that the masters proposed a new list, whereby no longer a uniform price was paid in all cases without deduction, but a price per lb. having been fixed for all twist manufactured by machines containing 336 spindles, a deduction was made at the rate of $1\frac{1}{2}$ per cent. for every twelve spindles beyond 336. This, in the extreme case (to which there is an obvious tendency) of a machine containing in all 1000 spindles, that is 664 extra spindles, would amount to 83 per cent. deduction of gross wages. Practically the wage would be reduced from a range of 28s. to 50s., to a range of 24s. to 40s., or to an average of 30s. per week. At least this was the masters' representation. An operative estimated the change to be a reduction upon the former scale of wages of 30 per cent. This list the masters justified in an address, issued by them to the public, on the score of necessity; the trade could not, they said, be continued in Manchester on any other method; cotton yarn had fallen in value; the current rates of labour were 15 to 40 per cent lower in the neighbouring districts than in Manchester; and, whilst the price of other labour had diminished, spinners' wages had been stationary for thirteen years.

On the list being issued, according to the representation of the secretary of the Union during the time of the strike, the men appointed a deputation to see the masters, to induce them, if possible, either to give up the proposed reduction, or to give time to the men to ascertain whether it was practicable to get the other masters in the surrounding districts to pay Manchester prices, and the deputation was authorized, in case these other masters refused, to consent to the proposed reduction. The masters, however, declined to allow any time for such inquiries, and, as is proved in the case of one master who was willing to compromise the matter with his men, compelled all the members of the Masters' Association at once to adopt, without deviation, the proposed list, by threats of enforcing a penalty bond of £500 against any refractory member and of underselling him in the market. The leaders of the Union thought a strike unadvisable, and, with a view to convince the men of this, proposed that every man who was likely to be called into the strike should send in a written statement of the number of weeks he could do without pay, and the name of the piece of furniture in his house he would consent to sell, and its probable value. Contrary to the expectation of the leaders, the returns showed an amount of £300 which the men were ready to contribute, besides the loss of their wages, and confirmed the men in their intention to strike. The strike accordingly took place of all the fine spinners in Manchester.

(8) *Articles of the Association of Operative Cotton-Spinners of Glasgow and Neighbourhood* (1833)

1. *Designation of the Association.* – This association to be termed the Association of Operative Cotton-spinners of Glasgow and neighbourhood; and to have for its only object the supporting of prices, and enabling its members to obtain a fair remuneration for their labour. . . .

2. *Government and Election.* – The affairs of the association to be conducted by the delegates, and a committee of 12, consisting of president, treasurer, and secretary, and nine directors, to be elected at the quarterly meetings. . . .

12. *Submitting to a Majority.* – Every member of this association binds and obliges himself to submit to a majority of his brethren in all cases connected with the association, which majority must, in all cases, relating to strikes, or altering the articles, bear 2/3ds of the votes returned; but in other cases, the majority will consist of one above the half of the votes returned.

13. *Strikes.* – No shop, individual or individuals in a shop considering themselves aggrieved, shall have the liberty to strike work upon any pretence whatever, without giving intimation at a delegate meeting in due form, as specified in Article 3d, when, after being fully considered, and a general vote taken (which must take place in all cases relating to strikes or threatened reduction), and if the vote be carried they shall cease work, as directed by the association, and be entitled to regular aliment for the period of 34 weeks from the date of their ceasing to work; and any member on a strike is at liberty to take wheels wherever he can find them, at the standard price; and odd spinners are entitled to aliment for a period of 17 weeks. . . .

15. *Instructing Spinners.* – This association binds and obliges every one of its members to refrain from instructing any individual in the art of spinning, except such as are sons or brothers of a spinner, who may have been, or is at present a member of this association; and it must be remembered that such persons can only be admissible by having served them as piecers; and that individuals having admissible piecers may not take advantage of their neighbour, they are strictly prohibited from allowing such piecers to spin in their absence, but must follow their draws, and overlook them in all their instructions and practice; and no person will be allowed to learn a male piecer, except such as are privileged as specified in this article.

(9) Home Office Papers, 40/27: Resolutions of the delegates at the Isle of Man Conference of Operative Cotton Spinners

3. That one grand General Union of all the Operative Spinners in the United Kingdom be now formed for the mutual support and protection of all.
4. That each nation shall manage its own affairs, always subject to the decisions and authority of a general or annual meeting of the delegates from each district who choose to send representatives to such meeting. . . .
7. That the sum of 10/- a week be paid to every member of this association when they are on strike against a reduction of wages.
8. That 10/- a week be paid to members contending for an advance of wages the same as when resisting reductions, but that no district or part of that district be allowed to strike for an advance without first having obtained the consent and authority of the other districts. . . .
25. That an address be prepared by Mr. Doherty to the operative spinners of the United Kingdom calling upon them to come boldly and manfully forward and support the attempt that is now being made to prevent any further depreciation of the value of their only property their labour, by repeated and unnecessary reduction of their wages. . . .
27. That it is not the intention of this Association either directly or indirectly to interfere with, or in any way injure the rights and property of employers or to assume or exercise any control or authority over the management of any mill or mills, but, on the contrary, will endeavour as far as in us lies to uphold the

just rights and reasonable authority of every master, and compel all the members of this association to pay a due obedience and respect to their respective masters, and all their confidential servants in authority under them, our only object being to uphold the best interests of our common country by averting all the horrid train of direful calamitites, which have already made too much progress amongst us and which are inseparable from cruel poverty, ignorance, degradation, pauperism and crime, and to obtain for our families the common comforts and conveniences of life.

There were numerous attempts to link unions of different trades. In Glasgow a committee of trade societies produced their own journal, *The Herald to the Trades' Advocate*, from 1830, and drew up plans for a general trades' union (10). The London unions formed a federal Metropolitan Trades' Union in March 1831, primarily to support parliamentary reform and statutory reduction of hours (11).

(10) *Herald to the Trades' Advocate*, no. 6 (30 Oct. 1830)

To us it is quite evident that the introduction of machinery, in competition with manual exertion, is the immediate cause of the reduction of wages; but while we are of this opinion, we by no means wish it to be understood that we are hostile to the introduction of machinery, if that machinery is properly conducted for the benefit of all. . . . To avoid the evil effects arising to the operatives, from the competition of machinery, it is necessary that in order to keep up their wages, that their numbers should be reduced in the labour-market; because labour, like every other marketable article, will rise and fall in proportion to its demand; and in order that the various operatives may maintain their high wages, it is absolutely necessary that their number should never exceed the demand; but should rather be below the number to be employed, by which means they would be certain of gaining an advance of wages, and of maintaining that advance when obtained. . . .

Rule 6. – That the great and only object of the whole Union should be to give employment to the idle and superfluous hands belonging to the different trades who contributed to the general fund. By this mode being adopted, the first object to be accomplished might be our intended newspaper, which would be the vehicle of communication for all. As soon as this was accomplished the next object might be the erection of an Operatives' Hall, with convenient committee-rooms, extensive bazaar, for the receipt of the produce of the members employed, or the United Operatives' Bank; and last, though not least, seminaries of learning for themselves and their hitherto neglected offspring.

(11) *Penny Papers for the People* (26 March 1831)

Let us henceforth adopt and practise a new principle: instead of every man living for himself exclusively, let us, in future, be ALL for EACH, and EACH for ALL. . . .

It is therefore proposed THAT A METROPOLITAN TRADES' UNION be formed.

Its first object, to obtain for all its members the right of electing those who make the laws which govern them, unshackled and uninfluenced by any Property Qualification whatsoever. Its second object, to afford support and protection individually and collectively, to every member of the METROPOLITAN TRADES' UNION; to enhance the value of labour by diminishing the hours of employment; and to adopt such measures as may be deemed necessary to increase the domestic comforts of working men.

In Yorkshire organisation grew among woollen and worsted workers following a strike in Bradford. The 'Leeds Union' spread throughout the county. One of its leaders, Simeon Pollard, recounted its history to striking Derby workers in 1834 (12).

(12) *The Crisis*, III, no. 21 (18 Jan. 1834)

The speaker then entered into the history of the origin of the Trades' Unions which took place in Yorkshire three years ago. A manufacturer of Bradford, in Jan. 1831, advanced the wages of his hands which, he said, the state of trade would allow, and he thought it but common justice that the operatives should partake of the benefits of an improved demand. Other masters did not follow the example; a meeting of operatives in the employment of Messrs. Gott was called, and an advance of wages was solicited. Messrs. Gott refused, and out of 239 hands, 219 turned out. A struggle commenced, which has been the cause of such consequences as no one could have anticipated. They waged war for eight months and then Messrs. Gott submitted to the demand of their work-people. Since that time many similar struggles had taken place on twenty times as more formidable scale, but the Union men had never been defeated, nor would they if their conduct was regulated by justice and a sound policy. At one time 108 masters said they would not employ Unionists – the men had a goodly sum ready for the contests – and the masters gave up the point. He then referred to contests at Idle, Helmsfirth, and Leeds, which he said terminated in favour of the men. The editor of the *Leeds Mercury* contended that the advance of wages, which the men obtained, was not the effect of their Union, but of an improvement in trade. But this was not the fact; the advance was given at a time when trade was flat. Another proof existed at this time that the editor of the *Leeds Mercury* was wrong. Although the Unions extended nearly throughout the manufacturing districts of Yorkshire, there were a few villages not in union, that had no advance of wages for the last four or five years. The inference was plain: the Union operated advantageously to the interests of the men in one case; in the other they had not united, and therefore they had not been advanced. – Union had not failed in the Potteries, it had not failed in Yorkshire, nor was it likely to fail.

Doherty's efforts to use his spinners' union as the nucleus of a general union, the National Association of United Trades for the Protection of Labour, were copied in other parts of the country (13).

(13) *Herald to the Trades' Advocate*, no. 34 (14 May 1831): 'Fundamental Laws of the Glasgow and West of Scotland Association for the Protection of Labour'

1st. That the miserable condition to which, by repeated and unnecessary reduction of wages, the working people of this part of the country are reduced, urges the imperative necessity of adopting some effectual means of preventing such reductions, and securing to the industrious workman a just and adequate remuneration for his labour.

2nd. That to accomplish this necessary object, a Society be formed, consisting of the various organised Trades throughout Glasgow and the West of Scotland.

3rd. That no Trade can be admitted members of this Association that is not regularly organised and united in itself.

4th. That every Trade, on applying to be admitted members of this Association be required to produce a copy of their articles, for the inspection of the Committee; and, if approved of, to be admitted at their next meeting.

5th. That each member of this society shall subscribe one penny per week to the funds of this Association, and an extra penny per quarter towards defraying incidental expenses.

6th. That the funds of this society shall be applied only to prevent reduction of wages, but in no case to procure an advance. Any Trade considering their wages too low, may exert themselves to obtain such an advance as they may think necessary, and can obtain by their own exertions.

7th. That each member of this society shall be entitled to eight shillings per week during the continuance of a strike against a reduction of wages. The money to be paid into the hands of the officers of the Trade whose wages may be attempted to be reduced.

8th. That no strike shall be allowed to take place, until an attempt be made to settle the dispute, or matter of contention, by a negotiation in an amicable manner.

The trauma of the Industrial Revolution brought about a social as well as an economic transformation of British society. Not everyone welcomed the development of a society based on the competitive system, and during the 1820s a number of thinkers sought alternatives to competition in a system based on co-operation. The best known of such men was the Lanarkshire master cotton spinner Robert Owen (1771–1858), but others built upon and developed his ideas. Owenism appealed particularly to those craftsmen who had found their wages, their status and their conditions deteriorating as a result of industrialisation. Encouraged by Owenites, groups of working men in many parts of the country experimented with co-operative production and co-operative selling. Gradually Owenites began to see the possibilities of using trade unions as the basis for their campaign (14).

(14) *The Crisis*, I, no. 41 (15 Dec. 1832): William Pare, Birmingham, to Robert Owen

You will perceive by the placards &c., sent herewith that we have not been idle in the Exchange business; quite the contrary, I assure you. We are agitating the whole town in every nook and corner. The different Trades Unions which we are meeting every night, are taking the matter up with spirit; and, being already organised, they are capable of doing us great good.

The plan they propose to pursue is this: Having had the system of Labour Exchange pretty fully developed to each particular trade, by some of our Committee, it is resolved that each shop shall elect two from their body, to form with a like number from each other trade, a grand Union Committee of Trades. The latter Committee will be in constant communication with the managers of the Exchange: and when any important communication is to be made, or any idle or false rumour to be contradicted, the two delegates from each trade assemble the general committee of their respective trade, and give them the requisite instructions, and thus, on the following morning it is known throughout the whole body of workmen. I conceive it to be of the utmost importance to cherish those trade unions. Only convince these fine-hearted men that our plan will really do them good, and you have an army on your side at once.

When you return to Birmingham we will have a meeting of all these Committees, who, of course, will be the very elite of their class, and you must address them. Already, they are so well pleased, that when you hold another public meeting in Birmingham, they declare they will honour you by getting up a grand procession with their new and beautiful flags, banners &c. All this will, of course, favour our cause, because it tends to form and consolidate a public opinion, which I believe will shortly become irresistible in our favour.

There is another affair connected with these said Unions, they are connected all over the country, and if we convince them here of the utility of our plans, which I am confident we will do, they will give you an excellent introduction to the other towns which you propose visiting. We have attended two meetings already, the Carpenters' and the Masons' and have cleared many difficulties which they at first had to the system, from ignorance, of course. They expressed themselves perfectly satisfied with our explanations, and determined to do all in their power to carry our plans into full execution.

Throughout 1833 Owenites assiduously worked among trade unions, particularly in Yorkshire, Birmingham and Liverpool. Owen himself addressed numerous meetings and stirred up enthusiasm about the possibilities of a 'new moral world'. He was particularly successful among the building workers in Lancashire and the Midlands, where in 1831 a number of craft unions federated to form the Operative Builders' Union. Owen was able to persuade the builders to establish an association to engage in co-operative production (15), though not all members approved of the use being made of their union (16).

(15) *To the United Working Builders of Great Britain and Ireland* (12 Sept. 1833):
'Proposals for the Establishment of a National Association of Building, to be
called "The GRAND NATIONAL GUILD OF BUILDERS" to be composed of
Architects, and Surveyors, – Masons, – Carpenters and Joiners, Bricklayers,
– Plasterers, – Slaters, – Plumbers and Glaziers, and Panters, – White-
smiths, – Quarrymen, – and Brickmakers'

OBJECTS OF THE UNION

1. The general improvement of all the individuals forming the Building Class;
   ensuring regular employment for all.
2. To ensure fair remuneration for their services.
3. To fix a reasonable time for labour.
4. To educate both Adults and Children.
5. To have regular superior Medical Advice and assistance, and to make
   provision for the comfortable and independent retirement of the aged and
   infirm.
6. To regulate the operations of the whole in harmony, and to produce a general
   fund sufficient to secure all these objects.
7. To ensure a superiority of Building for the Public at fair and equitable prices.
8. To obtain good and comfortable Dwellings for every Member of the Union –
   extensive and well arranged Workshops, – Places of Depot for Building
   Materials, – Provisions and Clothing, – Halls for the Meetings of the Lodges
   and Central Committees, – Schools and Academies for the instruction of
   Adults and Children in Morals and the useful Sciences.
9. And also the Establishment of Builders' Banks in the various districts in which
   the Grand District Lodges shall be established.

. . . These proposals to form a Grand National Company of Builders for the
United Kingdom, with the explanations for the Chair, being fully developed in
detail by Messrs. Hansom and Welch, were received by the whole meeting with
enthusiastic approbation.

(16) *The Crisis*, III, no. 16 (14 Dec. 1833)

PUBLIC MEETING   For the purpose of forming a branch of the National
Regeneration Society of Manchester. Mr. Austin called to the chair. . . .

It is impossible to give the reader even a summary of Mr. Owen's address,
which occupied more than an hour and a half; he took a discursive glance at
several political and commercial subjects; pointed out the errors of political
economists on the subject of population and private competition; good times and
bad times, which distinction he said might easily be removed, seeing they might
with the greatest care convert all bad times into good times. He then spoke of the
spirit of union which prevailed in the North, and the resolution which the
workmen had taken to amend their circumstances next year, by a general
demand for higher wages and less time. He concluded his address by reading a

copy of the resolutions which were to be proposed.

The first resolution – 'That it is most desirable to form an auxiliary society in connection with the parent society formed in Manchester for promoting National Regeneration' – was moved by Mr. Smith, who observed, that partial or detached unions in any part of the country would effect nothing; it must be a general union, and recommended the utmost toleration in respect to religious differences of opinion, otherwise they would throw barriers in the way of any union of interests.

Mr. *Phillips* objected to the use made of Trades' Unions, and said that none ought to interfere with them who were not members. Mr. Owen said, that the Trades' Unions did not as yet know the amount of their power, and what they were really destined to accomplish; they did know their power and their plans, but they did not mean to go so far as Mr. O., for they had no objections to work for masters that were well-disposed.

Owen saw trade unions not as bodies concerned with the day-to-day struggles of industrial relations, but as a means of bringing about a fundamental transformation of society. The basic conflict, according to Owen, was not between masters and men, but between producers and non-producers (17).

(17) *The Crisis*, III, no. 21 (18 Jan. 1834)

Mr Owen hoped the first meeting he attended in Derby of the operatives would be for good, and not for evil. He would, if he could, remove all angry feeling between the employed and the employers; he was quite sure the time was coming when they would regret there had been any angry expressions used between them and the manufacturers. They must admit that both parties were made of the same flesh and blood, and therefore, if the men were placed in the masters' circumstances, they would do as the masters had done; and the masters, similarly circumstanced, would do as the men had done. This consideration should promote the exercise of genuine charity between the parties. It had been his lot, in other places, to recommend, not division, but union, to the men, and union to the masters. The masters of Derby had decided against Union; he was quite sure they had done so under a mistake. Unions were forming in Great Britain and Ireland, with direct intention of equally benefiting the masters, the men, and the public; and if there were any masters present, he begged they would consider what he should state respecting those Unions. The present injurious system was destroying the capital of the workman – his labour – and the capital of the manufacturer; for although some large fortunes were amassed, it was his decided opinion, that seven out of ten of those who embarked their capital in manufacture, in a few years became bankrupt, or compromised with their creditors. Those who made fortunes stood prominently forth before the public; but those who failed were lost sight of, and sunk into poverty; it was better to receive the wages of the artisan, than to struggle with the difficulties of such masters. His object was not to promote Union for the protection of the working classes alone, but of the producing classes generally. . . .

Mr. O. then alluded to a society that had been established in Derby a few days previously, which we afterwards understood to be an auxiliary to the Manchester National Regeneration Society. It was established on just principles, and inculcated genuine charity, which would enable one man to make allowances for difference of sentiment in another. This charity, so much wanted in society, would discover itself in the every-day transactions of life. It gave a new heart, was observed in the tone of voice and the manners of mankind, and when it was universally understood they might date from that time the millennium of the world. He was very desirous that masters and men should never speak angrily to each other; that on all matters of dispute they should reason calmly, and make allowance for difference of circumstances. Then, he was quite sure before the end of another week a Union would be formed amongst the masters, and delegates appointed by both masters and men to confer together, and harmony and success would attend their future connexion. When he returned, which he should do in a few weeks, he hoped their differences would be terminated for ever.

While Owen's oratory may have inspired men to organise, most unions deviated from his utopian vision. Habits of secrecy died hard. The oath administered to members of the Builders' Union of 1831–4 was published by the hostile Poor Law official Edward Carleton Tufnell (1806–86) (18).

(18) E. C. Tufnell, *The Character, Objects and Effects of Trades Unions* (1834)

I do, before Almighty God and this Loyal Lodge, most solemnly swear, that I will not work for any master that is not in the union, nor will I work with any illegal man, but will do my best for the support of wages; and most solemnly swear to keep inviolate all the secrets of this Order; nor will I ever consent to have any money for any purpose but for the use of the Lodge and the support of the Trade; nor will I write or cause to be wrote, print, mark, either on stone, marble, brass, paper, or sand, anything connected with this Order, so help me God, and keep me steadfast in this my present obligation; and I further promise to do my best to bring all legal men that I am connected with into this Order; and if ever I reveal any of the rules, may what is before me plunge my soul into eternity.

Some of Owen's associates encouraged specifically class-conscious stances. At the forefront was James Morrison, the editor of the Operative Builders' Journal, *The Pioneer* (19).

(19) *The Crisis*, III, no. 27 (1 March 1834)

Mr. *Morrison* said he felt great pleasure in informing that numerous meeting that he was well acquainted with a great portion of the working classes, who had already been formed into Unions, and that he, with many others, had come to town for the purpose, if possible, of uniting all these in one great bond of union; and he would tell some parties, particularly those at Derby, that no family of the working classes need then be fearful of the consequences arising from the oppressive conduct of the masters. In their progress, they had had great prejudices to contend against, arising from the partiality of many of the operatives to their own particular trades, and from the pride which had sprung from the possession of larger funds, which had also given rise to the feeling that they ought to have superior power; but this was unbecoming. They had, however, been very successful in subduing their injurious views and feelings; and, in order that all might be included in the great union about to be effected, it had been proposed to constitute a miscellaneous lodge; and the whole will thus be cemented by wise arrangements, and will form the great regenerating power of society. Happily, too, the working classes had now discovered that violence was injurious, and altogether unnecessary to the success of the great cause; and although the Derby masters had succeeded in their object in a trifling degree, they would, in a few weeks, convince them, and those of Yeovil and Worcester, that they were for ever removed out of the reach of their oppressors. But the tyranny of the masters, in saying 'if you will not work for us, we will starve you to death,' had greatly contributed to the success of the union, for in one week after this circumstance had occurred, we established a manufactory. These gloves now on my hands are *Union gloves*, and to-morrow I expect we shall have large parcels up, ready for sale, of the very best qualities, and all the production of the Union turned-outs [tremendous cheering, which lasted for a considerable time]: – and to show you that the masters can quarrel as well as the men, I can inform you that they had a quarrel, and also a fight, and in the battle the mayor got a black eye! The various attempts of the masters, in different parts of the Kingdom, to put down the Unions, had caused the principles of general union to spread; and they had now attained that strength and power, which for ever prevents the capitalists of the country from wielding the productive power of the country to the total exclusion and injury of the producing many. And though the prejudices had been numerous, and a great many objections have been raised against the ceremonies of the Trades' Unions, yet have we not conventional ceremonies, religious ceremonies, freemasonry ceremonies? And though secrecy has also been objected to, and however well the objection might appear in theory, in practice it had been proved to be highly beneficial . . . .

The gap between the vision and the reality continued in 1834, when the Grand National Consolidated Trades' Union was formed (20, 21, 22). This union (GNCTU) grew from a meeting of union delegates in London held to gather support for the trade unionists of Derby, who had been engaged over many months in a struggle with their employers. It never succeeded in attracting really national support: the main provincial unions, such as the Builders' and the Potters', kept clear of it and the bulk of its support came from the London craft societies. Membership figures were much nearer 16,000 than the half a million or more that has sometimes been suggested. None the less, it did represent a serious attempt to co-ordinate union activity at a time when unions were coming under attack from organised employers, who had recovered from the shock of the 'explosion' of unionism in 1833.

(20) *The Tradesman* (12 April 1834): Address of Robert Owen

Men of industrious habits, you who are the most honest, useful, and valuable part of society, by producing for all its wealth and knowledge, you have formed and established the Grand National Consolidated Trades' Union of Great Britain and Ireland, and it will prove the palladium of the world. All the intelligent well-disposed, and superior minds among all classes of society, male and female, will now rally round the Consolidated Union, and become members of it; and if the irrationality of the present degraded and degrading system should render it necessary, you will discover the reasons why you should willingly sacrifice all you hold dear in the world, and life itself, rather than submit to its dissolution or slightest depression.

For your sakes I have become a member of your Consolidated Union; and while it shall be directed with the same wisdom and justice that it has been from its commencement, and its proceedings shall be made known to the public as you intend them to be, my resolve is to stand by our order, and support the Union to the utmost of my power. It is this Consolidated Union that can alone save the British Empire from greater confusion, anarchy, and misery than it has yet experienced. It is, it will daily become more and more, the real conservative power of society; for its example will be speedily followed by all nations; and through its beneficial example the greatest revolution ever effected in the history of the human race will be commenced, rapidly carried on, and completed over the world without bloodshed, violence, or evil of any kind, merely by an overwhelming moral influence, which influence individuals and nations will speedily perceive the folly and uselessness of attempting to resist.

(21) *The Crisis*, IV, no. 7 (24 May 1834), 'A Memorial from the Grand National Consolidated Trades' Union of Great Britain and Ireland, to the Producers and Non-producers of Wealth and Knowledge'

. . . Let no one, therefore, henceforth be deceived respecting the objects of the Grand National Consolidated Trades' Union of Great Britain and Ireland; for this association has not been formed to contend with the master-producers of wealth and knowledge for some paltry advances in the artificial money-price in exchange for their labour, health, liberty, natural enjoyment, and life; but to insure to everyone the best cultivation of all their faculties, and the most advantageous exercise of all their powers, physical and mental, that they may be enabled wisely to apply the inexhaustible materials provided by nature, to give to every human being the full extent of the happiness which his individual nature so cultivated and exercised is capable of receiving and enjoying, without interfering with the well-being and happiness of his fellow-men.

The Memorialists are therefore ready now to enter on general negotiations with the governments of Europe and America, to devise and decide upon the mode, the least injurious to all parties, by which this change may be at once effected in the principle and practice of governing; that the barbarous language, ignorant language, ignorant violence, and irrational legislation, now general throughout Europe and America, may cease and be for ever forgotten; that all men and parties may be instructed and employed in a superior manner to produce real wealth and sound wisdom; that by degrees these countries and every portion of the earth may be so well cultivated, and the inhabitants so much improved, that it shall become the terrestrial paradise, which the industry, skill, and knowledge of man are now competent to form.

And as old society is breaking up in all its departments, and rapidly advancing to general disorder, the Memorialists are desirous that the misunderstanding between the producers and non-producers of wealth and knowledge should be adjusted for the benefit of both parties, with the least possible delay.

On behalf of the Executive, in council assembled,

> John Brown,
> David Watkins,
> John Douthwaite.

(22) 'To the Operative Cordwainers' (letter from William Hoare), *The Pioneer*, no. 43 (28 June 1834)

Of the Grand National Consolidated Trades' Union of Great Britain and Ireland.

Brothers, – I feel particularly called on at the present moment to address you, on a subject of (to us) the most vital importance. The spirit of discord has reared its frightful head, and many of our London brothers have seceded from the Consolidated Union. It becomes necessary for me, as your responsible officer, to relate to you all the facts connected with the case, in order that you may not be deceived by partial or garbled statements; and in doing so, I am actuated alone by a zeal for the general good, convinced that the interests of one should be the interest of all – convinced also of the utter inutility and insufficiency of anything, short of a Consolidated Union, to effect the moral and physical regeneration of the industrious many.

Brothers, I am known to many of you – for mine has been the pleasing task of heralding forth the glorious principles on which our great Union is based. With heartfelt pleasure I have witnessed the reception and progress of those principles in England and Ireland; with feelings which I feel a difficulty in expressing, have I beheld the sons of industry by hundreds and thousands swelling the ranks of the Consolidated Union; with all the joy of a father for his first-born did I contemplate the mighty results of such a glorious combination, and hailed it as the early dawn of sacred freedom; and shall these hopes be dashed to earth by the opposition of blind infatuated ignorance and folly? Never! will be the answer of every true brother. The love of country, the love of family, of honour and liberty, forbid it.

Many of the brothers look to the Union *only* as a great power that will enable them to strike for a temporary advance in wages. Such men mistake the principle upon which we set out – such men cannot be acquainted with the report of the last delegated meeting, containing the great principles upon which the Consolidated Union is founded, and, in fact, must be utterly ignorant of its objects, namely, 'to establish the paramount rights of industry and humanity, by instituting such measures as shall effectually prevent the ignorant, idle, and useless part of society from having that undue control over the fruits of our toil, which, through the agency of a vicious money system, they at present possess'.

By the summer of 1834 unionism was breaking up almost everywhere. The savage sentences on the 'Tolpuddle martyrs' proved a strong deterrent to further activity. Union organisers had toured the low-wage southern agricultural counties in 1833 (23). Six labourers, headed by George Loveless (1797–1874), were sentenced to seven years' transportation in March 1834, for administering secret oaths (24, 25, 26). These sentences and the effective use of the 'document' by employers, to which was added the spiritual condemnation of the Roman Catholic Church (27), curbed the enthusiasm which had been so evident. Hopes of united action were dissipated as unions turned to a defence of their individual interests (28).

(23) *The Book of the Martyrs of Tolpuddle* (1934): Leaflet circulated in Dorset (Feb. 1834)

Brethren, This will inform you that there is a possibility of getting a just remuneration for your labour without any violation of the law or bringing your persons into trouble if men are willing to accept what is offered them. Labouring men may get two shillings or half a crown a day as easy as they now get one shilling, only let men be united and the victory is gained. After men are united and strike for advance of wages they will be supported all the time they are staying at home from a certain fund provided for the purpose, nor will there be a danger of others undermining you for you take the most cowardly man in the kingdom and let him be united, and he will stand firm as a rock. N.B. – Men are adopting this almost through the Kingdom.

(24) George Loveless, *Victims of Whiggery* (1837)

From this time we were reduced to seven shillings per week, and shortly after our employers told us that they must lower us to six shillings per week. The labouring men consulted together what had better be done, as they knew it was impossible to live honestly on scanty means. I had seen at different times accounts of Trade Societies; I told them of this and they willingly consented to form a friendly society among the labourers, having sufficiently learnt that it would be vain to seek redress either of employers, magistrates or parsons. . . .

    As to the trial, I need not mention but little; the cowardice and dastardly conduct throughout are better known by all that were present than could be by any description that I can give of it; suffice to say, the most unfair and unjust means were resorted to in order to frame an indictment against us; the grand jury appeared to ransack heaven and earth to get some clue against us, but in vain; our characters were investigated from our infancy to the then present moment; our masters were inquired of to know if we were not idle, or attended public houses or some other fault in us; and much as they were opposed to us, they had common honesty enough to declare that we were good labouring servants, and that they never heard of any complaint against us, and when nothing whatever could be raked together, the unjust and cruel judge, Williams, ordered us to be tried for mutiny and conspiracy, under an act of 37 Geo III Cap 123, for the suppression of mutiny among the marines and seamen, a number of years ago, at the Nore.

(25) *Morning Chronicle* (2 April 1834)

The *real* crime was the participating in the aggressive tactics of the Trades' Unions. Without intending in the least to justify the proceedings of these combinations, which are not only illegal, but the cause of infinite distress to the labouring classes themselves, we may observe that it is very hard to punish men for oaths whose real crime was very different.

(26) *The Spectator* (5 April 1834)

The Legislature a few years ago repealed the laws against combinations; but a judge has still the power of inflicting a severe punishment upon combinators, under the pretence of punishing them for an offence of a different kind – that is, for the breach of a law which poor and ignorant men see broken with impunity by hundreds of thousands of their fellow subjects of all ranks, from the King's brother to the chimney-sweep.

(27) *Catholic Magazine* (March 1834)

We ask . . . is the Union consistent with a good conscience, and can a member be admitted to the sacrament? If not, and usually the answer is in the negative, we must contend, that it is the duty of the clergy to guard their flocks against the danger, to which their souls are exposed, and in the discharge of this duty, they must expose themselves, if it be necessary to that imputation, which is most odious in itself, most revolting to their feelings, and most at variance with their sentiments and conduct, that of indifference to the sufferings and rights of the poor . . . It is, then, from . . . regard for their interest and their happiness, that we are induced to assure them of the evil of the Union, as at present constituted. To become a member of the Union, a candidate must take an oath. . . . He takes an oath, which may, for aught he knows, oblige him to commit a crime. In this case, he takes it; intending either to break it, in which case he is guilty of perjury; or to keep it, in which case he becomes criminal in the violation of some other branch of the moral law. . . .

But in addition to this objection, another arises from one of the laws of the Union, which, however it may be worded, obliges the members to prevent others from obtaining employment, and by employment, their subsistence. This is an obvious violation of justice; it is an act of violence; and emanating from a society, the professed object to which is to protect the poor man in the enjoyment of his rights, a palpable inconsistency. . . .

(28) *The Crisis*, IV, no. 11 (21 June 1834)

It will be seen, from a paragraph inserted from the *Leeds Mercury*, that the Unionists of Leeds have deserted the Union and returned to work. Many of them have also signed the declaration. The masters are exulting over this apparent temporary triumph, and we, ourselves, by no means experience any feelings of regret that such an event has happened, for the principle upon which the Union have hitherto been shaped ('if shape it might be called that shape had none') was a principle of division and discord, calculated only to sow the seeds of enmity amongst the higher and lower orders of producers, but never to effect any ultimate or permanent benefit to the poor. What some people, therefore, call the dissolution of the Unions, we call the dissolution of the 'striking' system only; a system which can no more be called a part of the Union system, that a wart, or a pustule, or a cancer can be called a member of the human body. The Unions will rise with increased health and energy after this dissolution as they call it; and instead of acting in detached bodies as hitherto, each following the impulse given by its own private isolated circumstances, the hope of gaining an additional sixpence per day, or perhaps the desire of gratifying some private feelings of hostility, in which the whole of the working population could not freely sympathize, the case of each Union, each Lodge, will be submitted to the investigation of a national council, and the head will assume control of the fingers and the toes. We shall always predict failure after failure till this takes place. We also now congratulate ourselves and the friends of the co-operative system upon the favourable aspect which the country presents for the propagation and adoption of our views of the production and distribution of wealth. The career of the people is straight forward to co-operation, and the stages seem to be very short, and the movements quick. Partial strikes are merely the competitive system, in direct opposition to co-operation, and we wonder at the countenance which many professed co-operators have given them; but probably they encouraged them as means to an end, thinking that the people could not otherwise be convinced of the necessity of adopting our ultimate measure. If the next step is not co-operation, it will be one stage nearer it, and there is one more stage to come.

As unionism collapsed, the Yorkshire factory reform leader Richard Oastler (1789–1861) condemned Leeds masters (29) and others (30) for their hostility to working-class organisations.

(29) Richard Oastler, *Serious Address to the Millowners, Manufacturers, and Cloth-Dressers of Leeds* (Huddersfield, 1834)

You are laying the foundation, upon which to build a nation of slaves, or a nation of criminals. . . . The first question I ask of you is – Whether are the LAWS of this Land, or the uncontrolled WILL of the 'United' Masters, to govern the Operatives? . . .

Who ever heard of an 'Union' of Landlords or Aristocrats, to compel their Tenants to sign away a natural or legal RIGHT, as a condition to the occupancy of their Houses and Lands? – Verily, my Good Sirs, ye have taught the people what Tyrants the Aristocrats were, but it has been reserved for the 'March of Intellect', to teach a 'Liberal' Millowner or Manufacturer, or Cloth Dresser, how to out Herod Herod, in Tyranny and Cruelty! . . .

The men have a RIGHT to unite, according to Law; – and you have no more right *to take advantage of their necessity*, and thus to *compel* them to abandon their RIGHTS – Than they have a RIGHT to take advantage of their numbers, and by force, to deprive you of your property, or of your lives! . . .

You teach them to seek for your blood – *when you starve them into submission!!* . . .

But you will perhaps say, 'the men when they unite, intimidate and otherwise act illegally'. – I suppose they do, – and who wonders? – I am sure I do not. – But, poor fellows, – the Law punishes them when they break it; though *you*, their Masters, taught them that trade, about three years ago; you taught them to despise the Laws, to insult the King and the Queen, and to 'Stop the Tap' against the Tax-gatherer. . . .

You are not taking a position you cannot maintain. I dare say you will beat the men, – but they will owe you a grudge!!! – and they will pay it you some day!! . . .

Never mention 'intimidation'. – You know you practise that much more than they.

(30) Richard Oastler, *A Few Words to the Friends and Enemies of Trades' Unions* (Huddersfield, 1834)

The Press of England seems to be engaged in a Crusade against 'Union', – and almost every class in society seems, at the present moment, to be persuading itself, that 'Trades' Unions' are the great cause of our national distress; – whereas the truth is, – *they are the legitimate offsprings of that distress*. . . .

The Land Owner, the Merchant, the Farmer, the Manufacturer, and the Shopkeeper, can never prosper, or be safe, *unless the Labourers are all well paid*. . . .

I believe it is the System (and not Individuals) which is the cause of our distress; employers cannot, if they would (under this system), act on Christian principles, to the employed; but they can, if they will, 'Unite' altogether to do justice.

Some organisations survived the general cataclysm and sought new roads to improvement. In 1834 some 700 Lancashire spinners established a 'quinquarticular system' of groups of five members, and in 1835 delegates issued an address from Preston (31). The spinners, under Doherty, were the most active unionists involved in Oastler's Factory Movement; indeed, they had supported the cause long before Oastler assumed the leadership in 1830 (32).

(31) *New Moral World* (3 Oct. 1835)

We are not for *confusion* and *bloodshed*, and therefore we speak thus plainly. Let not the trumpet of reasonable warning be disregarded, because it is sounded by a few Lancashire workers. We would despoil no man of his rightful property; we dream not of any absolute equality of condition; we entertain no visions of paradise below. We expect that the 'brow' of man must 'sweat' for his maintenance; but we expect also, according to the promise of the Most High, to live by it, to eat our bread by it.

(32) SC on Combinations of Workmen, *First Report, PP* 1837–8 viii: Evidence of John Doherty

Mr. *Pringle*. Will you state generally for what purposes the combination took place? – There were several objects of the Spinners' Association; the main one was to prevent reductions of wages; and next, if it be possible, and we hope it will be certain, to procure an Act of Parliament to lessen the hours of labour in factories. That point, I believe, in fact I know, during the whole of my connexion with the spinners of Manchester, has been one that has never changed. Our society has been abandoned at different periods, and our meetings given up, but we have never abandoned the hope and attempt to lessen the hours of labour by Act of Parliament.

Mr. *O'Connell*. You mean what is called the Ten Hours' Bill? – Yes; ten hours or less.

Mr. *Pringle*. You do not deprecate the interference of the Legislature with such a subject as that? – No, we do not; we seek it.

To what extent, then, do you deprecate the interference of the Legislature with the interests of the workmen? – With regard to the mode of carrying on their combinations or anything of that description.

Are there any other objects or purposes for which you associate? – The other object of combination would be in endeavouring to prevent certain harsh treatment, to which we find we are gradually becoming more and more subjected.

Lord *Ashley*. You say that what is technically called the Factory Question has been the main object of your combination for many years? – It has for more than 20 years, to my knowledge; I can state as a fact, that in 1818, when our combination was broken up, in consequence of a strike that was unsuccessful, in the year or two following that, when the men contributed nothing to the fund of the union, they contributed regularly for the purpose of procuring an Act of Parliament upon that question, and one was enacted in 1819.

Do you ever make contributions now for the purpose of carrying out that result? – Regularly; as soon as a notice appears of the question being mooted in Parliament, a discussion takes place, and so much money is set aside to defray the expense of attending to the proceedings in Parliament, and obtaining information.

Among the trades of the West of Scotland unionism continued to grow (33). The strongest union was the Association of Cotton Spinners (see (8) *supra*) which had, since about 1815, exercised a powerful influence on the industry by a combination of effective organisation and selective intimidation (34). Like the Manchester spinners, those in Glasgow made use of picketing against 'nobs' or 'blacklegs' (35, 36). At the end of 1837, after the assassination of a 'blackleg', the authorities acted. The leaders of the Glasgow Cotton Spinners' Association were arrested, brought to trial and sentenced to seven years' transportation (37). The extent of the spinners' leaders' involvement in the murder remains obscure (38), but, as in the case of the Dorset labourers in England, the trial of the Glasgow cotton spinners fulfilled the desire of the authorities to curb union growth in Scotland.

(33) W. Cleland, *Former and Present State of Glasgow* (Glasgow Statistical Society, 1836)

Of late Trades' Unions have been much in vogue in this city and neighbourhood, and it is strange that though these unions have, in many Trades, been successively overthrown, still new ones arise from the Unions. It bespeaks deplorable ignorance in the mass of the operatives who have allowed themselves to be led on by a few designing and selfish knaves.

(34) George Salmond, Procurator Fiscal of Glasgow, to D. Cleghorn (29 Aug. 1837) [MS. letter in Crown Agents' Papers, Scottish Record Office]

In following out a rather elaborate and difficult investigation and Precognition, as to the murder of John Smith a nob Spinner, by McLean who is understood to have been hired by the Secret Committee of the Combined Cotton Spinners, I learn that three of the accused who are in custody are said to have been deeply concerned in similar crimes on former occasions and that evidence to this effect is attainable – It being therefore of the greatest importance to make the case as strong as possible, I beg the favour of you to cause look out and send me

1. The precognition reported by the Glasgow Burgh Fiscal in Sept. or Octr. 1820 against Patrick Mellon for throwing vitriol upon and severely injuring, one Cairnie – Mellon was acquitted. Jas. McDonald one of the prisoners is said to have committed the crime.

2. Precognition reported by me against John Walker for shooting into the bedroom of Wm. Brown – Walker was tried at the Circuit court here and

convicted Spring 1827 – his accomplice John McCaffer is now in custody. In the production libelled on, there were 9 Schedules which it is extremely desirable you should recover from the Justiciary Clerk and send to me, as useful in the charge of conspiracy against the persons now in custody.

3. Precognition reported by me – December 1833 or shortly after, as to an aggravated assault committed on the Morning of Monday 16th December 1833 by some persons then unknown, upon the persons of Mr. Robert Millar, Manager of the Lancefield Cotton works near Glasgow – which Assault I am now assured can be proved to have been committed by *Wm. McLean* the prisoner said to have shot John Smith.

(35) E. C. Tufnell, *The Character, Objects and Effects of Trades Unions*

This system of picqueting mills has been carried to the greatest extent in Manchester; where the obnoxious factory is always watched by five or six men, unknown in the immediate neighbourhood, and who, on a given signal, can be reinforced to the extent of 300. . . . It is absolutely necessary for the protection of liberty, that some legal means should exist for removing these picquets. Any person connected with establishments so watched, or police-officer at the request of such person, might be authorised to apprehend, without warrants, any of these picquets, and take them before a magistrate, who should have the power of summarily convicting them in a penalty of three months' imprisonment.

(36) John Greig, Edinburgh, to Lord Advocate (16 March 1838) [MS. letter in Crown Agents' Papers, Scottish Record Office]

In the Autumn of 1834, I went to Glasgow to get some further experience in the engine and machine making. When I went to a shop to enquire for work, the Master asked if I belonged to the Union? When I said 'no' he said that 'he could not employ me, because if he did, all the rest of his men would leave him, but if he could get his shop filled with non-unionists he would be very happy', which shewed that he did not *willingly* submit to the Union's regulations. But in the shops where the Masters have defeated the Union, the Unionists still exercise their power with sufficient malignity to render the life of any poor obnoxious nob sufficiently miserable. When I wrought at Oakbank Foundry no sooner had daylight gone, than a regular battery of missiles was commenced and continued till we left the work. . . . After many generous, but unsuccessful attempts to protect me from the secret malice of the Unionists the master was at length obliged to dismiss me in order to prevent me being killed on his premises. In September 1836, I went to work at Manchester, and at the beginning of the second week I wrought there I was compelled to attend a meeting of the Unionists the purpose of which was to decide whether I ought to be allowed to work there or not; as might have been foreseen they decided that I ought not, and on my refusing to leave the shop to please them, they told me that I 'should not have the life of a dog', and they took special care that the truth should not fall short of prediction. I was there treated in the same manner as I was in Oakbank Foundry. There was one man who manifested an opposite demeanour, he behaved civilly and obligingly to me; the Unionists observed this and laid a letter on his bench informing him that if he was seen conferring any favours on, or speaking in a friendly manner to me he would be robbed of his tools and never have chance of redress.

(37) *A Voice from Prison. The Address of the Glasgow Cotton Spinners to Hugh Alexander, Chairman of Glasgow Committee of Trades, etc.* (Edinburgh, 1838)

Edinburgh Jail, 15 Jan. 1838

Our case, which has excited so much public interest, has now come to a close, and we have received in the language of one of the Judges, Lord McKenzie, '*an arbitrary sentence*'. How far that sentence is in accordance with the laws of the country; and the usages of our Courts of Justice, we leave the public to decide.

After having calmly examined the nature of the crimes of which a Jury has found us guilty, after minute and impartial investigation, we think it will be found, that those crimes amount in substance to neither more nor less than this, – That we, along with our fellow workmen, resolved, and did strike work against an enormous reduction of wages, determined upon by our employers; that a tumultuous crowd, or mob, of men, women, and children, of every grade and description, amongst which there were some Spinners assembled at Oakbank Factory, and that some stones, fish-heads and other missiles were thrown, and two men were thereby a little hurt; and that another crowd assembled near Mile End, Calton, where some Spinners were apprehended by the police, not for any offence, except as composing part of the crowd; and that one of them was summarily brought before the Sheriff, and convicted of what he never knew to be a breach of the law; since that the Cotton Spinners' Society resolved, at the request of their Agent, to use their influence with their own body, to prevent their members from joining in such assemblages in future. Yes, Dear Sir, this is all. A Jury after eight days attentive investigation, a period unparalleled in the history of criminal jurisprudence in this or perhaps any other country, could find against us; and what we think worthy of remark, no witness, or any one else attempted to say that any of us were near those places where the disturbances occurred, in fact, some of us were not in the kingdom at the time. Therefore you may see, Sir, *that our offence consisted entirely in our being members of the Spinners' Committee*, an offence, if it be one, that we have not at any time attempted to deny. . . .

(38) *The Monthly Liberator*, III (9 June 1838): 'Cotton Spinners' Case. *Truth* v. *Law*',

After all the mighty fuss that was made about the murder of Smith, and the nefarious attempts to fasten the guilt upon the united operatives, by a conspiracy of the bankrupt masters, who were anxious for an excuse to lie idle for a while, as

they could not meet their engagements for cotton, it is likely to turn out that the
Liberator was right, when it declared that Smith had either fallen victim to a just
revenge from the relative of some of those unfortunate children whom he abused,
or was assassinated at the request of the masters, in order to enlist against the
Spinners the sympathy of the public, and to furnish themselves with an excuse for
conduct so damning, that it could only escape execration during an excited state
of the public mind.

For some of the older crafts, decline was inevitable and no organisation could prevent it.
The introduction of power-looms, coming on top of overcrowding in the trade, and the
barriers to occupational mobility (39), brought the handloom weavers to a wretched state
(40). A few sympathetic men, such as G. S. Bull (1799–1864), Anglican priest and factory
reformer (41), Sir John Maxwell (1791–1865), a Scottish Whig MP, and others sought
State protection (42, 43). But radical views on the fatuity of looking to the State for aid
won the day. Francis Place (1771–1854), for example, the doyen of London liberal
radicals, had no sympathy with Northern demands for legislative protection (44). Many
handloom weavers were to be active in the Chartist movement.

(39) SC on Combinations of Workmen, *PP* 1837–8, VIII: Evidence of Sir
Archibald Alison, Sheriff of Lanarkshire

Mr. *O'Connell.* Is there any connexion in your opinion between the combination
of the cotton-spinners and the distress of the hand-loom weavers? – I gave some
evidence on that subject in a former examination, in answer to the questions of
my Lord Ashley; but I am strongly impressed with the effect it has had upon the
circumstances of the hand-loom weavers, and I was so much aware of it that I
recommended to Mr. Symons, the Government commissioner who is now
investigating the state of the hand-loom weavers of Glasgow, to turn his attention
particularly to that subject; but he told me just before I left Glasgow, that such
was the terror of the witnesses in the hand-loom line on the subject of strikes, that
out of the first 20 he had examined, he had only been able to get one who would
utter the words 'unions' and 'strikes' but in the twenty-first witness he did
stumble upon one who was less alarmed, and he gave important evidence on that
subject. I am perfectly convinced that the distress of the hand-loom weavers is
mainly and almost entirely to be ascribed to the exclusive monopoly established
by the forcible conduct of the trades in all other lines, which prevents their sons
getting into any other line.
    Preventing the free circulation of labour? – Preventing the free circulation of
labour; every trade is fenced round by prohibitions, which render it impossible
for a person to get into it, except a son or a brother, or some relation of an already
existing member; in short, it is the old spirit of monopoly revived in the persons of
the skilled labourers, with this difference, that it is not a few merchants, but a few
hundred or thousand workmen, who exclude a hundred thousand of unskilled
workmen.
    Who operate tyrannically upon all those who would wish to dispose of their

labour freely and without the influence of those unions? – Who operate so tyrannically that the lower orders find it impossible to oppose any resistance to it. . . .

(40) *Observations on Power-Looms* (Glasgow, 1826)

Power-looms stand upon a very different principle, they place the hand-loom-weaver in a situation, that requires him to do what it is not in the power of human nature to perform, and have brought him into a state of wretchedness; altogether unknown in Britain, or perhaps in the world.

[The hand-loom weavers] are the most numerous, the most industrious, and, perhaps, the most virtuous of your manufacturing operatives. Ay, and more than that, they are the bulwarks of your country. The weavers are as much the nursery of the army, as the merchant ships are of the navy.

(41) G. S. Bull, *The Cause of Industry* (Bradford, 1835)

The small Manufacturers of Employers of Hand Loom Weavers are the only remaining hope of this community – they form a link between labour and independence. Let them be destroyed by Capital and Steam, and we shall drive the labourer to despair. There is not a steady and clever Hand Loom Weaver who does not hope to become, at some day, a small employer. IS THIS BRIDGE TO BE BROKEN UP?

(42) *Report of Committee on Hand-Loom Weavers, PP* 1835 XIII

Of the combination of causes to which the reduction of wages and consequent distress of the Weaver may be attributed, the following appear to be the most prominent:–

1st. Increase of machinery propelled by steam.
2nd. Heavy and oppressive taxation, occasioned by the war.
3rd. Increased pressure thereof, from operations on the currency and con-tractions of the circulating medium in 1816, 1826, and 1829.
4th. The exportation of British yarn, and foreign competition created thereby, from the increase of rival manufactures abroad.
5th. The impulse given by low wages and low profits to longer hours of work.

Your Committee would also add the following suggestions from the Evidence, as worthy of adoption:

1st. A more exact specification of the length and breadth of the pieces of goods to be manufactured.
2nd. A cheaper legal form of indenture of apprentices, and a reduction of the stamp duty to 5s.
And 3rd. A more summary and effectual protection against embezzlement of weaving materials.

(43) Paisley United Weavers, Charleston District Meeting Minutes, Dec. 1834–Aug. 1835 [Paisley Museum]

5th January 1835

Resolved – That James Wood, John Wood and James Young form a deputation to call upon Mr. Speirs of Culcreagh and the Liberal County Candidate and ascertain their views respecting a Board of Trade.

2nd – That we publish a resolution in the Glasgow Chronicle and Liberator expressive of our approbation of Mr. John Maxwell's Parliamentary exertions in behalf our body in endeavouring to obtain a legislative enactment in our favour. . . .

4th – That any of James Parker's weavers who may be subjected to loss or expenses in consequence of refusing to comply with his request of withdrawing from the Union shall be supported from the funds.

(44) Francis Place, 'Handloom Weavers and Factory Workers', in *Pamphlets for the People*, no. 16 (1835)

You all know that the little master and the new master are the first to take advantage of the poverty of a workman, or of his want of employment. . . .

Leave off railing at others, and go seriously to work for yourselves. 'God helps those who help themselves', says the proverb; and you may depend upon it that you will never be helped by any but yourselves. . . . Your proposed remedy of a short time-bill, is even more than absurd. It never will be granted. It ought not to be granted. No Parliament will ever pass a bill to prevent any class of manufacturers from carrying on their business in any manner they may think most advantageous, save only as far as relates to the employment of children; and a short time-bill is not necessary for their protection. A short time-bill would make the condition of the 'factory workers' beyond all that they have hitherto endured, miserable indeed. . . .

I have never seen the inside of a cotton factory. It is almost certain that I shall never see the inside of one. . . . I cannot voluntarily submit to seeing the misery of working it before my eyes. I abhor such scenes of degradation.

The attitude of Chartists towards trade unions was often equivocal (45). However, they saw unions as a possible area of support if only they could be turned to the 'grander' purpose of the Charter. Joseph Rayner Stephens (1805–79), a violent Tory radical demagogue and dissident Methodist minister at Ashton, sought to stir the Glasgow workers to a revolutionary fervour (46), while in Lancashire William Benbow (1784–1850), a radical pamphleteer and itinerant orator, tried to incite a general strike, which he had been advocating since the beginning of the decade (47).

(45) *The New Liberator* (6 Jan. 1838)

Having thus stated our approval of unions, we will also state that we think they act not only injuriously to themselves, but also to the country at large. Whenever they interfere to prevent individuals, either by intimidation or otherwise, to enjoy free exercise of their rights to sell their labour at the highest possible prices, the union is no longer a protective body, but an active agent with a tyrannical tendency, hurtful to themselves and injurious to others. The rashness in which they have hitherto engaged in strikes had also been highly injurious. Strikes, like rebellions in a state, are of a very dangerous tendency. They ought to be carefully considered, well matured, and proper arrangements made to secure success, before being attempted, as every failure will only add to the grievances originally complained of, and to the insults formerly endured. They also are a direct loss to the community to the whole amount of the value of the labour while out of employment – a loss, never compensated by success. In order to be successful, indeed, a union of all trades ought to be formed – delegates from each, in proportion to their number, appointed as a committee, before whom all differences betwixt master and man should be laid, discussed, and disposed of, and each trade should be bound to abide by their decision. The cause of one trade would be defended by all, and, as greater caution would be adopted, the probability of success would be infinitely increased. Experience must have taught the trades before this that there must be something radically wrong in the structure of their unions, since after all their exertions – after all the sacrifices made – their situation is not one whit improved from what it was years ago. Why is this? Truly it is hard to say; but it appears to us that they have been wasting their energies in individual skirmishes, and *striking* sallies, instead of acting in one firm concentrated body, prudently, cautiously, and for the advancement of the interests, not of any particular trade, but of the whole labouring population, in the repealing of those laws which press upon all.

(46) *The New Liberator* (6 Jan. 1838): Speech of Joseph Rayner Stephens at Glasgow on the trial of the cotton spinners

I saw these men charged with unlawfully combining to save themselves, and the wives of their bosoms, and the children of their love from hunger, starvation and death – lingering, torturing death, by unappeased cravings for food in the land our God has given to all the people, that they may subdue it, and live in peace, plenty and happiness; . . . . Here I do not hesitate to say, that in the abstract, I do not approve of Trades' Unions; I look upon every union of working men, to raise the price of wages, as an evil; I denounce them as tending to destroy every kind, and generous, and Christian feeling; and to be, in fact, a constant civil war between people of different classes. I look upon every such union as a calamity. In no well governed society – in no well ordered community, where rightful laws prevail, ought such unions to exist; and I desire to see the unions of workingmen for ever put to an end to – aye, for ever buried in oblivion – provided – aye, provided that the masters, on their part, commence by setting the example (Cheers), and declaring that they will never combine to inflict torture by hunger and nakedness, on working men, their wives and children, by a hell-born conspiracy, to rob them of their property – their labour; by plundering them of their wages, which can alone ensure them and their families a comfortably and happy maintenance in the land which the Lord their God has given them. Much as I disapprove of trades' unions in the abstract, I approve of them in the present detestable state of society. (Cheers) The circumstances of the times imperatively demand them. (Cheers) Good men must combine when the wicked conspire. Working men who live by their own labour, must unite to protect themselves, when the capitalists, who live in luxury out of the labour of others, are banded together to starve the honest industrious operative. . . . To support the unholy devil-formed conspiracy of the capitalist against the labourer, is our whole land covered over with barracks, filled with armed soldiers, who, it is expected, will murder their brothers, who are trying to live by their labour. . . . Men of Glasgow, I am glad to tell you that the soldiers are with us (Cheers).

(47) William Benbow, *Grand National Holiday, and Congress of the Productive Classes* (1832)

The holiday signifies a *holy* day, and ours is to be of holy days the most holy. It is to be most holy, most sacred, for it is to be consecrated to promote – to create rather – the happiness and liberty of mankind. Our holy day is established to establish plenty, to abolish want, to render all men equal! In our holy day we shall legislate for all mankind; the constitution drawn up during our holiday, shall place every human being on the same footing. Equal rights, equal liberties, equal enjoyments, equal toil, equal respect, equal share of production: this is the object of our holy day – of our sacred day – of our festival! . . .

We must cut out the rottenness in order to become sound. Let us see what is rotten. Every man that does not work is rotten; he must be made to work in order to cure his unsoundness. Not only is society rotten; but the land, property, and capital is rotting. There is not only something, but a great deal rotten in the state of England. Every thing, men, property, and money, must be put into a state of circulation.

The high point of Chartist involvement with trade unions came in 1842. There had always been some close ties with the London crafts (48); but in July 1842 a strike movement starting in the Midlands spread to Lancashire (49, 50). Chartist leaders sought to channel the workers' demands to the Charter (51), but, as William Duffy, the secretary of the Manchester Trades' Delegates Committee during the strike, told his fellow tailors (52), the will to press for political change was often lacking.

(48) 'The West London Boot and Shoemakers' Charter Association to the Trades of London', *The Charter* (28 April 1842)

Most of us have hitherto, like too many of our class, regarded *politics* as something foreign to our interests, as a word of mystical meaning which concerned the rich and influential, and only of primary interest to those who had votes to sell, or ambition to purchase them. Hence we have been content to pursue our respective avocations with unremitting industry, to regard our trade affairs as a paramount interest, and to consider those only our enemies who sought to reduce our wages or infringe on our prices; without extending our inquiries to ascertain how far our trade, our wages, and the very feelings of our employers towards us, were dependent on, and subject to, superior influences – those of our POLITICAL *institutions*. While however we entertain the same favourable opinions of our trade associations, events have recently transpired to convince us, that we do not sufficiently direct our attention to the *source of our trade and domestic grievances*. . . . A political movement is now making throughout the length and breadth of the land to give the working men an equality of political rights, a right in making the laws they are compelled to obey. We would therefore call on you earnestly to join, as we have done, in this struggle for freedom.

(49) Midland Mining Commission, *First Report*, *PP* 1843 xiii: Evidence of Earl of Dartmouth, acting as Lord Lieutenant of the County of Stafford

Returning home from London on the 11th of July, I went to the Potteries, in consequence of letters from Sir James Graham endorsed with a letter of Saturday the 9th., which announced that they had struck work at the Potteries universally. The potters joined the strike after some time. The general opinion was that the potters were worse disposed than the colliers. I went into the Potteries on receiving Sir James Graham's letters.

The state of things in this country was such afterwards that I did not think it prudent to go again, as a strike was expected on account of notices of a reduction of wages by masters here. . . .

The chartists had hired rooms and established themselves at Bilston, and, I think Sedgeley, as long ago as last winter.

At the numerous meetings addressed by chartists, the charter was kept in the background, and they urged the miners to stand out and not give way, as a stepping stone to their own purposes.

The trade having been bad, and work short, though the wages were kept up, the chartists conceived the opportunity favourable for working discontent. It was not a preconcerted break out.

After the strike in the Potteries, the chartists' meetings at night were held in their hired rooms more frequently.

(50) *Manchester Guardian* (24 Aug. 1842): placard issued 'To the Power-Loom Weavers of Manchester and Salford, and the Surrounding Districts'

Fellow-weavers, now is the time, if ever there was one, to make a determined stand. Often have we made a stand versus reduction, but never did we stand in so glorious a position as the present. Nay, so bold is our present strike, that tyranny must, if we are united, fall before us. Will you then, we say, give up your birth-right, when it is within your grasp? No, we know you better. Everything is in your favour: the present demand for your labour is greater than for these last ten years. Warehouses are empty. The prices in the market are rapidly increasing. This, too, at a time when they are offering the most enormous reductions.

Our demand is not unjust, as the following list will prove:–

Reed	Breadth	Picks	Length	Prices
50	27	13	60	1s. 10d.
46	33	13	46	1s. 4d.
66	40	18	36	1s. 8d.
46	32	13	72	2s. 2d.

Fellow-weavers, the above list will not average more than 10s. per week from each pair of looms, and we consider that as being full low, and determined to have it. Be firm, then, – be united, and victory will most certainly be yours. Already some of our masters have consented to grant our just demand, while others seem unwilling to comply. Onward, then, ye toiling slaves – for such you are. Relax not one iota of your determination to have your rights. You know the consequences of defeat. Be men – be women, then, since everything depends upon every one doing their duty.

(51) *The Life of Thomas Cooper* (1872)

When I entered the railway carriage at Crewe, some who were going to the Convention recognised me, – and, among the rest, Campbell, secretary of the 'National Charter Association'. He had left London on purpose to join the Conference; and, like myself, was anxious to know the *real* state of Manchester. So soon as the City of Long Chimneys came in sight, and every chimney was beheld smokeless, Campbell's face changed, and with an oath he said, 'Not a single mill at work! something must come out of this, and something serious too!'

In Manchester, I soon found McDouall, Leach, and Bairstow, who, together with Campbell, formed what was called 'The Executive Council of the National Charter Association' . . . and it was agreed to open the Conference, or Convention, in form, the next morning at nine o'clock. We met at that hour, the next morning, Wednesday, the 17th of August, when James Arthur of Carlisle was elected President. There were nearly sixty delegates present; and as they rose, in quick succession, to describe the state of their districts, it was evident they were, each and all, filled with the desire of keeping the people from returning to their labour. They believed the time had come for trying, successfully, to paralyse the Government.

(52) *Manchester Guardian* (24 Aug. 1842): Meeting of Manchester tailors to receive report of William Duffy on proceedings of the trades' delegates

Gentlemen, called upon as your delegate to give a faithful and true account of my stewardship, I beg leave to say, that I will conceal nothing from you, or the public at large. I found hesitation, weakness, want of confidence, and indecision, on the part of all the delegates. Although the majority voted for the charter, still, as representatives of the trades, they were not able to carry into effect the vote which they had given. . . . Although no one is more anxious for the attainment of the charter than I am, or would go to a greater extent to make it the law of the land; yet, feeling I have a duty to discharge to you as a body, I must say, that I should only be deceiving you, were I to lead you to suppose that the delegates, or the trades they represented, had the courage, the energy, or the determination, so essentially necessary to the carrying out of their objects, and to setting an example to the Kingdom at large. Under those circumstances, I resigned the trust you have reposed in me. Under other circumstances, I might have been swayed by my own feelings and opinions; but, knowing, that many families were depending on the truthfulness of my statement, I have reported faithfully and according to my conscience. The Anti-corn-law League has opened our eyes to the extent of our miseries; the leaders of that body have convinced us, that it is the determination of the commercial classes to depress the working classes to the greatest possible extent, and, by lowering the wages of labour, to force us into a demonstration compatible with their views and interests; but you have already decreed, that you will not be ready tools or instruments in their hands. Men must be governed by circumstances; and under these circumstances I have noticed, you can no longer take a part in the present movement. The mechanical and other trades are about to abandon you, and therefore you should take advantage of the friendly communication already made to you by your employers.

3. *Towards Acceptance, 1843–67*

To a great extent both Owenism and Chartism were movements of the dispossessed and displaced manual workers, fighting a rearguard action against the onslaught of industrial change and capitalism. But throughout the period groups of workers had benefited from and adjusted to new circumstances. The printers (1, 2) and the engineers (3), for example, built up strong unions, which they used both to defend former positions and to gain advances. They were an 'aristocracy of labour' tentatively feeling their way towards 'respectability'.

(1) *The Jubilee Volume of the London Society of Compositors* (1898): Address of General Trade Society of Compositors of London, 1 May 1833

To those who are ignorant of the proceedings of the London General Trade Society from its establishment in 1826 to the present period (1833), it is considered advisable to state that, since its commencement, not one member has quitted it on account of its mismanagement, its tardiness, inefficiency, or illiberality – its numbers have always been increasing – its receipts have been augmenting every year, and never has it been found necessary to withdraw its money from the public funds, although it has always paid its full proportion of all trade expenses, and has invariably been the foremost to reward those who have been injured in their attempts to maintain the rights of the trade.

The proceedings of the Society are openly conducted – no secret and partial investigations – no party decisions have ever stained its records – no wasteful expenditure or embezzlement of its receipts can ever take place – its accounts are publicly audited every quarter – its acts, its funds, its laws, are under the control of its members, who can at all times investigate or take part in the direction of its affairs. . . .

The only security to the workman from injustice, oppression, and pauperism is a well-conducted Trade Society. . . .

(2) *The Compositor's Chronicle* (1 Feb. 1841): Tenth Annual Report of the Northern Typographical Union, Nov 1839 to Dec 1840

Gentlemen,

It is a matter of regret that I cannot commence this Report in the same strain of congratulation on the state of our funds as I did in that of last year. So far from this being the case, you will find that they have suffered a diminution of nearly one hundred pounds. You will, indeed, be aware, by the circulars which have been published, that we have been engaged in a great variety of struggles to maintain those rights for the support of which we are united – those rights on which hang the welfare of the profession and our means of subsistence. The battle against our adversaries has been nobly fought by many a brave and fearless warrior, bright examples of whom I could easily enumerate; and if we have failed, as doubtless we have in many instances, it must not be attributed to a want of courage or the abandonment of principle of our friends, but to the number and combination of our foes. The recent struggles in Wakefield and Doncaster afford an admirable illustration of these positions. It will be remembered, that just as the circular of September 24 was ready for the press, I received the intelligence that the proprietor of the Wakefield Journal had determined to take two additional apprentices. The circular I immediately issued through every part of Great Britain and Ireland; nothing could be more prompt, and yet, so numerous is the tribe of rats, that within a few days he received about twenty applications for the situations of his men. . . .

(3) *Rules and Regulations to be Observed by the Members of the Journeymen Steam Engine Makers and Millwrights Friendly Society* (1843)

PREFACE. . . . The Youth who has the good fortune and inclination for preparing himself as a useful member of society by the study of physic, or who studies that profession with success so as to obtain his diploma from Surgeon's Hall or the College of Surgeons, naturally expects in some measure that he is entitled to the privileges to which the pretending quack can lay no claim; and if in the practice of that useful profession he finds himself injured by such a pretender he has the power of instituting a course of law against him – such are the benefits of the learned professions. But the mechanic, though he may expend nearly an equal fortune and sacrifice an equal portion of his life in becoming acquainted with the different branches of useful mechanism, has no law to protect his privileges. It behoves him then, on all reasonable grounds, and by all possible and legal means to secure the advantages of a society like this to himself, not that it is intended to use any coercive or unlawful conduct towards our employers; on the contrary there is nothing as foreign to the intent of this society, nothing which this institution ought more to declaim against and suppress than such unwarrantable proceedings, which always tend to disunite and estrange that friendship which is so necessary to the interests of all parties; yet how many instances have we instanced in other societies from the very easy access into such of selfish and unprincipled characters, working themselves in, only that they may seize upon its vitals and poison and weaken its interests! But, we hope that this society is established on principles of sufficient strictness to preclude or exclude such characters. . . .

PREAMBLE. The Object of this society is to raise from time to time by subscriptions among the members thereof, various stocks or funds for the purpose of mutual support in case of infirmity, accident or superannuation, for the burial of members and their wives, and also for assistance to members out of work. It shall be called and known by the name of the Journeymen Steam Engine Machine Makers and Millwrights Friendly Society, and shall consist of members belonging to the following trades or branches viz.:– smiths, filers, turners, model makers, machine joiners and millwrights employed in the machine and steam engine business. . . .

Rule X. There shall be an acting branch elected every two years by a majority of branches, who shall see to the appointment of an Executive council of 22, seven of whom shall be appointed by the acting branch, six by Manchester 2nd. branch, and one from each of the following branches, viz. Stockport, Bury, Hyde, Ashton, Rochdale, Bolton, Stalybridge, and Petricroft. . . .

Rule XI. There shall be a general secretary appointed by the whole delegate meeting every two years; he shall devote the whole of his time to the business of the society; he shall be under the control of the Executive Council. . . . He shall draw up a monthly circular, stating the state of the trade in each town, as received from the branch secretaries. . . . He shall also cause to be printed with such report everything that may be considered of interest to the society. . . .

Rule XII. There shall be an equalisation of the funds in each branch every twelve months, immediately after the issuing of the February report, according to the number of members in each branch. . . .

The federal National Association of United Trades, founded in 1845, under the presidency of the radical MP Thomas Slingsby Duncombe (1796–1861), attempted to improve industrial relations and to establish co-operative workshops (4).

(4) SC on Masters and Operatives (Equitable Councils of Conciliation), *Report, PP* 1856 XIII: Evidence of Thomas Winter

1. *Chairman.* Will you state to the Committee what situation you hold? – I am the Corresponding Secretary of the National Association of United Trades for the protection of Industry.

2. Of how many individuals does this association consist? – Of from 5,000 to 6,000.

3. Whom do they represent? – They represent members in the wood trade, the iron trade, the salt trade, and the leather trade, and various other trades; I cannot call them all to mind.

4. Do they represent a variety of trades in the metropolis? – No, they are dispersed over different parts of the country.

5. How long had this association been established? – It was established on the 25th of March, 1845.

6. What were the objects of the association when it was first formed? – With the permission of the Committee I will state them from the rules of the association. The first object of the society is 'To secure, as far as possible, a general confederation or union of trades, to assure certain objects; first, to secure for each member, as far as practicable, a fair compensation for their industry, ingenuity and skill; or, as it is more generally understood, "a fair day's wages for a fair day's work".' The second object is 'To settle by arbitration and mediation all disputes arising between members, and between members and their employers.' The next object is 'To secure to each member the whole of his wages, without deductions, under any pretext, and to enforce all payments to be made in the current coin of the realm and not otherwise.' The next object is 'To employ members at their respective trades whenever practicable, who are thrown out of employment in consequence of resisting reductions of wages, or other acts injurious to their interests.' Another object is 'To regulate as far as possible the hours of labour, with a view to equalise and diffuse employment among the working classes, so that some shall not be overworked, while others may be starving from want of employment.' It is further intended 'To promote legislative reform in all laws that relate to the industrial, educational, sanitary and social progress of the people; to prevent abuses, and to procure the repeal of unequal laws between masters and workmen and capital and labour.' 'To promote the establishment of Local Boards of Trade or Courts of Conciliation and Arbitration for the purpose of adjusting disputes between employer and employed, empowering them to make bye-laws, rules and regulations, and to take cognizance of all questions affecting the interests of labour and trade.' 'To urge upon Parliament the expediency of appointing a Minister of Labour, whose duty it should be to direct and control all Commissions of Inquiry affecting the industrial and social condition of the people, and under whose authority the various enactments affecting the employer and employed should be carried into execution.' 'To secure properly lighted and ventilated workshops, and other sanitary arrangements for the prevention of premature disease and death of the members, and other physical evils that attach to various kinds of labour.' Those are the main objects of the society. . . .

A major development came in 1850 when several engineers' societies in Lancashire and London amalgamated to form the Amalgamated Society of Engineers. In its structure, aims, and wide range of benefits, it built itself on the two most important earlier engineers' unions, the Steam Engine Makers' Society (see ch. 2, (6), *supra*) and the Journeymen Steam Engine Makers' and Millwrights' Friendly Society (see (3) *supra*) (5, 6); under the leadership of William Allan (1813–74) it became the best-known and most powerful of mid-Victorian craft unions, and contrived to survive a major lock-out by the newly-organised engineering employers in 1852 (7, 8, 9). The dispute attracted wide attention from the press (10).

(5) *Rules* of the ASE (1851): Preface

'United we stand, divided we fall'

The Amalgamated Society of Engineers, Machinists, Millwrights, Smiths and Pattern Makers is established to concentrate the varied influences of the above-named branches of the trade upon some advantageous measures, which are calculated to confer benefits upon its members; and although objections are at times raised to Trade Societies, being associations of monopoly and of trade restrictions, they are nevertheless necessary adjuncts of a state of society which has inculcated feelings of selfishness almost beyond the control of our better nature, for by them only can the members of a trade be made to observe some rules, and to conform deferentially to many customs which are for the mutual benefit of all its followers. Members of a trade, who are in the habit of working together in large numbers, who, by their daily intercourse are made acquainted with the circumstances of each other, and who are cognisant of much of the misery which is attendant on a precarious employment, would be inhuman indeed, if they did not make some arrangement for relieving the distress of their fellow workmen, when sickness or a want of employment should befall them. . . .

Our object is not to do anything illegally or indiscreetly, but on all occasions to perform the greatest amount of benefit for ourselves, without injury to others; and if we should be constrained to make restrictions against encroachments on our interests by those who may not have earned a right by probationary servitude, we do so, knowing that such encroachments are productive of such awful consequences to a trade, that if they were persevered in unchecked they would result in reducing its condition to that of the ill-paid labourer without conferring a corresponding advantage on those who were admitted. It is our duty then to exercise the same control over that in which we have a vested interest, as the physician who holds his diploma, or the author who is protected by his copyright.

These then are our reasons for the establishment of a General Society, out of those which previously existed, in order that their various interests may be better protected . . .

(6) *Address of the Executive Council of the Amalgamated Society of Engineers to Their Fellow Workmen throughout the United Kingdom and British Colonies* (1855)

The advantages which are obtained by the Members of the Society are of two kinds, 1st, Personal Benefits which are received directly by each individual; 2nd, Trade Benefits which while they are of equal importance are not so directly or easily appreciated.

With respect to the individual advantages, the Society may be regarded as a great Assurance Association, founded on a broad and safe basis and managed advantageously, by the Members for themselves. The Association, however, offers benefits obtained by a single periodical payment, which ordinary

Assurance Companies do not present.

The Funds of this Society have been described as a general voluntary rate in aid of the Poor's Rate, and in their distribution form a striking contrast to the administration of the taxes for the relief of the poor. . . .

The Society gives security against want of work and the pauperism which is thus produced, – against the destitution which sickness may bring upon the most robust and industrious, – against the life-long dependence entailed by such calamities as disabling accidents, blindness, paralysis, or epilepsy, which incapacitate their victims for work, and against the helplessness of old age when failing powers render the continuous labour necessary to earn a livelihood impossible. This security is given for a contribution of 1s. per week and the benefits afforded by the Rules are as follows:– A Member out of employment through satisfactory circumstances is entitled to receive 10s. per week for fourteen weeks, and 7s. per week for other ten weeks, and after that he is entitled to receive 5s. per week until he obtains employment. A Member when sick (such sickness not being occasioned by drunkenness, disorderly conduct, or disease improperly contracted) is entitled to the sum of ten shillings for twenty-six weeks, and 5s. per week for other twenty-six weeks, after which he is entitled to 3s. 6d. per week so long as he continues sick. If a member is disabled by paralysis or epilepsy, he is entitled to receive £50. If he suffers from an accident or blindness, so as to be incapacitated from future labour, he is entitled to receive £100. The latter species of benefit is of considerable importance; the trade being one which renders men peculiarily liable to accidents.

A Member who has been eighteen years successively in the Society, and who is upwards of fifty years of age, and not able to follow his usual employment, is entitled to receive a Superannuation Allowance of 5s. per week for the remainder of his life. On the death of a Member, his widow, nominee, or next of kin is entitled to receive the sum of £10 to defray his funeral expenses, or a Member may receive £4 of this sum on the death of his wife, leaving £6 to be paid by the Society on his own death. . . .

(7) NAPSS, *Trades' Societies and Strikes* (1860): Declaration of the Executive Council of the Amalgamated Society of Engineers, 2 February 1852

In consequence of the demands and intentions which have been attributed to the Amalgamated Society, the Executive Council have thought it necessary publicly to declare what they have done, and publicly to deny what they have not done.

They have not demanded the discharge of unskilled workmen. They have not endeavoured to throw the skilled operative, not belonging to the Society, out of work, nor have they recommended others to do so. Neither have they countenanced a system of intimidation having that object. They do not seek to fix or to equalize wages, but hold to the doctrine that wages should be settled by individual agreement. They do not endeavour to prevent the introduction of machinery; but by their skill and labour perfect and multiply it.

They do not attempt to bring about any of those things; but in their Circular to the employers carefully limited themselves to the questions of overtime and piecework. To these they still rigidly confine themselves, and they conceive that the reasons for asking for the cessation of these practices are sufficient to justify them.

They look upon overtime as both a privilege and an evil. A privilege, because it holds out to men an opportunity of making more money; an evil, because that money is made at the expense of their own health, strength, mental powers and happiness, as well as the welfare and independence of others. It is not the first time in the world's history that a privilege has been an evil at once to those whom it seemed to benefit, and those whom it evidently injured. . . .

With regard to piecework, they wish it to be fully understood that their objections are to the system as it is, not as it ought to be. The Executive Council will continue to oppose piecework as it is, for the following reasons:– The price is arbitrarily fixed by the masters or middle-men, and often piece-masters or sweaters are introduced, who take a portion of that price themselves; thus making the workman pay out of his wages for the cost of direction and management. If the workman should, by dint of his own expertness and working very hard, earn much more than an ordinary week's wages, the price which was arbitrarily fixed is as arbitrarily reduced for the profit of the manufacturer, who refuses to pay the price originally agreed upon. . . .

The Executive Council of the Amalgamated Society hope that this explanation of their views and acts is sufficient to demonstrate that while they assert the rights of their members, and endeavour to secure their welfare, they do not attack the just claims or peril the prosperity of any other class. . . .

(8) Ibid: 'Representation of the Case of the Executive Committee of the Central Association of Employers of Operative Engineers, &c.'

On Saturday the establishments of all our members were closed. The conditions of an honourable pledge to each other have been faithfully fulfilled; and masters and men, free of their mutual engagements, will be once more called upon to settle the conditions of any new contract into which they may find it for their reciprocal interest to enter. . . .

ALL WE WANT IS TO BE LEFT ALONE. WITH LESS THAN THAT WE SHALL NOT BE SATISFIED. UNTIL WE ACCOMPLISH THAT, WE SHALL NOT RE-OPEN OUR ESTABLISHMENTS. With every respect for noble and distinguished referees, whose arbitration had been tendered to us, and with no reason to doubt that their award would be honest, intelligent, and satisfactory, we must take leave to say that *we* alone are the competent judges of our own business; that we are respectively the masters of our own establishments; and that it is our firm determination to remain so. To this principle we recognise no exceptions.

(9) 'Employers' Strike. Notice. To the Public and Working Classes of Keithley' [*sic*] (1852) [Keighley Reference Library]

[The Masters' Association was founded] not simply to refuse consent to them – but for the purpose of breaking up our valuable and provident institution. This was sought to be accomplished by means the most Despotic and Immoral. . . .

A sacred month was kept by the members of the Masters' Association by closing their workshops against all productive Labour hoping this Starvation method to accomplish that which could not be attained by the use of nobler weapons, such as were proposed by us, viz:– Arbitration, fair discussion, and appeal to the enlightened feelings of the British public.

(10) *The Times* (12 Jan. 1852)

The dispute can only be arranged by the men's withdrawing the notices served by their Council on the masters, or by the masters' relinquishing their demand for such withdrawal, or by a compromise between the two conditions. We will state in plain language why the masters cannot give way. They cannot give way, because by so doing they would admit and receive the notices before mentioned, requiring the abolition of overtime and piecework. If they admit these notices, one of two things must happen – either the notices are to remain a dead letter, or the demands they contain will be enforced. Of course the first of these suppositions is absurd, as it would be ridiculous for men to make such a stand in behalf of a circular which they never intended to come into operation. The Amalgamated Society, therefore, if its notices are allowed to remain un-withdrawn, will proceed at the fittest opportunity to employ its best means of coercion in bringing its desires to pass. These means have hitherto consisted in 'advising' the men to 'withdraw' from the firm refusing to yield; and as this, however disguised, is nothing more or less than a 'strike', the masters, after giving way for a month or two, would find themselves just where they are now. Clearly, this course would never answer.

The cotton workers of Lancashire, although organised in a large number of local societies, were none the less able to negotiate with their employers. In 1853, the East Lancashire Weavers' Association, centred on Blackburn, worked out with the employers an elaborate list of piecework rates (11). The Blackburn Standard List remained the basis of piecework rates in Lancashire for many years.

(11) W. A. Jevons, 'Account of the Weavers' Strike at Padiham in 1859', in NAPSS, *Trades' Societies and Strikes* (1860)

Blackburn is the leading manufacturing town in the East Lancashire district, and in Blackburn there is a powerful and well managed Union amongst the operatives, and also an Association among the masters. These two associations, in place of exhausting their strength in contests, in which *both* parties would inevitably be losers, have pulled well together – the result of which has been, that they agreed some years ago, upon lists of prices of the various descriptions of work in the cotton manufacture of the district, which lists are known as the Blackburn Standard Lists. Table number one of these lists gives the wages of the spinner, and was compiled and agreed to on the 1st of October, 1852. Another table gives the loomers' wages, and was agreed to on the 6th July, 1853; a third, containing the wages for winding, beam-warping, and tape-sizing, is dated the 17th of August, 1853. These tables do not constitute an invariably fixed rate, but form a sort of basis, on which the calculations of wages are made, and with reference to which every rise or fall is regulated. For example – the spinners at Blackburn now receive an advance of 15 per cent., and the weavers an advance of 5 per cent. on the printed tables. The advance of wages in Blackburn is agreed upon by the respective committees of the masters and men, and when adopted, is made uniformly and simultaneously throughout the branch of the trade affected by it.

The table of weavers' wages is a very complicated one, and the system of calculation upon which it is based, one which it would be in vain to attempt to explain fully on paper, without diagrams, to any one not practically acquainted with the machinery. The amount of labour of a weaver superintending a power-loom cannot be estimated by the mere number of pieces of cloth woven, without taking into consideration the nature of the machinery with which he is working, and the description of the cloth that he is weaving. A loom employed on a cloth of loose texture, would of course turn out a greater quantity than one employed on cloth of a fine and close texture; and, if the weavers were paid by the piece, without reference to the fineness of the cloth, a weaver employed on coarse cloth would receive three or four times the amount of wages earned by one employed on fine cloth. The object of the table in question is to give an easy means of rectifying this inequality, and equalizing the amounts earned by persons employed on different descriptions of cloth, fixing of course a low rate for coarse cloths and a high rate for fine ones. These rates vary for pieces of the same length and width, as much as from 3·98 of a penny to 15·37, and are expressed in decimals. In order to fix the amount of wages by this table, there must be ascertained, first the fineness of the reed, which determined the number of threads in the warp, and is expressed as a reed containing so many dwts. per inch; second, the thickness of the thread in the warp and in the weft; third, the number of threads in the weft, expressed in the number of picks per quarter of an inch of the cloth, each pick or thread of course representing one throw of the shuttle; fourth, the width of the loom; fifth, the width of the cloth; and sixth, the length of the piece of cloth.

The better-off workers became increasingly concerned with the 'elevation' and 'improvement' of their members and with creating an image of 'respectability' (12).

(12) *The Typographical Circular* (1 Jan. 1855)

We are glad to perceive the notion gaining ground that our society house should not be at a tavern. It is apparent to all that the cheerless, forbidding aspect of our call-room prevents nearly all our unemployed resorting to it, even in inclement weather, or when they are interested in the lottery of the present 'slate'. We consider it highly expedient for the London trade to have a couple of rooms in a private building, one for the secretary's room and the other for a respectable and comfortable *call-room* – a fit place of resort for any member of the society, in or out of employment.

The majoity of the London employers are never backward in aiding a beneficial trade object. We feel convinced that this *call-room* could be supplied with daily and weekly papers, publications, and useful popular works and books of reference, by appointing a committee to wait on the principal London firms. Depute them to solicit daily and weekly newspaper proprietors for subscriptions, in the form of copies of their papers; proprietors of publications for copies of them; proprietors of book-houses, publishers, and authors for copies of works; and the proper governmental department for parliamentary papers. And above all, we believe that a great number of the members of the profession would be ready to aid the project by presenting books, and thus a very useful library might be formed. . . .

A more extended use of the *call-slate*, now advocated by many members of the Society, we consider extremely desirable. All unemployed wishing to participate in its 'chances' might meet in the news-room, at 10 o'clock in the morning, and enter their names in the manner adopted at present; but we would have the trade secretary publicly to announce in the room all 'calls' at three stated periods during the day, say – 10, 2, and 6 o'clock. This plan is easy of accomplishment, and fraught with inestimable advantages, – it would show the care we take of the unemployed the manner in which the general trade conducts its business – its temperate tone – its non-antagonistic principles – its anxiety for elevation in the social scale. This would gain the respect of employers, would aid us in our self improvement, and the odium which has always rested on the words 'Trades' Unions' would gradually disappear; and not the least, – it would be the means of bringing within our ranks the comparatively few who still keep aloof, would consolidate the cause of unity, and be an example to the trades generally not to rely solely to the powers of numbers for the furtherance and the protection of their privileges.

The concern of workers in the mining areas was of a much more fundamental nature. In Scotland, Alexander McDonald (1821–81) formed the Scottish Miners' Association in 1852 to campaign against a whole range of grievances (13).

(13) Report of SC on Masters and Operatives (Equitable Councils of Conciliation), *PP* 1856 XIII: Evidence of J. C. Proudfoot

Prominent grievances complained of by the miners of Holytown district: 1st. That although we, as a class of workmen are engaged at so much per ton for mine, and 13 cwt. per cart for coal, yet in many works there are no such thing as steelyards or weighing machines of any description whereby to regulate the workmen's labour, and the whole matter is left to the avaricious and keen calculating eye of a menial of the employer who, it can safely be stated, will not be satisfied with less than 28 cwt per ton for mine, and from 17 to 19 cwt per cart for coal; and besides, very heavy deductions are made under various pretences, such as foul coal, brassey coal, &c., &c. And where they have weight the system adopted is so very oppressive that it often causes a strike; for suppose a workman was putting or sending 10 hutches, which is $3\frac{1}{2}$ carts, to bank, each hutch being $\frac{1}{4}$ cwt overweight, if one of this number is found only one pound deficient, the workman loses the whole price of the hutch, and nothing is allowed for the overweight which he has produced. 2nd. That though employed on piecework, the master generally fixes a certain quantum per day, and that labour is too heavy for us to perform. And if a united effort is made by us to reduce the quantity required by the employers to an ordinary day's labour, they (the employers) will not allow us to work, and therefore a strike is the immediate result. 3rd. That the employers, although in receipt of fair remunerative prices in the market for the material, often make unjust and unwarrantable reductions in the wages, thereby causing their workmen to enter upon a strike. It is therefore recommended, that a sliding scale of prices should be adopted between employer and employed. 4th. A code of laws, entitled 'Special Rules', containing no fewer than 43, the general drift of which is to throw all responsibility of accidents and other unskilful management on the shoulders of the workmen, inculcates a silent system, extra labour without promised fee or reward, and pains and penalties, the most tyrannical and vexatious ever heard of. In almost every work where this large book of rules has been served, it has caused a partial or procrastinated strike. 5th. The truck system is another grievance loudly complained of; in spite of all laws passed to the contrary, the employers manage to conduct a system almost purely truck as language can express it; for although they make a pretence to pay by cash, yet if any workman takes that cash to the best market, he is immediately discharged from employment; and all monies for house-rent, tools repairing, doctor's fees, and school-master's fees are retained by them in the pure essence of truck. 6th. That although the Government has enacted several important measures for the more safe conducting and better ventilating of mines and collieries, yet these laws are so much neglected, perverted, and misinterpreted, that their provisions are seldom brought into play for the benefit of the miner, which of necessity is the means of engendering discontent which often terminates in a strike. The proposed cure of these evils is some such measure as that now in operation in France, whereby all disputes arising between employer and employed would be settled by arbitrators mutually chosen by both parties.

Many unions were still largely concerned with organising relief for the artisan tramping in search of work. During the winter of 1859–60, Henry Broadhurst (1840–1911) future general secretary of the Trades Union Congress, travelled more than 1000 miles in search of work as a stonemason (14).

(14) *Henry Broadhurst MP. The Story of His Life from a Stonemason's Bench to the Treasury Bench, Told by Himself* (1901)

My trades-union had relieving stations in nearly every town, generally situated in one of the smaller public houses. Two of the local masons are appointed to act as relieving-officer and bed-inspector. The duty of the latter is to see that the beds are kept clean, in good condition, and well-aired, and the accommodation is much better than might be expected. When a mason or tramp enters a town, he finds his way to the relieving-officer and presents his card. On this card is written the applicant's name and last permanent address. In addition he carries a printed ticket bearing the stamp of the last lodge at which the traveller received relief. He was entitled to receive a relief allowance of one shilling for twenty miles and threepence for every additional ten miles traversed since his last receipt of relief money. Thus, if fifty miles have been covered the man receives one-and-ninepence. In addition he is allowed sleeping accommodation for at least one night, and if the town where the station is situated is of considerable size, he is entitled to two or three nights' lodging. Besides a good bed, the proprietor of the official quarters is bound to furnish cutlery, crockery, and kitchen conveniences for each traveller, so that the relief money can all be spent on food.

Not every commentator in the 1850s was convinced of the benefits of unionism (15). But by the end of the decade, with the help of middle-class sympathisers, in particular a group including the Christian Socialist lawyers J. M. Ludlow (1821–1911) and Thomas Hughes (1822–96), unions were achieving a measure of public acceptance. An inquiry by the influential National Association for the Promotion of Social Sciences found much of which to approve (16). There were, however, still those, such as Ernest Jones (1819–69), who tried to keep alive old Chartist ideals and to ally them with trade unionism (17, 18, 19).

(15) *Edinburgh Review*, cx (1859): 'Secret Organization of Trades'

The managers of Trades' Unions discountenance records. Their most stringent laws are unwritten; their most significant usages are unrecorded; their committees cannot be fixed with responsibility; their threats are not understood; their punishments are inflicted by invisible hands. . . . Their aim and object is, in every case which we have been enabled to investigate, to *stint* the action of superior physical strength, moral industry, or intelligent skill; to depress the best workmen in order to protect the inferior workman from competition; to create barriers which no Society-man can surmount, and which few non-Society-men dare to assail; and, in short, to apply all the fallacies of the Protective system to labour. Such a system injures first the individual, whom it robs of a free market for his labour; secondly, the class of manufacturers to which it belongs by increasing the cost and diminishing the efficiency of the workmen; and lastly the nation at large by curtailing the productive power, and consequently the wealth, of the community.

(16) NAPSS, *Trades' Societies and Strikes* (1860)

The character, ability and wisdom of the leaders of trade societies also naturally vary much in different trades. So far as this Committee have been brought into personal connexion with Societies' officers, their experience is, that the leaders are for the most part quite superior to the majority of their fellow-workmen in intelligence and moderation. Many of them have given most effective and intelligent aid in the prosecution of this inquiry.

The effect of trades' societies as an education in the art of self-government is important. Many of the societies have organizations of an elaborate character, and have a machinery for making the votes of the trade at once simple and effectual; and in many trades no strike can be authorized until the question has been discussed by several committees. This gives a habit of deliberation before action which cannot but have a good effect. . . .

The leaders of trades' societies are known and responsible men; they have the confidence of their own class. Through them prejudices may be dispelled, and the laws of that political economy which, correctly understood, is the workman's best friend, gradually acquiesced in and obeyed.

(17) *Notes to the People* (8 Oct. 1853)

I see only three great movements, having anything like extended influence, power, and cohesion: THE CHARTER, THE TRADES UNIONS, AND SHORT TIME. These three organisations are noble, salutary, and needful. . . .

We have a movement just started, or about to be, in North Lancashire for an act of Parliament to appoint boards of arbitration between employer and employed, to consist of an equal number of both classes. . . .

It looks very much like a trick of Tory factory lords to divide the people and to gain a little popularity on an impracticable question.

(18) *The People's Paper*, (15 Oct 1853)

Already some of the speakers of the 'Labour League', that seems under the especial patronage of Mr. Busfeild Ferrand, have openly advocated a higher duty on foreign Corn. . . .

No! no! the fault lies not in Trade's being *free* – but in Labour's being *enslaved*, – the remedy lies not in Trade's being fettered, but in Labour's being freed. Let Mr. Busfeild Ferrand and his new allies know that the people are not to be caught by any stale protective trick, although it comes clothed under the guise of 'sympathy for the industrious classes', and 'protection for Labour against Capital'. Although it is backed up by parsons, joined by a sprinkling of the ranks of toil. The protection of Labour is to set it free – so that it will want no artificial protection at all!

Free Trade, Free Land, Free Labour – founded on, and guarded by, the FREE VOTE – these are the securities for our future, and the redeemers of our present.

(19) Ernest Jones, 'Balance Sheet of Chartism', *Chartist Circular* (23 Oct 1858)

. . . I maintain that the concessions labour has achieved in other respects, are largely due to Chartist agitation. The Ten Hours' Bill, improved Combination Laws, the liberties of Trades Unions, the possibilities of organising co-operative societies, strikes, and of supporting 'turn-outs' or 'lock-outs', are largely, nay! mainly, due to the existence and conduct of the Chartist body. . . . Who ever heard, before Chartism became an organised reality, of the hours of labour – the health of the working man – the wages for his work – the truck system – the inspection of factories – the ventilation of mines – the education of factory children – the toil of women – and the thousand kindred matters that have since been discussed and legislated on, ever having been seriously considered by Parliament or the ruling classes? Had it not been for Chartism – for the fear of *Chartist pikes* – for the fear of Chartist plug-drawing – for the fear of an armed, terrible Chartist insurrection – not a trades union would have existed now in England; every strike would have been high treason – every combination and labour-subscription a conspiracy. And yet, blind, shortsighted and ungrateful, the very unions, the very men, whose organisation Chartism alone rendered possible, have tabooed politics, and banished Chartism from their councils and their halls. . . .

Struggles continued. Associated with the efforts to improve conditions was the demand for shorter working hours. It came to a head in the strike and lock-out of London building workers in the winter of 1859–60, but the campaign continued in 1861 (20).

(20) London Operative Bricklayers' Society, *Report and Balance Sheet of the Dispute Relating to the Attempt to Introduce the System of Hiring and Paying by the Hour* (1861)

One result of this desire was the Factory Act, restricting the hours of labour in factories to ten hours per day, which has done an immense amount of good. Another was the agitation in 1859 to reduce our working hours to nine per day. At that time the whole of the Building Trades formed a Conference to carry out this project. Public meetings were held, and pamphlets written, to show to the public the great good whch would accrue to us from the adoption of the nine hours' day. Public opinion was thus becoming more and more enlightened upon, and in favour of our measures, and at one time there appeared some prospect of success; but the employers, guided by avarice, formed a secret society, and with closed doors, formed the project of 'locking-out' their workmen, and ultimately of compelling them to sign the 'document'; and we are sorry to be compelled to say, that literature lent its aid in order to crush the noble efforts of the workman, and the name of Sidney Smith (not the witty dean and able essayist of the 'Edinburgh Review' and author of 'Peter Plymley Letter', &c.) a writer of the *Dispatch*, a man who more than once has used his talents to retard the progress of the masses: *his name* will be associated with the traitors and betrayers of our order, as one who added insult to injustice, thereby endeavouring the more completely to crush us.

But, notwithstanding the wealth of our opponents or the ability of their scribes, after a winter's suffering the document was withdrawn, and once more the workman could look his employer in the face without the badge of slavery. Again, in March, 1860, the workmen memorialized their employers for this reduction, and again silent contempt was the result. . . .

All the trades had now determined to send in a memorial (the masons included); they were all independent of each other. Our committee, seeing the determination of the other bodies to send in memorials, thought it best to back them up with one from ourselves, although we disagreed with the policy. Our fears were soon realised; for on the 15th of March a notice was posted on the various jobs of Kelk, Lucas, and Axford, and a notice went the round of the papers, with the names above attached thereto; and also of Mr. G. Smith of Pimlico, announcing, that 'on and after the 23rd of March they would pay all their workmen by the hour, instead of by the day as heretofore'. They thought the bait would take as there was a slight advance of wages by their offer; but the men perceived instantly the evils which would accrue from its adoption, and, without waiting for agitators to instruct them, met together upon their jobs and resolved to resist it at any risk. . . .

Arrangements were now made to hold a great meeting of the whole of the building trades in St. James's Hall, each society to pay its proportion of the expenses. This meeting took place on Wednesday evening, March 27th, and a most crowded and enthusiastic meeting it was. . . .

Several firms now tried to put in force the new system, and our men left at once; among the rest, Mr. Higgs, at the Chelsea Barracks. The employers were not in straitened circumstances for men, and the various large jobs seemed desolate. Mr. Higgs now applied to the War Office for some mechanics from the Corps of Royal Engineers, and, to the eternal disgrace of the Palmerston Government, they readily lent themselves to the capitalists, and supplied them with the men. . . . Earnest protests were entered against the Government, and a deputation of fifteen elected to wait upon the Secretary of War, to request him immediately to remove the grievances. . . . The result was, the Secretary for War promised, on Friday evening, August 2nd, in the House, that the Sappers should be withdrawn on the 1st of September, thus giving another month to our employers, in order to get men to supply the place of the Sappers when they left. The whole of this proceeding was a disgrace to the Government, and must never be forgotten by working men. . . .

We have thus given a running history of our struggle from the commencement; and the question may now be asked, how do we stand at present? to which we reply, our society is so extending itself that it will soon be as well-organized as any in the kingdom. Our laws are remodelled so as to meet every emergency; a circular is established to become the channel of communication between the different and distant branches; we have published a schedule of rules and customs of our trade, which every member must use the whole of his influence to get established. The hour system is restricted to twenty-five firms, and every opportunity must be taken to compel its withdrawal. But we deem it inexpedient to interfere with any other firms at present, but rather let our men keep on the old system until a favourable opportunity shall arise.

The need for some permanent link between trade societies in London had been forcefully brought home during the building workers' strike, and the London Trades Council was formed (21). It sought among other things to regulate the many requests for pecuniary aid which came to London from striking workers in the provinces (22). The LTC was under the influence of those large amalgamated societies with headquarters in London and encouraged the small unions to emulate them (23), as many carpenters' societies had done in 1860 by forming the Amalgamated Society of Carpenters and Joiners. With Robert Applegarth (1834-1925) as secretary from 1862, this society offered a similar range of benefits to those offered by the ASE (24).

(21) *A Short History of London Trades Council, by a Delegate*: Circular convening a conference of delegates from trade societies to be held in Shaftesbury Hall, Aldersgate, 18 May 1860

Are we not being continually made cognizant of either some actual or attempted encroachment on the rights of workmen? – now by some portion of the Public Press – some Member of Parliament – or some so-called 'Social Science' teaching Philosopher and Orator; our Unions being by such writers and speakers most grossly misrepresented, or denounced as institutions of unmitigated evil.

Besides, have we not our own deeply blameable demerits? Are we not grievously deficient in respect of our own duties? – our own means of self-help? – because so isolated; keeping aloof from co-operating with each other, as we in all cases should, and thus forgetting the grand principle – That Union is Strength.

From these causes therefore employers derive many advantages; are often enabled to reduce wages which otherwise would not occur; or curtail certain privileges which should be equally as dear to the working man as his wages. Hence, then, the necessity there is for establishing a Trades Council to strengthen and assist those who are united for securing the Rights of Labour, or are actually struggling in the cause. A Council to cheer, instruct and advise in any trade difficulty, and in the case of any delusive or false statements being made against our Unions, coming at once to the defence, so that the public mind may not be so easily and evilly poisoned against their existence and aims; and even still more than all these – because such a Council is most likely to have a very wholesome influence towards the prevention of many angry collisions which otherwise may, and which also continually, take place between employers and employed.

(22) Constitution of the LTC (1860)

Societies represented at the Annual General Delegate Meeting are recommended by the Council not to grant support to any trade appealing, unless they present credentials from the Council, who would not in any case recommend support to be given until the fullest investigation had been instituted. The Council believe that if trades adopt the above course, cases not actually deserving support would often be detected and often times money saved to the trades, as in the cases of appeal from the country. Before the Council recommend support to be given, they would expect the credentials from the Council of Trades where such trades (making appeal) should be located.

(23) *Bee-Hive* (26 March 1864): Fourth Report of the LTC

It is worthy to remark that societies after they amalgamate, or otherwise become large, steer clearer of strikes and yet raise and sustain their wages much easier and with less expense than small societies have done, or, we believe ever will do. This may be accounted for through the power, in the shape of men and money, which large societies have at their command, and which never fails to be appreciated by the employers, whenever the contending parties confront each other. We therefore would advise all societies to amalgamate should circumstances favour them so doing.

(24) RC on Trades Unions and Employers' Associations, *First Report, PP* 1867 XXXII: Evidence of Robert Applegarth, General Secretary of the Amalgamated Society of Carpenters

Does the 1s. per week entitle a man to all benefits you have specified? – a shilling per week and 3d. per quarter to a benevolent and contingent fund. The benefits are as follows: – Donation benefit for 12 weeks, 10s. per week; and for another 12 weeks, 6s. per week. For leaving employment satisfactory to branch or executive council, 15s. per week; tool benefit to any amount of loss, or when a man has been a member for only six months, £5; sick benefit for 26 weeks, 12s. per week, and then 6s. per week so long as his illness continues; funeral benefit, £12 or £3.10s. when a six months' member dies; accident benefit, £12 or £3.10s. when a six months' member dies; accident benefit £100; superannuation benefit for life, if a member 25 years, 8s. per week; if a member 18 years, 7s. per week; if a member for 12 years, 5s. per week. The emigration benefit is £6 and there are benevolent grants according to circumstances, in cases of distress.

The powerful national societies of engineers and carpenters projected an image of caution and moderation in their industrial activities. Large funds both gave strength and encouraged careful action (25, 26, 27). Even such a smaller London society as the Consolidated Bookbinders adopted similar attitudes, under the influence of its general secretary, T. J. Dunning (1799–1873) (28). In the important Midlands' glass trade the strong Flint Glass-makers' Society combined moderation with a firm control of the trade (29). While such societies relied on 'self-help' principles, the miners, united in a National Association in 1863, under Alexander McDonald, tended to look for State help (30).

(25) RC on Trades Union etc., *First Report, PP* 1867 xxxii: Evidence of William Allan, General Secretary of the ASE

826. Has the executive or central council or governing body of the society, in your opinion, done anything to prevent disputes from breaking into an actual strike? – The executive council does all it possibly can to prevent any strike, and where they have time or opportunity, generally, as I stated here the other day, they cause a deputation of the workmen to wait on their employers to represent their grievances, and then the council gives advice afterwards. We endeavour at all times to prevent strikes. It is the very last thing we would think of encouraging.

827. Do you find that the possession of very large funds, and the fact that they belong to a very powerful organisation, such as your society is, tends generally to make the members of your society disposed to enter into such a dispute, or the contrary? I am not asking now with regard to the council but the members? – I should say that the members generally are decidedly opposed to strikes, and the fact of our having a large accumulated fund tends to encourage that feeling amongst them. They wish to conserve what they have got, as I have heard it put here, the man who has not got a shilling in his pocket has not much to be afraid of, but with a large fund such as we possess, we are led to be exceedingly careful not to expend it wastefully, and we believe that all strikes are a complete waste of money, not only in relation to the workmen but also to the employers.

828. Have you found by experience that your society has done anything to promote the same feeling or the same practice in other trade societies? – Many of the societies (the Amalgamated Carpenters and others I could mention) have taken in fact our constitution and our mode of arrangement as their guide.

(26) Ibid.: Evidence of Robert Applegarth

As to the question what powers the council has over the branches, you will see on the first page of every monthly report the following words:– 'That in the event of the members of any branch of this society being desirous of soliciting their employers for any new privilege, they must first forward to the Council full particulars of the privilege required. The Council will immediately consider the same, and if circumstances warrant grant the application; but should the employers fail to comply with the request made, the branch so applying must again consult the council as to their future course. And under no circumstances will any branch be allowed to strike without first obtaining the sanction of the council, whether it be for a new privilege or against an encroachment on an existing one.' So that the council have the full and absolute power to grant support to members in case of strike, and if they struck against the decision of the council, then the council would withhold support from them.

(27) ASCJ, *Annual Report* (1867)

The men having heard what can be done by properly conducted trade societies by well-timed and wisely directed efforts, and tired of that system of individualism which gives Praxiteles his due and Arkwright, Brunel, and Stephenson 'full scope for the exercise of their extraordinary skill', but which leaves the thousands less skilful to scramble through a selfish world as best they can, have now resolved to try the humanising influence of such a society, and have joined one, the object of which is to lift up the less fortunate to their proper position and which challenges the proof of 'dragging down the skilful'.

(28) T. J. Dunning, *Trades Unions and Strikes* (1860)

We have endeavoured to trace out the cause which leads to the misuse of capital on the one hand and of Trades' Unions on the other. This we find to be an instinct of evil inherent in the very nature of man, belonging not merely to capitalists and workmen, but to the whole human family, which, for want of a better term, we have called the predatory instinct. Within due bonds this instinct, doubtless, lies at the root of all energy and enterprise; allowed to predominate, it is the source of every evil. To subdue this to its proper use should be the aim of all who would promote the well-being of their own and every other class of society.

Applying this to the employer and employed, it is of the highest importance that there should be a good understanding between them; that neither should vex or offend the other. Both are afflicted equally with this evil instinct, and each should learn to bear with the other. Neither class can injure the other without at the same time injuring itself. Both are so essential to each other, and so intimately connected, that one cannot be injured without the other feeling it, and, consequently, no triumph can be gained at the expense of justice by either class over the other with impunity.

(29) RC on Trades Unions etc., *Tenth Report, PP* 1867–8 xxxix: Evidence of T. J. Wilkinson, General Secretary of the Flint Glassmakers' Society

18,662. (*Mr Harrison*) Is it the practice when an employer is in search of fresh workmen and applies to the union, that he applies to someone outside of his own works? – The system of the society is this: There is a central secretary and executive; and a district secretary, and if there is anyone wanted in that manufactory if the employer just informs the factory secretary that he wants such and such a man he immediately applies to the district secretary to see if there is a man upon the roll competent to take the situation. This is done simply to facilitate the obtaining the man required.

18,663. But the employer practically deals with his own men? – With his own men. We keep a roll of unemployed men, and the first man upon that roll who is competent or supposed to be competent to undertake a situation when there is one applied for is the man we send for, if it is from the other side of the three kingdoms, and we pay his expenses to come to that situation.

(30) RC on Trades Unions etc., *Seventh Report, PP* 1867–8 XXXIX: Evidence of Alexander McDonald, President of the National Association of Coal, Iron and Limestone Miners

15,583. What is the number of members in your general union at the present moment? – About 35,000.

15,584. And what are the national association objects? – First, 'Legislation for the better management of mines to protect the miners' lives, promote their health, and to increase among them a higher moral status in society. Second, to obtain compensation for accidents where the employers are liable. Third, to assist all districts and members when unjustly dealt with by their employers in the point of law or legal rights. . . . Fifth, to make the hours of labour not more than eight in the 24 for all miners in the United Kingdom. Sixth, to assist all its members when permanently injured in the mines, by which they are rendered unable to follow any kind of employment. Seventh, a weekly allowance permanently to aged and infirm miners.' (I believe that has been removed), and Eighth, to establish a national agency to carry out the principles of the association. That has been removed also.

15,585. How are the funds raised? – By a penny per member per month.

Not everyone approved of the tactics of the leaders of the large societies. George Potter (1832–95), manager of the trade-union weekly paper the *Bee-Hive*, provided a lead to some of the smaller societies and from 1865 to 1867 maintained a bitter quarrel with Applegarth and other leaders of the LTC. Antipathy was mutual(31).

(31) ASCJ, *Monthly Report* (May 1865)

Of course, *all* our members are aware of the Lock-out in the Iron-trade, and *many*, of the differences which have arisen between the London Trades' Council and Mr. Potter. Had those differences been fairly stated in the *Beehive*, of which he (Mr. Potter) is secretary, manager, and treasurer, probably little difference of opinion would now exist. To enable our provincial members fully to understand the position of affairs, it will be necessary to state that on March 11 a notice appeared in the *Beehive* convening a meeting on the question of the Lock-out in the Iron-Trade. This meeting was held at the Sussex Hotel and there were about 130 present, Mr. Potter presiding. The Executive Council of the Bricklayers' Society attended and protested against Mr. Potter calling the meeting without having first consulted the Trades' Council, of which he is a member. They also declared the meeting to be illegally constituted and that it did not represent the trades of London. A noisy scene ensued – such as, in fact, always takes place at Mr. Potter's meetings if any unlucky wight, who, independent enough to think for himself, should have the courage to declare himself opposed to Mr. Potter's policy: he is instantly assailed by a storm of hisses and cries of 'Turn him out!' So much for 'freedom of speech' at Mr. Potter's meetings. Of course the bricklayers were unsuccessful. . . . Here then are two very serious questions arising out of Mr. Potter's conduct at that meeting – questions which every unionist ought seriously to consider: 1st, was Mr. Potter justified in calling that meeting without first having consulted the Trades' Council, whose legitimate business it is, and who are annually elected by the Trades' Societies of London 'to watch over the interests of labour in and out of Parliament?' 2ndly, Is it to be justified that any man shall call meetings (at which not a credential is seen, and none even demanded) and pass resolutions in the name of the Trades' Societies, who have never been consulted, and many of whom quite disapprove of the policy determined on? . . . A few days after the meeting above alluded to the Trades' Council called a meeting, at which a resolution was passed urging the men in North Staffordshire to accept arbitration as a mode of settling their differences. Mr. Potter opposed it; but as *that* meeting was not a meeting after his own heart, in-as-much as the whip had not been employed, he was left in a small minority. No doubt, if that meeting had been called by private circular – a practice constantly resorted to by Mr. Potter to pack meetings with irresponsible men – the decision might have been reversed. . . . On April 5, the Trades' Council convened a second meeting of delegates, at which fifty delegates produced credentials, and, after some discussion, the course the Council had pursued was approved, and the following resolutions were unanimously passed:–

> That this meeting tenders its best thanks to Lord Lichfield for the able and impartial manner in which he conducted the trust confided in him in relation to the strike and lock-out in the iron-trade, and hopes that the conduct of the men in refusing his suggestion will not deter him from using his good services in so noble a cause.

The resolution was unanimously carried.

> That the resolutions passed this evening be forwarded by the secretary to Lord Lichfield and to the executive of the men on strike, with their earnest wishes that Lord Lichfield's efforts be renewed, and become successful.

The resolution was unanimously agreed to. . . .

It is a well known fact that Mr. Potter, if he does not openly advocate, invariably pursues a policy that must inevitably lead to strikes. He has been the first to congratulate the men on having engaged in a strike, and the last to devise a practical mode of settlement. He has ridiculed and sneered at those who have advised a peaceful settlement of our difficulties; and, in some instances, when the men have effected a mutual and honourable settlement, they have been sneered at and their Societies ridiculed. And for why? Simply, because Mr. Potter knows full well that the circulation of the *Beehive* depends on the amount of strife and contention that exists between the employers and the employed. For our part, we regard strikes as one of the greatest curses that afflicts our social system; and it has been our object to impress upon our members the absolute necessity of engaging in them only when all moral means have been tried and failed. This, then, makes it a matter of little wonder that we have been so severely denounced by those whose interest it is to perpetuate them.

Outside London much important activity was being undertaken. The Glasgow Trades Council, formed in 1858, gave the lead in a campaign against the Master and Servant Acts, backed by the *Glasgow Sentinel* under the editorship of Alexander Campbell (1796–1871) (32). To obtain the necessary social reforms the Trades' Council urged unionists to consider political action' (33). Other councils soon developed, usually in response to some local crisis, as in Wolverhampton (34), or in imitation of the pioneers, as in Manchester and Salford (35).

(32) *Bee-Hive* (9 May 1863): Report of paper by Alexander Campbell

The statute 4th Geo IV Cap. 34, popularly known as the 'Workmen's Act' has been in force for nearly forty years, having been passed on 17 June 1823, and its provisions were still extended by Act 10th Geo IV Cap. 52. It is most comprehensive and is applicable to almost all trades, manufactures and occupations, the following being especially enumerated. Servants in husbandry, artificers, calico printers, handicraftsmen, miners, colliers, keelmen, pitmen, glassmen, potters, dyers, hatters, labourers, and all workmen employed in the woollen, linen, fustian, cotton, iron, leather, hair, flax, mohair and silk manufactures, or other person who shall contract with any person whatever from any time or times. Domestic servants, however, are excluded from the operation of the Act. Under the provisions of this statute any workman of the above description, who contracts, either orally or in writing, to enter the service of an employer, and who does not enter upon such services or, having entered upon it, leaves before the expiration of his contract, or is guilty of any misconduct while engaged on the execution of his contract, may be proceeded against criminally, either by the master or his manager.

Any master may avail himself of the provisions of the statute, by simply presenting a complaint to a justice of the peace and making oath that in his estimation the workman complained of has been guilty of one or other of the above offences, when the justice must at once issue his warrant for the apprehension of the workman to be brought before him for examination; and if he shall then be of opinion that the workman has not fulfilled his contract, or been guilty of any misconduct, he has the power to commit him to prison, with hard labour for any term not exceeding three months. Workmen are not entitled under the Statute to any notice of the intended proceedings against them before apprehension. Whether the charge be well- or ill-founded the justice has no discretionary power, but must on the oath of the master issue his warrant for the apprehension of the workman, and if the justice on examination be of opinion that the charge is unfounded or not sustained, the workman has no redress afforded him by the statute for the wrong he has been subjected to. Should a workman be convicted, there is no appeal the justice's decision being final. Although a workman suffers punishment by this act, such punishment does not dissolve the contract; and if at the expiration of his sentence there is any time of the contract unexpired, he must return to the master and fulfil it, or he is liable to be again proceeded against, and sent to prison a second and a third time, and so on, until the original term of his service has expired.

On the ground that the contract is a civil one the master is only liable under the act to a civil action for any breach of its provisions which he may commit; but he may prosecute criminally and punish as a common felon any of his workmen for what is acknowledged in his case to be a purely civil contract.

(33) *Reynolds's Weekly Newspaper* (10 Nov. 1861): 'Address of the Glasgow United Trades Councils'

We are aware that many are opposed to trades meetings being mixed with politics; we cannot coincide with such views so long as trade societies are amenable to the law.

There are several matters in law that affect them, such as those relating to combinations of workmen and the inequality of the law of master and servant; also, how many times have they been baffled in the attempt to establish councils of conciliation and arbitration? By what means are these measures to be rectified or obtained but by the possession of political power? – the want of which affects the whole labouring class. If these things be true, how can it be that working men, in their associated capacity, ought not to entertain politics?

(34) *Miner and Workman's Advocate* (16 Sept. 1865)

There having been a severe struggle going on for some time between the Plate Lock Masters and their employers, owing to the long continued practice of oppression brought to bear upon them, a few of the men, to the number of seven, started co-operation in the above trade, in a productive form, with a capital of £13, hoping thereby to better their condition, for up to that time the average wage were only 13s a week, for 14 hours labour per day. These men had for some time prospered in their undertakings, both in capital and members, and ultimately reached 100 men. When the masters saw that the men were likely to establish themselves, they started an unjust course of persecution against them in first, by victimizing a number of their workmen; next by combining together not to employ each other's workmen. Then by discharging those of their workmen who had been assisting the co-operators in establishing themselves in their noble undertaking; after which they attempted to influence certain merchants and manufacturers, not to supply them with the goods necessary to carry on their trade. Having been somewhat successful in the above attempts, they started an unfair and ruinous competition against the co-operators; such has been the effect of the competition that both masters and co-operators have been selling at less than cost price. The masters have (though not much to their credit) openly declared that they would make it a struggle between capital and labour; and, as capital always gained the victory, labour would have to succumb. This they have tried to accomplish for the last eleven months, and they have caused the co-operators to sell at a loss to the amount of £585.

In May last a meeting was called by some of the trades in Wolverhampton, to take into consideration the best means that could be adopted to render assistance to these men, when a conference of delegates representing the principal trades of the town, was formed and it was unanimously resolved to hold a public meeting for the further consideration of the subject, with a view to create a pecuniary sympathy on behalf of the Co-operative Plate Lock Manufacturers, to enable them successfully to withstand the course adopted and directed against them by the other employers in the plate lock-trade. There were the following trades represented at this Conference:– amalgamated engineers, tin-plate workers, carpenters and joiners, coach-builders, moulders, iron-workers, plasterers, cabinet workers, brassfounders, cabinet locksmiths, pattern-makers, painters and boilermakers. . . .

On 27 June the following resolution was unanimously passed:– 'That this conference of trades' delegates seeing the necessity for the establishment of a permanent trades council, as a means of social intercourse between the various trades of Wolverhampton, do hereby resolve respectfully to invite each of the several trades and co-operative societies to nominate and appoint two repre-sentatives to the first meeting of the before-named council.'

(35) *Bee-Hive* (25 Aug 1866): Circular from the Manchester and Salford Trades Council

The object intended in the formation of a trades council for Manchester and Salford, is to supply a want which has long been felt in this neighbourhood. Whilst London, Glasgow, Liverpool, Sheffield, Preston, Derby and other towns, possess associations or organised trades, and have derived great benefit and numerous advantages from their establishment, Manchester, although a great stronghold of Union principles, is comparatively weak, consequent upon the different trade societies being isolated in their operations, and not united for mutual protection against the encroachments of capital, – a want of sympathy being thus engendered, whenever any formidable difficulty presents itself, which ought not to exist. To remedy this defect and with a view of strengthening each others hands, by united action in delegation, the printing and issuing of appeals, and in keeping a correct register of trade secretaries addresses in the neigh-bourhood, it is proposed to form this Trades Council, based upon a simple code of rules, requiring a nominal subscription, and regular meetings of accredited delegates; and the frequent publicity of the principle of which will best conduce to prevent strikes and lock-outs and substitute, in lieu of these disastrous social revolutions of industrial progress, Courts of Conciliation and Arbitration, the principles of co-operation, together with general and determined support for those recognizing union principles in preference to employing those who decline to conform to the claims of trade societies. In furtherance of the above object, several preliminary meetings of trade representatives have been held on the 9th inst., at which 6,000 members of different trade societies were represented, a code of rules were adopted, as a basis for the consideration of the first meeting of the Council which will be held at Three Crown Inn, Salford on Thursday evening September 20 at 8 o'clock when the officers for the ensuing year will also be elected; and all delegates attending will be required to produce certificates of appointment in accordance with the 10th suggested rule. Signed,

> S. C. Nicholson, Chairman
> W. H. Wood, Secretary.

A great deal of opposition to unionism still persisted. In response to growing workers' organisation, associations of employers developed (36). Typical objections were made by an anonymous Manchester businessman (37).

(36) RC on Trades Unions etc., *Fifth Report, PP* 1867–8 xxxix Paper submitted by John Jones, secretary of the Iron Manufacturers Association and of the Ironmasters' Association

There are several ironmasters' associations; the oldest is the one in the South Staffordshire district. This association has held quarterly meetings for many years. At these the selling prices of iron for the district have been fixed, and wages were invariably regulated by these prices until recently, when some derangement of the system occurred. The principle is still adopted, however, and wages advance or recede 1s. per ton for puddling, and 10 per cent for other wages, for every change of £1. per ton in the price of iron, according as the 'list' prices of iron rise or fall. Thus, if iron goes up the men get an advance without any trouble or representation on their part. These list prices are not binding upon members of the association, and it not infrequently happens that makers are selling at more than £1 per ton under the list rates, though wages are regulated by the standard prices. The Staffordshire Association was modelled on the plan of the South Staffordshire society, but has been to some extent modified since that time. The North of England association first assumed a definite shape in 1863. It was established for the purpose of regulating prices and terms of selling iron. There were no rules or code of regulations. In 1865, after the masters of the northern district agreed to withdraw from the general compact on the under-taking of the men to sever their connexion with other districts, a set of rules was adopted, and the constitution of the association was defined. The men were to adopt such modifications in their rules as would make them conform to the spirit of the resolutions they had passed with reference to the separation from other districts.

(37) *Capital and Labour, By a Member of the Manchester Chamber of Commerce* (1867): Trade unions

1. That they have established a standing menace against all capital, and are making its employment impossible.

2. That they seek to destroy all unity of interest between the employer and the employed.
3. That they have made the operative class suspicious and discontented, by teaching them that their employers are deceiving and oppressing them.
4. That they have made them indifferent, if not opposed, to their employer's interest.
5. That they have taught them to consider their employer's loss their gain.
6. That they have made them wasteful in the use of materials, indifferent as to the quality of their work, and dilatory in the execution of it.
7. That they have made punctuality in the execution of contracts, and all prospective calculations of cost and profit impossible.
8. That they have stepped in between the employers and the employed, and prevented the association of interest that both instinctively desire.
9. That they have lowered the standard of English work.
10. That they deny the undoubted right of both employers and employed to make their own terms.
11. That they limit the work and profits of the operative by denying him the right to do as much, and as good work as he can.
12. That they seek to make every trade a close one by limiting the numbers employed in it.
13. That they have reduced the workmen as far as possible to an equality of mediocrity.
14. That they systematically deceive the men as to the true condition of labour at home and abroad.
15. That they advocate coercion and even terrorism in support of their policy.
16. 'That under their influence', to use Mr. Thomas Hughes' own words, 'the present relations between employers and employed are fast becoming insupportable.'

The most frequent grounds for attacking unions were their strikes and their defiance of the 'laws' of political economy. There was no place for unionism within the popularisations of classical economics, which were the prevailing orthodoxy (38). At least some unionists tried to adapt to this situation. Typical among them were the *Potteries Examiner* of William Owen and *The Operative* of William Newton (1822–76), founding father of the ASE (39, 40). Others sought to give a reasoned reply to their traducers (41, 42).

(38) G. H. Smith, *Outlines of Political Economy* (1866)

As already shown, the working man's skill and labour are his capital. They may be considered so much goods or merchandize, whose price varies with the supply and demand. No artificial means can either raise, or lower Wages, for any length of time. Before the laws of Political Economy began to be studied, Parliamentary and other Government enactments were frequently passed to fix the rate of Wages. But whether the object of such enactments was to maintain, to raise, or to lower the rate they invariably failed. Natural laws will ever override man's laws.

Men cannot be made to pay for labour more than it is worth to them; nor can men be forced to work for less than employers who are in want of hands, are willing to pay. When labourers are more abundant than work, Wages will fall. When work is more abundant than labour, Wages will rise. The great natural law of Demand and Supply mocks at all human interference.

But although Wages, like prices, follow this great law of Nature, it is the fact that, ordinarily, they are highest in those countries where the usual diet of the working classes is the most plentiful and most nutritive. Yet it must not be inferred from this that Wages rise with the price of provisions – the contrary being generally the case. The explanation of the fact simply is, that where working-classes have long been accustomed to live well, their capital must have largely accumulated and greater freedom have been enjoyed. Hence more employment because more means to pay for employment. Moreover, the labourer who is fed well and sufficiently can do more and better work in a given time, than the underfed; is better worth employing; can thus earn more. It is a common error to suppose that employers can always combine to keep down Wages; an error which leads to the contrary error of workmen's combining to raise Wages, or to maintain them at a given level. Hence, 'Lock-outs' on the one hand, and 'strikes' on the other. In particular instances, which as grammarians say, are 'the exceptions that prove the rule', such combinations may and do succeed for a time. But it is only for a time. Competition springs up among the employers, first their capital is lying idle; so they bid against each other for workers, and Wages rise in spite of their efforts to the contrary. On the other hand, in the case of 'strikes', want of means compels the workers to forego their claims, and Wages fall. The only universal regulators of price are Demand and Supply.

(39) *Potteries Examiner and Workman's Advocate* (22 June 1844)

For the last six months our Society has relieved the Poor Rates of these districts for some £60 or £70 per week, by supporting the unemployed members of the different branches from the funds of this society. This we shall continue to do as long as we have the means.

But the distress is more than temporary – it is caused by advancing powers of production and decreasing demand – in short surplus labour. It is in the knowledge of this that the Potters Emigration Society has been established, so that the £60 per week might be saved by removing the claimants to happy homes in the Western World.

It is intended to purchase 12,000 or more acres of land in or of the United States and pay for it in instalments in 10 years. To locate potters on the land.

(40) *The Operative* (12 April 1851)

We are willing, for the time, to submit to the competition principle of having wages regulated by the supply and demand of labour, therefore we are not desirous of dealing with wages at all, in a direct manner. We purpose rather to interfere with those principles that regulate wages, preferring to deal with the cause of the effect, rather than with the effect itself. If wages are to be maintained, it is not only by insisting upon a certain amount, without reference to the circumstances by which the trade is surrounded, but by surrounding the trade with such circumstances as will of necessity have a beneficial effect upon its condition. The wages of labour are influenced by the number of men out of employment, by the amount of competition that exists among the workmen themselves – and unless the number of unemployed is reduced and competition thereby destroyed, wages can never be increased nor privileges enhanced. To destroy then a redundancy in the labour market, ought to be the first object of a Trades Society. . . .

(41) T. J. Dunning, *Trades' Unions and Strikes: Their Philosophy and Intention* (1860)

It is superfluous to say that the price of labour, like that of everything else, is determined by the quantity or supply of it *permanently* in the market; when the supply of it *permanently* much exceeds its demand, nothing can prevent the reduction of wages; and, conversely, when the demand for it permanently much exceeds its supply, nothing can prevent their rise. In these two extreme points all contention is hopeless. . . . Trade Societies, however, rarely meddle with these two extremes. Leaving them, we come to the intermediate states that admit the operation of Trade Societies; and, indeed, which call them into existence. . . . In other words the trade might be for a good while 'slack'. If a reduction of wages took place during this period, this reduction would be very likely to remain when the trade got 'busy', the supply of hands not being then greater than the demand; and yet the temporary 'slackness' in itself would by no means be adequate to compel a reduction, and ought not to produce it. The undue competition among employers, bidding each other under the other, intending to make up the difference out of the wages of their men, – not from any compelling necessity in the trade, but from mere rivalry, – would inevitably cause a reduction, which, if not checked, might extend to the whole; not again from any compelling necessity arising from over-supply, but from taking advantage of the immediate necessities of their men being greater than their own. Hence the formation of Trade Societies, which become a necessity, to adjust the bargain for the sale and purchase of labour. . . . In this position as bargainers for the sale and purchase of labour stand the employer and employed. Singly the employer can stand out longer in the bargain than the journeyman; and as he who can stand out longest in the bargain will be sure to command his own terms, the workmen combine to put themselves on something like an equality in the bargain for the sale of their labour with their employers. This is the *rationale* of Trade Societies, which is very clearly indicated by Adam Smith in his 'Wealth of Nations'.

(42) Scottish History Society, *The Minutes of Edinburgh Trades Council 1859–1873*, ed. Ian MacDougall (Edinburgh, 1968) pp 107–8
James Hart, General Secretary of the Scottish Masons 21 October 1862

After a careful perusal of *The Workmen's Bane & Antidote* by Dr. John Watts of Manchester, I have arrived at the following conclusions: 1st, That the reasons alleged by him as being the occasion of strikes is erroneous: 2nd, That the cure proposed by him is utterly inadequate . . . and not at all practicable. . . .

But while admitting with Dr. Watts that strikes are an evil, I believe that they are necessary evils but by a little prudence properly exercised their occurrence would be less frequent, and the hardship endured on account of them would be greatly mitigated. I humbly suggest the following precautions on the part of those who have too good reason to resist the tyranny and avaricious selfishness of their employers: 1st, When a strike is in contemplation, three fourths of the number of those who are likely to be directly affected by it should be unanimous as to its necessity. 2nd, When a dispute arises between employer and employed offers should be made by the employees for arbitration. 3rd, The means at the disposal of the employers for prolonging the struggle should be ascertained as far as possible. 4th, The state and prospects of the trade and the position of the labour market. 5th, [the funds at the disposal of the society and the probable sums likely to be obtained] from other sympathising trades unions and the toiling millions generally.

In conclusion, I believe were these suggestions or others embodying the same sentiments but minute in detail faithfully carried out in practice, the number of strikes would be reduced and those that are absolutely necessary would stand a better chance of being crowned with success, thus raising the moral tone of Trades Unions in the opinions of those whose good opinions and co-operation are really worth having.

It was in response to mounting pressure on unionism from employers in the Midlands and the North that, at the suggestion of the Wolverhampton Trades Council, a national conference of unionists was held in Sheffield in July 1866. The outcome was the United Kingdom Alliance of Organised Trades (43), with the Sheffield unionists William Dronfield (1826–1914) and William Broadhead as secretary and treasurer. The association with Broadhead proved disastrous, when his violent role in Sheffield unionism was revealed in 1867 (44, 45). The saw-grinders' activities were merely the worst of numerous outrages among the cutlery trades.

(43) *Rules for the Government of the United Kingdom Alliance of Organised Trades as adopted at the Conference held in Manchester, January 1st. 1867 and three following days* (Sheffield, 1867)

Its primary *objects* are to render pecuniary and moral support to all Trades belonging to the Alliance, who may be exposed to the evils resulting from, or incidental to, *Lock-outs*, which entail such an incalculable amount of misery and suffering on so many of our fellow-men, as well as on their unoffending wives and families; which are alike an outrage, not only on the most clearly defined and generally accepted principles of political and social economy, but are calculated seriously to injure the trade and commerce of the country generally.

The Executive of the Alliance believes that its objects can be accomplished in various ways – by bringing about and perpetuating a better understanding and closer intercourse among the Trades at large – and by the dissemination of reliable information, through the medium of its Quarterly reports, on such topics as may be generally useful or interesting – and by a judicious exercise of the power invested in the Executive of using their endeavours when a lock-out appears imminent, of averting such a disastrous calamity, by conciliatory measures.

(44) RC on Trade Unions etc, *First Report, PP* 1867 XXXII

The earliest case is that of *Elisha Parker*, into which we inquired with the written sanction of Her Majesty's Principal Secretary of State for the Home Department.

Elisha Parker is a saw grinder living at Dore, about five miles from Sheffield. In the year 1853 Parker was working for Messrs. Newbould, who employed two non-unionist men, and he was repeatedly required by the union to discontinue working for Messrs. Newbould; this he refused to do.

In July of the same year a horse of Parker's was found hamstrung in a field where it had been grazing, and it had to be killed. Broadhead, the secretary of the Saw Grinders' Union, confessed that he had hired three members of the Saw Grinders' Union (Elijah Smith, John Taylor, and Phineas Dean) to commit this outrage. . . .

James Linley, who formerly had been a scissor grinder, had shortly before this period become a saw grinder, and kept a number of apprentices, in defiance of the rules of the Saw Grinders' Union.

He was shot by Samuel Crookes with an air gun on November 12th 1857, at the instigation of Broadhead, in a house in Nursery Street, and was slightly wounded.

1859, January 11th. *James Linley* was lodging with his brother-in-law Samuel Poole, a butcher, whose wife and family were living in the same house. Crookes, at the instigation of Broadhead, threw into Poole's house a can of gunpowder, which exploded and did some damage to the shop, but hurt no one.

1858 August 1st. Crookes and Hallam tracked Linley from house to house nearly every day for five or six weeks, intending to shoot him. On the 1st August they found him sitting in a public-house in Scotland Street, in a room full of people, the windows of which opened into a back yard, and from that yard Crookes shot Linley with an air gun. The shot struck him on the side of the head, and he died from the effects of the injury in the following February. Crookes and Hallam were hired by Broadhead to shoot Linley. . . .

Thomas Fearnehough, a saw grinder, had long been obnoxious to the union.

Having been a member of the union, he left it eight years ago, and shortly after joined again from fear of bodily harm. In 1865 he left the union a second time, and never rejoined it. He had been in the habit of working on his own tools instead of his master's (which was against the rules of the union), and at the time of this outrage he was working for Messrs. Slack, Sellars, and Co., who had a dispute with the saw handle makers. The saw grinders had in consequence been withdrawn, but Fearnehough had, notwithstanding the withdrawal of the grinders, persisted in working for the firm. Messrs. Slack, Sellars, and Co., aware of the danger which Fearnehough incurred by working for them, took power for him at Messrs. Butchers' wheel, to which there was no access except through a covered gateway which was carefully guarded. Fearnehough was therefore safe from being rattened.

Two or three months before October 1866, Henry Skidmore, secretary of the Saw Makers' Society, and Joseph Barker, secretary of the Saw Handle Makers' Society, called on Broadhead, and represented to him that Fearnehough was working for Slack, Sellars, and Co., and thereby injuring the trade, and asked him 'if something could not be done at him to stop his working'. They were aware that he could not be rattened at Butchers' wheel, but no plan was laid down by them by which Fearnehough was to be coerced, although they agreed to bear their share of the expense of compelling him to submit to the union. On the 8th October 1966 a can of gunpowder was exploded in the cellar under Fearnehough's house in New Hereford Street, in which he was then living with his family, consisting of two sons and a daughter. No one was hurt, but great damage was done to the house. Samuel Crookes was hired by Broadhead to commit this outrage, and was assisted by Joseph Copley, a member of the Saw Grinders' Union. A day or two after this occurrence, Barker and Skidmore, with the knowledge of Thomas Smith, secretary of the Saw Makers' Union, paid Broadhead £7.10s., the share of each union for the expense of committing the outrage. Joseph Barker found the money (the Saw Handle Makers' Union being then £18 in debt to the Saw Makers' Union), and Smith credited Barker with the amount in the books of the Saw Makers' Union. The entry of this amount was passed over by the auditors without inquiry in the December following; this could not have been done if the audit had been carefully and honestly conducted.

A reward of £1,100 offered for the detection of the perpetrators failed to elicit any information.

(45) Ibid.: Evidence of Samuel Crookes

Do you know Samuel Baxter of Langley? – Yes.
   Did you blow him up? – Yes
   By putting a quantity of gunpowder down the chimney? – Yes
   Who employed you to do that? – Broadhead.
   How much did he pay you? – Well, I cannot say, I think it was £15; that was about the regular sum I think generally. . . .

Early in 1867 unions found themselves threatened in the courts when the Court of Queen's Bench rejected an appeal by the Boilermakers' Society in the case of *Hornby* v. *Close*, against a decision of the Bradford magistrates (46). The court confirmed that if a union had certain functions 'in restraint of trade' then its funds could not be protected under section 44 of the Friendly Societies Act of 1855.

The decision placed in jeopardy the funds of the large amalgamated societies of engineers and carpenters, whose rules had been deposited with the Registrar of Friendly Societies. They therefore formed a Conference of Amalgamated Trades in January 1867 to press for legislative protection of their funds (47).

(46) *Hornby* v. *Close* (1867) LR 2QB 153

BLACKBURN, J.: Now, as the Lord Chief Justice has said, the purposes of a trades' union are clearly not analogous to those of a friendly society. A little deviation from the strict purpose of a friendly society might not take the society out of the scope of the act; but here a main object certainly – if not the main object, I think a main object – was that of a trades' union, and therefore the magistrates were fully justified in declining to act. Secondly, I go further, and think the rules illegal in the sense of void, according to the principles of *Hilton* v. *Ekersley* – a case of combination by masters, but the same principle must apply to combinations of men – that they are not enforceable at law. The Court of Exchequer Chamber in that case carefully avoid going further, and saying whether or not the objects of the masters were illegal in the sense of being criminal; and, acting on the authority of that case in the Exchequer Chamber, and adopting the view of Crompton, J., in the court below, I wish to guard myself from being supposed to express any opinion on the present case. I do not say the objects of this society are criminal. I do not say they are not. But I am clearly of opinion that the rules referred to are illegal, in the sense that they cannot be enforced; and on this ground, also, I think the society not within s. 44, as not being 'for a purpose not illegal'. Whatever the inclination of my opinion, it is unnecessary to decide whether the illegality of any of the rules would taint the whole, because here the illegal objects formed not a small part, but a principal, if not the whole, object of the society.

(47) LTC, *Annual Report and Balance Sheet, 1872–73*

The preparation of this Bill [to protect trade-union funds] and getting large support from Members of Parliament, proved to be a work of great labour and difficulty, and surpassing in importance all other trade society questions for the time being. To attend regularly, and at the shortest possible notice to that work, it was essential that a number of men should be appointed who would not have to leave their employers' work in the day time.

For this reason it was thought advisable to place the responsibility of this work in the hands of an 'Amalgamated Conference of Trades,' composed of secretaries of the various large Societies, as they would only have to consult their own officials. This was done and a representative of the Trades Council appointed to act with them. As there were, necessarily, expenses attending the labours of the Conference, and the Council, knowing the limited amount of subscriptions given by societies for all such purposes, resolved to suspend its labours until the Conference should have completed its undertaking.

Not to be outdone by Applegarth and his colleagues, George Potter's London Working Men's Association summoned a national conference of unions (48). By the time it met, a further crisis faced unionism, through the Government's decision to set up a Royal Commission on Trades Unions and Employers' Associations, but even this did not lead the Conference of Amalgamated Trades to associate with Potter's meeting (49).

(48) *Report of the Trades Conference held at St. Martin's Hall, London, on March 5th, 6th, 7th and 8th, 1867*: Report from the Committee of the Working Men's Association

Fellow Workmen, – The important crisis through which the Trade Unions of the United Kingdom is now passing is our justification for calling their representatives together on the present occasion, and we rejoice that our invitation has been so cordially and so generally responded to, resulting in one of the most numerous and influential trades' delegate meetings that has ever been assembled together. For the last few months the columns of a large portion of the public Press have been teeming with attacks upon Trade Unions and their leaders, never before equalled for violence and misrepresentation; every possible event that has occurred in connection with them has been distorted and misrepresented, with the evident object of exciting to a still greater extent the prejudice already existing in the public mind against these organisations. They have been accused, not only of being the direct cause of the distress now unhappily existing in many branches of industry throughout the country, but of driving, by their extortion and unjust demands, capital and trade into foreign countries. It would be an insult to the delegates now assembled for us to use any arguments to them in refutation of these fallacies, but we cannot shut our eyes to the fact that these statements, repeated over and over again, have had some effect on that portion of the public who form their opinions from leading articles in the public journals.

While these virulent attacks upon Trade Unions were daily taking place in the Press, a judgment was given in the Court of Queen's Bench which, unexpected in its character, struck at the very existence of trade societies, and placed the funds of every one of these societies at the mercy of any dishonest officer who might obtain possession of them. We allude to the decision given in the case of the Boiler Makers and Iron Ship Builders in the Court of Queen's Bench on the 16th of January last. By this judgment any trade society, although its rules may have been deposited with the Registrar-General of Friendly Societies, was deprived of any protection from the law of its funds, even of those funds which were expressly subscribed for a benevolent or charitable purpose. This judgment naturally created a sensation, and more than one of the London daily papers publicly expressed the belief and hope that by it Trade Unionism had received its death-blow. Under these circumstances, and after waiting for some days, and not seeing any action taken in the case by other bodies, the London Working Men's Association – a body composed mainly of Trade Unionists – instructed its committee to call the trades of the kingdom together in conference. . . .

In accordance with the promise made by Mr. Walpole . . . amongst the first measures introduced into Parliament by the Government was the Trades Union Commission Bill, appointing this Royal Commission of Inquiry into the Working of Trade Unions, and defining the powers of that Commission. This Bill has passed through the House of Commons, and will, doubtless, in a few days receive the Royal assent. The trades generally have made no objection to this Commission of Inquiry, feeling convinced as they do, that if only simple justice be done them, the unions will come out of that inquiry not only scatheless, but with honour and credit. But although there was no objection made to the issuing of the Commission, considerable dissatisfaction was felt at the manner in which it was composed, and a general desire was expressed that some workingmen – Trade Unionists – should be placed upon the Commission. Fully participating in this feeling, the Working Men's Association appointed a deputation, composed, with but one exception, of members of Trade Unions, to wait upon Mr. Walpole, the Home Secretary, for the purpose of inducing the Government to place two or three working men on the Commission. Mr. Walpole, however, after listening to their statements and reasons with great courtesy, informed the deputation that the point had been carefully considered by himself and his colleagues, and had been decided in the negative. Finding their efforts in this direction fruitless, the deputation then suggested that some gentlemen in whom the Trade Unionists at large had confidence, and who had made themselves practically acquainted with the working of trade societies, should be placed on the Commission. Mr. Walpole said he would not object to place any one gentleman the deputation might name upon the Commission, but that was the extent to which he could go, the names of the gentlemen forming the Commission having already received the sanction of Her Majesty. The deputation accordingly named several gentlemen, but ultimately Mr. Frederic Harrison, barrister-at-law, well and honourably known to Trade Unionists by his writings on their behalf, was accepted by Mr. Walpole, with the full concurrence with the whole of the deputation.

(49) MS. Minutes of the Conference of Amalgamated Trades, 8 March 1867 [British Library of Political and Economic Science]

This meeting was called in conformity with the expressed desire of the Provincial delegates that attended a conference at St. Martin's Hall, who at a meeting of the London Trades Council had appointed a deputation to meet and confer with this Conference with a view to Amalgamate the two conferences. The deputation consisted of

Mr. W. Dronfield   Sheffield
Mr. J. Kane   Ironworkers, Gateshead
Mr. J. C. Proudfoot   Glasgow Trades Council
Mr. W. Swan   Iron Shipbuilders Glasgow
Mr. W. H. Wood   Manchester Trades Council
Mr. W. Troup   Edinburgh Trades Council

A very animated discussion took place during which the promoters of the St. Martin's Hall Conference were denounced as meddlers in Trade Matters and Traders on the misfortunes of the Working class and as the 'Working-Men's Association' with which they were connected was composed of unionists and anti-unionists and systematic political agitators this conference expressed its determination of standing aloof from the St. Martin's Hall Conference and its promoters at the same time would be glad to co-operate with any Trade Society they thought proper to act with us.

4. *Investigation and Vindication, 1867–75*

Despite the Sheffield outrages trade unions were fast becoming 'respectable' (1) and an improved standard of living had eroded much of the earlier militancy (2). The Royal Commission on Trades Unions and Employers' Associations, sitting from 1867 to 1869, became exactly what Applegarth, Allan and other leaders of the amalgamated societies hoped that it would: a platform for further projecting the moderate image of the large unions. Working closely with the Positivist Frederic Harrison (1831–1923), they were able to present unionism in a most favourable light, to diessociate most unionism from the excesses of Sheffield and to refute much of the hostile case presented by some employers.

In 1869 the Commission produced two main reports: a majority report, signed by Sir William Erle (1793–1880) and most of the members, and a minority report, signed by Harrison and the Christian Socialist Thomas Hughes (1822–96) and largely supported by the 2nd Earl of Lichfield (1825–92). Even the majority report was more favourable to unions than might have been expected in 1867, though it still stressed the need for legal restrictions on their activities (3). The minority report called for complete freedom of association and for protection of unions (4) and became what Harrison intended it to be, a blueprint for future legislation.

(1) J. M. Ludlow and Lloyd Jones, *Progress of the Working Class, 1832–1867* (1867)

Trades' Unions . . . are becoming important influences for social improvement. No union. committee-man could be tolerated now if a drunkard. Without sobriety, intelligence and wisdom, no such man advances to influence. The action of the unions at Barnsley has been productive of almost miraculous improvement. Details are told of the brutality of the Barnsley roughs, even within these ten years, that could not now be tolerated by the lowest of themselves. And yet there is a marked difference between a district in the neighbourhood not in union and others which are. In the one, the men get the same pay as the unionists, but waste is uncontrolled. In the union districts, with better pay and shorter hours of work than heretofore, the men are turning their attention to garden plots, to pig-feeding; joining Co-operative and Building Societies. They are saving in Penny Banks, and the Post Office had many hundred of pounds of their money. It is found that though the men work shorter hours daily they do more work and earn more money, because they work more regularly, do not break time, and have no 'Saint Mondays' or 'play days'. There is a very decided improvement, both physical, moral, economic, and social in the whole Yorkshire district where union prevails. But when there is no union discipline, we have dog-fights and man-fights, riots, and manslaughters at every assize.

(2) *The Life of Thomas Cooper, written by himself* (1872)

In our old Chartist time, it is true, Lancashire working men were in rags by thousands; and many of them often lacked food. But their intelligence was demonstrated wherever you went. You would see them in groups discussing the great doctrine of political justice – that every grown-up, sane man ought to have a vote in the election of the men who were to make the laws by which he was to be governed; or they were in earnest dispute respecting the teachings of Socialism. *Now*, you will see no such groups in Lancashire. But you will hear well-dressed working men talking, as they walk with their hands in their pockets, of 'Co-ops' (Co-operative Stores), and their shares in them, or in building societies. And you will see others, like idiots, leading small greyound dogs, covered with cloth, in a string! They are about to race, and they are betting money as they go! And yonder comes another clamorous dozen of men cursing and swearing and betting upon a few pigeons they are about to let fly! As for their betting on horses – like their masters! – it is a perfect madness.

(3) RC on Trades Unions etc., *Eleventh and Final Report, PP* 1868–9 XXXI: Majority Report

(31) It does not appear to be borne out by the evidence that the disposition to strike on the part of workmen is in itself the creation of unionism, that the frequency of strikes increases in proportion to the strength of the union. It is, indeed, affirmed by the leaders of unions that the effect of the established societies is to diminish the frequency, and certainly the disorder, of strikes, and to guarantee a regularity of wages and hours rather than to engage in constant endeavours to improve them. But supposing such results to follow, as stated from the establishment and action of a powerful trades union in any trade or district, it is not unreasonable to assume that the diminished frequency of strikes may arise not from any want of disposition to strike on the part of the members of the union, but from the fact that its organization is so powerful as, in most cases, to obtain the concessions demanded without recourse to strike. . . .

(38) The chief expedients for repressing the competition among the workmen are rules, or a tacit understanding, prescribing a *minimum* rate of wages to be accepted and a *maximum* number of hours to be worked by the members of the union, and prohibiting them from working overtime or taking piecework. The opponents of overtime and piecework appear to us to hold that the man who works overtime takes so much from the common stock, and thus injures the rest;

and that the man who takes piecework, besides that he get more than his share of the common stock of work, is apt to show what may be done by skill and industry, and so raises the standard of expectation on the part of the employer. . . .

(41) ASSOCIATIONS OF EMPLOYERS. The associations of employers, to which our attention is directed by Your Majesty's Commission, are, though different in character, in principle the same with the associations of workmen hitherto referred to. They are, however, comparatively very few in number, and have, in general, been formed for the ordinary regulation of their respective trades, for the purpose of obtaining labour upon the most favourable terms, and for self-defence against the proceedings of the trades unions. The employers cannot fail to see the advantage which the trades unions, in the conduct of strikes, may have in attacking the employers in detail. The strike is with this view directed against a single employer, or against the employers in a single district, the workmen on strike being supported by those still in the employment of other masters; the intention being on the success of the first strike, to take other masters in succession. . . .

(48) Thus much only we intimate as the apparent result of our inquiries; that, whether the circumstance is to be regretted or not, the habitual code of sentiment which prevailed between employers and workmen in the times when the former were regarded by both law and usage as the governing class is now greatly relaxed, and cannot be revived. A substitute has now to be found for it, arising from the feelings of equity, and enlightened self-interest, and mutual forbearance, which should exist between contracting parties who can best promote their several chances of advantage by aiding and accommodating each other. . . .

(60) With regard to the general question of the right of workmen to combine together for determining and stipulating with their employer the terms on which only they will consent to work for him, we think that, provided the combination be perfectly voluntary, and that full liberty to be left to all other workmen to undertake the work which the parties combining have refused, and that no obstruction be placed in the way of the employers resorting elsewhere in search of a supply of labour, there is no ground of justice or of policy for withholding such a right from the workmen. . . .

All that, as it appears to us, the law has to do, over and above any protection that may be required for classes unable to protect themselves, such as women and children, is to secure a fair field for the unrestricted exercise of industrial enterprise. It should recognize the right in the labourer to dispose of his labour, the capitalist of his capital, and the employer of his productive powers, in whatever manner each of them, acting either individually or in association with others, may deem for his own interest; and that without reference to the question whether he is acting wisely for his own interest or advantageously to the public, or the contrary. The interest of the public will be best consulted by allowing each of these parties to do what he thinks best for himself without further interference of the law than may be necessary to protect the rights of others. . . .

(82) The registration of trades unions might be effected through the Registrar of Friendly Societies, and it would be his duty to see that the rules and byelaws of a society claiming to be registered were unobjectionable. . . .

(4) Ibid.: Minority Report

PROPOSITIONS RESPECTING AMENDMENT OF THE LAW

1. That the common law relating to combinations of workmen, as well as the interpretation of the statute 6 Geo. IV c. 129, and the effect of the joint operation of the common law and statute, appear to be involved in a considerable doubt, and have given rise to decisions sometimes conflicting with each other, and often unsatisfactory; and that in the opinion of eminent authorities the bulk of the existing unions are in some senses unlawful combinations, and are without any direct and adequate security for the safety of their property; and that an amendment of the law, and an explicit declaration of the law relating to combinations, are absolutely required.

2. That the principles of rules of law to restrict the liberty of workmen to demand their own terms in concert is contrary to the spirit of modern legislation; and that it is expedient to declare that workmen and employers may lawfully associate themselves for the purpose of obtaining any terms for their labour or capital that they think fit, and may lawfully withhold their labour or capital in concert upon such terms as they choose; and that no combination in pursuance of such agreement shall be indictable as a conspiracy or otherwise, unless it be made with intent to commit or to procure the commission of some offence punishable under the general criminal law.

3. That the doctrines respecting restraint of trade have been applied to remote consequences in the case of workmen, and with an uncertain effect, and require complete revision; that it is expedient to declare that whilst all combinations of workmen untainted with a criminal purpose are unlawful, certain agreements, to be defined, will not be directly enforceable at law, though they will not taint with an ulterior character of illegality combinations into whose purposes they may partially enter.

4. That the third section of the statute of 6 Geo. IV c. 129, and in particular the words 'threats', 'intimidation', 'molest', 'obstruct', involve a vagueness which should not exist in criminal law, and have received conflicting interpretations, which in some cases are harsh and unsatisfactory.

5. That the principle of combinations laws, or laws directed against associations of workmen and employers as such, and creating special offences in their case, is unsound, and the combination laws in general ought to be repealed, as at once

vexatious and inoperative; and that it is expedient to deal with all offences which may be committed by members of such associations under the general law of crime applying to all citizens alike.

6. That it is expedient to give full and positive protection to the property and funds of trades unions. . . .

Thos. Hughes
Frederic Harrison

While the Commission sat, the Manchester and Salford Trades Council, under two Conservative printers, S. C. Nicholson and W. H. Wood, sought to put the unions' case to the public by calling a trades union congress (5). The London-based Conference of Amalgamated Trades declined to take part (6) and continued to work on its own, through sympathetic Members of Parliament, to get suitable legislation.

(5) 'Proposed Congress of Trades Councils and other Federations of Trades Societies' [TUC Library; quoted in A. E. Musson, *Trade Union and Social History* (1974)]

Manchester, February 21st, 1868

Fellow-Unionists,

The Manchester and Salford Trades Council having recently taken into their serious consideration the present aspect of Trades Unions, and the profound ignorance which prevails in the public mind with reference to their operations and principles, together with the probability of an attempt being made by the Legislature, during the present session of Parliament, to introduce a measure detrimental to the interests of such Societies, beg most respectfully to suggest the propriety of holding in Manchester, as the main centre of industry in the provinces, a Congress of the Representatives of Trades Councils and other similar Federations of Trades Societies. By confining the Congress to such bodies it is conceived that a deal of expense will be saved, as Trades will thus be represented collectively; whilst there will be a better opportunity afforded of selecting the most intelligent and efficient exponents of our principles.

It is proposed that the Congress shall assume the character of the annual meetings of the British Association for the Advancement of Science and the Social Science Association, in the transactions of which Societies the artizan class are almost entirely excluded; and that papers, previously carefully prepared, shall be laid before the Congress on the various subjects which at the present time affect Trades Societies, each paper to be followed by discussion upon the points, advanced, with a view of the merits and demerits of each question being thoroughly ventilated through the medium of the public press. It is further suggested that the subjects treated upon shall include the following:–

1. – Trades Unions an absolute necessity.
2. – Trades Unions and Political Economy.

3. – The Effect of Trades Unions on Foreign Competition.
4. – Regulation of the Hours of Labour.
5. – Limitation of Apprentices.
6. – Technical Education.
7. – Arbitration and Courts of Conciliation.
8. – Co-operation.
9. – The present Inequality of the Law in regard to Conspiracy, Intimidation, Picketing, Coercion, &c.
10. – Factory Acts Extension Bill, 1867: the necessity of Compulsory Inspection, and its application to all places where Women and Children are employed.
11. – The present Royal Commission on Trades Unions: how far worthy of the confidence of the Trades Union interest.
12. – The necessity of an Annual Congress of Trade Representatives from the various centres of industry.

All Trades Councils and other Federations of Trades are respectfully solicited to intimate their adhesion to this project on or before the 6th of April next, together with a notification of the subject of the paper that each body will undertake to prepare; after which date all information as to place a meeting, &c., will be supplied.

It is also proposed that the Congress be held on the 4th of May next, and that all liabilities in connection therewith shall not extend beyond its sittings.

Communications to be addressed to Mr. W. H. Wood, Typographical Institute, 29 Water Street, Manchester.

By order of the Manchester and Salford Trades Council,
s. c. NICHOLSON, President.
w. h. wood, Secretary.

(6) Robert Applegarth to Charles Williams, General Secretary of the National Association of Operative Plasterers, 13 March 1868 [Picton Library, Liverpool]

It was absolutely necessary that a plan or policy or bill, which ever you like to call it should be issued to the country. That we have done, in the shape of our Bill and its provisions are such as the experience of some of the oldest Trade Societies officers, and the ablest lawyers could suggest, and its issue was considered to be the very best plan to elicit the opinions of all whom it would concern. It has done its work well and now we are receiving the opinions and suggestions of the Trades of the country which will be placed in the hands [of those] who will attempt to get us a law passed so that in committee of the House of Commons the Bill may be made the most Liberal and desirable Bill that the House will pass. Our object is to get security and protection and as much of it as possible. But depend upon it if we are not prepared to make a united effort and if we '*bother the House*' with Bills from two or three different quarters the chances are we shall defeat the very object we are aiming at. I hear of another *Conference in London* but I think the Provincial Societies have had enough 'St. Martin's Hall Conferences'. You ask if our conference is going to co-operate with the Manchester Conference. My reply is that to secure protection for our funds and the general protection of Trades Societies need we shall gladly co-operate with an *Conference* or *Council* constituted of *Trade Unions*.

Pressure for new legislation was maintained by such unionists as John Allen (1804–88) of the boilermakers (7) and by such sympathisers as Harrison (8).

(7) The Boiler Makers' and Iron Ship Builders' Society, *Monthly Report* (April 1869)

Petition, Petition, must be your cry: your action and unceasing exertions to get the Bill of Mr. Thomas Hughes and Mr. Mundella passed. Neglect this and the doom of your children and your future freedom and happiness is sealed, to give place to your enemies, that they may still augment *the one hundred and fifty millions a year* which they are at present dividing among themselves from the labour of the working classes in the three kingdoms. . . .

We must have laws that will give us power to deal with our employers, and which will give to us and our families much more of the £15,000,000 a year than we have ever received. It lies with us to make the effort. . . .

(8) Frederic Harrison, 'The Trades Union Bill', *Fortnightly Review* (1 July 1869).

The Trade Union question is another and the latest example of the truth, that the sphere of legislation is strictly and curiously limited. After legislating about labour for centuries, each change producing its own evils, we have slowly come to see the truth, that we must cease to legislate for it at all. The public mind has been of late conscious of serious embarrassment, and eagerly expecting some legislative solution, some heaven-born discoverer to arise, with a new Parliamentary nostrum. As usual in such cases, it now turns out that there is no legislative solution at all; and that the true solution requires, as its condition, the removal of the mischievous meddling of the past.

Not until 1871 was legislation giving full legal recognition to trade unions passed (9) and it was accompanied by the Criminal Law Amendment Act, which still retained the vague offences of 'intimidation' and 'molestation' (10). If Parliament believed that it had freed unions from prosecution as conspiracies, it was quickly disillusioned by Mr. Justice Brett, when he sentenced five London Gas Stokers to a year's imprisonment (11). There were widespread demonstrations against what the unions regarded as 'class legislation' and all the techniques of the pressure group were applied (12).

Times were good for trade union activities with the economy experiencing the greatest boom of the century in the first three years of the 1870s. Workers took advantage of the demand for their labour to press for shorter hours. The Newcastle Nine Hours' Movement (13) triggered off a generally successful demand for shorter hours among skilled unionists, and there was an 'explosion' of organisation among many groups of unskilled workers (see Ch. 5 *infra*). The advance of unionism brought a reaction from some employers, who sought in the National Federation of Employers to build 'a rampart' to keep back 'an advancing army' (14).

(9) The Trade Union Act, 1871, 34 and 35 Vic., c. 31

2. *Trade union not criminal.*   The purposes of any trade union shall not, by reason merely that they are in restraint of trade, be deemed to be unlawful so as to render any member of such trade union liable to criminal prosecution for conspiracy or otherwise.

3. *Trade union not unlawful for civil purposes.*   The purposes of any trade union shall not, by reason merely that they are in restraint of trade, be unlawful so as to render void or voidable any agreement or trust.

4. *Trade union contracts, when not enforceable.*   Nothing in this Act shall enable any court to entertain any legal proceeding instituted with the object of directly enforcing or recovering damages for the breach of any of the following agreements, namely,

(1) Any agreement between members of a trade union as such, concerning the conditions on which any members for the time being of such trade union shall or shall not sell their goods, transact business, employ, or be employed:
(2) Any agreement for the payment by any person of any subscription or penalty to a trade union:
(3) Any agreement for the application of the funds of a trade union (a) To provide benefits to members; or (b) To furnish contributions to any employer or workman not a member of such trade union, in consideration of such employer or workman acting in conformity with the rules or resolutions of any such trade union; or (c) To discharge any fine imposed upon any person by sentence of a court of justice; or
(4) Any agreement made between one trade union and another; or
(5) Any bond to secure the performance of any of the above mentioned agreements.

But nothing in this section shall be deemed to constitute any of the above-mentioned agreements unlawful.

(10) The Criminal Law Amendment Act, 1871, 34 and 35 Vic., c. 32

1. Every person who shall do any one or more of the following acts, that is to say, (1) Use violence to any person or any property, (2) Threaten or intimidate any person in such manner as would justify a justice of the peace, on complaint made

to him, to bind over the person so threatening or intimidating to keep the peace,
(3) Molest or obstruct any person in manner defined by this section, with a view
to coerce such person, –

1. Being a master to dismiss or to cease to employ any workman, or being a
   workman to quit any employment or to return to work before it is finished;
2. Being a master not to offer, or being a workman not to accept any
   employment of work;
3. Being a master or workman to belong or not to belong to any temporary or
   permanent association or combination;
4. Being a master or workman to pay any fine or penalty imposed by any
   temporary or permanent association or combination;
5. Being a master to alter the mode of carrying on his business, or the number or
   description of any persons employed by him,

shall be liable to imprisonment, with or without hard labour, for a term not
exceeding three months.

A person shall for the purposes of this Act be deemed to molest or obstruct
another person in any of the following cases; that is to say,

1. If he persistently follow such person about from place to place:
2. If he hide any tools, clothes, or other property owned or used by such person,
   or deprive him or hinder him in the use thereof:
3. If he watch or beset the house or other place where such person resides or
   works, or carries on business, or happens to be, or the approach to such house
   or place, or if with two or more persons he follow such person in a disorderly
   manner in or through any street or road.

(11) *Regina* v. *Bunn* [1872] 12 Cox CC 316

Brett, J. said to the jury: I tell you that the mere fact of these men being members
of a trade-union is not illegal and ought not be pressed against them in the least.
The mere fact of their leaving their work – although they were bound by
contract, and although they broke their contract – is not sufficient ground for
you to find them guilty upon this indictment. This would be of no consequence of
itself, but only as evidence of something else. But if there was an agreement
among the defendants by improper molestation to control the will of the
employers, then I tell you that would be an illegal conspiracy at common law,
and that such an offence is not abrogated by the Criminal Law Amendment Act,
which you have heard referred to. This is a charge of conspiracy at common law,
and if you think that there was an agreement and combination between the
defendants, or some of them, and others, to interfere with the masters by
molesting them, so as to control their will; and if you think that the molestation
which was so agreed upon was such as would be likely, in the minds of men or
ordinary nerve, to deter them from carrying on their business according to their
own will, then I say that it is an illegal conspiracy, for which these defendants are

liable. That, gentlemen, is as to the first set of counts. But this conspiracy is charged in another form, and in that other form the real charge is that they either agreed to do an unlawful act, or to do a lawful act by unlawful means; and it seems to me naturally to fall under the latter class. I shall, therefore, ask you whether there was an agreement or combination between these and others to hinder and prevent the company from carrying on and exercising their business, by means of the men simultaneously breaking their contracts of service which they had entered into with the company. And I tell you that the breach without just cause of such contracts as have been proved in this case is an illegal act by the servant who does it. It is an illegal act, and what is more, it is a criminal act – that is to say, it is an act which makes each of them liable to the criminal law . . . .

(12) LTC, *To Trade Societies on Repeal of the Criminal Law Amendment Act Demonstration, Whit-Monday, June 2nd 1873*

In calling upon the Trades of London to join the forthcoming Demonstration, we have to remind them that both the Trades' Union Congresses, held in Nottingham and Leeds, declared decisively for nothing short of the repeal of the 'Criminal Law Amendment Act', and such alteration in the 'Master and Servants' Act', and 'Law of Conspiracy', as shall secure precisely the same punishment to the Employer for the same acts as is inflicted on the Workman. The collective opinion of the Unionists, as expressed in clear and definite resolutions at the Congresses referred to, was followed up last year by great demonstrations of the Trades in most of the large Towns of England; but London in this respect has been silent. It is now time, however, for the Workmen to speak plainly and emphatically on the subject of Class Legislation, and to follow it up by the necessary action for its removal.

This course is now rendered more than ever imperative. Already the attitude of Employers is both ominous and threatening. Two meetings have just been held, one in London, the other in Manchester, representing powerful and wealthy organisation of Employers, with the avowed object of opposing Mr. Vernon Harcourt in the effort he is about to make in Parliament, to effect the just alteration in the Law which we desired.

These circumstances induced the London Trades Council to convene a Delegate Meeting, at which it was decided to hold a great demonstration in Hyde Park, on Whit-Monday, June 2nd. . . .

(13) Nine Hours' Movement in the North of England, E. Allen, *The North-East Engineers' Strikes of 1871* (Newcastle, 1971) p. 114

To the Working Men of Great Britain. – After a strike of three or four weeks' duration, the Employers of Engineering Labour in Sunderland, on the 2nd of May, yielded to the demands of their workmen, in regard to a reduction of the hours of labour from fifty-nine to fifty-four per week.

The men of Newcastle and Gateshead, inspired by the success of the

Sunderland men, have resolved to come out on strike, in order to attain the same object, and, as the position of the Employers in these Towns is almost the same as that occupied by the Sunderland Employers before the strike, we have every hope of success.

We have not come to this resolution rashly, or with undue haste, but have tried every means to gain our object without having recourse to the last dread resource of a strike. Our Employers, however, have treated all our advances with contempt, and have left us no alternative but a strike. And as a strike cannot be carried on without funds, we apply to you for pecuniary assistance.

Our object is not a merely selfish one, for if it is attained by us it will be rendered more easy of attainment by you, and indeed by the working men of Britain generally, so that, in fact, we feel that as we are out on strike, not only for ourselves but for the whole of the working population of this kingdom, we have a claim upon our sympathy and support, which we are confident you will not refuse to acknowledge.

Our need is urgent, as we will have ten thousand men out on strike on June 1st, not the 12th part of that number being members of any Trade Society.

Trusting that you will contribute to our support as liberally as ever possible.

We remain, Gentlemen, yours respectfully,

THE ACTING COMMITTEE OF THE NINE HOURS' LEAGUE.

Newcastle-on-Tyne, 22nd May, 1871.

(14) *Capital and Labour* (31 Dec. 1873), The National Federation of Associated Employers of Labour

We beg to call attention to the enclosed rules of this Federation, and to explain why it has been formed, what are its objects, and how it proposes to attain them.

It has been formed in consequence of the extraordinary development – oppressive action – far-reaching, but openly-avowed designs, and elaborate organization of the Trade Unions.

Its object is, by a defensive organization of the employers of labour, to resist these designs so far as they are hostile to the interests of the employers, the freedom of the non-unionist operatives, and the well-being of the community. . . .

[The trade unions] have a well-paid and ample staff of leaders, most of them experienced in the conduct of strikes, many of them skilful organizers, all forming a class apart, a profession, with interests distinct from, though not necessarily antagonistic to, those of the work-people they lead but, from their very *raison d'être*, hostile to those of the employers and of the rest of the community. . . .

They have, through their command of money, the imposing aspect of their organisation; and partly also, from the mistaken humanitarian aspirations of a certain number of literary men of good standing, a large array of literary talent, which is prompt in their service on all occasions of controversy. They have their own press as field for these exertions. Their writers have access to some of the leading London journals.

They organize frequent meetings, at which paid speakers inoculate the working-classes with their ideas, and urge them to dictate terms to candidates for Parliament. . . .

They have the attentive ear of the Ministry of the day, and their communications are received with instant and respectful attention. . . .

The necessary and legitimate result of this powerful organization, – of the sacrifices, pecuniary and otherwise, which the workpeople make in its support, – of the skilful and ceaseless energy with which it is directed, must be to give it, to a large extent, the control of the elections, and consequently of parliament; the power to dictate terms everywhere between employers and employed, and the mastery over the independence of the workmen, as well as over the operations of the employers.

These results are the deserved reward of the superiority of the Trade Unionists over the employers in these high qualities of foresight, generalship, and present self-sacrifice for the sake of future advantage, which form necessary elements in the success of every organized society.

It is more than time for the employers to emulate the example thus set in energy and devotion, but in pursuit of more legitimate and less selfish ends. . . .

The disadvantage of there being no adequate organisation charged with the special duty of vindicating employers' interests is made prominent when the Trade Unions seek to force through Parliament some desired change in the law, such as. . . . 1st. The repeal of the Criminal Law Amendment Act; 2nd. The repeal of all penal laws affecting workmen; 3rd. The Conspiracy Law Amendment Bill; 4th. The revision of the Masters and Servants Act; 5th. The promotion of the Payment of Wages Bill; 6th. The promotion of the Compensation of Workmen Bill.

Should the Unions be unresisted in these efforts, a period of legislative change adverse alike to employers, to the independent workmen, and to the interests of the whole community, will be brought in with the new Parliament. . . .

John Robinson, President. . . .

The Trade unions had considerable political success in their campaign against the Criminal Law Amendment Act in the election of 1874. Many newly-elected MPs were pledged to support repeal, including the new Home Secretary, R. A. Cross. The Conservative Government's first decision, however, was to set up yet another commission to look at the labour laws. Only with great difficulty were labour representatives found to sit upon it (15). Its report was inconclusive, but Cross pressed ahead with an extensive programme of labour legislation. The Criminal Law Amendment Act was repealed and, at long last, by the Conspiracy and Protection of Property Act, trade unions were removed from the charge of criminal conspiracy (16); the Employer and Workman Act replaced the unequal Master and Servant legislation (17); and the Trade Union Act Amendment Act of 1876 smoothed out the anomalies of the 1871 Act (18). The

Parliamentary Committee of the TUC had reason to be satisfied with its endeavours.

(15) A. J. Mundella to R. Leader, Sheffield, 21 March 1874 [Sheffield University Library]

It is evident that the Government succeeded in obtaining their Commission just as they had abandoned all hope of doing so. At the eleventh hour, before the paragraph in the Queen's speech was expunged (as it was certain to have been) Hughes and Macdonald gave a qualified assent to join the Committee. In Hughes' case it was weakness; in Macdonald's worse. Hughes actually assisted the day before in drawing up the protest against the Commission, and even strengthened the words they proposed to use. There is but little excuse for him, and yesterday he met the working men from all quarters of England, Rolley amongst the number, and Hughes' defence was his worst accusation. He and Macdonald are now re-considering what course they shall pursue. They both express regret at having been entrapped by intrigue on the part of the Government, and that they assented to the Home Secretary's proposals. The way the thing was managed was singularly ingenious and crafty, and Burt's account of the whole story and Hughes' and Macdonald's subsequent relation was as good as a play. Indignant as the men were at finding themselves betrayed, they screamed with laughter at the clever trickiness of the whole thing. Hughes was put in one room at the Home Office. Burt in another; one was played off against the other, and both against Macdonald till two had given their assent.

(16) Conspiracy and Protection of Property Act, 1875, 38 and 39 Vic., c. 86

3. An agreement or combination by two or more persons to do or procure to be done any act in contemplation or furtherance of a trade dispute between employers and workmen shall not be indictable as a conspiracy if such act committed by one person would not be punishable as a crime.

Nothing in this section shall exempt from punishment any person guilty of a conspiracy for which a punishment is awarded by any Act of Parliament.

Nothing in this section shall affect the law relating to riot, unlawful assembly, breach of peace, or sedition, or any offence against the State or the Sovereign. . . .

4. Where a person employed by a municipal authority or by any company or contractor upon whom is imposed by Act of Parliament the duty, or who have otherwise assumed the duty, of supplying any city, borough, town, or place, or any part thereof, with gas or water, wilfully and maliciously breaks a contract of service with that authority or company or contractor, knowing or having reasonable cause to believe that the probable consequences of his so doing, either alone or in combination with others, will be to deprive the inhabitants of that city, borough, town, place, or part, wholly or to a great extent of their supply of

gas or water, he shall on conviction thereof by a court of summary jurisdiction, or on indictment as herein-after mentioned, be liable either to pay a penalty not exceeding twenty pounds, or to be imprisoned for a term not exceeding three months with or without hard labour.

5. Where any person wilfully and maliciously breaks a contract of service or of hiring, knowing or having reasonable cause to believe that the probable consequences of his so doing, either alone or in combination with others, will be to endanger human life, or cause serious bodily injury, or to expose valuable property whether real or personal to destruction or serious injury, he shall on conviction thereof by a court of summary jurisdiction, or on indictment as herein-after mentioned, be liable either to pay a penalty not exceeding twenty pounds or be imprisoned for a term not exceeding three months, with or without hard labour.

7. Every person who, with a view to compel any other person to abstain from doing or to do any act which such other person has a legal right to do or abstain from doing, wrongfully and without legal authority,

(1) Uses violence to or intimidates such other person or his wife or children, or injures his property; or,
(2) Persistently follows such other person about from place to place; or,
(3) Hides any tools, clothes or other property owned or used by such other person, or deprives him of or hinders him in the use thereof; or,
(4) Watches or besets the house or other place where such other person re-sides, or works, or carries on business, or happens to be, or the approach to such house or place; or,
(5) Follows such other person with two or more other persons in a disorderly manner in or through any street or road,

shall, on conviction thereof by a court of summary jurisdiction, or on indictment as herein-after mentioned, be liable either to pay a penalty not exceeding twenty pounds, or to be imprisoned for a term not exceeding three months, with or without hard labour.

Attending at or near the house or place where a person resides, or works, or carries on business, or happens to be, or the approach to such house or place, in order merely to obtain or communicate information, shall not be deemed watching or besetting within the meaning of this section.

(17) Employers and Workmen Act, 1875, 38 and 39 Vic., c. 90

3. In any proceeding before a county court in relation to any dispute between an employer and a workman arising out of or incidental to their relation as such . . . the court may, in addition to any jurisdiction it might have exercised if this Act had not passed, exercise all or any of the following powers: (that is to say),

(1) It may adjust and set off the one against the other all such claims on the part either of the employer or of the workman, arising out of or incidental to the relation between them, as the court may find to be subsisting, whether such claims are liquidated or unliquidated, and are for wages, damages, or otherwise; and,

(2) If, having regard to all the circumstances of the case, it thinks it just to do so, it may rescind any contract between the employer and the workman upon such terms as to the apportionment of wages or other sums due thereunder, and as to the payment of wages or damages, or other sums due, as it thinks just; and,

(3) Where the court might otherwise award damages for any breach of contract it may, if the defendant be willing to give security to the satisfaction of the court for the performance by him of so much of this contract as remains unperformed, with the consent of the plaintiff, accept such security, and order performance of the contract accordingly, in place either of the whole of the damages which would otherwise have been awarded, or some part of such damages. . . .

4. A dispute under this Act between an employer and a workman may be heard and determined by a court of summary jurisdiction, and such court, for the purpose of this Act, shall be deemed to be a court of civil jurisdiction. . . .

(18) Trade Union Act Amendment Act, 1876, 39 and 40 Vic., c. 22

1. This Act and the Trade Union Act, 1871, herein-after termed the principal Act, shall be construed as one Act, and may be cited together as the Trade Union Acts, 1871 and 1876, and this Act may be cited separately as the Trade Union Act Amendment Act, 1876. . . .

12. Any two or more unions may, if in the case of each or every such trade union, on a ballot being taken, the votes of at least fifty per cent of the members entitled to vote thereat are recorded, and of the votes recorded those in favour of the proposal exceed by twenty per cent or more the votes against the proposal, became amalgamated together as one trade union, with or without any dissolution or division of the funds of such trade unions, or either or any of them; but no amalgamation shall prejudice any right to any creditor of either or any union party thereto. . . .

16. The term 'trade union' means any combination, whether temporary or permanent, for regulating the relations between workmen and masters, or between workmen and workmen, or between masters and master, or for imposing restrictive combinations on the conduct of any trade or business, whether such combination would or would not, if the principal Act had not been passed, have been deemed to have been an unlawful combination by reason of some one or more of its purposes being in restraint of trade.

5. *The Unskilled*

The trade unions of the mid-nineteenth century were predominantly organisations of craftsmen, whose 'skilled' position often stemmed from their membership. A substantial gap existed between the world of the skilled man and that of the unskilled labourer (1, 2). In the boom of the early 1870s, unions began to flourish among the previously unorganised. Those most depressed of workers, the agricultural labourers, organised societies in the Midlands, East Anglia and in the South East, often supported by middle-class sympathisers (3, 4). Joseph Arch (1826–1919), a Primitive Methodist lay preacher and labourer at Barford in Warwickshire, probably deserves the title of 'founding father' by organising local labourers on 7 February 1872 (5) but there were others and rivalries developed (6, 7). Organisation appeared among many other groups of workers, in the docks, in shops, and among gas workers. Middle-class sympathisers were particularly important in the formation of unions among railwaymen (8) and among women workers (9).

(1) *Bee-Hive*, (2 July 1864): Editorial Comment

The working classes, by which I mean those who labour a certain number of hours per day for a certain weekly wage, are divided into two large sections, one comprising the skilled artisan and mechanic, and the other the labourer, the costermonger, the men who get their daily living by means which they themselves would find it difficult to describe, although yet honest with all, and the 'roughs' of all description. These two sections, although strictly working men, are very dissimilar in their tastes, habits and feelings, and it is a common mistake made by writers and speakers in what is called the higher classes, when writing and speaking about the working classes, to confound both those sections together. A fatal mistake, and one that has been productive, in many instances, of much evil.

(2) *Bee-Hive* (25 Feb. 1865)

There is undeniably a strong aristocratic feeling amongst working men; the skilled mechanic looks down with a feeling akin to contempt upon the unskilled labourer; the printer looks down upon the builder, the builder in his turn looks down upon the shoemaker, and so on; although, at the same time, neither the engineer, the printer, nor the builder, are above sending, in their time of need, a deputation to a shoemakers' society for the purpose of obtaining contributions. Working men in the mass are not yet prepared to receive the truth, that what concerns one concerns all, and that no department of industry can be injured without that injury more or less being felt by all other departments.

(3) *Bee-Hive* (2 March 1872)

Sir – The labourers from nearly twenty Parishes assembled on 26th February, in the British School, to form themselves into an association for their protection against farmers, who are grinding them down, and refuse to advance their wages. About 700 assembled; several of them told most pitiable tales of the way in which they were treated by their employers, and how owing to the lowness of their wages, they were obliged to go often with an empty stomach.

They demand 3s. per day, and 10 hours' work. The manner in which they conducted themselves was praiseworthy. Knowing your sympathy with the movement, and that you try to assist the working man, I write to ask you if you will furnish me with particulars to form an association, and if you can do, to furnish me with the rules of some society, by which we can go by. I am the only one who has taken up their cause in any official way, and if you advise me I shall be glad. I wish you to understand they are entirely of the agricultural class, and if they obtain their demands I want them to remain banded together, for their mutual benefit, especially in the case of sickness. I hope you will help us,

Yours respectfully,

Charles H. Leakey, Secretary to the Horncastle Agricultural Protection Society

(4) *Stamford Mercury*, (3 May 1872): 'Labourers' Association Conference at Grantham'

On Saturday a meeting of delegates representing the labourers' associations in Lincolnshire was held at the Spread Eagle Inn, Grantham, to consider the desirability of forming an amalgamated association. The Hon. A. Herbert, M.P for Nottingham presided, and Ald. Carter, M.P. for Leeds was present.

(5) Joseph Arch, *The Story of His Life* (1898)

We settled that I should address the meeting under the old chestnut tree; and I expected to find some thirty or forty of the principal men there. What then was my surprise to see not a few tens but many hundreds of labourers assembled; there were nearly two thousand of them. The news that I was going to speak that night had been spread about; and so the men had come in from all the villages around within a radius of ten miles. Not a circular had been sent out, not a handbill printed, but from cottage to cottage, from farm to farm, the word had been passed on. . . .

We passed a resolution to form a Union there and then, and the names of the men could not be taken down fast enough.

(6) *Labourers' Union Chronicle*, (21 Aug. 1875)

Sir, When the Labourers' Union first started Joseph Arch being a farm workman, seeing it was to benefit his class, he of course took a part in promoting it. Being a Primitive Methodist local preacher he had considerable experience in addressing congregations of people, therefore it was no wonder that the labourers in his own neighbourhood should at once put him forward as a public speaker on the union question, and eventually adopt him as their leader. When the agitation commenced in Warwickshire, and Joseph Arch stood forth to advocate Unionism among his fellow-workmen, it was not anticipated, either by the labourers or himself, that he would be anything more than the leader of a section of Unionists organized in the locality in which he lived; in fact it was not expected that the agitation would so suddenly become general. As if by magic, however, in almost every part of the country, men sprang up, who although then in good and easy circumstances, had been originally farm labourers or had been either eye witnesses or actual partakers of their poverty, hardships and difficulties, and consequently ardently sympathised with the movement, to improve what they knew to be an oppressed and down-trodden class. Many other, like myself, found the funds for commencing and carrying on the agitation, employed and paid men to assist in organizing for years, were found nightly on village greens and town market places, addressing large gatherings of labourers, giving both advice and encouragement, and thus large districts were formed, studded with branches and for this neither fee nor reward was expected. Seeing the movement thus spreading, Messrs. H. Taylor and others were placed at the head of an Executive, who took the leadership of a district in Warwickshire, Mr. Arch being chosen president. At that time the 'Labourers' Union Chronicle' newspaper was started, by the circulation of which the proceedings of the Warwickshire body was made public, and as all other daily and weekly papers, both local and otherwise, entirely ignored the agitation, the doings of other but the Leamington district was not heard of, hence the public sympathizers gave their subscriptions to Warwickshire, believing the whole movement to be represented there. Instead of Messrs. H. Taylor and Co. setting out at once to spread the Union in places where no organizations existed, they set about trying to oust from their positions men who had organized districts, seize their labours and annex their possessions. There being no other paper but Mr. Vincent's to chronicle Union events, and it being the organ of the Leamington section, the meetings attended by Mr. Arch were regularly reported, and hence he soon became a very prominent figure. . . . This, of course, gave him considerable power and influence with a large body of labourers, and the middle and upper classes having peculiar views and crochets which they desired to push amongst working men, observing this, seized upon Mr. Arch as the means of commnication; he thus became the platform companion of many. . . .

(7) *The Labourer* (30 June 1877)

The Amalgamated Labour League was formed in January, 1871, and has secured an advance of wages for all its members of from 3s. to 5s. per week. About £15,000 has been paid for death grants to the relatives of members, for legal aid to members, and in various other benevolent objects. The entrance fee is 1s. and the contribution 2d. per week. A copy of rules and contributions card, 4d. Benefits – legal aid free, assistance to emigrate or migrate, weekly payments during a strike or lock out, a grant of £2.10 at the death of a member to his widow or relations etc. etc.

Each district manages its own local affairs, and retains its own funds, paying its own share according to membership of all the expenditure for general welfare of the members at large. The paid officials do not vote. None but working men are elegible for office, and no honorary or consultative committee formed.

In addition to these valuable benefits, a Sick Club has been formed in connection with the League for the use of its members only. . . . Each district has to pay its own sick benefit, but all districts are bound to help each other in case of need. . . .

(8) *Bee-Hive* (9 Dec. 1871): Objects of the ASRS

To promote a good and fair understanding between employers and employed; to prevent strikes; to protect and defend members against injustice; to secure ten hours for a fair day's labour and one day's extra pay for eight hours overtime; the payment of the same rate for Sundays; to afford a ready means by arbitration or otherwise of the settlement of disputes; for granting temporary assistance to its members, and to provide legal assistance when necessary; to make special grants to members who desired to emigrate, and to found a superannuation fund for old and disabled members.

(9) TUC *7th Annual Report* (1875)

The Chairman read a letter from Mrs. Emma Patterson, of London, calling the attention of the congress to the subject on the increased employment of women in various trades, and the necessity for the formation of trades unions amongst them, to ensure a 'fair day's pay for a fair day's work'. The attention of the congress was directed to the efforts now commenced for the formation of women's unions. In one trade – that of bookbinding – there were 4,000 or 5,000 women employed, and a trade union was formed amongst them three months ago, which was steadily progressing. In its formation, the women were assisted by a trade union of men, in London, engaged in the same employment, and it was asked that other trades unionists would show a willingness to assist in a similar manner the women of other trades in any effort they might make to organise their labour.

With the onset of the depression in trade at the end of the decade, many unions collapsed and others had their membership greatly depleted. It is clear, however, that in most areas some nucleus of unionism among the unskilled remained ready to reappear when the economic situation improved or when the right leader emerged, as Havelock Wilson (1858–1929) of the seamen and Ben Tillett (1860–1943) of the London dockers explained (10, 11).

(10) RC on Labour, *PP* 1892 xxxv, Group B, 1: Evidence of J. Havelock Wilson, General Secretary of the National Amalgamated Sailors' and Firemen's Union of Great Britain and Ireland

9176. . . . The condition of the seamen in the year 1851 was much about the same as the condition of the seamen prior to the formation of our present National Union. Wages were very low and the ships were seriously under-manned. The men were so much oppressed by the shipowners that they were compelled by their tyrannical conduct to bind themselves into a Union . . . which was named the Seamen's United Friendly Society. . . .

9179. Was the Union instrumental in securing any advantages for the men? – Yes, the Union at that time became a very powerful one, branches were formed in about 30 different ports in the country, but they were not an amalgamated Union, they were a number of branches or separate societies federated together, their rules were not perfect and there was no perfect system of central government. . . .

9182. How long did this Union last? – The Union lasted about 11 years. I think it finally collapsed in 1859 or 1860. . . .

9188. Do you know whether its collapse was in consequence of the owners' opposition, or to what cause was it due? – Entirely in consequence of the opposition of the owners. . . .

9189. . . . In 1879 we formed a Union which is now in existence, and is known as the North of England Sailors' and Sea-going Firemen's Friendly Association. After the formation of this Union, the wages being very low and freights being very good, we thought we had a right to have a share of the profits. We were only a very small Union in one port only at that time, and we resolved to approach the owners. . . .

9193. . . . When all efforts of conciliation had failed, the men resolved to strike, with the result that they got their demand for 32s. per week conceded to the extent of 31s. 6d. per week, which sum the men accepted.

9194. . . . We made considerable progress with this North of England Union up to about 1882. We had formed branches of this Union in other adjacent ports, but eventually these branches collapsed. As soon as the employers found that the men's organisation had gone down, they commenced to decrease their wages – reductions took place all round, not because freights were bad, because it can be proved that freights at that time were actually better that they are to-day although the owners are paying nearly 30 per cent. more wages than they did at that date. . . .

9227. . . . In what way was the next attempt at organisation made? – In 1886, a considerable number of men enrolled themselves in this way: We then made another attempt to reorganise this North of England Society, which had got very low, and to do this we issued at that time what we called a privilege card. It had certain rules upon the back, and every member who would enroll as a privilege member without paying entrance fee got one of those cards on condition that he would act up to the rules of the Union. We enrolled a large number of men as privilege card members. . . .

9232. . . . There was some small attempts made in 1886 to form a Union in London known as the Vigilance Association. They enrolled, I believe, about 1000 members, but it did not last more than about 18 months: it died a natural death. . . .

9236. Will you state what steps were taken for the formation of the existing Union? – I had been a member of this North of England Union for about nine years at that time, and I found that if the seamen wanted to improve their condition it could only be done by a national movement. We had tried local efforts for many years and they had always failed, of course. Then I tried to induce the committee of the North of England Sailors' and Firemen's Union to extend their organization, but they were afraid to do so; they could not see how a National Sailors and Firemen's Union would work. Therefore I resolved a draft a code of rules, which took me some considerable time, and I founded this present Union, with branches now in every port of the United Kingdom, 15 branches on the continent, one branch at Constantinpole, and another one at Malta.

(11) Ben Tillett, *Memories and Reflections* (1931)

Even before we began to organise there were innumerable small strikes which we were forced to participate in as a protest against the intolerable exploitation to which we were subjected. In the South-West India Dock there was a system of surplus wages established. It was called the 'Plus System'. Some unknown method of working out quantities and tonnage, on a given basis of cost, might leave a surplus to be paid out in addition to the ordinary pay of the workers. Two things made this basis nothing but systematic robbery. One was that no docker know anything of the basis of cost. There was no check, no access to accounts, and as the labour was casual from hour to hour and from day to day, a big minority, if not the majority of the men, would not come back to the job on the second or following days.

This outrageous robbery went on in every one of the dock quays where the system applied. On ship after ship work was stopped to ascertain costs, but never once did I hear of a proper account to men individually or groups. It was this abuse that really led to the dock strike of 1889. Just before that great upheaval occurred, there were months and years of haphazard and sporadic agitation; street corner work and propaganda in which I bore a part. . . . I cherished a secret ambition to be a barrister, and might indeed have achieved my ambition if a bigger brief – bigger than I realised at the time – had not been placed on my hands on a day in July, 1887.

On that day a workmate, a man called Fleming, whose name was really Flanagan, but who had adopted an alias during the Anti-Irish time, when the advertisement 'No Irish need Apply' was a common sight, brought me a card announcing a meeting of the tea operatives, called by the employees of the warehouse in Cutler Street, where the management sought to impose a reduction in the wages paid for handling the new season's tea. There were grievances also in other tea warehouses.

A herald of a new wave of activity among the unskilled workers came in July 1888 when the low-paid girls at Bryant and May's match-factory successfully struck against bad conditions, fines and victimisation. The main figure behind the strike was the redoubtable Mrs Annie Besant (1848–1933), freethinker, socialist, later theosophist and Indian nationalist, with her journal *The Link*. She had the help of the LTC (12). The nascent dockers' unions were less successful in attracting support from the craft unionists (13), but it was the London dock strike of August 1889 which came to symbolise the 'new unionism' (14).

The dock companies were dependent on casual labour. For some workers the ports offered a better living than farm-work (15), but for most they were 'the last refuge of the destitute' (16) and the misery of conditions is well attested (17).

(12) *The Link* (21 July 1888)

On Tuesday the strike Committee accompanied members of the London Trades' Council into the presence of the directors, and put their own case. It was finally agreed that; (1) all fines should be abolished; (2) all deductions for paint, brushes, stamps, etc., should be put an end to; (3) the 3d. should be restored to the packers; (4) the 'pennies' should be restored, or an equivalent advantage given in the system of payment to the boys who do the racking; (5) all grievances should be laid directly before the firm, ere any hostile action be taken; (6) all the girls to be taken back. The firm hoped the girls would form a union; they promised to see about providing a room for meals away from the work; and they also promised to provide barrows for carrying the boxes, which have been hitherto carried by young girls on their heads, to the great detriment of their hair and their spines.

It is small wonder that these terms were enthusiastically endorsed by the girls as a whole, when they were submitted to them at a meeting held at 6 p.m. the same day. Mr. Shipton received warm applause as he explained the details of the settlement, and the acceptance was carried amid wild cheering, the girls feeling that they had won a victory which would materially better their conditions.

(13) Minutes of LTC, 5 Oct. 1888

Mr. Tillett, Secretary of Dock Labourers' Society wrote to ask the assistance of the Council for the Labourers out on strike at the Tilbury Docks, but as the letter gave no particulars of a definite character and considering that the place was more than twenty miles from London, it was outside the Metropolitan District. Together with other appeals then before the Trades – that in the absence of accurate and detailed information the Council cannot at present see its way to take action upon the application.

(14) Tillett, *Memories and Reflections*

This Conference [with the chairman of the Dock Company], though it proved abortive of any result, enabled me to present the demands for which the strike had been called: two regular calls per day, and one call for night work; fixed meal times; day wages and night wages also to be defined; minimum scale of hours to be worked; minimum rates of pay to be prescribed; travel time to be counted as work time; access to accounts on all wage rates; payment at properly appointed times and places, and under guarantee; honest accountancy; number of men to constitute a gang; safety in gear; efficiency in all the lifting and running gear used for loading and unloading – I included safety slings on chains or ropes; – a limit of overtime; systematic organisation in calling on and engagement of labour; special rates for Saturday afternoons and Sundays, holidays and holy days; and recognition by the management of Organised Labour and its representatives.

In those claims I summarised the grievous wrongs and discontents of the dock worker, to be assuaged by the dockers' 'tanner' and by the importation of a little humanity, order, and commonsense in the organisation of dock labour. . . .

The scheme of picketing itself was Napoleonic in proportion, for by now 100,000 London workers were affected by the Strike. We had 16,000 pickets on at one time under their Captains, Lieutenants, and Sergeants, divided and subdivided with military precision. At Tilbury, where night pickets had to be posted, as sometimes elsewhere, we paid for picket duty, but by day the picketing was done freely, loyally, and effectively, by volunteers who were systematically organised. . . .

We learned to make good use of the Press, in maintaining public interest in the Strike, and keeping their purse strings open and in presenting the case against the Dock companies.

(15) RC on Labour, *PP* 1892 xxxv, Group B, I: Evidence of John Polhill, free labourer

6003. What part do you come from? – From Romney Marsh and Dungeness.

6004. How long have you worked at the docks? – Seven months.

6005. As a free labourer? – As a free labourer.

6006. Have you been in employment the whole of that time? – The whole of that time.

6007. And your wages have averaged what? – 36s. a week.

6008. What did they average before you came to the docks at London? – I should not think anything more than 12s. or 13s. a week.

(16) SC on the Sweating System, *PP* 1890 xvii

Of all the overcrowded, laborious, and uncertain callings in England, that of the casual dock labourer is one of the most miserable. It is open to everybody without apprenticeship or training, and all who are reduced to extremities fly at once to it. It is the last refuge of the destitute, the only halting place which intervenes between the friendless outcast and the workhouse.

There is regular employment for the picked hands at the docks, and the companies have a large proportion of their men who remain permanently in their service. But the 'casual' is in a most helpless and wretched condition. Artisans out of work, agricultural labourers who have come to London in the old belief that its streets are paved with gold, engineers, tailors, shoemakers, bakers, painters, costermongers, all flock to the docks when their own employment fails them. Thus, surplus labour in any trade, from whatever cause produced, instantly makes itself felt at the dock gates, and the men who were brought up to that occupation, as many were, find it more and more difficult to get a living by it.

(17) H. A. Mess, *Casual Labour at the Docks* (1916)

Men are engaged in the Victoria and Albert Docks either at or near the offices of the various shipping companies, or at one or two recognised centres of employment. Of these centres Custom House Railway station is the chief; it stands about half-way down the Victoria Dock on the north side. At a quarter to seven on an average morning some hundreds of men may be seem turning towards it from the neighbouring streets; whilst large numbers arrive by tram and train, often from a considerable distance, as for instance, from King's Cross or from Walthamstow. A glance at these men suffices to reveal the presence of a social problem of some magnitude. To begin with, very few of them are well clad.

They have not the look of self-respecting mechanics. Their clothes are patched and makeshift, and their boots are often in a deplorable condition. It is quite obvious that many of them are ill-nourished. Altogether they seem inadequately equipped for the work they have to do.

Such as they are they line up along the road which runs inside the dock area, skirting the quays. If it is a busy morning there will be a half dozen or more groups at intervals of a few yards; each group will contain anything from forty to a couple of hundred men. A little before seven the foremen appear, and proceed to select from the various groups the men they want. The methods differ from company to company, and from foreman to foreman, but usually they start by reading down a list of 'preference' men. As each man is called he steps across from the crowd. One can notice growing anxiety on the faces of those who remain. If it is a slack time the list of names may not be exhausted; but if on the other hand a great many hands are required the foremen may proceed to call men from the crowd. An experienced foreman knows a good many casuals by name, in some cases as many as 400, and when he no longer remembers names there will be faces which are familiar to him. . . .

At one 'call' which the writer attended there were some sixty men waiting. The foreman stood on the raised ledge of a warehouse and eyed the crowd all over as if it were a herd of cattle. Then very deliberately he beckoned a man with his finger, and after a considerable interval a second and a third, until he had taken ten in all. There was an evident enjoyment of a sense of power, understandable enough as human nature goes, and the whole proceedings were horribly suggestive of the methods of a slave market. . . . At one of the big calls on the south side of the Albert Dock the men wait to be taken on in a kind of cattle pen. The foremen mount into booths, not unlike pulpits in appearance, and from them they distribute metal tallies which are a token of engagement. The spectacle of some scores of men struggling violently is by no means infrequent here. Occasionally a foreman will toss a tally to a man at the rear of the crowd, just as a morsel of food might be thrown to a dog.

The attitude of the skilled workers to the new unionists was a strange mixture of sympathy and suspicion (18, 19, 20). Much of the suspicion stemmed from doubts about the methods of the new unionists and about the people who were leading them (21, 22). The new unions attracted the help of socialists and as such saw unionism as having a specifically socialist goal (23, 24, 25).

A touchstone of socialism and anti-socialism in the late 1880s had been the issue of the legal eight-hour day. The Parliamentary Committee of the TUC had made no secret of its hostility to legislative intervention (26), but gradually attitudes changed (27) and the important debate on the issue by the 1890 congress was less a victory for socialism or for new unionism than for new attitudes stirring 'old' unionists (28).

(18) F. Harrison, 'The New Trade Unionism', *Nineteenth Century*, CLII (Nov 1889)

The 'new' element is this. The trades have stood by one another as they never did before. The skilled workmen have stood by the unskilled workmen in a wholly new spirit, and public opinion supported the men as it has never done yet. In all the thirty years that I have closely studied the labour movement, I have never before known the best-paid and most highly skilled trades strike out of mere sympathy simply to help the unskilled, where there had been no dispute of their own. The skilled trades have often offered generous aid in money to other trades. But they never have struck work themselves, without asking or expecting any direct advantage from the sacrifice. In the strike of Dock Labourers the whole brunt of the struggle lay in the turn out of the stevedores, lightermen, sailors, and engineers, and other skilled men. . . . Without the stevedores and other skilled officers, unskilled labour, even if it could be found, would have been useless in the Docks.

(19) *TUC, 23rd Annual Report* (1890): Report of Parliamentary Committee

The past year has been one of remarkable activity in the labour world. There are many and various reasons for this increased life. In the first place combination is perfectly free and recognised by law in the Trade Union Acts, and the law of contract, if not perfect, at any rate leaves little to be desired. Increased interest is taken in workmen's movements by the press and enormous prominence is now given to labour agitation by newspapers, which in the days which have scarcely passed, had nothing but sneers and misrepresentation when they did not utterly ignore the efforts of the workers to better their condition. Ministers of all denominations, and representatives of various classes of society, have joined in the cry of better life for the people. These forces, a few years back, when not actively against us, certainly gave us neither encouragement nor assistance.

The success of the movement of the London dock labourers, which was nearly assured at our last Congress, was shortly afterwards consummated. Other labour movements followed in all parts of the country in varied and quick succession, some successful, others disastrous. The agitation of the metropolitan police and postmen are fresh in the memory of all, and it is sufficient to say that the result seems in many respects to be similar to a like movement in these two bodies some twenty years ago, namely, premature and enthusiastic action, followed by sudden collapse and then a sacrifice of victims. We think it will be very difficult to consolidate organisation in any body where a system of deferred pay either in the form of perquisites or pensions prevails. We have always contended that men should have full scope for combination for mutual aid and protection in all branches of industry, and we claim the same rights for policemen and postmen.

We welcome the increase of trade-unionism, and hope that the new unions that have been formed and which are being formed, will be based on such sound principles of organisation and finance that they will not prove broken reeds in the day of their trial, but will fulfil to the utmost the functions which trade unionism should and does fulfil when the first principles of organisation are observed and carried into effect.

(20) Liverpool Trades Council, *Annual Report 1890–91*

Liverpool Trade Unionists, through their Trades Council, may justly claim to be the pioneers of this great social change, as evidenced by their action in espousing the cause of the Seamen and Firemen in the primitive struggle wrought by this, the first great arm of the new Unionism, during the summer of 1889.

Although the objects of the Old and New Unionism are identical, yet, a certain amount of friction and clashing has existed which, however, has been unjustifiably magnified by irresponsible charlatans under the subtle 'aristocracy of labour' cry. A diagnosis of the evolution of latter-day unionism, imports the fact that the ardent spirits of the ancient order have had a self-imposed dual task to perform; on the one hand they had to imbue and educate the unskilled labourer into the principles and benefits of combination, whilst, on the other hand, they had to cultivate their older associates to tolerate and recognise these new champions to their devoted cause.

(21) George Howell, *Trade Unionism New and Old* (1891)

The distinguishing trait in the conduct of prominent 'new leaders' has been, and is, their persistent, cowardly, and calumnious attacks upon the old leaders, upon men who have borne the brunt of labour's battles, many of whom are still the trusted officials of the several Unions. For several years some of these men have attacked such representatives as Thomas Burt, Charles Fenwick and John Wilson, in the mining districts of their own constituencies; to such an extent was this pursued that Mr Burt offered to place his resignation in the hands of his council, and of his constituents. Mr Broadhurst was attacked so vehemently and persistently that he retired from the post of Secretary to the Trades Union Congress, a post held by him for about fourteen years. An effort was similarly made to get rid of Mr Shipton, Secretary of the London Trades Council, a post he held for nearly twenty years. The attacks upon Mr C. J. Drummond, the Secretary of the London Society of Compositors, were of such a character that he also resigned, but in this case he was entreated to withdraw the resignation, and continue at his post as secretary. Mr Robert Austin, the Secretary of the Amalgamated Society of Engineers, has been subject to similar attacks, though he has not gone so far as to tender his resignation. . . .

The effect of slanders, so ruthlessly and persistently circulated, has been to foment discontent among the members of societies represented by those named, and others occupying positions in other Unions. Some of the new leaders have openly proclaimed their mission is to preach the gospel of discontent. Of course there is discontent *and* discontent. In so far as discontent leads to emulation, to vigorous effort to better the condition of the workers, it is healthful; it stirs the stagnant pool. But there is discontent of another kind, which aims at lawlessness and license; we have seen examples of it during the last few years in strikes, without reason; in the exercise of brute force, without compunction; and in capitulation without honour. Violent methods are, or rather, they should be, things of the past. They belonged to an age when freedom of association was denied; when persecution drove men to something like frenzy; when long hours, low wages, dear provisions, scarcity of work, and demoralising conditions, had degraded the working classes almost to the level of brutes.

(22) *Dundee Year Book, 1891* (Dundee, 1892):

(a) Evidence of the Rev. H. Williamson, President of the Dundee Mill and Factory Operatives' Union, to the RC on Labour

The members of the Union had not received any assistance from the Dundee Trades Council, who had only taken an interest in the Union by finding fault with it. There was no other organisation of women in Dundee, though there was one in Forfar, but the Unions did not work harmoniously together. The fact was that he was, as it were, the father of these Unions. He had established them in Arbroath, Montrose, Brechin, and Kirkcaldy, and he had been rather freely criticised by one or two of the leaders of the outside Unions, which had alarmed a good many people. The fathers and brothers of the women had sometimes been afraid that the Union was not on a very sound basis, and therefore witness had been very anxious all along to hand over the Union to any competent person who was ready to take it up.

(b) Evidence of James Reid of the Dundee Trades Council

Might I ask you, have the Trades Council of Dundee come to any resolution upon the question of shortening the hours? – They have voted two or three times in favour of an eight hours day.

How to be obtained? – By means of legislation.

Mr Williamson told us that the women's Trades Union was not in connection with your Trades Council. You have spoken of the many things in which women are interested. Do you think that if Mr Williamson's Union was affiliated with your Trades Council some of those things might be undertaken by you? – Yes.

The CHAIRMAN – But you do not want to interfere with the women's Union do you? – We do not particularly desire to interfere with it. We should be glad to work with them. We should be glad to welcome the women's Union into the Trades Council. When they applied for admission to the Trades Council Mr Williamson was sent as their representative, but the rules debarred him from obtaining admission as a delegate because he was not a man engaged in the trade. The Council are quite willing to accept representatives from the Society if they send some of the actual workers.

But you don't dispute the success of the organisation with which Mr Williamson is connected? – No.

Mr COURTNEY – You object to the professional agitator? (Laughter.) – I would not apply that name to Mr Williamson. But we do certainly object to professional agitation.

You want to deal with the trade direct? – According to the rules, only members of the trade can represent them.

And the rule is the law of the Medes and Persians? – Yes.

The CHAIRMAN – And cannot be altered? – It will not, at any rate, be altered.

(23) Tom Mann and Ben Tillett, *The 'New' Trades Unionism* (June 1890)

Mr. Shipton has been Secretary of the London Trades Council for 18 years past, and the balance sheet issued by him for the year ending 1888, shows that the number of trade unionists affiliated to that Council was 25,949. In the early part of 1889, however, the London Society of Compositors withdrew their delegates, being dissatisfied with the reactionary character of the Secretary and Executive Council, thus reducing the affiliated membership to 18,824; and this was the position of the Council a year ago. Several other Societies also decided to withdraw their delegates. The reason for this was to be found in the fact that an increasing number of trades unionists of London had lost any confidence they previously had in the Council, but especially its Secretary, as it was rarely mentioned except contemptuously, in times of labour difficulties. The Council generally, and its Secretary particularly, had shown a decided inclination to be associated with those who were 'superior' to workmen, whilst to take part in labour struggles or to assist in the organisation of the unskilled, was entirely opposed to their principles and practice. Thus when the great strike was on in August last year, the two most advanced men of the Executive Council requested the Secretary to call that body together to render such assistance, as they might be able. But no, East End labourers are not in George Shipton's line; he can and often does, give forth a vague expression of sympathy, but as to doing some real work to assist dock labourers, or any other labourers, especially in the East End, it is 'all off' with the Secretary of the London Trades Council. Picnics to the Channel Tunnel, Sandringham and deputations in connection with various semi-politico and patriotic demi-semi-trade unionist and pseudo-philanthropic movements, such as the Sugar Bounties agitation and the Bimetallic cry, are much more agreeable, and after a few years of this one does not want to be bothered with the petty details of new societies.

(24) Tom Mann, *Tom Mann's Memoirs* (1923), quoting *The 'New' Trades Unionism – A Reply to Mr. George Shipton*

Many of these who are identified with the 'new' trades unionism have been connected with their own trade societies for many years past, and it was a continual source of bitter grief to them that so much poverty should exist amongst workers of all sections, but especially among the unskilled and unorganised, and that the old Societies should be so utterly callous to this poverty as not to make any special exertion to alter matters for the better. . . .

The methods adopted by us of determining a change in our present industrial system, are on a strictly trade-union basis. All our public utterances, all our talks to our members, have been directly towards cultivating a sturdy spirit of independence, and instilling a deep sense of responsibility. In fact we have been at pains to discredit appeals to the legislature, contending that the political machine will fall into our hands as a matter of course, so soon as the educational work has been done in our labour organisations. We are convinced that not until Parliament is an integral part of the workers, representing and responsible to industrial toilers, shall we be able to effect any reform by its means. . . .

The statement that the 'new' trade unionists look to Governments and legislation, is bunkum, the keynote is to *organise* first, and take action in the most effective way, so soon as organisation warrants action, instead of specially looking to Government. The lesson is being thoroughly well taught and learned that we must look to ourselves alone, though this, of course, does not preclude us from exercising our rights of citizenship.

It is quite true that most of the newly-formed unions pay contributions for trade purposes only, leaving sick and funeral benefits to be dealt with by sick and insurance societies. The work of the trade unionist is primarily to obtain such a re-adjustment of conditions between employers and employed as shall secure to the latter a better share of the wealth they produce, in the form of reduced working hours and higher wages, and our experience has taught us that many of the older unions are very reluctant to engage in a labour struggle, no matter how great the necessity, because they are hemmed in by sick and funeral claims, so that to a large extent they have lost their true characteristic of being fighting organisations, and the sooner they revert to their original programme the better for the well-being of the working masses. We, therefore, advocate strongly the necessity for labour organisations dealing with trade matters.

At every opportunity that presented itself we have paid our willing tribute to our old leaders, the *real fighters*. We attribute the apathy of many of the wealthy unions to the lack of new vitality, many of them up until recent years not being in advance of the stage where they have been left by the men who suffered imprisonment and starvation for their convictions.

Our ideal is a *Co-operative Commonwealth*. This we believe will be reached by honest effort in various directions, chief among which will be the efforts of the trade unionists; and while striving for the ideal, we are glad to know that we need not wait for years before further advantages can be obtained, but that by discreet conduct on our part, we can be continually gaining some advantage for one or other section of the workers.

(25) Harry Quelch, *Trade Unionism, Co-operation and Social Democracy* (Sept. 1892)

Trade unionism is not, for the unskilled worker, so much a weapon for fighting capitalists as a means of securing a weapon wherewith to fight them. The utility of the 'New Unionism' lies less in the little gains of wages or leisure it has secured for the worker – of which, in the first opportunity, they may be deprived – than in its political effects. It represents the workers as a political force. It is in this direction mainly that the new unions must progress if they would succeed in achieving any permanent material advantage. They must become more political and re-volutionary, not from a party but from a class point of view. To go on following the old beaten paths of trade unionism is simply to go on exhausting the possibilities of error for an indefinite period. If the new unions are simply to play the part of regulators of wages, as trade and prices rise and fall, they will be of very slight advantage to the workers compared with what they might accomplish if they took a broader view of their opportunities and their duties. What they have to do, and that now, is to use the power which organisation gives them to get control of the political machinery of the country and use it for the advancement of their class. By this means, they could if they chose, achieve as much in a year or two as would be gained in a century by the old methods of trade agitation and strikes.

(26) *Alliance Cabinet Makers' Monthly Report*, no. 153 (March 1888): 'Questions on Eight-Hour Working Day from the Parliamentary Committee of T. U. C.'

1. Are you in favour of an eight hours limit of the day's work – total 48 hours per week? or, as an alternative to this
2. Are you in favour of a total cessation of work on Saturdays?
3. Are you in favour of Parliament enforcing an eight hours day by law, or enforcing a Saturday holiday by law, or,
4. Are you in favour of obtaining either of these privileges by the free and united efforts of the organised trades of the Kingdom?

The points necessary to be considered in voting upon the above questions are as follows:–

Would you be willing to make the necessary sacrifice in your total week's wages which such an alteration might involve?

It is necessary for you to bear in mind that in case of an eight hours law being obtained, all overtime would by necessity cease.

In case of your being in favour of asking Government for such a law, it must not be forgotten that capital, which is much more powerful and better organised than labour, will have the same right to ask for regulation by Parliament of the conditions under which you and your labour are paid, as you have to invoke Parliamentary assistance against capital.

Is it your opinion, keeping the fact that on the continent of Europe the prevailing number of working hours per week are very much greater than in competing trades in this country, that we are at this time justified in seeking the reduction suggested?

We express no opinion in this circular upon the policy of these proposals, but leave you to form an unbiased judgment and decision.

(27) *North British Daily Mail* (2 Feb. 1888)

The Aberdeen Trades Council last night formally adopted the principle of 8 hours work per day, but agreed that instead of dividing the 48 hours per week into five days the period of labour should be spread over 6 days. It was resolved by 17 votes to 3 to communicate the result to the Parliamentary Committee of the Trades' Congress, and to ask the body to take steps for securing legislative interference in preference to voluntary efforts.

(28) *TUC, 23rd Annual Report* (1890)

Mr. C. J. Marks [London Society of Compositors] moved –

That, in the opinion of this Congress, the time has arrived when steps should be taken to reduce the working hours in all trades to eight per day, or a maximum of forty-eight hours per week; and while recognizing the power and influence of trade organisations, it is of opinion that the speediest and best method to obtain this reduction for the workers generally is by Parliamentary enactment. This Congress, therefore, instructs the Parliamentary Committee to take immediate steps for the furtherance of this object.

He believed every man in the room was in favour of a reduction in the hours of labour. He would devote his attention to the method of obtaining that reduction. . . . There were two methods suggested as to how this should be brought about. The first was that it should be brought about piecemeal by the various trade organisations, some already existing, and many yet to be born; and the second was that it should be brought about by one united effort of all section of workers as represented in this Congress by Parliamentary action. He was of opinion that if they were to wait for the piecemeal method of bringing about this reduction in the hours of labour they should never see it thoroughly established, or the advantage of the reduction secured to all workers. . . .

Mr. A. Matthews [London Society of Compositors] (London), in seconding, said his society had felt so strongly on the matter that they gave him but the one instruction to the Congress – to press for an eight hours day. (Applause.) They had been told that an eight hours day was an impossibility, but that was what employers only had said. In printing offices it was said they could not do with an eight hours day, but they could have shifts, as in other trades, and then an employer could carry on his business all the twenty-four hours round, and the men would not be living on each other, as they were now. At present his society (compositors) had 500 men on the books, and they were simply living on their fellows. This he objected to as long as they could put them all in the way of earning their own living. . . .

Mr. Knight [Boilermakers] (Newcastle) said they were all agreed as to the necessity of a further reduction in the hours of labour. . . . The way to reduce the hours of labour was by building up their organisations. (Applause.) If they got an Eight-Hours Bill passed, were they to be compelled to work eight hours per day? Eight hours were too long for some people. To shorten the hours they should dispense with overtime. Each trade by making itself strong would be more likely to obtain what the members required. (Cheers.) . . .

Mr. Holmes [Northern Countries Amalgamated Association of Weavers] (Burnley) . . . asked them to be careful, and to hesitate before enforcing eight hours in the textile trades during the present condition of affairs in India and on the Continent. . . .

Mr. G. J. Davies (Manchester and Salford Trades Council) said he had been instructed to support the legal eight hours day. So far as his constituents were concerned, this movement was not a reflection of Socialism. They were old-trade unionists, and when he spoke on their behalf he spoke for men who had considered this matter. . . .

Mr. Mosses [United Pattern Makers' Association] (Glasgow) held that a legal eight hours day was pernicious in principle, impracticable in operation, and detrimental to the best interests of trade unionism. It had been proved up to the hilt that the trade unions of the country were well able to secure, if they wished, not only an eight hours day, but a seven hours day, and even a six hours day. (Cries of 'Oh, oh.') . . .

The original resolution was then put to the vote, when the figures were:–

For the resolution		193
Against		155
	Majority	38

The initial success of the new unions provoked a counter-attack by both private and municipal employers (29, 30, 31). The Shipping Federation 1890 (32) was perhaps the most effective organisation aiming to break union power by using 'blacklegs' during disputes. Trade Unionist reactions were sometimes violent (33), but a sizable force of anti-unionist workers was recruited by various 'Free Labour' groups, notably by William Collison (1865–1938) and his National Free Labour Association of 1893 (34). Because of their vulnerability to such groups, many 'new unionists' endeavoured to gain a 'closed shop' (35). However, unity was difficult to achieve and even more difficult to maintain, as the Liverpool dock labourers found in 1893 (36).

(29) Manningham Strike Fund, *To the Trades' Unionists of the United Kingdom* (Bradford Trades and Labour Council, 1891)

Fellow-workers, We venture to make an appeal for your sympathy on behalf of the 2,000 hands now on strike or lock-out at Messrs. Lister & Co.'s Ltd., Manningham Mills.

The cause of the dispute is Messrs. Lister's who have declared a dividend this half year of 8% proposal to reduce their Weavers, Female Warp Dressers, Spoolers and Winders from $12\frac{1}{2}\%$ to 30% on wages that have not, for men weavers who have worked overtime 26 weeks, averaged more than 17s. per week during the 50 weeks previous to the Strike breaking out. Women weavers have earned less than this. The Female Warp Dressers have not earned so much as the Weavers, and the Winders and Spoolers even less than either of these classes of operatives.

Since the dispute broke out, Mr. Lister has publicly claimed to be paying higher wages than any other firm in the textile industry. This being so, the operatives offered to accept the same rate of wages as ruled their fellow-workers at Saltaire, who are employed on similar work, this was refused by the Directors. The Directors were then offered the selection of three firms making the same class of goods, the operatives also to select three firms, the average rate paid to these six to form the basis of a settlement. This Mr. Lister, acting for the Directors, again refused, and, in refusing, Mr. Lister claims in future to have the wage rate paid to Manningham operatives ruled by those rates paid to Continental workers, making special reference to the operatives at Crefeld. We believe this to be the first attempt on the part of a manufacturer to enforce continental wage rates upon English workers.

The struggle is now in its eighth week, and help is needed very pressing. . . .

(30) E. A. Pratt, *Trade Unionism and British Industry* (1904)

The story of the South Metropolitan Gas Company and their men is well worth recalling at the present moment because it shows alike how aggressive trade unionism may become, how great is the aversion of trade union officials to any scheme that tends to bind masters and men together, and how successfully trade union tactics can be defeated when the employers represent a compact and determined body. In 1889, on the suggestion of the Gas Workers' Union, the Company granted to their men (to whom they had themselves offered it on two previous occasions) a three-shift instead of a two-shift system, and the concession was made so readily that the officials of the union thought they had only to ask for more and they would get it. Finding that the stokers were filling up some of their leisure moments by oiling the retort lids, carried on levers, they insisted that this was not stokers' work – although the stokers themselves raised no objection to it – and that special men should be put on this trivial bit of work. In this and in other matters the object seemed to be to find all sorts of little jobs which would afford an excuse for getting more men put on the wages list. Having secured all the stokers as members, the union next tried to get the yard men and the mechanics, while the policy of interference carried on rendered the position of affairs altogether intolerable. Thereupon the company introduced their profit-sharing scheme, hoping thereby to create a closer bond between themselves and their men. This was so little to the taste of the union that it withdrew all its members at a week's notice, thus causing a difficulty which involved the company in expenditure and losses to £100,000. When the strike was at last over the company took back the union men, but their secretary threatened that the next time there would be no week's notice given. The company then decided that they would employ no more union men for the future, and to this resolve they adhered, with the result that, since then, employers and employed at the South Metropolitan Gas Works have been quite a happy family. The business, too, is conducted more cheaply there than at other London gas works which are still under trade union domination.

(31) Will Thorne, in *NUGMW, Souvenir History* (1929)

The splendid success of the London Gas workers for an eight hours day stirred the imagination, and Leeds was one of the first to respond. The credit of taking the initial steps to organise the Leeds men belongs to the little band of Socialists of the time, and in this connection occur the names of Tom Maguire, Tom Paylor, Alderman Ben Turner and Alf Mattison.

Six weeks after the Union was formed, most important concessions were obtained for gas workers. The Leeds Gasworkers' Branch was formed in October, 1889, the first branch formed in Yorkshire. At the time the Leeds gasworkers' conditions were: twelve hours' work in one shift per day for stokers, wheelers, yardmen and purifiers; wages, 5s. per day for stokers, 3s. 4d. per day for wheelers, yardmen, and purifiers, and one-fourth extra for one shift on Sundays, but after negotiations with the Leeds Gas Committee, who, finding that the spirit of the Union was so strong in the men that resistance to their just demands would be useless, agreed reluctantly and with very bad grace, to the following conditions: a reduction of hours from twelve to eight for stokers and wheelers, and the making of a new class (firemen) with eight hours per day and 5s. wages. All classes got time-and-a-half for Sunday work. The wheelers received an advance to 4s. per day, and the yardmen and purifiers, who had to still work 54 hours per week, received 2s. per week advance in wages. The stokers only did two hours less work, and the coal wheelers 20 per cent. less work in the eight hours than in the twelve. The extra Sunday pay, also, instead of being paid to one twelve-hour shift, was paid to three eight-hour shifts – from 6 a.m. on Sunday to 6 a.m. on Monday.

In June, 1890, the Gas Committee thought, as some of them said, that 'Their turn had come'. They demanded (1) that the men should engage themselves for four months at a time, and to have no power to strike within that period; (2) that the stokers' work within the eight hours should be increased. The men refused these terms, and were locked out on the 30th June. Three days before the stokers were locked out all the other hands struck work. Blacklegs were brought in from various places outside the town. The population was at once exasperated, and encounters of the most violent nature took place between the police and military on the one hand, and the general mass of the townspeople on the other. After four days' struggle, the Gas Committee gave way, all blacklegs were discharged, and the old hands reinstated.

How the gas gave out and Leeds for five nights was in complete darkness; how public feeling became incensed against the Committee; how hundreds more police and a regiment of mounted soldiers were sent for; how, when a convoy of blacklegs protected by the latter was on its way through the town to the new Wortley Gasworks, and passing under one of the railway bridges, it was attacked by a crowd of thousands of people. How the people got the possession of the bridge and poured down tons of brickwork and stones upon the enemy, and how a pitched battle – in which the women played no inconspicuous part – lasted till nightfall in the streets – all this is a matter of history. Such fighting was not common, but in many places the struggle was bitter, and sometimes prolonged.

(32) RC on Labour, *PP* 1892 xxxv, Group B, 1, appendix viii: 'Circular Giving the General Scope of the Operations of the Shipping Federation, 20 October 1890'

The Federation intends primarily to secure to every man freedom to work at his own terms without interference, and whether he belongs to any union or not.

Where attempts are made to prevent men (whether sailors, labourers, or others) from engaging to work or to cause them to break engagements they have made, the Federation will proceed against those who break the law, and will protect those who are threatened or supply substitutes.

It will specially protect masters and officers and other members of a crew who are threatened in any way in consequence of their not belonging to any union, and will prosecute those who threaten.

The Federation, in the event of a dispute respecting wages, will assist owners in procuring crews and labourers at market rates.

It is arranging to establish registry offices at various points for the purpose of registering those who desire employment.

The Federation does not aim at excluding members of any union from any employment.

It proposes, as above indicated, to assist owners who join it, and compensate them if they detain or lay up their vessels by *agreement* with the Federation.

Owners are strongly recommended to insert in all charters, &c the following clause:–

'Ship not to be responsible for any loss, damage, or delay directly or indirectly caused by or arising from strikes, lock-outs, labour disturbances, trade disputes, or anything done in contemplation or furtherance thereof, whether the owners be party thereto or not.'

(33) Ibid.: Evidence of E. A. Earnsby, free labourer

5861. Now could you tell us something as to the class of men who were imported by the Shipping Federation during the late strike; what sort of men were they?– In my opinion they were very good men indeed, with the exception of a very few; the majority of the men who were employed during the last strike were men from the country – men recruited from the agricultural labouring class and fishermen,

and I think that on the whole there was no complaint whatever to be made about
them. . . .

5864. We understand that you have some evidence to give us as to assaults and
intimidation practised by union men, could you tell us what you know on the
subject? – I cannot give you the exact dates. I think the first was an attack on the
'Scotland'. I noticed on that day one man in particular; I have since been told,
but I cannot find out his name, that he is some official or someone of some note in
one of the Unions. This man with four or five more went round to the different
ships and the different barges where men were at work, and those were union
men who were at work, and called them together asking them to come and storm
and turn the blacklegs out of the 'Scotland', and the men assembled to do it.
This was done in a matter of about an hour and a half, sufficient time to organise
in a body and get them together in one lump. The first thing they did was to
besiege the small tug we had in use; when taken about 60 men went into the
Victoria Dock to the ship 'Transition', where they went to work. They assembled
there at the entrance of the dock from the Albert Dock to the Victoria Dock, and
picked up everything they could lay their hands to – lumps of coal, iron bolts,
lumps of iron, stones, and one thing and another – and they began to pelt and do
all they could to harm and to injure our men if they could.

(34) William Collison, *The Apostle of Free Labour* (1913)

When I saw that New Unionism was bad, I declared war upon it. . . .

The National Free Labour Association is a commercial as well as an industrial
organisation run on a business basis, and being fraught with danger from the
enemies it is sure to make, we act on the principle that the labourer is worthy of
his hire, a remark which applies with added force to those employers who only
seek our services when in trouble.

Violence frequently occurs and always is a possibility which necessitates the
elaborate protection plan and organized Emergency staff incorporated in the
system.

We have representatives in every manufacturing centre through the country.
These men are thoroughly informed on general and local labour conditions, and
are ready at a moment's notice to 'jump' to the nearest place from the station
where a strike is likely to occur. If the situation is ominous, the Chief Office is
communicated with by telephone – for quick action is the first requisite of the
business – our object being either to avert a strike, or to prevent the strikers
obtaining too strong a position. If the information received warrants it, I
personally leave for the scene of trouble and place myself in touch with the
employing concern. . . .

A contract is then made with the employing company or firm, at a rate of so
much a day for each man's services during the duration of the strike, such rate
being the district rate paid for the particular work. . . . The ordinary man in the
street would naturally ask where a sufficient number of competent and fearless

men, as they must be to brave the Pickets, could be obtained at such short notice. Under our Free Labour Exchanges system it is easy. Each has a 'live' register of competent men averaging eighty thousand, embracing one hundred and fifty different trades, in all parts of the country.

(35) RC on Labour, *PP* 1892 xxxv Group B: Evidence of Harry Quelch, representing steamship workers of South Side Labour Protection League

2396. You have said that your society objected in self-defence to non-unionist workers. In what manner have they shown their objection? – As far as possible they refuse to work with them. Whenever they are sufficiently numerous – sufficiently strong – they refuse to work with the man who has not got a union card.

2397. Do they take any other active steps to make it disagreeable for the non-unionist? – I scarcely understand that question.

2398. Do they make it personally disagreeable to non-unionists who are working or attempting to obtain work? – I could not say that they never do such a thing. I expect they do. What I mean is that a man working under those circumstances would probably find himself in a rather uncomfortable position, by the epithets which would occasionally be addressed to him, and the way in which generally he would be treated. If he were in a public-house and the men knew he did not belong to the organisation, and that he worked at a certain place, they would call him a blackleg probably, they would refuse to drink with him, and so on, and, as far as possible, send him to Coventry. . . .

2408. . . . We are prepared to give a man the fullest possible liberty to combine, but we are not prepared to give him liberty not to combine. . . .

2411. . . . I do not believe in the right of any man to have the liberty to injure me.

2632. . . . Ours is an open labour market and there is just one point which perhaps it would be as well to clear up now. In our union we do not object to work with any man as long as he is a unionist. I am one of the officers of the branch in that particular neighbourhood, and we are not at all severe on a stranger. If a stranger comes in the neighbourhood and he gets work, I, or some responsible person sees him, and says, 'Our branch is so and so, and we shall expect you to come and join.' The only ones we are harsh upon, and perhaps you will say cruel to, are men in our immediate neighbourhood, who have got benefits equal with our own, and perhaps more, and who will not belong to us. We are obliged to put a little pressure on such men, but to a stranger we are never at all harsh.

2633. I suppose by putting a little pressure you mean without the use of violence you make his life unpleasant to him? – No; what happens is this. If he does not have his card stamped he will not be employed; the foreman will not employ him. We do not need to bring any pressure. That is the pressure. If he has not his card stamped showing that he is a *bona fide* member he will not get employment.

2634. I do not understand how that agrees with your memorandum, that the attitude of employers towards the unions is one of passive hostility, and in some cases active opposition? – Quite so. While we have the majority it will be the other way. Seeing that in nearly every case we are unionists, at present we have got a whip hand.

2635. As I understand you then, the employers will not take on a non-unionist because of the objection the other men feel to working with him? – That is so, and he does not want his work to be stopped. He knows if he employs a non-union man the work will be stopped, and that is a loss to him.

(36) J. Sexton (General Secretary of the National Union of Dock Labourers), *Sir James Sexton, Agitator. The Life of the Dockers' M.P.* (1936)

To put it bluntly, things in the Union were in a most unholy mess, and I and my reforming colleagues quickly discovered that our fight was to be with the chaotic want of discipline, the ignorance and petty jealousies within our own ranks, rather than with the employers.

Not the least of our manifold difficulties arose from the prevalence of what I can only describe as the caste system throughout the dockers' fraternity, which led to the creation of almost innumerable small clubs and societies all hostile to each other. Some of these were sick and funeral clubs, which divided the available funds amongst their members at Christmas time, trusting to luck and the generosity of members, with perhaps a 'tarpaulin muster' at the pay table, to meet any emergencies that arose before the society was again in funds.

Quite frequently religious and political differences kept those bodies apart, and, indeed, alive. Thus the coal heavers had one society at the north end, another at the south. The leader of one was a North of Ireland Orangeman, the leader of the other an equally perfervid Irish Home Rule Catholic. The League of Nations itself could not reconcile two such organisations. The only point on which they were united was a mutual objection to mere cargo hands handling coal.

Salt heavers took up the same attitude as to the exclusiveness of their job; if you weren't one of them you couldn't touch bulk salt. . . .

Similarly, those whose work was the loading and discharging of railway bars to and from barges and steamers – in which there was at that time enormous traffic – had their two societies. One was 'the Cabbage Club' – though how it got that title Heaven alone may know; the other, the 'Clarence Dock Club', was for men engaged only in the coasting trade.

Within the ranks of the TUC the debate between 'new' and 'old', socialist and non-socialist, continued through the 1890s. The alteration of the Congress's standing orders in 1895 to exclude trades councils and to introduce the card vote (37) was part of this debate since trades councils tended to send a high proportion of militant delegates. The new system left power at the TUC firmly in the hands of the big battalions of miners and cotton workers, and, although all trades councils protested, only these in Scotland found an alternative, in the long-talked-of Scottish TUC, inaugurated in 1897 (38).

(37) Minutes of the Parliamentary Committee of TUC: Adjourned meeting of Parliamentary Committee, 10 Oct 1894

Present. Messrs. Holmes, Burns, Cowey, Inskip, Broadhurst, Mawdsley, Wilson, Harford, Sheedon, Jack, Tillett, Thorne and the Secretary. Mr. Holmes occupied the chair.

re Standing Orders. Some discussion arose with regard to the Standing Orders when it was moved by Mr. Mawdsley and seconded by Mr. Broadhurst: 'That in accordance with resolution of Congress remitting a number of resolutions and amendments to the Standing Orders, to the Parliamentary Committee, It is hereby agreed that a sub-committee be appointed to revise the Standing Orders, which said Standing Orders shall be submitted for approval to a meeting of the full Parliamentary Committee, and after adoption they shall be sent out to the Trades and shall become the standing orders governing the proceedings next year.'

It was moved, seconded and carried 'That Messrs. Holmes, Burns and Mawdsley (with the Secretary ex-officio) be appointed as the sub committee. . . .'

(38) Glasgow United Trades Council, *Annual Report 1895–96*

Mr George Shipton sent out a circular to ascertain the views of trades councils as to the desirability of convening a National Conference of Representatives from them. Nineteen Councils replied favourably and 21 opposed such a conference, leaving 110 Councils from whom no answer was received. Under these circumstances, the London Trades Council at a General Delegate Meeting held in March 1896 decided to abandon the project of a Conference. The prevailing opinion of the letters received was that efforts should be made to broaden the Standing Orders of the present Trades' Congress so as to admit qualified representatives from Trades Councils, but we fear it may be safely said that there is no likelihood of any change being made in the Standing Orders passed by the Parliamentary Committee and confirmed by the Congress at Cardiff, which enabled them to shut their doors against the Trades Councils of the United Kingdom, and practically hand over the business of Congress to a few large Trades' Societies.

At a Conference of delegates from the Scottish Trades Councils held at Falkirk on 25th of April, under the auspices, and at the invitation of the Local Council (at which this body was represented), held principally to consider the subject of Trade Federation, a resolution was passed recommending the formation of a Trades Union Congress for Scotland, and at a subsequent large and representative gathering of delegates from Trades Councils, Trades Societies, and other Labour bodies (at which we were again represented), held in Edinburgh on 11th September last, this resolution was approved of and confirmed, and a Committee representing the various districts and the leading Trade Unions of Scotland, was appointed to carry out the necessary arrangements. The first Congress will be held in Glasgow on Thursday, Friday and Saturday, the 25th, 26th and 27th March 1897, when the Trades Council will be represented. It seems generally felt that the time has come for this step, and that this Congress will give an opportunity for the full consideration of matters more particularly affecting Scottish labour interests.

Considering the existing differences between Scotch and English labour conditions, and in view of the fact that in nearly every bill brought before Parliament, special provisions have to be made for Scotland, it is obviously desirable that Scottish labour men should have a full opportunity for the ventilation of their views on such matters, and that there should be some organisation of Scottish labour opinion on questions of local and national importance, and some common understanding in respect of them.

In the limited time at the disposal of the British Congress, obviously, in the nature of things this cannot be had. At this Scottish Congress opportunity will also be taken for discussing the scheme of a National Trades Federation, which was before the Edinburgh and Falkirk Conferences.

Throughout the 1890s unionists, and particularly those new unionists who made extensive use of picketing, found themselves up against the courts where judges and lawyers were developing the concept of civil conspiracy (39). The process came to a head with the House of Lords decisions in the cases of *Taff Vale Railway Co.* v. *ASRS* (40) and *Quinn* v. *Leathem* (41), when Unions found themselves liable for damages for the action of their members during strikes.

(39) *J. Lyons & Sons* v. *Wilkins*, [1896] 1 Ch 811

Lindley, L. J.: . . . Courts are not to treat as 'watching and besetting' any 'attending at or near a house in order merely to obtain or communicate information'. That is to be allowed; and picketing (if you call it so) for that limited purpose, and conducted in that way for that simple object, is not made a criminal offence, and must therefore be taken to be a lawful act. . . . But it is easy to see how under colour of so attending a great deal may be done which is absolutely illegal. . . . Now, they are not there merely to obtain or communicate information: that is not their function. They are there to put pressure upon Messrs Lyons by persuading people not to enter into their employment; and that is watching or besetting within clause 4, and is not attending in order merely to obtain or communicate information. Under these circumstances they have gone too far, and have gone beyond what the Act of Parliament authorizes, and I do not hesitate to say that it is a case in which from the necessity of the thing a quick remedy is actually and absolutely required.

(40) *Taff Vale Railway Co.* v. *ASRS* [1901] AC 426

Farwell, J.: Now, the Legislature in giving a trade union the capacity to own property and the capacity to act by agents has, without incorporating it, given it two of the essential qualities of corporation – essential, I mean, in respect of liability for tort, for a corporation can only act by its agents, and can only be made to pay by means of its property. The principle on which corporations have been held liable in respect of wrongs committed by its servants or agents in the course of their service and for the benefit of the employer . . . is as applicable to the case of a trade union as to that of a corporation. If the contention of the defendant society were well founded, the Legislature has authorised the creation of numerous bodies of men capable of owning great wealth and of acting by agents with absolutely no responsibility for the wrongs that they may do to other persons by the use of that wealth and the employment of those agents. They would be at liberty (I do not at all suggest that the defendant society would so act) to disseminate libels broadcast, or to hire men to reproduce the rattening methods that disgraced Sheffield thirty or forty years ago, and their victims would have nothing to look to for damages but the pockets of the individuals, usually men of small means, who acted as their agents. . . . If, therefore, I am right in concluding that the society are liable in tort, the action must be against their registered name. The acts complained of are the acts of the association.

(41) *Quinn* v. *Leathem* [1901] AC 495

Lord Brampton: It has often been debated whether, assuming the existence of a conspiracy to do a wrongful and harmful act towards another and to carry it out by a number of overt acts, no one of which taken singly and alone would, if done by one individual acting alone and apart from any conspiracy, constitute a cause of action, such acts would become unlawful or actionable if done by the conspirators acting jointly or severally in pursuance of their conspiracy, and if by those acts substantial damage was caused to the person against whom the conspiracy was directed: my own opinion is that they would. . . .

Lord Lindley: . . . My Lords, it is said that conduct which is not actionable on the part of one person cannot be actionable if it is that of several acting in concert. This may be so where many do no more than one is supposed to do. But numbers may annoy and coerce where one may not. Annoyance and coercion by many may be so intolerable as to become actionable, and produce a result which one alone could not produce. . . . But coercion by threats, open or disguised, not only of bodily harm but of serious annoyance and damage, is *prima facie*, at all events, a wrong inflicted on the persons coerced; and in considering whether coercion has been applied or not, numbers cannot be disregarded.

6. *The Growth of Collective Bargaining*

The mid-nineteenth century saw numerous efforts to regulate industrial relations by the establishment of courts of conciliation and arbitration. As the Webbs pointed out, what many contemporaries really meant by these terms was in fact collective bargaining. Among the most ardent advocates of a structured system of industrial relations was the Nottingham hosiery manufacturer A. J. Mundella (1825–97) (1), but a whole variety of plans for conciliation was devised, sometimes for particular trades, sometimes for particular regions (2, 3).

What was involved was a recognition, by employers, of the usefulness of trade unions in bringing order into industrial bargaining, and by unions of the value of attaining a bargaining role (4, 5, 6). By the middle of the 1870s, Mundella had reason to congratulate himself on the extension of his system (7).

(1) RC on Trades Unions etc., *Tenth Report, PP* 1867 8 xxxix, Evidence of A. J. Mundella, Nottingham hosiery manufacturer

19,375. . . . I will tell you what has been the effect of our board of arbitration. The very men that the manufacturers dreaded were the men that were sent to represent the workmen at the board. We found them the most straightforward men we could desire to have to deal with; we have often found that the power behind them has been too strong for them; they are generally the most intelligent men; and often they are put under great pressure by workmen outside to do things which they know to be contrary to common sense, and they will not do them. They have been the greatest barriers we have between the ignorant workmen and ourselves, and I know that is so. I have found it in my correspondence with trade union secretaries and leaders; all over England I have found that so. . . .

19,383. . . . We have nearly 5,000 different articles to deal with and have to regulate them all. We are continually fluctuating up or down, but not down much, because the tendency of wages had been slowly upwards for the last 500 years. Men require higher money wages because the purchasing power of money gets less. Instead of wages fluctuating downwards we generally let things remain as they are, and that has made things much more equal. I will give you an instance of that. Mr. Samuel Morley, who is one of the largest employers in our trade, for he employs 5,000 people, has told me over and over again: 'in good times I can lay up stock now; before I could not do that, because I was always afraid of some unscrupulous employer cutting me out with lower prices'.

(2) *The Ironworkers' Journal* (1 May 1876): Paper by B. Samuelson MP on 'The Board of Arbitration and Conciliation for the North of England Manufactured Iron Trade', read to the British Iron Trade Association

The manufacture of iron had in the course of less than ten years assumed dimensions which placed the North of England in the front rank amongst the producing districts of the Empire. Labourers had been collected hastily from all parts, and recruited from various occupations, strangers to each other and to their employers, for the most part illiterate, earning higher wages than those to which they had been accustomed, unable to appreciate the difficulties incidental to a trade so liable as the iron trade to great and sudden vicissitudes. It is not surprising that, under such conditions, serious disturbances should have arisen, which culminated in 1865–66 in a lock-out and strike; the latter of four months duration. Between that time and the winter of 1868–69 repeated reductions in wages became necessary; and gave rise to feelings of resentment, which rendered it more than probable that any considerable increase in the demand for iron would be the signal for peremptory demands on the part of the workmen, tending to a renewal of the confusion of previous years, and to the destruction of the prosperity which all might otherwise hope to share. It is due to the leaders of the workmen to state that they were at least as ready as their employers to accept the suggestion of the establishment of a Board of Conciliation and Arbitration, which was accordingly formed, after several preliminary meetings, on the 22nd March, 1869.

The Board consists of two representatives of each of the works joining it, one chosen by the owners, the other by the operatives, the latter being elected by ballot, and each serving during the calendar year. The decisions of the Board, if they can agree, or in case of difference, of the independent umpire, whom they are directed in such case to choose, are binding on their constituents.

The Board elects a President and Vice-President and two Secretaries for the year. These offices have always been filled in equal number by the employers and the operatives, to whom, with the President and Vice-President, all differences are in the first instance referred for investigation, and whose recommendations are, in minor matters, generally accepted by the parties interested. The Standing Committee has, however, no power to make an award. All questions not settled by it are brought before the Board for adjustment as quickly as possible. The Committee meets whenever there is any business, and the Board twice in each year unless specially summoned at other times. At the Board all votes are taken by ballot, and no casting vote is allowed to the Chairman. The expenses are borne equally by the employers and the operatives, and the members of the

Standing Committee are paid 10s. for each attendance, and their travelling expenses.

This system has now been in operation nearly seven years, and except that it has been the practice, on some occasions of the readjustment of wages over the whole pay sheet, to interpose between the Board and the 'independent umpire', two arbitrators representing opposite parties, no change has taken place in its constitution, or in its mode of operation, since the time when it was first established.

(3) *The Reformer* (31 Oct. 1868)

The Manchester Chamber of Commerce and the Manchester Trades Council have agreed to establish a 'Court of Arbitration and Conciliation' to be open to all trades in the Parliamentary boroughs of Manchester and Salford. The Court is to be composed of 16 members, – 8 to be selected by the Chamber of Commerce, and 8 by the Trades Council. The following rules are agreed upon for the working of the Court: – 'That the objects of the said court shall be to arbitrate on any question relating to wages or other matters that may, by mutual agreement, be referred to it from time to time by the employers and operatives, and, by conciliatory means, to interpose its influence to put an end to any disputes that may arise. Such court only to be appealed to when the employers or employed have failed to effect an amicable settlement of any dispute by other means.' . . . The decision of the Court is to be binding in all cases referred to it, in accordance with Lord St. Leonards' Act.

(4) Thomas Brassey, *Lectures on the Labour Question* (1878)

The constant meeting of employers and representatives of the operatives at the same table must naturally facilitate peaceful negotiation, where a desire for peace exists on both sides. With constant discussion, coming events will cast their shadow before, and disputes are not likely suddenly to arise. Again, employers will acquire the habit of giving more unreserved explanations as to the condition and prospects of trade. . . .

When the memorable struggle was commenced in Newcastle for a reduction in the number of hours, I ventured to suggest, in an address delivered at Birkenhead, that the solution of the difficulty which had arisen in the engineering establishments, might be found in employing relays of mechanics to succeed each other at the same machine. My friend Mr. (now Sir George) Elliott, is pushing the system of a succession of labour in collieries, with every advantageous results to all parties concerned. Comparing a Durham colliery, workmen on the double-shift system, with a colliery in Glamorganshire, worked by one set of miners, he ascertained that twice the quantity of coal per day was being raised in Durham. The prejudices of the miners in South Wales against the double-shift have presented a serious obstacle to its introduction. Mr. Elliott hopes that this may eventually be overcome by the influence of Mr. MacDonald and other representatives of the men, whose superior intelligence will enable them to appreciate more readily the advantages of new and improved systems of working. . . .

The existence of trades unions must be accepted as a necessary consequence of the new phases into which productive industry has entered; and the only practical question is, how to direct this important and extensive organisation into a useful channel. The working classes must always be more or less in a state of uncertainty as to the profits, which their employers may from time to time be realising. This must, however, be known, in order to decide whether they have a right to demand an advance of wages, or, what is the same thing, a reduction in the hours of labour. It is evident that the problem cannot be solved without an intimate knowledge of the state and prospects of trade. Highly qualified commercial advisers are needed to guide the deliberations of trades unions on these matters.

(5) ASE, *25th Annual Report* (1875): First report from John Burnett as General Secretary

A few words as to our relations with the Iron Trades Employers' Association. Upon one occasion during the past year, representatives from that Association and ours met in friendly conference at Manchester. The interview which then took place was without immediate result, and failed to settle the dispute it was called to consider. Still it was deemed on our part, and on the part of the employers present, a good thing to settle disputes where possible, by friendly conference and mutual conciliation.

(6) John Kane, Foreword to Amalgamated Ironworkers' Association, *Rules* (Darlington, 1870)

. . . I assure you Brother Members that every illegal stoppage of work retards your progress by giving encouragement to enemies of your union; to brand you as incompetent of self government. I am determined to give no encouragement to men who refuse to obey and to abide by the written laws of our Association. I shall prefer their censure so long as I act according to our rules in preference to their applause, which too many have sought to earn by pandering to ignorance, prejudice, and disorder.

(7) A. J. Mundella to R. Leader, Sheffield (24 Feb. 1876)

The Meeting of the Iron and Steel Institute [on conciliation and arbitration] was very interesting and important. It was a great triumph to hear one after another who had been prejudiced opponents, get up and support our plans. Markham of Stavely came to me in the evening and made a curious statement. He said that in '68 he did all he could against me and wrote letters in the 'Telegraph', signed 'A Voice from the Hive' but that he was so satisfied I was right and so pleased with my speech that he desired to make the amends, etc., etc.

Mr. Schneider of Barrow, Hurst of S. Stafford and others came to shake hands and say congratulations and in this body of ancient antagonists I found nothing but kindness and a warm reception.

One major development of bargaining came with the introduction of sliding scales by which the wages of workers was directly related to the price of the product. This system was particularly popular in parts of the coal industry (8). It could, in fact, be a deterrent to trade-union growth, since it left little ground for actual bargaining over wages – the main *raison d'être* of unions. However, as the *Ironworkers' Journal* pointed out, there was still usually room for manoeuvre and the prerogative of management continued to be eroded (9).

(8) J. R. Raynes, *Coal and Its Conflicts* (1928): A South Wales sliding-scale agreement, 11 Dec. 1875

1. That the minimum wages to be paid at the several collieries shall be fixed at five per cent above the prices paid in the same collieries in 1869, adjusted to the imperial ton and determined as follows: For the steam coal collieries, the cutting price of the Upper Four Feet seam in the Aberdare Valley should be the standard: for the Bituminous collieries of Monmouthshire and the Caerphilly district, the cutting price of the Mynyddislwyn and the Tillery seam shall be standard: for the Bituminous collieries of Glamorganshire, which includes all the collieries in the Neath and Swansea districts, with the exception of the Cross-Lands, California, Cawdor, and the Hendreforgan collieries, the cutting price of the No. 3 Rhondda seam shall be standard.

2. The minimum standard of wages payable in the several seams – that is, the Upper Four Feet seam in the Mynyddislwyn and Tillery seams and the No. 3 Rhondda seam, as fixed, by adding five per cent to the several cutting prices paid for them in the year 1869, shall be the equivalent wages for the following net minimum selling prices for the several descriptions of colliery-screened large coal, delivered free on board in the ports of Cardiff, Newport and Swansea, that is to say,

Steam Coal	12s a ton
Mynyddislwyn and Tillery Coal	11s a ton
No. 3 Rhondda Coal	11s a ton

3. The foregoing minimum selling prices and minimum cutting prices and wages are to include all claims of the work people in respect to the extra cost of getting coal due to the Mines Regulation Act.

4. The wages payable as and from the 1st day of January, 1876, being determined as hereinafter provided for, shall be regulated according to the following scale, that is to say: As soon as the average nett prices obtained for large colliery-screened coal free on board at the ports of Cardiff, Swansea, and

Newport, advance one shilling above the respective minimum prices on Clause 2, the wages payable to the workmen for the succeeding six months shall be advanced seven-and-a-half per cent for every shilling advanced on such selling prices up to a maximum of 21 . . . it being understood that wages shall also be reduced according to the same scale down to the aforesaid minimum of 12s. nett and 11s., as mentioned in Clause 2.

5. The average selling price of the several descriptions of colliery-screened large coal free on board in Cardiff, Newport, and Swansea, during the months of November and December, 1875, shall determine wages payable according to the foregoing scale for the six months commencing January 1st, and terminating June 30th, 1876. At the end of the period, and of each succeeding half-yearly period of six months, ending 31st December and the 30th June, the books of the owners and workmen, and the average nett prices realised, free on board, for the preceding six months shall determine the wages for the ensuing six months.

(9) *Ironworkers' Journal* (1 Feb. 1877)

Voluntaryism is one of the most characteristic features of arbitration, as contradistinguished from ordinary legal procedure, and one of the most natural and obvious effects of this characteristic is that each side is comparatively free to adduce such evidence as it cares to bring forward, and to let alone that which is not consistent with its own notions of propriety. . . .

The kind and extent of evidence produced in a case of industrial arbitration will necessarily depend very much upon the basis adopted. In practice it is found that the men are usually prone to contend that the employers withhold information not only relevant but absolutely essential to the issue. It is rather unfortunate that upon this as upon most other phases of industrial arbitration, there is a great lack of uniformity and agreement. In one case the employers produce information which they withhold in another. In one case the issue is decided upon oral evidence, and in another written statements alone are admitted. In other cases, again, both written and oral evidence is adduced. In the Arbitration (Master and Workmen) Act of 1872, prepared by Mr. Rupert Kettle and introduced by Mr. A. J. Mundella, M.P., there is a provision which requires the introduction of books, documents and accounts, on demand by the arbitrators or umpire, subject to such conditions concerning the mode of production or examination as either side may impose. . . .

In all cases of arbitration as to the value or price of labour it must be assumed, *ab initio*, that the workmen on the one hand consider themselves entitled to more having regard to the profits made by the employers, or, conversely that the employers deem the workmen entitled to less in view of the inadequacy of profit or its entire absence. Hence, although it may not exactly be put in that form, it is manifest that the whole issue submitted to arbitration is the amount of wages that the employers can afford to pay the workmen, having regard to the cost of production on the one hand, and the net average realised selling price of the commodity produced on the other. In other words, it has practically come to this, that wages are to be regulated by prices, as the only standard available. . . .

Despite the substantial advances made in the early 1870s, by the end of the decade unions were under great pressure. Many of the gains of the previous years were lost. In engineering wages fell and the nine-hours' day was threatened and in many cases lost (10). In the cotton industry, twenty years of negotiation gave way to bitter confrontation (11).

(10) ASE, *Abstract Report of Proceedings of Executive Council* (1878–9)

At no time in our history have we had such a number of industrial disturbances throughout the country. Bad trade has prevailed; and our employers, now better organised than ever before, seem to have made it their aim to raise as many points of contention with us as ever possible. In one place sweeping reductions of wages would be carried out or attempted; and in others the sales paid for overtime were sought to be reduced, while in many cases the hours of labour have been attacked, and in the Clyde district successfully, three hours being, as a result, added to the week's work all over Scotland. . . . Another notable feature of the depression has been the continued oppression by the employers of the men in the most submissive districts, where conciliatory measures were adopted, and where little objection was made to any innovation. The Clyde district has been a notable example of this fact, passing in the first instance through two considerable reductions of wages almost passively, only to be almost immediately after the victims of desultory attacks upon the hours question. Irregular attacks appear almost to have been the system adopted by the employers in preference to the development of any general movement by their Associations.

(11) *Manifesto of the Lancashire Weavers* (June 1878) in S. and B. Webb, *History of Trade Unionism* (1894)

Fellow-workers – We are and have been engaged during the past nine weeks in the most memorable struggle between Capital and Labour in the history of the world. One hundred thousand factory workers are waging war with their employers as to the best possible way to remove the glut from an overstocked cloth market, and at the same time reduce the difficulties arising from an insufficient supply of raw cotton. To remedy this state of things the employers propose a reduction of wages to the extent of ten per cent below the rate of wages agreed upon twenty-five years ago. On the other hand, we have contended that a reduction in the rate of wages cannot either remove the glut in the cloth trade or asist to tide us over the difficulty arising from the limited supply of raw material. However, this has been the employers' theory, and at various periods throughout the struggle we have made the following propositions as a basis of settlement of this most calamitous struggle:

1. A reduction of ten per cent, with four days' working, or five per cent with five

days' working, until the glut in the cloth market and the difficulties arising from the dearth of cotton had been removed.

2. To submit the whole question of short time or reduction, or both, to the arbitrement of any one or more impartial gentlemen.

3. To submit the entire question to two Manchester merchants or agents, two shippers conversant with the Manchester trade, and two bankers, one of each to be selected by the employers and the other by the operatives, with two employers and two operatives, with Lord Derby, the Bishop of Manchester, or any other impartial gentleman, as chairman, or if necessary, referee.

4. To split the difference between us, and go to work unconditionally at a reduction of five per cent.

5. Through the Mayor of Burnley, to go to work three months at a reduction of five per cent, and if trade had not sufficiently improved at that time, to submit to a further reduction.

6. And lastly, to an unconditional reduction of seven and a half per cent.

Unions – and others – sought in vain to explain the 'depression' (12, 13). Certainly, they could recognise the erosion of traditional work patterns and standards (14, 15). The Royal Commission on Labour (1892–4) heard similar evidence (16), together with information on the current state of union organisation (17, 18). Technological changes continued to weaken the craftsmen's status. Demarcation disputes were common (19), and unions sought to ensure that new processes and machines were worked by their members (20).

(12) Edinburgh Trades Council, *Annual Report, 1879–80*

This depression, which was to a great extent the natural sequence of the mad speculation and over production engendered by the unprecedented prosperity, in the uncertainty of our political relations with other countries, and also, by the fact that, while our individual incomes were getting reduced, the national expenditure was gradually growing in the hands of those who seemed to care more for national vain glory abroad than the prosperity of the masses at home, and who spent in barbarous wars for scientific frontiers the treasures that might have fostered industry at home or been used to assuage to some extent the misery, caused by want of work, of the millions who are the bone and sinew of the nation.

(13) RC on Depression of Trade and Industry, *Second Report, PP* 1886 xxii, appendix D, pt. 2: Evidence of the Edinburgh Trades Council

That in the opinion of this Council the present depressed state of trade and industry is largely due to the manner in which the land of this country is tied up in the hands of comparatively few persons, and that this state of affairs is greatly intensified by the vast and increasing numbers of non-producers who live upon the wealth produced by the industrial class. That unless steps are at once taken to bring about a general diffusion of the soil among the people, and to reduce the number of non-producers, at no distant period this country will be the scene of a social revolution brought about not by means of peaceful legislation, but by a great uprising of the people in the demand for justice.

(14) George Howell, 'Trades Unions, Apprentices, and Technical Education', *Contemporary Review*, xxx (1877)

In the Amalgamated Society of Engineers there is no rule with regard to apprentices, whether as to limitation or restriction; practically, no such system is enforced as a condition of membership in the society; the rule as to the admission of members is to accept all persons who have worked at the trade for five years successively, and who are nominated by two full members who having worked with the proposed member, are able to vouch for him as being able to earn his living at the trade, and to command the current wages of the district in which he is proposed. . . . The masons, by reason of their extensive and at the same time compact organization, have by their rules been more restrictive than any other body, but even with them there is now no rule as to limit, any reasonable number being allowed; no actual apprenticeship is really needed in order to obtain admission into the society; competency as a workman, and the ability to earn the current wages of the district as a journeyman, are the only conditions required, no matter how these are obtained. . . . The Scottish Society does not attempt in any way to interfere with either the number of apprentices or the term of service, so that throughout Scotland the trade is essentially open to all comers without let or hindrance of any kind. . . . The bricklayers have practically neither limitation nor restriction. . . . In the London district, and in the southern and eastern counties, the trade is practically open without restriction.

(15) Extract from Ironfounders' Society, *Report* (Feb 1885) [in E. Belfort Bax, 'Address to Trades' Unions', issued by the Council of the Socialist League, *The Socialist Platform*, no. 1 (1885)]

. . . look at the increased speed we are compelled to work at. The moment any work comes into a shop the pressure is put on and men are compelled to hurry on, and what for? – Why, to hasten our discharge. . . . Quantity and quantity is the cry. Quality is getting to be a thing of the past. . . . Reckless competition is doing its full work. Riches and wealth will never compensate for the decay of men.

(16) RC on Labour, *PP* 1893–4 xxxii, Group A, vol. iii: Evidence of J. Swift, General Secretary of the Steam Engine Makers' Society

23,611. Has your Society in the engineering trade affected any improvement in the working hours or wages? – They have. In some parts of Lancashire wages for artisan engineers have advanced 4s per week within the past 21 years, and hours reduced $3\frac{1}{2}$ and $4\frac{1}{2}$ per week. On the north-east coast even a greater advance in wages has been secured in the same period, and the working hours reduced one hour per day. The societies have also secured higher rates for overtime, better terms for outwork, and prevented excessive reductions in wages during times of depression, and then in times of revival took the earliest opportunity of again securing any concession they had previously lost. In addition to this, material assistance is rendered by the Society to its members in assisting unemployed members and removing them from low paid to higher paid districts.

23,612. Then, comparing the present conditions with those of, say 20 years ago, what do you say? – The men àre much harder worked and kept under closer surveillance, whilst the preference for young and strong men is very marked, rather than men of mature years, ability and experience, and the need for spectacles by a workman, in many firms, results in his removal. Improved appliances and machinery have led to a division of labour that does not give the youth or apprentice an opportunity of learning the trade or making such an experienced or general worker as was the case 20 or 30 years ago.

23,613. Is there any difference within your experience between employment by private firms and employment by companies? – Yes, the difference is generally in favour of private firms, where the employer comes in direct contact with his workmen. In companies this is not the case, as they relegate the supervision to a manager, who has not the same interest as an employer, whilst the excessive number of officials, as a rule, taxes the cost of production, and the workman suffers in consequence.

(17) Ibid.: Précis of the evidence of R. Knight, General Secretary of the United Society of Boilermakers and Iron Shipbuilders

This Society was established in August 1834. It has its headquarters at Newcastle-on-Tyne, and extends over the whole of the United Kingdom. At the present time, the number of its members is 37,300 among whom are included the five classes of mechanics connected with iron and steel shipbuilding, viz. angle-iron smiths, platers, rivetters, caulkers, and holders up. Platers do not represent more than 1/5 of the whole. The subscription is now 1s. 3d., though originally only 1s. per week. There are three grades of membership. First class members must have served an apprenticeship to the trade, and second class members must have worked in the industry for five years, while the third class is open to all members of the five trades enumerated above who have not sufficient standing to entitle them to a place in the higher classes. The latter receive no benefits except strike allowance, and pay only 6d. a week subscription. Labourers are altogether excluded, and a member proposing for election any person with whom he is not perfectly acquainted is liable to a fine of 30s.

The administration of the affairs of the union is vested in an executive council, composed of seven members, each of whom is elected by one of the branches established within a certain area, the councillors must have been members of the union for at least 10 years, and must have held official positions as presidents or secretaries of branches. Their appointment holds good for twelve months, three members retiring at the end of the first and four at the end of the second half of the year. Any member, however, can withdraw at the expiration of his first six months of office by giving one month's notice of his intention to the general secretary. Ex-councillors are not eligible for re-election. As a guarantee that the union funds shall not be spent in unnecessary disputes, the members of the executive council have full control over them. In no case can one penny be spent in a dispute without their sanction, and before granting it, they make every effort, generally with success, to get the difficulty adjusted peaceably. Even if a strike proves inevitable and does occur with their sanction, they have power to declare it settled, if they consider the terms offered by the employers to be acceptable.

(18) RC on Labour, *PP* 1892 xxxvi pt 1, Group B, vol. ii: Evidence of J. Keir Hardie

12, 965. How is it that [miners' unions] have failed in the past? – Well, I should say partly through the opposition of the employers which was not then so great as it is now, and partly through the injudicious action of the men in rushing into strikes for which they were not prepared and which the circumstances did not justify, and thereby draining the Union of its funds and causing the men to lose confidence in it.

12,966. What are the objects for which you think a Union ought to be constituted? – The objects of our Union, as stated in the rules, are to obtain the best possible wages, to have a short day, an eight hours' day at most, and to secure the passing of legislation to protect the life and health of the miner, and such other laws as may be necessary to protect his well-being.

13,164. [Asked to account for decline of organisation in some Scottish districts.] . . . One cause is the want of unity among the leaders of the men, they do not seem to agree very well; perhaps I should say we do not seem to agree very well; being one, and that undoubtedly has an effect. Another cause is the want of – I scarcely know what term to apply to it, unless it is *esprit de corps*, amongst the men in certain districts, they are not attached to the district, they come here and work for a short time and then shift to other districts. The places where the Unions are strong are the places where the Unions are old residenters, and have been mining districts for generation. That is another cause. Then the opposition of the employers is to me the chief cause; these others have been overcome in other places, and could be, and would be, in Scotland, but for the determined opposition of the employers, chiefly in Lanarkshire, and in certain districts of Ayrshire.

(19) RC on Labour, *PP* 1893–4 xxxiii, Group A, vol. iii, appendix xliii: 'Arbitration Proceedings on the Question of the Apportionment of Work to be

done by the Shipwrights and Joiners in the Shipbuilding and Repairing Yards of the River Tyne. 28 October 1889. Umpire's Award. R. Burt, Umpire'

The questions at issue on Tyneside are numerous and complicated. Under any circumstances it would have probably been difficult to arrive at a just decision, but the difficulties have been enormously increased by the parties being in direct conflict, not only in the claims they put forward, but also in the facts upon which the claims are based. As a first step, therefore, it was necessary to ascertain the facts. To find out the actual practice in the shipbuilding yards in the Tyne, forms were carefully prepared by the Arbitrators and sent to be filled by the representatives of the respective trades. These forms when returned, showed variance on many important points – both Shipwrights and Joiners stating that they were doing the same kind of work. At this stage a few witnesses were examined, but without settling the differences. Ultimately we deemed it best to visit the yards to take evidence in the presence of the manager (whenever practicable) and always in the presence of the foremen and representatives of the workmen. Several days were occupied in the investigation, but the time was well spent. The facts, so far as they were procurable, were thus ascertained. After this sifting process the differences were reduced, but they were still considerable. This extreme difficulty in getting at the facts did not arise in any great degree from any wish to conceal the truth – still less from any intentional misrepresentation. In many classes of work there is really no uniformity. In one yard shipwrights do the work that Joiners do in another; in a second, both are doing precisely the same; while in a third a complete reversal may have taken place within a few years or a few months – the work done at one time by Shipwrights, being done by Joiners, or *vice versa*.

With these conflicting claims, and with no recognised line of demarcation between the respective trades, it is not surprising that disputes occur. The wonder is that they are so few. In the majority of the shipyards there is a good deal of give and take, the work as a rule going on with comparative smoothness and satisfaction. One department may be brisk while the other is slack, and it is better for all parties that the Shipwrights and Joiners should work to each other's hands, rather than that additional outside labour should be introduced, often probably for a very short period. . . .

To minimise the inconvenience, I would strongly advise that wherever the present arrangements are at all satisfactory and the work 'is proceeding harmoniously, no alteration be made merely through a desire to comply with the Award. Let the Award be kept, as it were, in the background to be appealed to only when differences arise which cannot be otherwise amicably adjusted. . . .

(20) *Rules of the United Society of Boilermakers and Iron Shipbuilders* (1901): Rule 43. – Members Acting Contrary to Trade Interests

Section 1.–Any member of this society, either angle-iron smith, plater, rivetter, caulker, holder-up, or sheet-iron workers, instructing anyone not connected with our society (except legal apprentices) by allowing him to practise with his tools, or otherwise instructing him in other branches of the trade, shall, on proof thereof, be fined for the first offence 10s.; for the second, £1; and the third, be expelled the society.

Section 2.–All riveting machines used in shipbuilding where piecework is done must be worked by a full set of riveters, who must be members of our society. Any member working shorthanded, or any member working on such with a non-member, shall be fined 5s. for each offence.

All riveting machines used in boiler shops or bridge yards must be worked by our members at riveters' rates.

Caulking, cutting, and other machines, whether hydraulic, electrical or pneumatic, etc., to be worked by our members at recognised rates.

All light holes, manholes, and all holes appertaining to riveting and caulking must be cut by our members, whether by machinery or hand. Members refusing to do such work when requested shall be fined for the first offence 40s., second offence £4.

Section 3.–All work done at punching machines, hydraulic presses, and rolls must be done by our members, but platers' wages must be paid. . . .

Section 4.–It is not in the interest of this society that piecework should be done, but when members are compelled to do it, members of one branch of the trade shall not take work from another. . . . Any member taking work by the piece and not sharing equally, in proportion to his wages, any surplus made over and above the weekly wages paid to members working such job, shall be summoned before his branch or committee of his branch, and, if he does not comply with the above regulation, he shall be fined, in the first instance £5; second £10; and, in the third instance be excluded, subject to the approval of the Executive Council.

The Royal Commission, after extensive inquiry, could see no alternative to the extension of voluntary collective bargaining (21), which remained the norm, despite some support for further state intervention (22, 23). The cotton industry continued to pioneer advances in industrial relations with the famous Brooklands Agreement of 1893 (24); the boot and shoe industry achieved a major settlement in 1895 (25); and the printers at length devised an agreement on manning the new linotype machines in 1898 (26). There was an increasing elaboration of industrial relations machinery during the last decade of the century and the early years of the twentieth century, as employers strengthened their organisations (27) and unions sought to balance them through the activities of the General Federation of 1899 (28). However, traditional structures and aspirations continued to be dominant in some industries (29). In others organisation was strengthened through amalgamation (30) and experiments in new techniques were also made (31, 32).

(21) RC on Labour, *Final Report, PP* 1894 xxxv: Majority Report

303. Although we are unable to agree in supporting any proposal for

establishing, at the present time, any system of State or public boards for intervening in trade disputes, we think a central department, possessed of an adequate staff, and having means to procure, record and circulate information, may do much by advice and assistance to promote the more rapid and universal establishment of trade and district boards adapted to circumstances of various kinds. It was proposed by a Bill brought into the House of Commons in the session of 1893 by Mr. Mundella on behalf of the Government . . . to authorise the Board of Trade to take the initiative in aiding by advice and local negotiations the establishment of voluntary boards of conciliation and arbitration in any district or trade, and, further, to nominate upon the application of employers and workmen interested a conciliator or board of conciliation to act when any trade conflict may actually exist or be apprehended.

304. The following clause was added to the Conciliation Bill as re-introduced in the session of 1894, viz:–

Where a difference exists or is apprehended between an employer, or any class of employers, and workmen, or between different classes of workmen, the Board of Trade may, if they think fit, exercise all or any of the following powers, namely, –

(a) inquire into the causes and circumstances of the difference, and make such report, if any, thereon as appears to the Board expedient; and
(b) invite the parties to the differences to meet together, by themselves or their representatives, under the presidency of a chairman mutually agreed upon or nominated by the Board of Trade or by some other person or body, with a view to the amicable settlement of the difference.

We think that discretionary powers of this kind may with advantage be exercised by the Board of Trade. There seems no legal reason why the Board of Trade should not, even without legislation, take steps of the kind indicated in the Bills of 1893 and 1894, but a statutory provision of this character will probably be of use in giving to the Board a better *locus standi* for friendly and experienced intervention in the case of disturbed trade relations, and would make it easier to employ a staff suitable and adequate for the purposes in question. . . .

320. To establish by law a maximum working day of a fixed number of hours applicable to all trades and occupations alike does not appear to us to be a proposal which bears serious examination.

321. The proposal that any trade should be enabled to decide by vote its own maximum hours of labour, and to obtain legal sanction to that decision, appears to us to be more worthy of consideration. No schemes, however, have been produced which solve the practical difficulties . . . of defining in all cases a trade, and of ascertaining its collective decision, especially in the case of the less well-organised industries. . . .

325. With regard to mines . . . we do not think that a special case has, so far as the evidence in our possession goes, been made out for exceptional legislation upon the ground that the length of the hours now worked leads to an increase in accidents or to injury to health. The miners are, moreover, in almost every district a very powerful and highly organised body of workmen, and we do not think that it has yet been proved that they are unable to obtain by voluntary agreement with employers the hours which are best suited to the circumstances and interests of the industry in each district.

(22) Ibid.: Minority Report signed by William Abraham, Michael Austin, James Mawdsley and Tom Mann

The fundamental cause of disputes between employers and employed is to be found, we believe, in the unsatisfactory position occupied by the wage-earning class.

Notwithstanding a great increase in national wealth, whole sections of the population comprising, as we believe, at least five millions, are unable to obtain a subsistence compatible with health and efficiency. Probably two millions are every year driven to accept Poor Law Relief in one form or other. In London, the wealthiest and most productive city of the world, we learn from Mr. Charles Booth's researches, that 32 per cent. of the total population falls below the 'Poverty Line' – that guinea per week of regular earnings below which no family can live in decency and health. And when we find that in certain districts of the metropolis one-half and even three fifths of the entire population fall below that minimum, and that this state of things arises from no exceptional distress, but represents the outcome of 50 years of steady improvement, we cannot but regard the situation as calling for the gravest consideration of the Government. Nor is this destitution confined to unskilled or specially degraded classes of workers. Even in those grades in which labour is better paid, the statistics of the Labour Department show that a large number of competent mechanics are at all times out of employment whilst in periods of trade depression many thousands of men are in the same condition.

But whilst many competent and industrious artisans find no work to do, thousands of others are kept to labour for unnecessarily long periods. In nearly every branch of manual labour the length of the working day is greater than is compatible with the proper discharge of the duties of parentage and citizenship. The returns presented to the Commission by the Amalgamated Society of Engineers show that 71 per cent of its members are in the habit of working overtime averaging nine hours a week. The evidence laid before us proves that many of the chemical workers, the railway and tramway servants, the shop assistants, the iron and steel smelters, and many grades of women workers habitually labour for at least 12 hours a day, whilst many exceed 15.

Many thousands of workers still toil under circumstances which make disease and accident an inevitable accompaniment of their lives. Insanitary conditions still prevail in many workshops, and to a greater extent in the houses in which the sweated industries are carried on. Phthisis still decimates the badly ventilated workplaces of the compositors. Except perhaps, in coal-mining and one or two other trades regulated by special legislation, no systematic attempt had yet been made to utilise the resources of science for the prevention of death or disease in industry. We cannot believe it to be necessary, in the present state of scientific knowledge, that the occupation of a railway worker should be more hazardous than that of a soldier, or that potters and file-makers should die at three times the rate of clergymen. And if we turn from occupation of the workers to the homes in which they live, the state of things appears to us equally unsatisfactory. We do not here refer so much to the insanitary state of the slums as to the actual amount of house accommodation which each family obtains. Nearly two and a half millions of persons in England and Wales alone, live in tenements which the Registrar-General declares to be overcrowded. The statistics of the census, and those of Mr. Charles Booth, indicate that probably from 20 to 33 per cent of the whole population of some of our largest towns dwell in one-room homes. . . .

Finally we have the fact that of all who survive to the age of 70, one out of every three is believed to be in receipt of poor relief. . . .

It is impossible to refrain from connecting this deplorable condition of the working class with the fact that two-thirds of the annual product of the community is absorbed by one fourth of its members, and that the annual tribute of rents, royalties, and dividends levied upon the industry of the nation amounts to nearly five hundred millions sterling.

With economic conditions such as we have described, the relations between employers and employed cannot, in our view, fail to be unsatisfactory. Strikes, and other signs of resistance on the part of the wage earners, however inconvenient they may be in themselves, are only symptomatic of a discontent with existing social conditions, which we regard as healthful and promising. . . .

We think it high time that the whole strength and influence of the collective organisation of the community should be deliberately, patiently and persistently used to raise the standard of life of its weaker and most oppressed members. We regard this as one of the primary functions of democratic government, whether national or local, and whilst leaving on one side as beyond our scope such fundamental matters as the nationalisation of the land, and the taxation of unearned incomes, we have suggested, in some detail, various practicable reforms in this direction.

(23) Ibid.: *Final Report*. Observations by Chairman and seven members

The object of this Act [Trade Union Act, 1871] appears to have been, while freeing Trade Unions from the last remains of their former character of criminal conspiracies, and giving full protection to their property, (1) to prevent them from having any legal rights against their members, or their members against them; and next (2) to prevent their entering into any legally enforceable contracts as bodies with each other or with outside individuals except with regard to the management of their own funds and real estate.

In our opinion the experience of the period which has elapsed since the year 1871 justifies some relaxation of these statutory restrictions. We think that the extension of liberty to bodies of workmen or employers to acquire fuller legal personality than that which they at present possess is desirable in order to afford, when both parties wish it, the means of securing the observance at least for fixed periods, of the collective agreements which are now, as a matter of fact, made between them in so many cases. . . .

(24) W. M. Wiggins (President of the Federation of Master Cotton Spinners' Associations), 'Survey of Industrial Relations in the Cotton Industry of Great Britain', in F. E. Gannett and B. F. Catherwood, *Industrial and Labour Relations in Great Britain* (1939)

A prolonged and costly strike occurred in November of 1892 when the spinners refused to accept a reduction of 5 per cent in their wages, which the conditions of the trade rendered necessary. This strike lasted until the end of the following March, when both employers and operatives, realising the waste and futility of such a disastrous stoppage of work, took steps to compose their differences and to seek some method of avoiding frequent stoppages in the future. The result of these efforts towards conciliation was the framing of the famous Brooklands Agreement. This Agreement, dated March 24th 1893, marked a new and more enlightened approach to the settlement of disputes within the industry. In the first clause, it was stated that 'some means should be adopted for the future whereby such disputes and differences may be expeditiously and amiably settled, and strikes and lock-outs avoided'. It provided for the settlement of the dispute then proceeding by a reduction in wages of 7d. in the £ and for the immediate resumption of work. The all-important provisions of this Agreement referred to procedure to be adopted for the settlement of future disputes without recourse to strike action. It provided that the secretary of the local employers' association should give to the secretary of the local Trade Union, or vice-versa, one month's notice in writing of any demand for a reduction of wages in the one case or for an advance of wages in the other case. It also provided that no strike or lock-out should be countenanced or supported by either the employers' association or the Operatives' Trade Union, until the matter in dispute had been fully considered by the Secretaries of the local employers' association and the local Trade Union or by a committee consisting of three representatives of each of these bodies. If such action failed to produce a settlement of the points in dispute within a period of seven days, the matter had to be referred to a committee of four representatives of the Federation of Master Cotton Spinners' Associations and four representatives of the Amalgamated Association of the Operatives' Trade Unions, with their secretaries.

The manner in which the provisions of this Agreement are carried out can be best understood by tracing the procedure in practice. It is presumed that a dispute concerning the conditions of employment has arisen at a certain mill. In the first place the operatives concerned report their complaints to the management of the mill, and an endeavour is made to settle the matter. In practice, the majority of minor troubles never get beyond this stage. If, however, the trouble cannot be settled satisfactorily between the management and the operatives within the mill, the case is reported to the local trade union secretary, who generally visits the mill as soon as possible and, after enquiring into the facts, interviews the management and a settlement is attempted between these parties. If this effort is unsuccessful the trade union secretary reports the case to the secretary of the local employers' association who, in turn, enquires the facts from the management of the mill, after which the two secretaries usually visit the mill together and try to effect a settlement. If this fails, a local joint meeting is arranged. The employers' representatives for this meeting are usually managers of other mills in the district and the operatives' representatives are usually employed in other mills in the same district. The points in dispute are discussed by this meeting and every effort is made to arrive at a settlement. If this is unsuccessful, the dispute passes to the next stage of negotiation – the central meeting. This meeting is composed of members nominated by the central employers Amalgamation. If it proves impossible for this central committee to reach an agreement, the available means of conciliation under the Brooklands Agreement will have been exhausted, but this does not mean that, in practice, a conflict is inevitable. When matters have reached this stage, a breakdown of negotiation would be a serious matter, for the central bodies would now be committed more or less, to support the local bodies and the conflict would probably become general to the whole of the spinning industry. . . .

The Brooklands Agreement was entered into only by the employers' and operatives' organisations in the spinning section of the industry, but it became the model for a later agreement covering the weaving section.

(25) Terms of Settlement of the Boot and Shoe Trade Dispute, 1895 in A. Fox, *A History of the National Union of Boot and Shoe Operatives* (Oxford, 1958)

We the undersigned representatives of the Federated Associations of Boot and Shoe Manufacturers and of the National Union of Boot and Shoe Operatives agree to the following terms of settlement of the dispute in the Boot and Shoe Trade on behalf of those whom we represent:–

PIECE-WORK STATEMENTS

(1) This Conference is of opinion that a piece-work statement or statements for lasting and finishing machine workers, and those working in connection therewith are desirable. Such statements to be based on the actual capacity of an average workman. Any manufacturer to have the option of adopting piece-work or continuing day work; it being understood that the whole of operatives

working on any one process shall not be changed oftener than once in six months. Heeling and sewing to be regarded as separate processes.

(2) This Conference is of opinion that a piecework statement for welted work at Northampton should be prepared on the principle laid down in the above resolution. 'The statement shall be based on the actual capacity of an average workman' – employers having option as laid down in that resolution with regard to payment by the time or piece.

(3) That for the purpose of carrying into effect the last two resolutions Joint Committees be appointed as follows:–

(a) Joint Committee of representatives of the Employers and workmen, 4 of each, to determine the principles and methods of arrangement and classification on which piece-work statements for machine workers shall be based. . . .

(b) Joint Committees composed of representatives of Employers and Employed, 4 of each, to prepare such statements for their respective localities in accordance with the principles laid down by the above Joint Committee. Such Committees to hold their first meetings with the least possible delay after the completion of the work of the above Joint Committee.

(c) A Joint Committee to prepare a statement for welted work for Northampton. . . .

Such Committees shall take such evidence and obtain such information as they may think fit for the purpose, and, each shall appoint an umpire to determine points on which they fail to agree. Failing agreement on the part of any of the Committees as to the appointment of umpires the appointment shall be made by the President of the Federation and the General Secretary of the Union or if they fail to agree by Sir H. James.

BOARDS OF ARBITRATION

(4) That the various local Boards of Arbitration and Conciliation consisting of equal numbers of representatives of employers and workmen in the district be immediately reconstituted and their rules be revised so far as necessary with a view to great uniformity by a Joint Committee of representatives of employers and employed, 4 of each, to be appointed forthwith. . . .

(8) No strike or lock out shall be entered into on the part of any body of workmen or any manufacturer, represented by the National Union or any manufacturer, represented on any local Board of Arbitration.

(9) That if any provision of this agreement or of an award agreement or decision be broken by any manufacturer or body of workmen belonging to the Federation or National Union and the Federation or the National Union fail within ten days either to induce such members to comply with the agreement decision or award

or to expel them from their organization the Federation or the National Union shall be deemed to have broken the agreement, award, or decision.

(26) *Minutes of Evidence Taken Before the Industrial Council in Connection with Their Enquiry into Industrial Agreements*, Cmd 6953 (1913), appendix XXIII

Rules for Working Linotype Machines on 'stab as mutually agreed upon in conference between the Committee of the Linotype Users' Association and the representatives of the Typographical Association, on Tuesday December 13th, 1898.

1. The rate of wages shall be arranged to give operators on the Linotype machine an advance of nearly as may be, $12\frac{1}{2}$ per cent, on the existing case rates payable in the various towns.
2. The hours for Linotype operators shall be in future 48 hours for day and 44 hours for night work. Operators may be required to work the hours in force in their respective offices for case hands at ordinary machine rates without charge for overtime.
3. All skilled operators shall be members of the T.A., and, on the introduction of composing machines into any office, preference shall, as far as possible, be given to the members of the companionship into which they are introduced.
4. Members of the T.A. learning to become machine operators shall work for a period of not more than three months at the ordinary 'stab (case) wages of the town'.
5. That duly recognised apprentices who have served three years of their apprenticeship shall be allowed to work on the machines, but such apprentices to be reckoned in the number allowed by rule to each office.
6. Apprentices shall not permanently occupy machines beyond the proportion of one machine to each three in the office, but where there are less than three machines, or in case of an irregular number of machines, the time in which apprentices may be employed on them shall not be more than one-third of the time the machines are worked.

The above rules apply to the area covered by the Typographical Association, except Ireland.

Signed on behalf of the Linotype Users' Association,

Lascelles Carr, President
E. Taylor Thomlinson, Secretary

Signed on behalf of the Typographical Association,

O. Waddington, President
Richard Hackett, Secretary

(27) Ibid.: 'The Engineering Employers Federation'

Evidence to be submitted to the Industrial Council by Allan MacGregor Smith, M.A., LL.B., Solicitor, Secretary to the Federation, 6th November 1912.

The Federation is a combination of Employers' Local Associations in 52 districts throughout the United Kingdom.

The individual firms, of whom there are over 800, are members of the Local Associations.

The federated firms employ in their various departments between 500,000 and 600,000 work-people and pay annually in wages between £40,000,000 and £45,000,000.

Since the dispute in the engineering trade in 1897–98 the Federation has been organised on its present basis and has, as a Federation, made agreements with many of the Trade Unions representing the work-people employed.

In the main the agreements are on general principles and are applicable to all Federated firms.

The principle one is the agreement with the Engineering Trade Unions, made in the first instance at the termination of the dispute, and re-enacted in 1907 and still in operation.

Local Agreements are made by the Local Associations with the local officials of the Unions.

It is not the experience of the Federation that the Unions with whom they have agreements do not conform to the provisions of those agreements.

There are instances where individuals or sections have acted in breach, but these are in the main the effect of human nature and in all cases have not received the sanction of the Unions.

Similarly the Federation has, when called upon, exercised discipline.

Happily these instances are few.

Amongst the elements which have contributed to this satisfactory working are the following:–

1. Effective organisation of the trade both as to employers and workmen.
2. Organisation sufficiently strong to enforce discipline on their members.
3. No agreement entered into under the guidance of outsiders.
4. No agreement entered into without the clauses being the subject of full and serious discussion between the parties.
5. Provisions of agreement as reasonable as foresight can make them.
6. Willingness of both sides to confer or any question arising.
7. The incorporation in the agreement of "Provisions for avoiding disputes" as follows:–

PROVISIONS FOR AVOIDING DISPUTES

'With a view to avoid disputes, deputations of workmen shall be received by their employers, by appointment, for mutual discussion of any question in the settlement of which both parties are directly concerned, or it shall be competent for an official of the Trade Union to approach the Local Secretary of the Employers' Association with regard to any such question, or it shall be competent for either party to bring the question before a Local Conference to be held between the Local Association of Employers and the Local Representatives of the Trade Unions.

In the event of either party desiring to raise any question a Local Conference for this purpose may be arranged by application to the Secretary of the Employers' Association, or of the Trade Union concerned, as the case may be.

Local Conferences shall be held within twelve working days from the receipt of the application by the Secretary of the Employers' Association, or of the Trade Union or Trade Unions concerned.

Central Conferences shall be held at the earliest date which can be conveniently arranged by the Secretaries of the Federation and of the Trade Union or Trade Unions concerned.

There shall be no stoppage of work, either of a partial or of a general character, but work shall proceed under the current conditions until the procedure provided for above has been carried through.'

8. The consulting of the membership on both sides prior to an agreement being completed.

Where constituents have refused to carry out agreements made it is in some cases feared that the trouble is due to some personal influence or consideration.

(28) W. A. Appleton, *Trade Unions. Their Past, Present and Future* (1925)

The General Federation of Trade Unions is in fact, though perhaps not intentionally, based upon a recognition of this belief [in 'an ultimate commonalty of industrial interest'], of the contemporaneous existence of particular rights which conflict, and general interests which attract. It provides for the fullest exercise of antonomy on the part of its affiliated unions; they may even fight each other if they choose; though such fights are discouraged by a refusal on the part of the Federation to pay financial benefits in demarcation or similar disputes. Its affiliated unions receive general or personal advice and assistance, together with statistical, historical and legal information. They receive also financial backing on an insurance basis, but there is no interference with management, finance, policy or politics.

The General Federation of Trade Unions is in a peculiar sense a creation of the Trades Union Congress, but the success of the former body has not in recent years met with the unqualified approval of the latter. . . .

The Federation was formed to undertake a function which the Congress, both in 1899 and in 1924, was incapable of performing. The Congress was primarily a political organisation. It existed to influence opinion and not to finance strikes. But there was, amongst trade unionists, indeed, there has been from the earliest days of the trade union movement, a strong body of opinion favourable to forms of common support for particular disputes. . . .

It was, therefore, determined to form an organisation with a constitution sufficiently elastic to permit the involvement of all types of trade unions desirous of attaining *bona fide* trade union objectives, and sufficiently cheap to attract. It was to be business-like enough to insist upon the cardinal trade union principle of continuous financial preparation for the struggle which must ensue between employers and employed; and that principle of regular contribution to insure the regular payment of specified benefits. . . .

The Federation proclaimed in its rules its belief in, and its desire for, industrial peace, but declared at the same time that its main objective was the maintenance of wages and the improvement of working conditions. The Federation began to function in July 1899, to accumulate funds and to acquire influence in trade union affairs. . . .

The formation of the Labour Party and its assumption of the political functions of the Trade Union Congress left the latter without much excuse for continued existence. It had delegated the strictly trade union function of providing funds against strikes to the General Federation, and a year later it delegated its most pertinent political functions to the Labour Party.

The probabilities are that it never intended to divest itself of so much authority. But it was several years before the real situation became generally apparent. Then attempts were made to modify, or at least to keep under control, the antagonism which arose through each of the national organisations pursuing different aims. What was called the Joint Board came into existence for this purpose. It was composed of an equal number of representatives of the Trades Union Congress, the Federation and the Labour Party.

The responsibility for this attempt at reconciliation belongs to the General Federation, and for a time the efforts promised good results; but a complaint of blacklegging, preferred by the Federation on behalf of a small, against a large, union, provoked animosities which ultimately led to the Board being destroyed, the main object of the resolution moved at the Birmingham Conference in 1916 being the exclusion of the General Federation from participation in general labour affairs. . . .

The General Federation, through Colonel John Ward, in 1922 submitted its Bill for Unemployment Insurance by Industry. This Bill, while it proposed to keep unemployment insurance in the hands of the two parties to industry – the trade unions and the employers' associations – suggested arrangements for those who might, either temporarily or permanently, find themselves outside particular industries. It praised an equalising scheme as between the successful and unsuccessful organisations, but it was officially opposed by the Labour Party, whom political exigencies had driven from the 1911 position.

The General Federation, while maintaining its right to make political pronouncements, has always had regard to the differing political opinions of its membership. It has, consequently, refrained from subordinating itself to any particular party. No attempt is made to encourage the doctrine that the workman, when joining a trade union, loses his political or religious independence. The rules of the Federation give no one power even to question the right of any workman to vote and to pray exactly as he pleases.

(29) Scottish National Federation of House and Ship Painters, Dundee branch, *Payment Card, 1895–6*

The objects of this Association are to effect a general union of the OPERATIVE PAINTERS of Dundee and vicinity; to establish a better feeling between employers and employed; to redress as far as possible the various abuses now existing in the trade – above all that degrading system of employing lads without having served a proper apprenticeship, a system the prevalence of which has produced a class of tradesmen disgraceful to the profession; to raise by entrance fees and weekly contributions such funds as will provide for the protection of the trade, and funeral and accidental benefits.

Our objects are also to endeavour gradually to improve the moral, intellectual, and physical condition of our Members by establishing a Reading-room for their use during the Winter months, and such other means as may be within our power; also that we obtain for our labour the highest remuneration that the state of the market may warrant us in demanding.

(30) Amalgamated Association of Card and Blowing Room Operatives, *First Annual Report* in Alfred Roberts, *After Fifty Years* (Ashton, 1936)

The 13 weeks strike in Oldham in 1885 against a reduction of 10 per cent in wages, though the Members of the existing Societies in Oldham and district received liberal support from their kindred and other Trade Societies, showed the want of a closer combination amongst Card and Blowing Room Operatives than had hitherto existed, for the struggle against a reduction of wages effected not only the Operatives engaged in it, but the majority of Operatives engaged in Cotton Spinning, and the result was anxiously looked for by thousands of operatives outside Oldham; showing clearly that the interest of Operatives in one district was the interest of all engaged in the same branch of labour.

That Strike taught many a bitter lesson, and at its conclusion the existing societies in Oldham and district formed themselves into one province, having one central fund. After perfecting their own society, the Oldham Provincial at the earliest opportunity took the initiative steps to form an amalgamation of all Card and Blowing Room Operatives' Societies, and for that purpose issued invitations asking local societies to send representatives to a meeting that was being held in Oldham for the purpose of discussing the basis on which an organisation could be formed.

The result showed that an earnest desire existed amongst all for the speedy formation of an amalgamation. At a subsequent meeting officers *pro tem.* were appointed, together with a committee, to draw up a Code of Rules for the government of the Amalgamation on the lines agreed upon at the meetings, and on the adoption of which, and levies agreed upon, the foundation of our present organisation was founded.

(31) *The Seamen's Chronicle* (24 Oct. 1896)

What is Ca' Canny? It is a simple and handy phrase which is used to describe a new instrument or policy which may be used by the workers in place of a strike. If two Scotsmen are walking together, and one walks too quickly for the other, he says to him, 'Ca' canny, mon, ca' canny', which means, 'Go easy, man, go easy.'. . .

If the employers persist in their refusal to meet the workmen's representatives in order to discuss the demands sent in, the workmen can retort by marking their ballot paper in favour of adopting the 'Ca' canny', or 'Go easy', policy until such times as the employers decide to meet and confer with the men's representatives.

(32) LTC, *Government Contracts! Fair Wages and Sub-Contracting* (1891)

On February 13th 1891, Mr. Sydney Buxton M. P. in an able speech, moved the following resolution in the House of Commons – 'That clauses be inserted in all Government contracts requiring that the contractor shall, under penalty, observe the recognised customs and conditions as to rate of wages and working hours that prevail in each particular trade, and that the contractor should, under penalty, be prohibited from sub-letting any portion of his contract except where the department concerned specifically allows the sub-letting of such special portion of the work as would not be produced or carried out by the contractor in the ordinary course of business' The motion was seconded by Mr. C. Fenwick, M. P. After an interesting debate, Mr. Plunket (First Commissioner of Works), on behalf of the Government, declared that the Government were in entire sympathy with the proposals involved in the motion, but were not able to accept the wording of the hon. Members' resolution. They proposed instead the following –

'That, in the opinion of this House, it is the duty of the Government in all Government contracts to make provision against the evils recently disclosed before the Sweating Committee, to insert such conditions as may prevent the abuse arising from sub-letting, and to make every effort to secure the payment of such wages as are generally accepted as current in each case for competent workmen.'

Mr. Buxton, while expressing regret that the question of hours was excluded from the terms of the motion of the Government accepted the motion proposed in lieu of his own in order that the House of Commons might come to a unanimous decision.

7. *The Militant Years*

The first decade of the twentieth century witnessed the first sustained fall in the level of real wages for almost a century (1). This, together with the aftermath of the Taff Vale judgement, initially restrained militant industrial action by the unions, but collective bargaining continued to expand, sometimes under the aegis of the Labour Department of the Board of Trade, set up under the Conciliation Act of 1896 (2). Following a Royal Commission report (3), the Trade Disputes Act of 1906 combated the Taff Vale judgement by extending unions' legal immunities. (4).

(1) A. L. Bowley, *Wages and Income in the United Kingdom since 1860* (Cambridge, 1937) Index of money wages and the cost of living, 1880–1914 (1914 = 100)

Year	Wages	Cost of Living	Quotient
1880	72	105	69
1885	73	91	81
1890	83	89	93
1891	83	89	92
1892	83	90	92
1893	83	89	94
1894	83	85	98
1895	83	83	100
1896	83	83	100
1897	84	85	98
1898	87	88	99
1899	89	86	104
1900	94½	91	103
1901	93	90	102
1902	91	90	101
1903	91	91	99
1904	89	92	97
1905	89	92	97
1906	91	93	98
1907	96	95	101
1908	94	93	101
1909	94	94	100
1910	94	96	98
1911	95	97	97
1912	98	100	97
1913	99	102	97
1914	100	100	100

(2) Conciliation Act, 1896, 59–60 Vic., c. 30

An Act to make better Provision for the Prevention and Settlement of Trade Disputes [7 August 1896].

Be it enacted . . . .

1. – (1) Any board established either before or after the passing of this Act, which is constituted for the purpose of settling disputes between employers and workmen by conciliation or arbitration, or any association or body authorised by an agreement in writing made between employers and workmen to deal with such disputes (in this Act referred to as conciliation board), may apply to the Board of Trade for registration under this Act. . . .

2. – (1) Where a difference exists or is apprehended between an employer, or any class of employers, and workmen, or between different classes of workmen, the Board of Trade may, if they think fit, exercise all or any of the following powers, namely, –

   (a) inquire into the causes and circumstances of the difference.
   (b) take such steps as to the Board may seem expedient for the purpose of enabling the parties to the differences to meet together, by themselves or their representatives, under the presidency of a chairman mutually agreed upon or nominated by the Board of Trade or by some other person or body, with a view of the amicable settlement of the difference.
   (c) on the application of employers or workmen interested, and after taking into consideration the existence and adequacy of means available for conciliation in the district or trade and the circumstances of the case, appoint a person or persons to act as conciliator or as a board of conciliation.
   (d) on the application of both parties to the difference, appoint an arbitrator. . . .

4.   If it appears to the Board of Trade that in any district or trade adequate means do not exist for having disputes submitted to a conciliation board for the district or trade, they may appoint any person or persons to inquire into the conditions of the district or trade, and to confer with employers and employed, and, if the Board of Trade think fit, with any local authority or body, as to the expediency of establishing a conciliation board for the district or trade. . . .

(3) RC on Trade Disputes and Trade Combinations, *Report*, *PP* 1906 LVI

MAJORITY REPORT

Our recommendations may be summarised as follows:–

(1) To declare Trade Unions legal associations.

(2) To declare strikes from whatever motive or for whatever purpose (including sympathetic or secondary strikes), apart from crime or breach of contract, legal, and to make the act of 1875 to extend to sympathetic or secondary strikes.

(3) To declare that to persuade to strike i.e. to desist from working, *apart from procuring breach of contract*, is not illegal.

(4) To declare that an individual shall not be liable for doing any act not in itself an actionable tort only on the ground that it is an interference with another person's trade, business, or employment.

(5) To provide for the facultative separation of the proper benefit funds of Trade Unions, such separation if effected to carry immunity from these funds being taken in execution.

(6) To provide means whereby the central authorities of a Union may protect themselves against the unauthorised and immediately disavowed acts of branch agents.

(7) To provide that facultative powers be given to Trade Unions, either (a) to become incorporated subject to proper conditions, or (b) to exclude the operation of Section 4 of the Trade Union Act, 1871, or of some one or more of its sub-sections, so as to allow Trade Unions to enter into enforceable agreements with other persons and with their own members.

(8) To alter the 7th Section of the Conspiracy and Protection of Property Act, 1875, by repealing Sub-section 4, and in lieu thereof enacting as a new Sub-section (which would also supersede sub-section 1): 'Acts in such a manner as to cause a reasonable apprehension in the mind of any person that violence will be used to him or his family, or damage be done to his property.'

(9) To enact to the effect that an agreement or combination by two or more persons to do or procure to be done any act in contemplation or furtherance of a trade dispute shall not be the ground of a civil action, unless the agreement or combination is indictable as a conspiracy notwithstanding the terms of the Conspiracy and Protection of Property Act, 1875.

MEMORANDUM BY SIDNEY WEBB

... I cannot accept the assumption underlying the Report that a system of organised struggles between employers and workmen, leading inevitably now and again to strikes and lock-outs – though it is, from the standpoint of the community as a whole, an improvement on individual bargaining – represents the only method, or even a desirable method, by which to settle the conditions of employment. ...

A more excellent way is, I believe, pointed out in the experimental legislation of the past decade in New Zealand and Australia. We have in the factory, mines, shops and sanitary legislation of the United Kingdom, long adopted the principle of securing by law, the socially necessary minimum, as regards some of the conditions of employment for certain classes of labour. The various industrial conciliation and arbitration laws of New Zealand and Australia carry this principle a step further, so as to include all the conditions of employment and practically all classes of labour. Such a system appears to offer, to the general satisfaction of employers and employed, both a guarantee against conditions of employment that are demonstrably injurious to the community as a whole, and an effective remedy for industrial war.

(4) Trade Disputes Act, 1906, 6 Ed. VII, c. 47

1. The following paragraph shall be added as a new paragraph after the first paragraph of s. 3 of the Conspiracy and Protection of Property Act, 1875:

'An act done in pursuance of an agreement or combination by two or more persons shall, if done in contemplation or furtherance of a trade dispute, not be actionable unless the act, if done without any such agreement or combination would be actionable.'

(1) It shall be lawful for one or more persons, acting on their own behalf or on behalf of a trade union or of an individual employer or firm in contemplation or furtherance of a trade dispute, to attend at or near a house or place where a person resides or works or carries on business or happens to be, if they so attend merely for the purpose of peacefully obtaining or communicating information, or of peacefully persuading any person to work or abstain from working.

(2) Section seven of the Conspiracy and Protection of Property Act, 1875, is hereby repealed from 'attending or near' to the end of the section.

3. An act done by a person in contemplation or furtherance of a trade dispute shall not be actionable on the ground only that it induces some other person to break a contract of employment or that it is an interference with the trade, business, or employment of some other person, or with the right of some other person to dispose of his capital or his labour as he wills.

4. (1) An action against a trade union, whether of workmen or masters, or against any members or officials thereof on behalf of themselves and all other members of the trade union in respect of any tortious act alleged to have been committed by or on behalf of the trade union, shall not be entertained by any court.

(2) Nothing in this section shall affect the liability of the trustees of a trade union to be sued in the events provided for the Trades Union Act, 1871, s. 9, except in respect of any tortious act committed by or on behalf of the union in contemplation or in furtherance of a trade dispute.

On the railways the unions had never succeeded in gaining general company recognition, despite attempts over many years (5). From November 1906 the 'All Grades Movement' started to develop among railway unionists and in January 1907 presented a set of agreed demands to the companies (6). Almost all the companies refused to negotiate and by the end of the year a national railway strike seemed ominously close. Lloyd George, the

President of the Board of Trade, personally intervened and a conciliation scheme was adopted (7).

In the civil service, organisation among postal workers at last received official recognition (8) and the right to 'fair wages' was reasserted (9).

(5) *Bee-Hive* (15 Sept. 1866): notice – 'Union of Railway Servants'

It having been reported to the directors of several railway companies in Scotland that certain meetings have been held, and that others are in contemplation, for the express purpose 'of attainment of our (railway servants) rights' etc., the directors hereby give notice to the engine drivers, firemen and passenger and goods guards, passenger and goods porters, and pointsmen, that while they with their several officers are most desirous of meeting the legitimate demands of their employees, they will most firmly withstand all dictation by the men; and they give notice that any attempt at combination by the respective employees, will be met by the directors in such a manner as may to them seem fit. The directors take this opportunity of cautioning the men in their employ against combination, or joining any union for the avowed purpose of dictating to their employers.

> Thomas K. Rowbotham, General Manager,
> North British Railway Company.
> W. Johnstone, General Manager,
> Glasgow and South Western Railway Company.
> C. Johnstone, General Manager,
> Caledonian Railway Company.

(6) G. R. Askwith, *Industrial Problems and Disputes* (1920): Demands of the 'All Grades Movement'

Hours. –
(a) That eight hours constitute the standard day for all men concerned in the movement of vehicles in traffic, viz. drivers, firemen, guards (goods and passenger), shunters, and signalmen; also for motormen, conductors, and gatemen on electric railways.
(b) That ten hours a day be the maximum working day for all other classes of railwaymen, except platelayers.
(c) That no man be called upon to book on more than once for one day's work.

Rest. – That no man be called out for duty with less than nine hours rest.

Overtime. –
(a) That each day stand by itself.
(b) That a minimum of rate and a quarter be paid for all time worked over the standard hours.

Sunday Duty. –
(a) That Sunday duty be regarded as distinct from the ordinary week's work.

(b) That a minimum of rate and a half be paid for all time worked between twelve midnight Saturday and twelve midnight Sunday.

(c) That Christmas Day and Good Friday be regarded as Sundays.

Guaranteed Week. – That, independent of Sunday duty, a week's wages be guaranteed to all men whose conditions of service compel them to devote their whole time to the companies.

Wages. –
(a) That an immediate advance of 2s. per week be given to all grades of railwaymen who do not receive the eight-hour day.

(b) That all grades in the London district be paid a minimum of 3s. per week above the wages paid in the country districts.

One Man in Motor Cab. – That the system of working with only one man in motor-cab be abolished on electric railways.

(7) Ibid.: Conciliation scheme for railways, 1907– 'General Principles'

(a) Boards to be formed for each Railway Company which adheres to the Scheme to deal with questions referred to them, either by the Company or its employees, relating to the rates of wages and hours of labour of any class of employees to which the Scheme applies, which cannot be mutually settled through the usual channels.

(b) The various grades of the employees of the Company who are governed by the Scheme, to be grouped for this purpose in a suitable number of sections, and the area served by the Company to be divided if necessary, for purposes of election into a number of suitable districts.

(c) The employees belonging to each section so grouped to choose from among themselves one or more representatives to form the employees' side of the Sectional Board, to meet representatives of the Company to deal with rates of wages and hours of labour exclusively affecting grades of employees within that section.

(d) The first election of representatives to be conducted in the manner set out in the Rules of Procedure. Subsequent elections to be regulated by the Boards themselves.

(e) Where a Sectional Board fails to arrive at a settlement, the question to be referred on the motion of either side to the Central Conciliation Board, consisting of representatives of the Company and one or more representatives chosen from the employees' side of each Sectional Board.

(f) In the event of the Conciliation Board being unable to arrive at an agreement, or the Board of Directors to the men failing to carry out the recommendations, the subject of difference to be referred to Arbitration. The reference shall be to a single Arbitrator appointed by agreement between the two sides of the Board, or in default of agreement to be appointed by the Speaker of the House of Commons and the Master of the Rolls, or in the unavoidable absence or inability of one of them to act, then by the remaining one. The decision of the Arbitrator shall be binding on all parties.

(8) Post Office circular (13 Feb. 1906) quoted in *Official Recognition: The Story of Postal Trade Unionism* (n.d.)

Mr. Sydney Buxton desires to repeat the assurance that all servants of the Post Office have full liberty of making representations to the Post Master General in regard to any matter which affects them.

He is prepared frankly to recognise any duly-constituted Association or Federation of Postal Servants. He is willing to receive representations from the members or representatives of the Association if they be in the Service, or through its Secretary (whether he be a member of the service or not) on matters relating to the Service as a whole, or matters affecting the class or classes of which the Association is representative.

In regard, however, to matters solely affecting an individual, and not his class or branch of the Service, the appeal is to come from the individual himself.

Postmasters are instructed that the Secretaries of the Branches of the various associations of Postal Servants are at liberty to make representations relating to the Service and affecting the class of which the branch of an Association is representative, and that such representations are not to be refused on the ground that they are not signed by the whole or a section of the class affected.

(9) F. E. Gannett and B. F. Catherwood, *Industrial and Labour Relations in Great Britain* (1939): Fair Wages

House of Commons 10 March 1909.

That, in the opinion of the House, the Fair Wages Clauses in Government Contracts should be so amended as to provide as follows:–

The contractor shall, under penalty of a fine or otherwise, pay rates of wages and observe hours of labour not less favourable than those commonly recognised by employers and trade societies (or, in the absence of such recognised wages and hours, those which in practice prevail amongst good employers) in the trade in the district where the work is carried out. Where there are no such wages and hours recognised or prevailing in the district, those recognised or prevailing in the nearest district in which the general industrial circumstances are similar shall be adopted. Further, the conditions of employment generally accepted in the district in the trade concerned shall be taken into account in considering how far the terms of the Fair Wages Clauses are being observed. The Contractor shall be prohibited from transferring or assigning, directly or indirectly, to any person or persons whatever, any portion of his contract without the written permission of the department. Sub-letting, other than that which may be customary in the trade concerned, shall be prohibited. The Contractor shall be responsible for the observance of the Fair Wages Clauses by the Sub-Contractor.

Government action on the railways was a foretaste of further intervention in industrial relations matters. In 1908 an Act gave the coal miners a statutory eight hours day (10) and in the following year the Government established a network of Trades Boards with powers to fix minimum wages in 'Sweated' industries and the first Employment Exchanges (12). Increasing Governmental involvement in industrial affairs encouraged some unions' affiliation to the emerging Labour Party. Once again, the Amalgamated Society of Railway Servants faced legal troubles when a Walthamstow official, W. V. Osborne, sought to prohibit it from collecting a political levy (13). Osborne won his case in the House of Lords in 1909 (14), and the decision was not reversed until the passing of the Trade Union Act of 1913 (15).

(10) *Parl. Debs* (22 June 1908)

Mr. W. Abraham (Glamorgan, Rhondda): . . . The public must understand that all the miners are seeking is that they should be relieved of a little of the time that they are forced to spend underground. It is suggested that the miner has more than he wants, in fact, more than really necessary if we listen to the arguments that are advanced. It is said that the miners want their wages advanced. It is said that the miners want their wages advanced for the same amount of work. That is not the case in South Wales. What the South Wales men want is that the coal that they produce should be cleared away in time and they would give the same amount of coal as they have done hitherto. . . . I say again that we are not seeking to get this Bill passed for the sake of advancing wages. We want more time, more leisure; we want to enjoy ourselves in the open air, in the light of the sun. It is not a question of wages. We are not grumbling at the wages; we are thankful that they are as good as they are. . . .

We are asked why we come to Parliament. Is there not a reason why? It is sad in a sense that we should have to come here to find fault with some of the best employers in South Wales, but for thirty-five years they have been breaking the law – breaking the Mines Act – in the case of the boys who could not in any way defend themselves. Why are we here? We are here because we cannot help ourselves and are compelled to be here. It is said that we have made no effort before. Here stands one before you who has three times made appeal to the colliery owners, and though my appeal has in every other respect been conceded, yet the moment we came to the question of the hours we were told to stand aside, because that was no occasion for dealing with the subject. If the Conciliation Board of the Sliding Scale Committee was not the place to deal with the hours of labour where is the place unless we come to this House. And we are here now to ask this House to do for us what we have failed to do for ourselves. It is necessary that something should be done to compel some of our own men to leave work. It is not always the fault of the employers. A man may desire to increase his wage a little, and he continues to work in a bad place instead of fighting for his rights, and oftentimes he was in danger.

Mr. Markham (Notts, Mansfield): . . . The effect of this Bill, so far as South Wales is concerned, is going to be very serious, and there is going to be a large reduction in the output there. The honourable baronet, the member for the Bosworth Division, and myself are directors of a large company in South Wales which produced over 1,500,000 tons of coal per annum. The House is aware what the honourable baronet said about the profits of the coal trade, and I should like to give my own experience of the profits of mines in which I have been concerned during the last five years. The honourable member for South Glamorganshire gave the case of two collieries in South Wales as if they were typical of the whole coal mining industry. They did not show even a fair average of the coal mining industry. The honourable member ought to have taken the whole of the South Wales mines if he wished to show what was the fair average. Instead of doing so he took two of the best mines. In the case of one of the mines the whole of the capital has been built up by not spending any money on capital account, and by paying no dividends for a long series of years. All these matters seem never to have occurred to honourable members who talk on this question. The collieries I am connected with during the last five years have raised £13,802,149; they have paid in wages £3,596,190, and in dividends £433,600. The average profit over the past five years amounts to 7·7d. per ton in dividends. The Socialist party tell us that the men receive 5 per cent. and the owners 95 per cent. The figures I have quoted show that for every £1 paid in wages the companies get 2/6, or, in other words, for every £100 paid in wages the profit was £15 10s. If a Socialistic Government took over the mines, as the honourable member for Merthyr Tydvil desires, there would only be an addition of £12.10s. on every £100 paid in wages at the present time. That is, of course, after allowing for all the cost of equipping and sinking collieries and interest on the capital involved. In addition to that I contend that in many cases collieries do not set aside sufficient money for depreciation. There is no use of referring to special collieries. Coal mining depends on whether the conditions are favourable. Good collieries can make money, while other collieries adjoining lose money. What we can only arrive at is the average, and, though my own experience may be wrong, I believe that the profit made in coal mining on the average is not 6 per cent. on the capital value. It is not more in the companies with which I am associated. I believe that the profit made in coal mining has not been more on the average, during the last twenty years, than 6 per cent. on the capital involved. . . . I am not saying that the profits in the last year or two have not been large, but the honourable member ought to have given a fair average of the profits made over a reasonable period. The honourable member must be aware that these large companies have for years seen their shares continually depreciating in value.

(11) Askwith, *Industrial Problems and Disputes*: Report of Select Committee on Sweated Trades, 1908, under Sir Thomas Whittaker

If 'sweating' is understood to mean that work is paid for at a rate which, in the conditions under which many of the workers do it, yields to them an income which is quite insufficient to enable an adult person to obtain anything like proper food, clothing, and house accommodation, there is no doubt that sweating does prevail extensively. We have had quite sufficient evidence to convince us (indeed it is almost common knowledge) that the earnings of a large number of people – mostly women who work in their homes – are so small as alone to be insufficient to sustain life in the most meagre manner, even when they toil hard for extremely long hours. . . . While our evidence has been chiefly concerned with home workers, it has been shown that very low rates of remuneration are by no means confined to them, but are not infrequently the lot of factory workers also in the trades in which home work is prevalent. . . .

In the opinion of your Committee, the second proposal – for the establishment of wages boards – goes to the root of the matter, in so far as the object aimed at is an increase in the wages of home workers. No proposals which fail to increase the income of these people can have any appreciable effect in ameliorating their condition. Improved sanitary conditions are important and necessary; greater personal and domestic cleanliness in many cases is very desirable; but the poverty, the miserably inadequate income, of so many of the home workers is the great difficulty of the situation. With the increase in their earnings many of the other undesirable conditions which intensify and in turn are aggravated by the ever-present burden of grinding poverty would be very appreciably modified and improved. . . .

The conclusions at which your Committee have arrived are that it is desirable –

(1) That there should be legislation with regard to the rates of payment made to home workers who are employed in the production or preparation of articles for sale by other persons.

(2) That such legislation should at first be tentative and experimental, and be limited in its scope to home workers engaged in the tailoring, shirtmaking, underclothing, and baby-linen trades, and in the finishing processes of machine-made lace. The Home Secretary should be empowered, after inquiry made, to establish wages boards for any other trades.

(3) That wages boards should be established in selected trades to fix minimum time and piece-rates of payment for home workers in those trades. . . .

(12) Memorandum on Labour Exchanges, July 1908, prepared for W. S. Churchill by William Beveridge (in R. S. Churchill, *Winston S. Churchill*, vol. II Companion pt 2 (1969)

A 'Labour Exchange' may be defined as an office for registering on the one hand the needs of employers for work people, and on the other hand the needs of work people for employers. Properly organised, it should serve two distinct though connected purposes: – (1) the closer adjustment of the demand for, and the supply of, labour by the concentration of the labour market for any given area at a single known centre; and (2) the supply of immediate information as to the state of the labour market and as to industrial conditions generally. . . .

The principal object of a well-equipped system of Labour Exchanges would be . . . to decasualise labour as much as possible by dovetailing the casual work of the different employers in the area, so that the same man, though constantly passing from one employer to another, should yet be able to obtain a reasonable continuity of work in a group of similar firms where he cannot find regular employment under one employer alone. . . .

A system of Labour Exchanges would automatically register the beginning, depth and ending of trade depressions; it would show the need or the absence of need at any given time for emergency measures or relief; and furnish much valuable information at present only inadequately obtained as to the conditions of the labour market, especially amongst those trades which are either entirely unorganised or only partially and loosely organised.

(13) W. V. Osborne, *Sane Trade Unionism* (n.d.)

In 1902 this society [the ASRS] took a ballot of the whole of its members, amounting to 54,443, as regards their willingness to subscribe one shilling per year for the purpose of promoting Parliamentary Representation. Although the question of affiliation with an outside political association was not mentioned, only 14,239 voted in favour of such levy.

The Executive Committee met to consider the result, and adopted a scheme which amongst other proposals provided that 'A fund should be established to be called the ASRS Parliamentary Representation Fund, and that it should be formed and maintained by a *voluntary* subscription of one shilling per year, to be paid quarterly, and to be forwarded to the head office with the quarterly dues.'

Had the political levy rested upon the *voluntary* basis here suggested no real injustice would have been done, although the wisdom of linking Trade Unions up with political associations might have been doubted. But when this scheme was being embodied in the rule book, the Annual Meeting of the Society struck out *voluntary* and made the scheme read as follows: –

1. For the maintenance of Parliamentary representation a fund shall be established by the society. The subscription to be one shilling per member, to be paid quarterly, and forwarded to the head office with the quarter's dues.
2. The objects of the fund shall be: –

  (a) To provide for the representation of railway men in the House of Commons as the Annual General Meeting may from time to time determine.
  (b) To contribute to the Labour Representation Committee such sums as the

Executive Committee or Annual General Meeting may from time to time direct, so long as the society remains affiliated to such Committee.

3. A separate account shall be kept of this fund. . . .
4. Candidates adopted in accordance with object (a) must be and remain *bona fide* members of the society . . . no candidate shall contest a constituency whose candidature has not been endorsed by the Trades Council and Labour Representation Committee.
5. In the event of a candidate being selected for a constituency, his election expenses shall be defrayed. Should he be unsuccessful at the poll and be unable to resume his ordinary work, he shall be found employment by the head office at a salary not exceeding £150 per year, until such times as a constituency can be found to return him to the House of Commons.
6. Should a candidate be elected he shall be paid a salary of £250 per year and third class return fare to his constituency so long as he remains a member of parliament. He shall reside at such place as the Executive or Annual General Meeting may consider necessary for the proper discharge of his duties. During the time Parliament is not sitting his services shall be at the disposal of the society. . . .

(14) *ASRS* v. *Osborne*, [1910] AC 87

Lord Atkinson: . . . it is clear, in my view, that [trade unions] are, when registered, quasi-corporations, resembling much more closely railway companies incorporated by statute than voluntary associations of individuals merely bound together by contract or agreement, express or implied. And it is plain that, as soon as this character was given to them and the rights and privileges they now enjoy were conferred upon them, it became a matter of necessity to define the purposes and objects to which they were at liberty to devote the funds raised from their members by enforced contributions. A definition which permitted them to do the particular things named and in addition all things not in themselves illegal would be no definition at all and would serve no purpose at all. There must be some limit. The question for decision, therefore, is whether parliamentary representation falls within or without that limit, or, in other words, whether the Legislature, expressly or by fair implication, has conferred upon registered trade unions power and authority to subsidize, in the manner provided by the impeached rule, a scheme of parliamentary representation. . . . Trade unions are in this respect in precisely the same position as all corporations, municipal or commercial. If . . . the intention never has been and cannot be imputed to the Legislature to confer upon such corporations as these powers or authority to devote their funds to the procurement of parliamentary representation in the manner in this case contended for, how can such an intention be imputed to it in the case of quasi-corporations such as registered trade unions?

(15) The Trade Union Act, 1913 2 and 3 Geo. V, c. 30

1. *Amendment of Law as to objects and powers of trade unions.*

(1) The fact that a combination has under its constitution objects or powers other than statutory objects within the meaning of this Act shall not prevent the combination being a trade union for the purposes of the Trade Unions Act, 1871 to 1906, so long as the combination is a trade union as defined by this Act, and, subject to the provisions of this Act as to the furtherance of political objects, any such trade union shall have power to apply the funds of the union for any lawful objects or purposes for the time being authorized under its constitution. . . .

2. For the purposes of this Act, the expression 'statutory objects' means the objects mentioned in section sixteen of the Trade Union Amendment Act, 1876. . . .

3. *Restriction on application of funds for certain political purposes.*

(1) The funds of a trade union shall not be applied, either directly or in conjunction with any other trade union, association, or body, or otherwise indirectly, in the furtherance of the political objects to which this section applies (without prejudice to the furtherance of any other political objects), unless the furtherance of those objects have been approved as an object of the union by a resolution for the time being in force passed on a ballot of the members of the union taken in accordance with this Act for the purpose by a majority of the members voting. . . .

(a) That any payments in the furtherance of those objects are to be made out of a separate fund (in this Act referred to as the politics fund of the union) and for the exemption in accordance with this Act of any member of the union from any obligation to contribute to such a fund if he gives notice in accordance with this Act that he objects to contribute.

(b) That a member who is exempt from the obligation to contribute to the political fund of the union shall not be excluded from the benefits of the union, or placed in any respect either directly or indirectly under any disability or any disadvantage as compared with other members of the union (except in relation to the control or management of the political fund) by reason of his being so exempt, and that contribution to the political fund of the union shall not be made a condition for admission to the union.

By 1910 economic conditions had started to improve, and the pent-up discontents of previous years exploded in a wave of strikes (16, 17, 18). In the docks a major complaint was the continued casual nature of the work (19, 20), and the dockers' militancy was infectious among other workers at the ports (21, 22); in some industries the new management techniques associated with the American F. W. ('Speedy') Taylor provided a further abrasive element (23).

(16) Askwith, *Industrial Problems and Strikes*: The Cambrian mining strike

The third large dispute of 1910 lasted for a whole year, and was the forerunner of the disputes of 1911. Ostensibly it arose over the refusal of Welsh coal-owners to entertain one of the proposals made earlier in the year, when the Conciliation Board was formed, to give payment of a fixed wage to workmen employed in 'abnormal places'; a difficulty not reduced till the passing of the Coal Mines (Minimum Wage) Act at a later date, but it indicated other symptoms. It showed that South Wales miners would not accept, under certain conditions, either the proposals made by agreement between both sides of the Conciliation Board, or the assurances of the owners or the advice of their own Executive or the Miners' Federation of Great Britain, or the suggestions and efforts made by the Board of Trade. A large section of 10,000 men, when support was withdrawn by their own Association, and the National Association to which they belonged, still held out by themselves for months, ultimately accepting, in August, the very terms put before them by me in January, and in the result finding that those terms worked satisfactorily; but resuming work with a feeling of bitterness. It showed that there was serious and growing revolt in South Wales against owners and against their older leaders, a new spirit of disaffection among the younger men, which the events of subsequent years have not dispelled.

(17) Ibid., quoting Philip Snowden MP

The year 1910 has been an exceedingly trying time for all who have had any responsibility for the management of trade unions and the direction of the labour movement. The men connected with a number of important trade unions have shown a good deal of dissatisfaction with the actions of their responsible officials, and this dissatisfaction has expressed itself in some cases in rebellion against the agreements entered into by the Union executive and in unauthorised strikes. Trouble of this sort has been chiefly active in the North-East of England, on the Clyde, and in South Wales. On the North-Eastern Railway, a matter of the most trivial character was made the excuse for the men in a Newcastle goods yard to stop work, and this immediately led to a general cessation, which for a few days paralysed the railway system. This unauthorised and spontaneous action on the men's part was a way of expressing their general discontent. The company conceded the immediate demands of the men, so that their action in taking matters into their own hands and overriding the authority of the Union Executive may, like the actions of the locked-out boilermakers, be considered to have been justified by its success. But victories of this sort may be bought too dearly. Discipline in trade unionism is too vital a thing to be injured by violation, and although an occasional irresponsible movement may succeed, such a practice must, if frequently adopted, be destructive of collective bargaining and of trade unionism itself; for no executive could retain office if its authority were not respected. By the side of the success of the North-Eastern strike may be put the complete failure of the unauthorised stoppage of work of the Durham and Aberdare Valley miners. . . .

In 1910– a year of record trade – wages remained practically stationary. The cost of living increases, and the working people's desires rightly grow. But with stationary wages, the real condition of the workers is one of diminishing power to satisfy desires. This is one of the causes of the unrest in the Labour world. With the spread of education, with the display of wealth and luxury by the rich, it is certain that the workers will not be content. It is the duty of statesmanship to acknowledge the justice of the desire of the workers for a more human and cultured life, and to satisfy this unrest by concessions of reform. If employers and politicians are so unwise as to ignore the demands of Labour, then what might be done by safe and constitutional methods will, by great suffering and loss, be accomplished by industial strife, and through social anarchy.

(18) Tom Mann, 'The Transport Workers', *The Industrial Syndicalist*, 1 (Aug. 1910): The London dockers

TWENTY YEARS AFTER: Now that 21 years have elapsed since the strike, it is necessary to take stock of the situation and see whether the advantages obtained at that time have been maintained or lost.

As regards London it must be admitted that, whilst the number of permanent men have been slightly added to, and the wage is a little higher than prior to the '89 strike – the minimum being 6d. per hour instead of 5d. – nevertheless as regards the conditions of employment, the make-up of the gangs, the persistent rush, corresponding to the 'speed and feed' movement in engineering shops, and the taking-on of men and payment of them for as little as two hours, instead of a minimum of four hours as fixed by the conditions of settlement of the strike, in all these important matters, the conditions of the *pre*-strike days obtain at present.

One of the greatest advantages to port workers that followed upon the settlement of the great strike was the proper make-up of the gangs. There was always a tendency to work short-handed on the part of the contractors and shipowners, and frequently six men had to do the work that eight men ought to have been doing. This short handedness not only reduced the total wages that went to the men, but was also a danger to life and limb.

NEW METHODS. Since the '89 period many changes have taken place in the method of unloading vessels. In the discharge of grain in bulk, for instance, which prior to '89 in all the London docks except Millwall was done by hand; since that time the suction elevator, or else the cup elevator have been in general use, which has added enormously to the unemployed. A very moderate statement is that two men out of every three formerly employed in the discharge of grain are now dispensed with, i.e. thrown into the ranks of the unemployed. The system now resorted to is to have as few handlings of cargo as possible, and as little storage as possible. Thus at the Victoria Docks there are two flour mills. The grain is hauled in at one side of the mill from the vessel or lighter, and it goes through all the necessary processes almost without the aid of the man. It is then lowered as flour from the other side of the mill into the barge ready for delivery; and every time an improved method of handling is resorted to it means more profit for the Capitalists and more starvation for the Workmen.

(19) H. A. Mess, *Casual Labour at the Docks* (1916)

The Dockers' Union has had bad days since [1889] as well as good, its members and its authority have fluctuated, its leadership has often been criticised not least by the men themselves; but in its very worst days it has remained the nucleus of an organisation, and the dockers have never again been the undisciplined rabble they were before 1889. The Dockers' Union has voiced many claims, prevented many petty encroachments, called attention to defects of gear and lack of inspection, protested against the bullying of foremen, secured further increases in pay, and in many other ways helped to raise the standard of the docker's life.

But in the matter of casual engagement, which after all is the chief evil of the docker's life, the union has not accomplished a great deal. It has not been able to secure the abolition of three morning calls at intervals of an hour which necessitate so much mischievous loafing. It has not been strong enough to enforce for any length of time over the whole area of the docks the 'ticket', that is to say to insist on only union men being employed, and consequently it has not been able to check the continual drift of labour to the docks and the maintenance of a huge surplus. Its very success in obtaining increases in the hourly rate of pay have tended to aggravate the evil. The increase from fivepence in 1872 to sixpence in 1889, sevenpence in 1894 and eightpence in 1911 has meant substantial gain and an improved standard of living to those men who are fairly sure of work, the permanent men and the preference men high up a foreman's list. But to the casual labourer in intermittent employment the changes have been of doubtful advantage. With each increase in the rate of pay the competition for work has increased also.

(20) Ibid.

The *Board of Trade Labour Gazette* publishes monthly a return of the number of labourers who have been employed each day in the docks and at the principal wharves of London. In 1913 the greatest number employed on any one day was 18,228 on January 7, and the two smallest numbers were 11,164, on December 27 and 12,335 on August 2, the Saturday before the Bank Holiday. The lowest figure, it should be noted, was 13,222. With the exception of a very few days in the year the range of variation is between 13,000 and 17,000. The average daily number employed in 1913 was 15,060.

(21) *The Transport Worker* (15 Aug. 1911): Liverpool transport strike

A large number of sailors, firemen, ships' stewards, cooks, butchers, and bakers, engine men, crane men, train men, railway workers, mill and warehouse workers, canal men, flat men, and in fact every conceivable branch and section of the transport industry, fell into the possession and marched orderly down London Road. . . .

At the opening of the address on No. 1 platform. Bro. Tom Mann said that the railway workers had been without representatives on the Strike Committee, but, having regard to the conditions of their labour, no one could blame them for striking.

In some branches of work, men were receiving from 20s. to 24s. per week for working excessive hours, and others were getting as low as 17s., 15s., and even 13s. 6d., and upon this they were asked to support their wives and families.

The Strike Committee was compelled to have regard to their conditions, to look upon them as comrades, and to do its best to get their grievances adjusted.

He then announced the decision that the Strike Committee had come to in the morning as communicated to the railway companies. He said: 'We have decided on the Strike Committee, adequately representative of other sections of the transport workers, to adopt a peaceful attitude and to show our wish for a speedy settlement by sending a letter to all the companies. There shall be no excuse for them. They will know that there is some one willing to receive communications from them, and to help in arriving at a settlement. If that brings forth no reply to-morrow, if they ignore us or refuse to take action with a view to a settlement, the Strike Committee advises a general strike all round.' At this moment cheering continued for at least five minutes. Bro. Tom Mann remarked: 'We cannot, in the face of the military and extra police drafted into the City, have effectual picketing, and we cannot but accept the display of force as a challenge. We shall be prepared to declare on Tuesday morning a general Strike, that will mean a strike of all transport men of all classes; of railway workers, passengers as well as goods men, drivers, stokers. It will mean all connected with the ferry boats, tug boats, river tender men, dock board men, the Overhead and Underground Railways, flatmen, barge men, dockers, coal heavers, crane men, elevator men, warehouse workers, carters, and in fact every conceivable section and branch of the great transport industry in Liverpool will down tools until this business is settled.' (Raising his voice to a pitch that could be heard on the top of the steps of the Plateau, he shouted): 'If you are in favour of that action, if we get no favourable reply from the railway companies, please hold up your hands.' The response to that request was unanimous.

(22) Ben Tillett, *Memories and Reflections* (1931): London Dock Strike 1912

As I wrote at the time, the transport workers had held up every service. Coal and water, gas and electricity, meat, flour, ice and vegetables, all the materials of the commerce, products of the workshop and factory and the mill, borne on the railway, or transported by road, canal, and river, arrested in their movements. Yet I was able to say with truth, and without challenge, that in no case was there any failure or deliberate malice imported into the strike.

'Not only were the electric light, hydraulic power, gas lighting, and coaling at the mercy of the men, but in no single case do I know of any sinister attempt at wrecking which might easily have emptied the docks of water, and committed irreparable damage. Any appeal for public service, any appeal for provision, medicines, and necessaries were not only readily sought, but readily given; and although the strict code of war demanded firmness even to brutality, no single case can be cited, against the Strike Committee or the men of any act of riot, recklessness, or violence. In the name of the Strike Committee I congratulate all our comrades who associated themselves in the fight. I desire to point out to the capitalist class and the great public that our side was more honourable, just, and merciful in the use of their power, and in their conduct towards the great, brutal, British public, (or that portion of them who are well off and who are indifferent to the well-being of the rest of their fellows) than they are.'

(23) L. Urwick and E. F. L. Brech, *The Making of Scientific Management* (1949), vol. II: 'A Note on the Trade Union Attitude to the Premium Bonus System, 1910'

It is doubtful whether the British Trade Union Movement was familiar with Taylor's teachings at any time prior to his death in 1915. A fairly wide search has not produced any references, and in the Special Report referred to below, Taylor is not mentioned at all by name though presumably his 'system' was among those covered in the conclusions. That the trade unions were interested – and strongly interested – in the increasing development of workshop planning and piece-work schemes is evidenced by general condemnation expressed at the 1908 Congress and by a formal resolution passed unanimously at the Nottingham Congress in 1909. The resolution ran as follows:

This Congress strongly condemns the modern method of increasing output by the introduction of the premium bonus system of working, regarding it as utterly opposed to the principles of trade unionism, inasmuch as it creates a form of sweated labour, and acts as a factor in increasing the number of unemployed, and hereby recommends that societies should use every effort to stop the further development of the system, also to take steps to abolish it wherever it has been introduced.

In a subsequent paragraph specific mention is made of the Admiralty and War Office establishments at which premium bonus schemes had been introduced and had apparently roused such concern that the T. U. C. Parliamentary Committee had arranged for deputations to wait on the Department concerned in 1908.

The sequel to the 1909 resolution was the appointment by the T. U. C. of a Committee of Enquiry which collected information as to the working of premium bonus schemes from a number of engineering and allied unions and examined individual witness from a number of localities. Eventually in 1910 a report was published, and its tenor may be judged from the following extract:

> The Committee concur in the whole of these conclusions (see following). They are of the opinion that the premium bonus system, by encouraging individual selfishness, is demoralising to the workman. That, by destroying craftsmanship and encouraging specialisation it is harmful to the industry, which moreover is burdened by a horde of supervising officials, whose maintenance as non-producers imposes a considerable tax upon its profits; and that further, the system is a menace to the community at large, owing to the abnormal and continuous increase in unemployment, which is directly due to its working and which is bound to become intensified as the system extends.

The conclusions were that the system was extending, but that almost all who have had practical experience of its working condemned it for the main reasons that:

(1) It destroys the principle of collective bargaining;
(2) It is destructive of trade unionism and encourages disorganisation;
(3) It is one of the causes of unemployment;
(4) It leads to scamping of work;
(5) It prevents the proper training of apprentices;
(6) It promotes selfishness in the workshop;
(7) It promotes workshop favouritism.

An important though immeasurable factor in the bitterness of the pre-war unrest was the spread of ideas of syndicalism, industrial unionism and workers' control of industry, on which much propaganda was published (24, 25, 26). The influence of these ideas was significant in *The Miners' Next Step*, published by the South Wales Miners' Reform Committee in 1912 (27) and in the even stronger sentiments expressed in Tom Mann's publications (28). Industrial unionism reached a peak with the establishment of the National Union of Railwaymen in 1913 (29), but arguments long continued over rival forms of union organisation (30, 31, 32). The notion of the 'sympathetic strike' was simultaneously developed, most notably by the 'Triple Alliance' of railwaymen, transport workers and miners in 1914 (33). While most of the unrest was explicable in terms of purely British experience, it was also seen as part of an international phenomenon (34).

(24) *The Socialist Labour Party: Its Aims and Methods* (Edinburgh, 1908)

Industrial Unionism, the propaganda of which has spread over the whole country during the last few years, is the negation of all that trade unionism stands for. It proposes to organise the working class *as a class*, 'in an organisation formed in such a way that all its members in any one industry, or in all industries if necessary, cease work whenever a strike or lock-out is on in any department thereof, *thus making an injury to one an injury to all*.' The said organisation to have as

its object the bringing together of the workers 'ON THE POLITICAL AS WELL AS
ON THE INDUSTRIAL FIELD, to take and hold that which they produce by their
labour.'

A very brief outline of the industrial form of the organisation is as follows. The
unit is an organisation formed of all the workers in a given plant, factory, mine,
or railway system. The workers will be arranged in branches corresponding to
the sub-departments of the said industrial plant. The workers in the same
industry throughout the country will compromise an Industrial Union. . . . The
industrial Unions of the several departments of industry are in turn federated
together, so as to form an organisation of the entire working class. . . .

The Industrial Unions will constitute a body of men and women at once
intensely practical and uncompromisingly revolutionary. It can never degenerate
into a sect, which is the danger to which political organisations representing the
revolutionary position have hitherto been exposed, but will palpitate with the
daily and hourly pulsations of the class struggle as it manifests itself in the
workshop. . . . When in the fulness of its strength, it is able through its political
ambassadors to demand the surrender of the capitalist class, it will be in a
position to enforce its demands by its organised might, and, in place of the strikes
of former days, institute the General Lock-out of the capitalist class. Finally,
having overthrown the class State, the united INDUSTRIAL UNIONS WILL
FURNISH THE ADMINISTRATIVE MACHINERY FOR DIRECTING INDUSTRY IN
THE SOCIALIST COMMONWEALTH.

(25) Tom Mann, 'Prepare for Action', *The Industrial Syndicalist*, 1, no. 1 (July
1910)

The growth of Capitalist industry has compelled this class to organise perfectly.
In the case of the large Trusts a decision given at a Board meeting often affects
hundreds of thousands of workmen. The Masters' organisations cover all
connected with the Industry. In the case of the Engineering and Shipbuilding
Industry the action of the Masters is aimed to cover, and succeeds in covering,
the whole of those workers in the establishments owned by them, no matter how
many trades there may be. It is the entire Shipbuilding Industry they are after,
and so they take care to act concertedly over the whole – and this covers some
twenty different trades, organised into some twenty-four different unions. These
twenty-four Unions have never been able to take combined action against the
capitalists. Hence this weakness!

The unit of organised efficiency must be the whole of the workers connected
with an Industry, no matter how many trades there may be. For fighting
purposes the Boiler Makers, Moulders, Fitters, Turners, Coppersmiths,
Blacksmiths, Patternmakers, Drillers, Strikers, Machinists, Handymen and
Labourers, no matter what the occupation – even the clerical staff and drawing
office – must combine, and, for fighting purposes, act as one man.

This is the meaning of Industrial Unionism!

It is not in Britain only that this urgency for Industrial solidarity exists. It is in every country alike.

In 1905 there was held a Convention in Chicago, U. S. A., to consider the faultiness and inefficiency of the Trade Union Movement in that country. The outcome of that convention was the formation of a new organisation known as the 'Industrial Workers of the World' – the essence of which is the organisation of all workers on the basis of working class solidarity irrespective of occupation. It declared that the old method of organising to protect the interests of those connected with a particular craft or trade is essentially mischievous, and harmful to working class interests as a whole. It creates and perpetuates divisions, instead of making for the unity of the working class. They therefore held that organisation on the lines of the 'American Federation of Labour' was essentially reactionary, maintaining craft and sectional bias amongst the workers. Worse still, that the Unions of the A. F. of L. were not aiming at the overthrow of Capitalism but were compromising with capitalists and merely seeking, at best, to patch up the increasing holes made by that system. The Conveners stated in a circular that their object was to be able to take united action and present a solid front to the enemy – as was being done in some of the European countries.

(26) S. and B. Webb, *What Syndicalism Means. An Examination of the Origin and Motives of the Movement with an Analysis of its Proposals for the Control of Industry* (1912)

The Syndicalist Movement in Great Britain, as well as in France, is a reaction from past optimisms, the culmination of successive disillusionments – the disillusionment of the manual working wage-earner with the present order of things, his disillusionment with orthodox Trade Unionism, his disillusionment with the Co-operative Movement, and his disillusionment with the Parliamentary action advocated by the State Socialists. . . .

The manual working wage-earner has lost faith in the necessity, let alone the righteousness, of the social arrangement to which he finds himself subjected. He sees himself and all his fellow wage earners toiling day by day in the production of services and commodities . . . . He sees the services and commodities that he feels that *he* is producing, sold at prices far exceeding the amount which he receives in wages. He has, of course, been told that this price has to pay large salaries to managers and other officials, and has to cover payments of rent and interest to the owners of the land and the capital. But to-day, in his disillusionment, this statement seems to him merely another way of describing the fact: it does not satisfy him of the reasonableness of the enormous and constant inequality between the wage he receives and the incomes enjoyed either by the owners of the instruments of production or by their managers and agents who rule his life. And this inequality of income is not personal to himself and his employer: it is true of all wage earners and all employers . . . . The workman who has become what the Syndicalists term 'class conscious' – aware of the economic, legal, and political subjection to which his whole class is condemned – his position seems scarcely distinguishable from that of slavery. The basis of Syndicalism is an acute 'class consciousness' of this sort.

Against this control of the owner of the instruments of production the less depressed of the wage-earners have, wherever the Capitalist system has prevailed, spontaneously banded themselves together in Trade Unions–that is to say, in organisations formed exclusively of the workers in each trade. . . . Nowhere has it proved to be within the power of more than a small minority of the wage-earners (and these not the sections most in need of it), to organise any effective Trade Unionism at all. Nowhere has even this small minority succeeded in doing more, by its 'collective bargaining' and its 'Courts of Conciliation and Arbitration' than increase wages at infrequent intervals by fractional increments. . . . The Trade Union, in fact, of the orthodox type, assumes and accepts as permanent the very organisation of industry against which the 'class conscious' wage-earner is now revolting. . . .

As they become aware of the necessary limitations in the Trade Union Movement, the more 'class conscious' of its members have always desired to take the 'next step', and, somehow or other, to secure for the manual workers, not merely a larger share in the product, but (with due participation of all who have contributed by hand and by brain), the whole product of their joint labours and complete control of their own employment. . . .

Meanwhile the Socialist movement had arisen, to hold out high hopes to the wage-earners of the world. . . . [But] when 'Socialism' was worked out to mean the transfer of industry from private to public ownership, it became plain that it by no means meant handing industry over to the manual workers. . . . Nor do the Syndicalists see that the progress of this sort of 'Socialism' has, in itself, any tendency to lead to any other state of things. To them it seems that its tendency is to induce the manual workers to put their reliance on the promises of the politicians, who are necessarily, for the most part, not of the manual working class; whilst such working class members as are elected quickly fall away, with the great change in the circumstances of their lives, from that full 'class consciousness' which is bred of the wage-earner's insecurity, impecuniosity and subjection to the orders of others.

(27) South Wales Miners' Reform Committee, *The Miners' Next Step* (1912)

COLLECTIVE BARGAINING OLD AND NEW

So long as the system of working for wages endures, collective bargaining remains essential. From the men's side we cannot permit individual bargains to be made. Such individual bargains have a tendency to debase wages and conditions. On the employer's side there is no great desire for change in this matter. As will be seen by recent speeches by Mr. D. A. Thomas and Lord Merthyr, they realize its value, *in its present form*, to them. They have no time to bother with individuals, but prefer to purchase their labour power in bulk, on an agreed schedule. On the men's side, however, it is being realized, that collective bargaining can be made so wide-reaching and all-embracing, that it includes the whole of the working class. In this form the employers and the old school of labour teachers have no love for it. The employers, because they realize its dangers to their profits. The labour leaders, because it will degrade their power and influence by necessitating a much more stringent and effective democratic control than at present obtains. Let us, in order to clearly realize this, examine at close quarters the labour leader and his functions.

ARE LEADERS GOOD AND NECESSARY?

This is not a double question, since if leaders are necessary, they are perforce good. Let us then examine the leader, and see if he is necessary. A leader implies at the outset some men who are being led; and the term is used to describe a man who, in a representative capacity, has acquired combined administrative and legislative power. As such, he sees no need for any high level of intelligence in the rank and file, except to applaud his actions. Indeed such intelligence from his point of view, by breeding criticism and opposition, is an obstacle and causes confusion. His motto is 'Men, be loyal to your leaders'. His logical basis: Plenary powers. His social and economic prestige, is dependent upon his being respected by 'the public' and the employers. These are the three principles which form the platform upon which the leader stands. . . .

PROGRAMME

Ultimate Objective
One organization to cover the whole of the Coal, Ore, Slate, Stone, Clay, Salt, mining or quarrying industry of Great Britain, with one Central Executive. . . .

Immediate Steps – Industrial
1. That a minimum wage of 8s per day, for all workmen employed in or about the mines, constitute a demand to be striven for nationally at once.
2. That subject to the foregoing having been obtained, we demand and use our power to obtain a seven-hour day.

Programme – Political
That the organization shall engage in political action, both local and national, on the basis of complete independence of, and hostility to all capitalist parties, with an avowed policy of wresting whatever advantage it can for the working class. . . .

General
Alliances to be formed, and trades organizations fostered, with a view to steps being taken, to amalgamate all workers into one National and International union, to work for the taking over of all industries, by the workmen themselves. . . .

Industrial Democracy the Objective

Today the shareholders own and rule the coalfields. They own and rule them mainly through paid officials. The men who work in the mine are surely as competent to elect those, as shareholders who may never have seen a colliery. To have a vote in determining who shall be your foreman, manager, inspector, etc., is to have a vote in determining the conditions which shall rule your working life. On that vote will depend in a large measure your safety of life and limb, of your freedom from oppression by petty bosses, and would give you an intelligent interest in, and control over your conditions of work. To vote for a man to represent you in Parliament, to make rules for, to assist in appointing officials to rule you, is a different proposition altogether.

(28) Tom Mann, *Tom Mann's Memoirs* (1923): Open Letter to British Soldiers. First printed in the *Syndicalist* (Jan. 1912)

Men! Comrades! Brothers!

You are in the army.

So are we. You, in the army of Destruction. We, in the Industrial, or army of Construction.

We work at mine, mill, forge, factory, or dock, etc., producing and transporting all the goods, clothing, stuffs, etc., which makes it possible for people to live.

You are Workingmen's Sons.

When we go on Strike to better our lot, which is the lot also of Your Fathers, Mothers, Brothers, and Sisters, YOU are called upon by your Officers to MURDER US.

Don't do it.

You know how it happens. Always has happened.

We stand out as long as we can. Then one of our (and your) irresponsible Brothers, goaded by the sight and thought of his and his loved ones' misery and hunger, commits a crime on property. Immediately you are ordered to murder Us, as You did at Mitchelstown, at Featherstone, at Belfast.

Don't You know that when you are out of the colours, and become a 'Civy' again, that You, like Us, may be on strike, and You, like Us, be liable to be Murdered by other soldiers.

Boys, Don't do It. . . .

(29) G. D. H. Cole, *The World of Labour* (1913)

Amalgamation . . . may proceed along the lines of either 'occupational' or 'industrial' Unionism. The attempt to apply these two methods at once over the whole of industry can only end in bickering and disunion. The great new organisations thus created will at once become involved in squabbles and recriminations that may well prove a greater danger to Trade Unionism than the whole demarcation problem has ever been. Knowing how employers have used the question of demarcation to sow dissension among the workers, we have every reason to fear that they will not be slow in grasping their new advantage, and turning the weapon of solidarity against the workers themselves. An instance will make the danger plainer. The General Railway Workers' Union, now fused in the National Union of Railwaymen, catered for all classes of workers employed by Railway Companies. The Amalgamated Society of Railway Servants on the other hand, made no attempt to organise workers employed in Railway construction shops! When fusion was proposed, the General Railway Workers' Union refused to come into any scheme which did not provide for complete 'Industrial' Unionism. They carried their point, and membership of the N. U. R. was made open to all employees of Railway Companies. There was, at the time, a great deal of ill feeling on the question, and Mr. J. H. Thomas, M. P., of the A. S. R. S., definitely declared that no attempt would actually be made to organise workers in the sheds. This remark, on representation from the G. R. W. U., he was at once compelled to withdraw. However, pressure from Industrial Unionists and the views of individual organisers have forced the hand of the N. U. R., and in some centres a campaign is being waged to enrol all Railway workers in the one organisation. This at once gives rise to a difficult problem. The skilled mechanics of all crafts employed in the Railway sheds have long been organised, for the most part, in the Amalgamated Society of Engineers, the Boilermakers, the Steam Engine Makers, the United Machine Workers, and certain 'craft' Unions of a similar type. As soon, therefore, as the N. U. R. attempts to touch the skilled workers in the 'shops' it will come into direct conflict with the A. S. E. Such a conflict, between two Unions of enormous strength, can end only in disaster.

(30) A. Bellamy JP (President of the NUR), 'Industrial versus Craft Unions', *Labour Year Book* (1916)

One of the objects of the National Union of Railwaymen is 'to secure the complete organisation of all workers employed on or in connection with any railway in the United Kingdom' (Rule 4), and in consequence of that object it is provided that 'any worker on or in connection with any railway in the United Kingdom shall be eligible for membership' (Rule 5).

The railway transport industry is a distinct unit of industry in all its manifold ramifications necessitating the application of scores of crafts and trades, the specific object of the labour of those employed by railway companies being the maintenance of the railway system of transport and its continuation as an indispensable complete national unit.

The ramifications of the industry are so great and its variety of classes of industry are so many that the line of demarcation between the callings, crafts, or trades is indefinable, and, following a line from the latest boy recruit to the general manager, it is found that railway labour in its practical application is interchangeable, and the railway industry thereby lends itself to a subtle form of involved replacement in ordinary working or in exigencies that no effort and no organisation can resist, even if it were considered wise to offer any resistance. The industry is kept moving by the continual but barely noticeable inter-changeability of the units of labour from end to end of the system, and this is one of the reasons why the National Union of Railwaymen has declared itself an industrial union, and opened its doors to all persons of any capacity employed on or about a railway. The organisation of railwaymen by craft or grade has proved unsuccessful, and experience has shown that the development of the railway transport industry necessitates the organisation of those employed in its manipulations in one Trade Union in order to bargain collectively with the one association of employers. Whatever may be the specific craft or trade a worker may follow his labour is being applied to the running of the transport machine: the objective of the work is to that one end. In whatever direction he may apply his craft skill he is bound up with and carrying on the work of the railway transport industry, and while so employed is distinctly and definitely a railway worker irrespective of his craft classification or denomination. In many respects his craft skill is peculiar to the railway system.

The principle of elementary craft unionism in the railway industry, if ever such were possible, has become obsolete. The tendency to co-ordination between railways, as in other industries has rendered craft industrialism ineffective. . . .

The co-operation of four of the railway unions in the successful strike of 1911 gave a great impetus to this movement, and in the spring of 1913 three out of four unions come together and formed the nucleus of the new body which was called the National Union of Railwaymen. Whether as a recruiting agency or as a fighting organisation the new policy has achieved remarkable success. It is its very success which has led to its being attacked. For some time before the Trades Union Congress of 1915 the matter had been before the Joint Board, and that body had tried its utmost to prevent a collision and to produce a settlement. But the craft unions insisted on a total reversal of the policy before they would enter into any negotiations. . . .

As all the world now knows, the Trades Union Congress by a narrow majority, upheld the contention of the craft unions, but the battle is only just beginning. The new policy will not be relinquished, although the N. U. R. is quite ready to meet the legitimate complaints of the craft unions and to enter into arrangements with a view to a reasonable settlement.

(31) Fred Bramley (National Amalgamated Furnishing Trades Association), 'Craft versus Industrial Unions', *The Labour Year Book* (1916)

Arising out of past experience, and as a consequence of numerous examples of men employed in one section of industry being used during trade disputes to assist the employers to defeat their fellow Trade Unionists in another, we naturally witness a growing desire to put an end to any method of industrial organisation which makes its possible for the enemies of Labour to use one group of men to assist them in their attacks on another and the principles which it is the duty of all, irrespective of craft or trade, to defend.

The attempts made to end this danger have taken the form of passing resolutions at the Trades Union Congress calling upon the Parliamentary Committee to promote amalgamation wherever possible of all unions representing workers employed in the same industry. The interpretation placed upon these resolutions by the craft unions differs very considerably from the interpretation used in justification by such unions as the National Union of Railwaymen of a policy which by being applied has brought them into conflict with 25 of the principal craft unions, and a conflict which because of its dimensions is likely to prove an event of historic importance to the Trade Union movement.

The policy referred to as applied by and contained in the rules of the N. U. R. is *that any worker employed on or in connection with any railway is eligible for membership in their organisation*. The importance of this policy from the craft union point of view is not determined by the effect on craft unions due to its application by one union, however large, but is due to serious consideration of its effect if applied and extended to other organisations which have as much right to claim all craftsmen employed in their respective industries as the N. U. R. The miners, the textile workers, the printing, clothing and the shipping trades may make the same claim. A certain section of the building trades are already making the attempt, and find themselves in a state of war with every established union in the industry.

(32) G. N. Barnes 'Trade Unionism and Strikes', *The Socialist Review*, IX, no. 54 (Aug. 1912)

There are, however, some Labour leaders of anarchical proclivities who are leading newly organised labour into the ditch by strikes. They have become obsessed in favour of the strike policy, and in order to make it more attractive they present it in a fancy name imported from France.

When a section of Labour is coming into organised line it should be the aim of those responsible for its guidance to see the husbanding of its resources and the careful strengthening of its Trade Union capacities. They should indulge as little as possible in irritating filibustering tactics and in personal expressions regarding matters that do not relate to their duties as Trade Union leaders. . . .

The Syndicalist sometimes justifies strikes with or without preparation; he assumes – without any regard for the issues involved – that the larger area covered by strikes the better, and he sometimes advocates their being waged against the community. One of the miners' leaders, on the resumption of work after the recent strike in the coal fields, advocated strikes on all these grounds. The next strike, he said, would come like a thief in the night; it would be a strike of all trades, and it would be a strike against the community. He justified that pronouncement on the plea that the community had just made war upon Labour, and that, therefore, Labour would make war upon the community.

That, I say, is fool's talk. I for one will be no party to a policy of that kind, because I know that nothing but disaster can come of it. A general strike may be justifiable in certain cases – in cases, that is to say, where the object was one the attainment of which would outweigh the evils of civil war, and in which Labour was so strongly organised as to have some chance of success. But contingencies of that nature can only arise in some grave event even when Labour is impelled by an urgent need imposed from without. To talk of a general strike as a general policy for organised Labour is sheer madness. Labour can only wage war upon the community by waging war upon itself. Labour *is* the community. Other classes are mere excrescences or special organs falling into atrophy, which it is the mission of Labour to hasten by disuse into decay.

(33) Robert Smillie, 'The Triple Industrial Alliance', *The Labour Year Book* (1916)

One definite concrete result of the industrial unrest of recent years is the formation of the Triple Industrial Alliance proposed at a conference of the Miners' Federation of Great Britain, the National Union of Railwaymen, and the National Transport Workers' Federation, held on April 23rd, 1914.

The idea of such a conference was first brought into prominence at the Miners' Annual Conference in 1913, when a resolution was passed 'That the Executive Committee of the Miners' Federation be requested to approach the Executive Committee of other big Trade Unions with a view to co-operative action and the support of each other's demands.'

The meeting of the three Executives, held in April, 1914, to consider ways and means of working in common and so avoiding the evils of disjointed action, was enthusiastic and unanimous. It resolved that a working agreement should be drawn up, and appointed a committee, consisting of the presidents and secretaries of the three organisations, for the purpose. [MFGB: Robert Smillie and T. Ashton; NUR: Albert Bellamy and J. E. Williams; National Transport Workers' Federation: Harry Gosling and Robert Williams.] The idea behind this agreement is not in any way the formation of a federation. The new body is not to be a rival to any other. Nor is it to be sectional in any sense. There is no suggestion, for instance, that if one section of the miners determines to strike they will receive the assistance of the new alliance. Action is to be confined to joint national action. Further, no action will be taken until all three partners have men in conference and have agreed upon the course to be adopted. Sympathetic action, in fact, is no longer to be left to the uncontrolled emotions of a strike period, but is to be the calculated result of mature consideration and careful planning. The predominant idea of the alliance is that each of these great fighting organisations, before embarking upon any big movement, either defensive or aggressive, should formulate its programme, submit it to the others, and that upon joint proposals joint action should then be taken.

(34) G. D. H. Cole, *World of Labour*

Unrest, the unrest of which we have been speaking, is almost purely a national phenomenon. Strong though the bonds that bind the commercial doings of nations together have grown, they have not yet caused either Labour or the employers to organise, or even to feel, to much purpose, internationally. Doubtless there is on both sides a realisation that the interests of either party is at bottom the same in every country, and that national development may often be stimulated or retarded by conditions overseas. Certainly too, feeling in these matters is destined to become, in the near future, far more international, and international sentiment is certain to be followed, at a respectful distance, by international organisation. But at present such causes are wholly insignificant beside the special industrial circumstances of each particular country; and it is on these, and not on international feeling, that the ebb and flow of unrest will for some time continue to depend. . . .

There is, however, another sense in which the international question is highly relevant to our subject. Even if the dispossessed of different nations cannot do much to help one another, they have at bottom the same battles to fight, and the same enemy to overthrow. Everywhere exploiter and exploited face each other in a social system which, more or less complicated in different instances, is always fundamentally the same.

8. *The First World War and After*

In spite of the bitterness of industrial relations in the years before the outbreak of war in August 1914, the leaders of the trade-union movement were anxious to co-operate with the Government in the war effort. The needs of war-time production required a rapid expansion of the labour force in munitions industries, and Government and employers pressed for a lifting of those well established restrictive practices by which unions insisted that certain jobs had to be done by skilled, time-served workmen. It was to discuss this and the general problems of maintaining industrial peace that the 'Treasury Conference' was summoned in March 1915 (1). Among many rank-and-file workers there was less enthusiasm about making concessions and Clydeside became the seat of much unrest, organised by an unofficial group of shop stewards (2), but supported by workers who were aware of the inequality of sacrifice being asked in the early months of the war (3).

In June 1915 Lloyd George became the all-powerful Minister of Munitions and he proceeded to incorporate the Treasury Agreement in legislation, the Munitions of War Act, and again met stiff resistance from rank-and-file unionists, who feared the effect of dilution of labour (4). An inquiry into unrest on the Clyde found much in the Act that required revision (5).

(1) *The Labour Year Book* (1916): The Treasury Conference

On 17 March 1915, representatives of the chief Trade Unions in industries producing commodities for the war were invited to a conference with the Chancellor of the Exchequer (Mr Lloyd George) and the President of the Board of Trade (Mr Runciman) 'to consider the general position in reference to the urgent need of the country in regard to the large, and a larger, increase in the output of munitions of war, and the steps which the Government propose to take to organise the industries of the country with a view to achieving that end'. . . .

To this conference Mr Lloyd George made a speech in which he first dealt with the power of the Government to assume control of factories under the Amended Defence of the Realm Act passed the previous day. This power it could only exercise if it had the complete cooperation of employers and workers. A limitation of profits would be considered as a counterweight to the relaxation of Trade Union rules. He then appealed to them to accept arbitration and to relax the Trade Union rules under adequate safeguards.

After Mr Lloyd George's speech a Sub-Committee of seven was appointed to draw up proposals for submission to the conference. The Sub-Committee was as follows:–

Arthur Henderson, M. P. (Ironfounders)
C. W. Bowerman, M. P. (Parliamentary Committee)
John Hill (Boilermakers)
W. Mosses (Patternmakers)
A. Wilkie, M. P. (Shipwrights)
Frank Smith (Cabinetmakers)
J. T. Brownlie (Engineers)

The proposals were submitted to the conference next day and agreed to by the officials of all the unions present except the Amalgamated Society of Engineers. The agreement ran as follows:–

The workmen's representatives at the conference will recommend to their members the following proposals with a view to accelerating the output of munitions and equipments of war:–

1. During the war period there shall in no case be any stoppage of work upon munitions and equipments of war or other work required for a satisfactory completion of the war:–

All differences on wages or conditions of employment arising out of the war shall be dealt with without stoppage in accordance with paragraph 2.

Questions not arising out of the war should not be made the cause of stoppage during the war period.

2. Subject to any existing agreements or methods now prevailing for the settlement of disputes, differences of a purely individual or local character shall unless mutually arranged be the subject of a deputation to the firm representing the workmen concerned, and differences of a general character affecting wages and conditions of employment arising out of the war shall be the subject of conferences between the parties.

In all cases of failure to reach a settlement of disputes by the parties directly concerned, or their representatives, or under existing agreements, the matter in dispute shall be dealt with under any one of the three following alternatives as may be mutually agreed, or in default of agreement, settled by the Board of Trade.

(a) The Committee on Production
(b) A single arbitrator agreed upon by the parties or appointed by the Board of Trade.
(c) A court of arbitration upon which labour is represented equally with the employers. . . .

The relaxation of existing demarcation restrictions on admission of semi-skilled or female labour shall not affect adversely the rates customarily paid for the job. In cases where men who ordinarily do the work are adversely affected thereby, the necessary readjustments shall be made so that they can maintain their previous earnings.

A record of the nature of the departure from conditions prevailing before the date of this undertaking shall be kept and shall be open for inspection by the authorised representatives of the Government.

Due notice shall be given to the workmen concerned, whenever practicable, of any changes of working conditions which it is desired to introduce, as a result of this arrangement, and opportunity of local consultation with men or their representatives shall be given if desired.

(2) W. Gallacher, *Revolt on the Clyde* (1934): Clyde strike, Feb. 1915

The strike was, and still is, wrongly referred to as an 'unofficial' strike. Such a term is entirely misleading. Branch officials, district officials and in some cases, executive officials (like myself) were involved. The more correct term for such a strike is 'spontaneous strike'. Such strikes have played an important part in the development of the trade union movement and are often recognized and supported by national officials. Such a strike is necessary when something occurs, leaving only the option of submitting or fighting. It may be the introduction of a non-unionist, where trade union membership is insisted on by the union as a condition of employment. It may be a cut in a recognized rate or, as was the case at Weir's the introduction of privileged workers from outside at the expense of Weir's own employees. . . .

In order to escape the threats of the Defence of the Realm Act, we formed, instead of a 'Strike' Committee, a 'Labour-Withholding' Committee, with myself as chairman and J. M. Messer as secretary. At our first meeting we had to take note of the fact that the Government had hurriedly called together the national officials of the bigger unions and had given them their instructions – 'Call off this strike'.

Representatives of the national committees rushed to Glasgow and did their utmost to break the strike. But they got a tough reception.

(3) D. Lloyd George, *War Memoirs* (1938): Memorandum of I. H. Mitchell of Industrial Commissioners Department, June 1915

I am quite satisfied that the labour difficulty has been largely caused by the men being of opinion that, while they were being called upon to be patriotic and refrain from using the strong economic position they occupied, employers, merchants and traders were being allowed perfect freedom to exploit to the fullest the Nation's needs. This view was frankly submitted to me by the leaders of the Clyde engineers' strike in February last. As soon as Labour realised that nothing was being done to curtail and prevent this exploitation by employers, it let loose the pent-up desire to make the most they could in the general scramble. This has grown until now many unions are openly exploiting the needs of the Nation. If the work is Government work, it is the signal for a demand for more money. Trade union leaders who, from August last year until February this year, loyally held their members back from making demands, are now with them in the rush to make the most of the opportunity.

(4) Gallacher, *Revolt on the Clyde*: Meeting of the Clyde Workers' Committee with Lloyd George, Dec. 1915

I said a few words to the effect that all he had told us was already well known; and then called on Johnny Muir to state our case.

Johnny was masterly in the handling of the subject. He dealt very briefly with the development of capitalism and with the fact that the one and only concern of the employers was profit; that in pursuit of profit every change in the method of production was used to cheapen the cost, and that this took the form of continually introducing new types of semi-skilled or unskilled labour at the lowest possible rate of wages. Thus he showed that dilution had always been a feature of capitalist development.

Now, however, he continued, the speeding of production necessitated by the war had made an extraordinary acceleration of this process an urgent necessity. All this we understood. We weren't trying to stop the process. On the contrary, we were all in favour of encouraging it. But we had to take note of the fact that large-scale dilution would be used by the employers to bring in cheap labour and by this means force a general all-round lowering of standards. Against anything like this we would fight with all our power. The position therefore stood as follows: the Minister wanted a large influx of new labour-dilution. We had no objection to this. The only question at issue between us was: who was going to control the process – the employers or the workers? The Minister had said he held no brief for the employers. His one concern was to win the war. We therefore proposed that the Government take over the factories, right out of the hands of the employers, and put the full control of all matters relating to wages, working conditions and the introduction of new labour, into the hands of factory committees.

(5) 'Clyde Munitions Workers. Report of the Rt. Hon. Lord Balfour of Burleigh, K. T., G. C. M. G. and Mr. Lynden Macassey, K. C., 1915', *PP* 1914–16 XXIX

6. The first question is the important one of clearance certificates, and we state below in summarised form some conclusions to which we have so far come: –

(A) It should be provided that no employer shall enter on a clearance certificate given to a dismissed workman the reasons for dismissal.
(B) An employer should be bound to give a clearance certificate to a dismissed

workman immediately on dismissal, unless the workman acted improperly
so as to secure dismissal.

(C) In cases where an employer has unreasonably refused any workman a
clearance certificate, jurisdiction should be conferred upon Munitions
Tribunals to award the workman reasonable compensation to be paid by
the employer for any want of employment suffered by the workman in
consequences of the refusal of the certificate. . . .

7. We think the definition of 'munitions work' in the Munitions of War Act,
1915, is too restricted. Employers are forced by the exigencies of the manufacture
of munitions to give the term a wider meaning than it bears in the Act. This has
led to differences with munitions workers. . . .

8. Before the Munitions of War Act, 1915, piece-prices were determined by
mutual agreement between employers and workmen. Under the Act, although
that position is nominally continued, a workman may in practice be compelled,
for a time, to work at piece-prices to which he objects. Work rules should provide
for determination locally of any dispute in regard to piece-prices, either under
Part I of the Act or in some other prompt and effective manner. . . .

11. An employer should not be allowed to dismiss a munition worker without
reasonable cause. . . .

16. A number of cases were brought before us where it was alleged that
employers were treating differentially the original tradesmen and the introduced
tradesmen in a trade into which other tradesmen had since the War been
introduced, as for instance in the allotment of overtime to the introduced
tradesmen and the refusal of it to the original tradesman. . . .

17. As we have already observed, many of the differences brought before us
would never have grown into disputes affecting the whole of the employers and
munitions workers in the Clyde District had they been promptly dealt with in
their embryo stage.

Problems of maintaining production in coal-mining brought increased Governmental
intervention in the industry (6). The introduction of conscription in 1916 meant further
problems of 'dilution'. Women undertook many more jobs (7) and there was often a great
deal of bitterness over those who were exempted from call-up.

  Lloyd George's need to find posts for Labour Members in his Government resulted in
the establishment of a Ministry of Labour (8). None the less, throughout 1917 industrial
unrest continued and a commission of inquiry found many causes of discontent common
to most parts of the country (9).

(6) *Mines and Quarries: General Report, with Statistics, for 1918, by the Chief
Inspector of Mines*, Cmd 490 (1919), pt II

The patriotism of the miners was so great, that by the beginning of 1915 no less than 40 per cent of those of military age in the coal mines had joined the colours, while others had left the mines and gone to munition factories. This depletion of labour resulted in a serious reduction in the output and, in view of the importance of the output of coal being, if possible, increased, a Departmental Committee was appointed by the Secretary of State in February, 1915, consisting of the following members: – Sir Richard Redmayne, K. C. B., Chief Inspector of Mines (Chairman), the Earl of Crawford & Balcarres, Mr. Vernon Hartshorn, Mr. Arthur Francis Pease, Mr. Charles Edward Rhodes, Mr. Robert Smillie, Mr. Stephen Walsh, M. P. – to enquire into the conditions prevailing in the coal-mining industry, with a view to promoting such organization of work and such co-operation between employers and workmen as, having regard to the large number of miners who were enlisting for military or naval service, would secure the necessary production of coal during the war.

The Committee continued its labours until the Government decided to control the coal mines and a Controller of Mines was appointed, when it, with additional members, became the Advisory Council to the Coal Controller. It did much good work, and to it is largely due that the output of coal was, on the whole, well maintained. . . .

In July, 1915, the Home Office arranged for a National Conference of representatives of the Industry, at which the need of united efforts on the part of the owners and men to increase the output of coal was urged. It was held at the London Opera House on the 29th July, and was addressed by the Home Secretary (Sir John Simon), the Minister of Munitions (Mr. Lloyd George), and representatives of owners and men. Their speeches were printed in pamphlet form and widely distributed by the Home Office through the Miners' and Owners' Organizations. In October 1916, it was considered necessary to convene another National Conference of owners and miners to emphasize the importance of regular work. It was held at Central Hall, Westminster, on the 25th October, and the Prime Minister (Mr. Asquith) and the Home Secretary (Mr. Samuel), and others spoke at it.

At a large number of collieries where the multiple shift system was in vogue before the war, single shifts were adopted to enable them to carry on in the altered conditions, and now when more labour is available, the colliers are not inclined to revert to the former practice in this respect.

Miners returned from the army were not sufficiently recovered from injuries, or the shock and horrors of war to be able to produce as large an output as they did before the war.

It is with these and many other difficulties that the mining industry finds itself confronted on the dawn of Peace. . . .

(7) *Labour Year Book* (1916): 'Women and the War'

After clerical work the replacement of men by women has occurred to a larger extent in the distributive trades – and especially in grocery – than in most other trades and occupations. Practically the only limitations to the openings for women in these trades have been in work requiring physical strength or technical knowledge. It should be noticed that the National Amalgamated Union of Shop Assistants, Warehousemen, and Clerks, which includes over 20,000 women among its 90,000 members, refused at its annual conference this year (1915) to demand equal pay for men and women on the ground that the work was not equal, but it in no way raised objections to the extension of women's employment. Where women's labour is introduced the union has sought to enforce a minimum scale based on four-fifths of the rates paid to men.

In industry proper by far the most important developments have been in engineering and the metal trades. The chief change is that women have found their way into the engineering shops, and are now working together with the male operatives, even if they are engaged on different processes. This gave rise to the proposal that women should be admitted to the Amalgamated Society of Engineers, but at the delegate meeting, in June 1915, the suggestion was definitely rejected. Instead, the society decided to regard the women as emergency workers only, and came to an agreement whereby they should be organised by the National Federation of Women Workers. It is too early yet to make any comments on the effect of this policy, or indeed with any certainty on the extent to which women are entering general engineering. The cotton industry, which has been depressed, has shown little change, but the agitation for the introduction of women in the spinning processes is being renewed. Consequent upon enlistment there has been, and still is, a more acute shortage of piecers – a poorly paid and almost blind alley process – but the Spinners' Amalgamation, which resists the entrance of women, has pressed instead for an extension of child labour.

(8) *Labour Year Book* (1919): The Ministry of Labour

Of the numerous new Departments which we owe to the *coup d'état* of Mr. Lloyd George in December, 1916, one is of particular interest to Labour, viz., the Ministry of Labour. For years the creation of a Ministry of Labour had been advocated by Royal Commissions and social reformers; pious resolutions had been passed at Trades Union Congresses; and in 1909 the 'National Committee for the Prevention of Destitution' undertook a campaign in which the establishment of a Labour Ministry to deal with the unemployed problem played a leading part. This country was one of the few countries without a Minister of Labour; but what in time of peace was regarded as too drastic a change in our administration is created in time of war with no friction and very little trouble, although the transference of power from other Departments to the Ministry of Labour is still by no means complete, and a number of other Departments have still important functions relating to Labour.

The first step towards the creation of a Ministry of Labour was the appointment of Mr. Arthur Henderson as Labour Adviser to Mr. Asquith's

Government in August, 1916. The duties assigned to the office were unknown and ill defined, and in fact the appointment was made in the first place to find a post for Mr. Henderson when, on the reorganisation of the Government, he resigned his post as Education Minister. The Department, as might have been expected, did little, and was almost forgotten when the crisis of December, 1916 occurred. Labour was then definitely asked to join the Government, and was offered six posts, including that of Minister of Labour. Mr. John Hodge was the first Minister, but it was not till the passing of the New Ministries and Secretaries Act in February, 1917, that definite powers were allotted to the Ministry. By this Act there were transferred to the Ministry of Labour the powers and duties of the Board of Trade (Employment Department), the Trade Boards Department, and the Chief Industrial Commissioner's Department. The Ministry thus had charge of the Labour Exchanges (re-christened Employment Exchanges), Unemployment Insurance, Trade Boards for 'sweated' trades, and trade disputes. An attempt was made by the Labour Party to bring in also the Factory Department of the Home Office – a Department enforcing the conditions of Labour laid down by the Factory Acts, and obviously a legitimate function of a Labour Ministry, but this was postponed, like many other things, 'till after the War'. Another Department – the Labour Statistics Department of the Board of Trade – whose function is to publish statistics as to Trade Unionism, strikes, unemployment, cost of living, etc., successfully held out for some time, but the 'vested interests' of the Board of Trade were ultimately defeated. The absurdity of a 'Labour Gazette' published by the Board of Trade was too apparent, and after six months this Department was transferred to the Ministry of Labour. In December, 1916, Mr. (now Sir) David Shackleton was appointed Permanent Secretary, and when, after the Stockholm crisis of August 10th, Mr. Hodge became Minister of Pensions, he was succeeded by Mr. George Roberts. In July, 1918, there began the publication of 'The Month's Work'. The Department has been in existence too short a time to say either good or evil of it, but the true testing time will come at the end of the war.

(9) *Commission of Inquiry into Industrial Unrest,* Report on Wales, *PP* 1917–18 xv

Amongst the causes of unrest due to War conditions may be mentioned the following:–

(a) The suspicion that a portion of the community is exploiting the national crisis for profit. This suspicion, rightly or wrongly, was one of the factors that brought about the South Wales strike of 1915. The allegations of profiteering were applied at first to employers in the various productive industries, especially coal mining and shipping. Latterly the indignation has been focused on the agencies engaged in the production and distribution of food commodities. This is undoubtedly the chief immediate cause of unrest, and nearly every witness raised the question. The abolition of profiteering and the provision of adequate food supplies at reasonable prices are essential if industrial peace is to be maintained. The workers are prepared to bear their portion of the War burden, but they decline to do so whilst, as they believe, a favoured few are exploiting the national necessity.

(b) Lack of confidence in Government pledges generally. The view is also widely accepted that the Government has encouraged profiteering by their policy in respect of the Excess Profits Tax. . . .

(c) In some industries inequalities of wages as between skilled workmen in cognate industries, or skilled and semi-skilled or unskilled workers, have been greatly accentuated since the war, and this has given rise to much discontent. The disparity, for example, is particularly pronounced in the shipyards, where ship repairers and boilermakers working on piece rates receive often three or four times the wages of skilled engineers. The high wages paid to boys, again, as compared with skilled men of many years' experience has induced considerable unrest. . . .

(d) A condition of nervous strain produced by over-work, uncertainty as to combing-out, restrictions on liberty and the like, has also tended to ruffle the tempers of the men and to make them highly sensitive to real and fancied injustice. . . .

(e) A fruitful source of unrest also is to be found in the restrictions on individual liberty necessarily imposed, for the safety of the State, under the Defence of the Realm Act, the Munitions of War Act, and the Military Service Act. . . .

An outstanding feature of our enquiry has been the unqualified hostility on the part of witnesses both on the men's and the employers' side to Government interference. This has arisen from two main causes:–

(1) The multiplicity of Government Departments dealing with labour and the lack of co-ordination between them.

(2) The delays that have arisen in the settlement of disputes by the Committee of Production and other Government bodies and the interference of departments with settlements that have already been amicably arranged by employers and men.

Although the outcome of the war was still far from certain, the unions and the Government were, as early as 1916, looking to the post-war world. The president of the TUC indicated some of Labour's demands (10) and the Government appointed a committee under J. H. Whitley to look at future relations in industry (11).

When the war ended it was hoped that the Whitley recommendations would form the basis of future relations in industry (12, 13, 14, 15). A Restoration of Pre-War Practices Act sought to allow the return of trade practices put aside during the war (16) and an Industrial Courts Act sought to encourage settlement of disputes by arbitration (17). The Government also extended the range of occupations covered by the 1909 Trade Boards Act (18).

However, many bitter disputes took place. A demand for a 40 hour week in Glasgow ended in violence (19). A national railway strike was seen as a test for the future (20). An inquiry into the coal-mining industry did nothing to settle the industry's problems (21, 22, 23). The Government declined to accept the recommendations of Mr Justice Sankey and the demands of the miners, backed by the TUC (24), for state control of the industry.

(10) TUC, *Annual Report* (1916): Presidential Address by Harry Gosling

But we hope for something better than a mere avoidance of unemployment and strikes. We are tired of war in the industrial field. The British workman cannot quietly submit to an autocratic government of the conditions of his own life. He will not take 'Prussianism' lying down, even in the dock, the factory, or the mine. Would it not be possible for the employers of this country, on the conclusion of peace, when we have rid ourselves of the restrictive legislation to which we have submitted for war purposes, to agree to put their businesses on a new footing by admitting workmen to some participation, not in profits but in control?

We workmen do not ask that we should be admitted to any share in what is essentially the employers' own business – that is in those matters which do not concern us directly in the industry or employment in which we may be engaged. We do not seek to sit on the board of directors, or to interfere in the buying of materials, or with the selling of the product. But in the daily management of the employment in which we spend our working lives, in the atmosphere and under the conditions in which we have to work, in the hours of beginning and ending work, in the conditions of remuneration, and even in the manner and practices of the foreman with whom we have to be in contact, in all these matters we feel that we, as workmen, have a right to a voice – even to an equal voice – with the management itself. Believe me, we shall never get any lasting industrial peace except on the lines of democracy.

(11) Committee on Relations between Employers and Employed, *Final Report*, Cd 9153 (1918)

The Committee was appointed by the Prime Minister in October 1916, with the following terms of reference:–

(1) To make and consider suggestions for securing a permanent improvement in relations between employers and workmen.
(2) To recommend means for securing that industrial conditions affecting the relations between employers and workmen shall be systematically reviewed by those concerned, with a view to improving conditions in the future.

This reference might be held to invite us to recommend in detail schemes applicable to varied industries. From this we have refrained, in the belief that it is wiser to indicate a ground plan only, and invite the persons actually engaged in the several industries to build the fabric suited to their own conditions.

2. We have presented four Reports. In our first Report on Joint Industrial Councils (Cd. 8606) we recommend the establishment for each of the principal well-organised industries of a triple form of organisation, representative of employers and employed, consisting of Joint Industrial Councils, Joint District Councils, and Works Committees, each of the three forms of organisation being linked up with the others so as to constitute an organisation covering the whole of the trade, capable of considering and advising upon matters affecting the welfare of the industry, and giving to labour a definite and enlarged share in the discussion and settlement of industrial matters with which employers and employed are jointly concerned.

3. In our second Report on Joint Industrial Councils (Cd. 9002) we proposed for trades where organisation is at present very weak or non-existent an adaptation and expansion of the system of Trade Boards working under an amended Trade Boards Act; and for trades in which organisation is considerable, but not yet general, a system of Joint Councils with some Government assistance which may be dispensed with as these industries advance to the stage dealt with in our first Report. In the second Report we proposed also a plan whereby the Joint Council of an industry when it has agreed upon a minimum standard of working conditions for those employed in the industry may have the means of making those conditions general in any district or over the whole country.

Taking our first and second Reports together they constitute a scheme designed to cover all the chief industries of the country and to equip each of them with a representative joint body capable of dealing with matters affecting the welfare of the industry in which employers and employed are concerned, and of caring for the progressive improvement of the industry as an integral part of the national prosperity.

4. We have considered it no less important that in each factory or workshop, where the circumstances of industry permit, and when the conditions which we have stated are fulfilled, there should be a Works Committee, representative of the management and the men and women employed, meeting regularly to consider questions peculiar to the individual factory or workshop, which affect the daily life and comfort of the workers and in no small degree the efficiency of the work, and in which practical experience will bring a valuable contribution to the improvement of methods. This question was the subject of our third Report (Cd. 9085). . . ..

6. In our fourth Report (Cd. 9099) we have made recommendations on Conciliation and Arbitration. Relying in the main on the methods built up by agreement within the various industries and looking to an expansion and improvement of these methods resulting from the habit of dealing with common questions in Joint Council, we have limited our new proposals to the establishment of a small standing Arbitration Council, on the lines of the present Committee on Production, to deal with cases where the parties have failed to

come to an agreement under their ordinary procedure and wish to refer their differences to this Council.

In this connection we have made suggestions designed to minimise the occurrence of conflicting awards and to secure an interchange of knowledge and experience between persons called upon to act as Arbitrators. . . .

(12) Labour Research Department, *Monthly Circular*, iii, 6 (1 Dec. 1918)

The War Cabinet adopted the principle of the first Report, and issued it to all Trade Unions and Employers' Associations, with a letter from the Minister of Labour urging them to put it into practice. At the same time the Government was strongly urged by the Post Office and Civil Service Unions to set a good example by introducing the principle of the Report throughout all Government service. The railwaymen, also, as members in a State-controlled industry, asked immediately for representation on the Railway Executive Committee as an instalment of control.

The railwaymen received no reply of any kind, and to the date of writing Labour remains unrepresented on the governing body of the railways in this country. The Post Office and Civil Service Unions were told at first that 'the Civil Service is not an industry'; and subsequent deputations, protests, and questions in Parliament, extending over a period of nearly a year, elicited the illuminating information that 'the matter was receiving the consideration of the Post Office in conjunction with other Departments'. . . . The great Trade Unions, for the most part, took little notice of the Report, preferring their own methods of negotiation; and the Councils have therefore been set up in trades which only a very elastic interpretation could include under the term 'well-organised'. There are now actually in being National Industrial Councils for the following trades: baking, bedstead-making, bobbin-making, building, heavy chemical, china clay, furniture-making, gold, silver, and allied trades, hosiery (with a special council for the Scottish section), leather goods and belting, match-making, paint and varnish, pottery, rubber, saw-milling, silk, vehicle building, and the Scottish section of the woollen and worsted trade. Committees are also engaged in drafting constitutions for the boot and shoe trade, commercial road transport, electrical contracting, electrical power and supply, heating and domestic engineering, the non-trading side of municipal employment, needles and fish-hooks, newspapers, printing, roller engraving, surgical instrument making, tin mining, the tinplate trade, tramways, waterworks.

(13) *Report of Provisional Joint Committee, Presented to Meeting of Industrial Conference, Central Hall, Westminster (April 4 1919)*, Cmd 139

The views of the Committee on the questions with which they have been able to deal in the time at their disposal, may be summarised as follows:–

Hours
(a) The establishment by legal enactment of the principle of a maximum normal working week of 48 hours, subject to –
(b) Provision for varying the normal hours in proper cases, with adequate safeguards.
(c) Hours agreements between employers and trade unions to be capable of application to the trade concerned.
(d) Systematic overtime to be discouraged and unavoidable overtime to be paid for at special rates.

Wages
(a) The establishment by legal enactment of minimum time-rates of wages, to be of universal applicability.
(b) A Commission to report within three months as to what these minimum rates should be.
(c) Extension of the establishment of Trade Boards for less organised trades.
(d) Minimum time-rates agreements between employers and trade unions to be capable of application to all employers engaged in the trade falling within the scope of the agreement.
(e) Wages (Temporary Regulation) Act 1918, to continue for a further period of six months from 21st May, 1919.
(f) Trade Conferences to be held to consider how war advances and bonuses should be dealt with, and, in particular, whether they should be added to the time-rates or piece-work prices or should be treated separately as advances given on account of the conditions due to the war.

Recognition of, and negotiations between, organisations of employers and workpeople

(a) Basis of negotiation between employers and workpeople should be full and frank acceptance of employers' organisations and trade unions as the recognised organisations to speak and act on behalf of their members.
(b) Members should accept the jurisdiction of their respective organisations.
(c) Employers' organisations and trade unions should enter into negotiations for the establishment of machinery, or the revision of existing machinery, for the avoidance of disputes, with provision for a representative method of negotiation in questions in which the same class of employers or workpeople are represented by more than one organisation respectively, and for the protection of employers' interests where members of Trade Unions of workpeople are engaged in positions of trust or confidentiality, provided the right of such employees to join or remain members of any Trade Union is not thereby affected. . . .

National Industrial Council
(a) A permanent National Industrial Council should be established to consider and advise the Government on national industrial questions.

(b) It should consist of 400 members, 200 elected by employers' organisations, and 200 by trade unions.

(c) The Minister of Labour should be President of the Council.

(d) There should be a Standing Committee of the Council numbering 50 members, and consisting of 25 members elected by and from the employers' representatives, and 25 by and from the trade union representatives, on the Council.

(14) T. Williamson, 'Trade Unionism and Negotiating Machinery in the Gas Industry of Great Britain', in F. E. Gannet and B. F. Catherwood, *Industrial and Labour Relations in Great Britain* (1939)

1919. National Joint Industrial Council for the Gas Industry.

CONSTITUTION
(A) – FUNCTIONS

1. The functions of the council shall be to secure the largest possible measure of joint action between employers and workpeople for the safeguarding and development of the Industry, for the general improvement of working conditions, and for the attainment of improved output with a view to promoting the best interests of all employers and workers engaged therein. The Council may take action as to any matters which are within the scope of this general definition and particularly as to the following matters:–

(a) The consideration of wages, hours and working conditions in the Industry as a whole. In order to enable the Council to deal with these matters as far as they concern workers in the Industry who are members of an organisation not represented upon the Council, the Council may take steps to secure the co-operation or representation of such workers' organisation for these purposes.

(b) The consideration of measures for securing maximum production and employment.

(c) The consideration and establishment of means for securing the speedy settlement of difficulties between different parties and sections in the Industry.

(d) The consideration of measures for encouraging the inclusion of all employers and workpeople in their respective Associations.

(e) The improvement of the health conditions obtaining in the Industry and the provision of special treatment, where necessary, for the workers in the Industry.

(f) The encouragement of the study of processes and of research, with a view to perfecting the products of the Industry, the most effective utilisation of such products, and the promotion of a high standard of efficiency.

(g) The provision of facilities for the encouragement, consideration and utilisation of inventions and improvements in machinery and methods and for the adequate safeguarding of the rights of authors of such inventions and the designers of such improvements.

(h) The supervision of the entry into, apprenticeship to and training for the Industry and co-operation with educational authorities in arranging and stimulating education in all its branches for the Industry.

(i) The collection and publication of statistics and information on matters appertaining to the Industry, as and when agreed, and to industries whose existence affects the Industry.

(j) The study of special problems of the Industry, including the comparative study of the organisation and methods of the Industry, and of industries whose existence affects the Industry, in this and other countries, and where desirable the publication of reports. The arrangement of lectures and the holding of conferences on subjects of general interest to the industry.

(k) The issue to the press of authoritative statements upon matters affecting the Industry of interest to the general community.

(l) The periodical publication and circulation among workers in the Industry of a journal containing matters of general interest to the Industry.

(m) The representation of the needs and opinions of the Industry to Members of Parliament, the Government, Government Departments, Local and other Authorities, and particularly setting up of such arrangements as shall ensure that the Council is consulted before the introduction of governmental legislation or administrative measures which affect or may affect the Industry.

(n) The consideration of such matters as may be referred to the Council by the Government, Government Departments or other Authorities. . . .

(15) L. H. Green (Secretary of the Flour Milling Employers' Federation), 'Labour Problems in the British Flour Milling Industry', F. E. Gannett and B. F. Catherwood, *Industrial and Labour Relations in Great Britain* (1939)

The leaders of the flour milling industry recognised that with the improved status of their workmen after the War, pre-War rates of pay and hours and conditions of work were no longer tolerable. As there was no national organisation to deal with labour conditions on either side, it was decided to form a federation of employers on the one hand, and on the other to encourage the workpeople to join their Trade Unions.

Accordingly in the autumn of 1918 the Flour Milling Employers' Federation was established; and six months later both sides were sufficiently organised to warrant the setting up of a National Joint Industrial Council for the Flour Milling Industry, an event which took place at the Ministry of Labour in March, 1919. With the Flour Milling Employers' Federation were associated the English and Scottish Co-operative Wholesale Societies. On the other side of the table were the representatives of thirteen Trade Unions. Today (1939) the Federation and the two Co-operative Wholesale Societies still form the employers' side of the joint body, but the number of Trade Unions has, by a process of amalgamation, been reduced to three, namely the Transport and General Workers' Union, the National Union of General and Municipal Workers, and the National Union of Distributive and Allied Workers.

The employers encouraged their men to join their Unions because they realise that stable working conditions are impossible in industry unless each side is able to make agreements which its constituents will keep. An employer may employ 10 men or 10,000 men, but in each case he has to come to terms with them. If he is fixing a rate of wages, that rate does not depend merely on what he says he can afford. He has to take into account not only the prosperity of his own industry as well as the cost of living to his workpeople and the rates that his competitors are paying. In other words, he has to make an agreement and each of the two parties has to sign that agreement and see that it is carried out. This cannot be done by irresponsible individuals, but only by official representatives who are properly elected by their constituents and are in a position to ensure that their side of an agreement is carried out.

(16) Labour Research Department, *Monthly Circular*, IV, no. 6 (2 June 1919)

Restoration of Pre-War Practices Bill. – . . . Under the Bill, which is to be carried through immediately, an obligation is placed directly on every owner of an establishment, two months after the passing of the Act, to restore the pre-war customs which have been suspended during the war. Failure to do this renders the owner liable to prosecution after a week's notice has been given, by the Trade Union or individual concerned, of the intention to prosecute. It is a good defence for the owner if he can prove that an agreement has been arrived at with the Trade Union or Trade Unions concerned substituting new conditions in lieu of the practice prevailing before the war. Except where such an agreement has been arrived at, the obligation is general, and applies not only to munitions factories, but to all work on which departures from Trade Union custom have occurred, whether under the Munitions Act, or the Treasury Agreements, or any other war-time agreement of a similar character. It also applies to Government establishments. The Trade Union Committee which has been negotiating with the Government will remain in being, both to watch the Bill in its passage and to deal with any grievance or difficulties which may arise in the working of the act.

(17) Ibid., v, no. 6 (1 Dec. 1919)

In spite of the protests of Labour, the Industrial Courts Act is now law. The clauses which virtually set up compulsory arbitration and which made Trade Union funds liable for strikes of the members against the decisions of arbitrators have been removed; but it should not therefore be assumed that the danger of compulsory arbitration has gone. The Act in its present form sets up an

Industrial Court, appointed by the Minister of Labour from employers, workmen, women, and 'independent' persons. To this Court the Minister may refer any trade dispute of any kind which either exists or is apprehended; or he may refer the dispute to the decision of an arbitrator or arbitrators appointed by him or to a board of arbitration representing the employers and workmen, with a chairman nominated by himself. In a trade in which conciliation or arbitration machinery already exists disputes may not be referred to the Court without the consent of both sides. No penalties at present attach to any failure to comply with the Court's award. Part II of the Act sets up Courts of Inquiry. These are to consist of persons nominated by the Minister, who may refer any existing or apprehended dispute to such a Court, whether it has been reported to him under Part I or not. The Court will then sit in public or private as it thinks fit, and take evidence on oath, which may be published by the Minister during or after the inquiry (in the case of confidential information, not without the consent of the person or organisation supplying it). The Court may issue interim reports. All reports and minority reports shall immediately be laid before Parliament. Part III represents the jam round the pill. It prolongs the provisions of the Wages (Temporary Regulation) Act so far as relates to the enforcement of the 'prescribed rate of wages' until September, 1920. There is, however, no power to substitute a higher rate of wages than is now obtaining. The effect is to stabilise wages at their present level, without variation either way.

(18) Ibid., III, no. 6 (1 Dec. 1918)

The new Trade Boards Act (passed in the face of vehement opposition on the part of certain employers) gives the Minister of Labour the right to apply the Act of 1909 by Order to any trade in which he considers it desirable, without passing a fresh Act. The machinery is also speeded up, so as to bring a Trade Board into existence within three months instead of nine. Under this Act the Minister of Labour has announced his intention of setting up a Trade Board for the tobacco trade.

(19) *Evening News* (Glasgow, 31 Jan. 1919)

STRIKE BATTLE

RIOT ACT READ

Police Charge the Mob

WILD GLASGOW SCENES

About 30 Persons Injured

LEADERS ARRESTED

Quite a battle started in George Square, Glasgow, shortly after noon to-day, between the police and a great mob of strikers.

The police found it necessary to make a baton charge, and strikers and civilians – men, women, and children – were felled in the melée that followed.

Sheriff Mackenzie proceeded to read the Riot Act from the Municipal Buildings, and in doing so he was struck with a bottle.

Kirkwood, Gallacher, and other of the strike leaders are reported to have been arrested, some of them requiring surgical attention.

In Bellshill district this morning a procession of strikers from Blantyre are reported to have attacked the police and caused damage to property. Near Bellshill Cross they were confronted by a strong body of police with batons, and the demonstrators fled, eight men being arrested.

(20) NUR Central Strike Committee, Edinburgh District, *Strike Bulletin* (4 Oct. 1919)

THE ISSUE

YOUR FIGHT IS YOUR FELLOW-WORKER'S FIGHT

TRADE UNIONISM AT STAKE

WHICH WAY 'THE KNOCK-OUT BLOW'?

Mr. Lloyd George:– 'Whatever we lay down for the Railwaymen, you may depend upon it, is going to be claimed throughout the country, and therefore we have to consider not merely your case, but we have to consider the cases of all other trades in the Kingdom.'

Mr. J. H. Thomas:– 'Of course, as you know, that equally applies on our side, and we feel equally in coming down that we are doing something for the rest of the workers.'

(21) *Coal Industry Commission Act 1919. Second Stage. Reports*, Cmd 210 (20 June 1919)

1. *Mr. Justice Sankey*

REASONS FOR STATE OWNERSHIP OF COAL MINES

XXII Coal mining is our national key industry upon which nearly all other industries depend. A cheap and adequate supply of coal is essential to the comfort of individuals and to the maintenance of the trade of the country. In this respect, and in the peculiar conditions of its working, the coal mining industry occupies a unique and exceptional place in our national life, and there is no other industry with which it can be compared.

XXIII The other industries and consumers generally are entitled to have a voice in deciding the amount of coal to be produced and the price at which it is to be sold, which they have not had in the past.

xxiv The export trade in coal has greatly increased, and the system of competition between many private colliery owners and exporters to obtain orders frequently prevents the industry getting the full value for the article.

xxv The inland trade in coal has greatly increased, and the system of distribution through the hands of many private individuals prevents the consumer getting the article as cheaply as he should do. It has been estimated that there are 28,000 retail distributors of coal in the United Kingdom.

xxvi In other words, there is underselling in the export trade and overlapping in the inland trade.

xxvii Passing to another phase of the difficulty, the lack of capital in some mines and the lack of proper management in others prevent the development of coalfields and the extraction of coal to the best advantage for the benefit of the Nation.

xxviii There are in the United Kingdom about 3,000 pits owned by about 1,500 companies or individuals. Unification under State ownership makes it possible to apply the principles of standardization of materials and appliances and thereby to effect economies to an extent which is impossible under a system where there are so many individual owners.

(22) *Coal Industry Commission Act 1919. Report by Messrs. R. Smillie, Frank Hodges, and Herbert Smith, Sir Leo Chiozza Money, Messrs. R. H. Tawney and Sidney Webb,* Cmd 85 (20 March 1919)

The miners' plea is essentially one for justice. They claim that the conditions under which they live and work are not such as the conscience of the nation can approve; that their wages, reckoned in commodities, are now actually less than before the war; that the way in which they and their families are housed is, in the majority of cases, nothing less than scandalous; that in spite of their convincing public opinion and the House of Commons in 1908 that so much toil was excessive, the so-called Eight Hours Act of that year was, through Parliamentary exigencies, finally couched in such terms as practically to impose on them, unknown to the public, a working day underground of nine, and in some cases even more than ten hours, and that these are still their hours of labour; that thousands of them who have been totally incapacitated by accidents are existing on Workmen's Compensation Act allowances of no more than half their pre-war wages, with a statutory maximum of 20s. (now 25s) per week, which the rise in the cost of living has made insufficient for maintenance; that during the war they have foregone all movements for an improvement in their conditions, although under the accustomed Conciliation Board arrangements some of the districts would have normally been entitled to advances even exceeding what is now asked for; and that taking into account the arduous and hazardous nature of their calling in comparison with workmen in other industries, where hours of labour have lately been reduced, and whose rates of pay have been increased, they are equitably entitled to such an increased share of the product of their industry as will afford them a substantial advance in their standard of life.

We think that these claims are, broadly speaking, justified. Notwithstanding the fact that the miners' calling is one of those to which public opinion and the House of Commons readily concede exceptional consideration, we cannot avoid the conclusion that it has now fallen behind some other industries. But even in doing justice we cannot rightly ignore what may be the economic effects of our decisions upon the industry itself, upon the nation's trade, and upon the whole community of consumers. It is fair to say that the Miners' Federation does not overlook this point; and it is, we apprehend, very largely on this ground that its application for improvements in wages and hours is inextricably bound up with its claim that the existing methods of organisation, both of the production and distribution of coal, are so extravagant and wasteful, and result at present in so many unnecessary charges on the industry, as easily to permit both of greater productivity and of a lower cost per ton to the consumer. It is accordingly, in our judgment, impossible, in dealing with their claims, to separate nationalisation from hours and wages.

(23) *Coal Industry Commission Act 1919. Interim Report by Messrs. R. W. Cooper, J. T. Forgie, and Evan Williams*, Cmd 86 (20 March 1919)

The Miners' Federation of Great Britain demand that the wages at present paid to colliery workers exclusive of the war wage provided by the Order of the Board of Trade shall be increased by 30 per cent, on the ground that this increase is necessary to enable them to attain a higher standard of life and not merely to meet the increased cost of living at present resulting from the war, which it must be assumed will gradually be reduced as the war conditions disappear.

It was proved in evidence before us that the average annual earnings of all colliery workers both men and boys were, in the year 1913, £82, and in the September quarter of 1918 at the rate of £169, so that the increase of wages since the date of the outbreak of the war was £106 per cent.

According to the 'Labour Gazette' of the 16th March, 1919, the increase in the cost of living amongst the working classes is at present 115 per cent, but in the case of the colliery workers this percentage is reduced by the fact that they either receive a supply of coals and the use of a house free of charge or a supply of coals at a reduced rate, and except in rare cases no change was made in these respects during the war.

Your Majesty's Government have already offered the miners an increase of 1s. per day, which is equal to 10 per cent on their earnings.

The question we have had to decide is not what amount we would desire colliery workers to receive to enable them to attain a higher standard of living, but the amount to which their existing wages ought to be increased, regard being had to a reasonable standard of living amongst the colliery workers and the effect of any increase of their wages in the development of the coal industry and the economic life of the country. . . .

In our judgment no addition can be made to the present export prices. Upon the evidence before us we are of opinion that the existing abnormal prices of coal exported to neutrals cannot be maintained, and that if we are to maintain our trade with foreign markets there must be a substantial reduction in export prices. We can, therefore, only look to our home consumption for any increase of price.

After considering the question we have come to the conclusion that no greater increase than 1s. 6d. per day worked for persons 16 years of age and upwards and 9d. for persons under that age can be made in the existing wages of colliery workers without seriously affecting our home industries, which are dependent upon our coal supply. Such an advance will have the effect of bringing the present average earnings of the colliery workers to over 130 per cent in excess of their earnings at the outbreak of the war.

(24) TUC, *Annual Report* (1919): Resolutions on coal-mining industry

(a) This Congress having received the request of the Miners' Federation to consider the Government rejection of the Majority Report of the Coal Industry Commission, and the adoption in its place of a scheme of District Trustification of the industry, hereby declares that, in conjunction with the miners, it rejects the Government scheme for the governance of the industry as a scheme contrary to the best interests of the nation, and it expresses its resolve to co-operate with the Miners' Federation of Great Britain to the fullest extent, with a view to compelling the Government to adopt the scheme of national ownership and joint control recommended by the majority of the Commission in their report.

(b) To this end the Congress instructs the [Parliamentary Committee], in conjunction with the Miners' Federation, to immediately interview the Prime Minister on the matter, in the name of the entire Labour Movement, to insist upon the Government adopting the Majority Report.

(c) In the event of the Government still refusing to accept this position, a Special Congress shall be convened for the purpose of deciding the form of action to be taken to compel the Government to accept the Majority Report of the Commission.

Assisted by the Trade Union Amalgamation Act of 1917(25) a number of important federations and amalgamations continued to develop, notably among iron and steel workers, general workers, engineers, builders and transport workers (26, 27, 28). Guild socialists like G. D. H. Cole wanted a more fundamental reconstruction of industry (29, 30, 31).

(25) Trade Union Amalgamation Act, 1917, 7 and 8 Geo V, c. 24

Be it enacted etc. . . .

1. (1) Any two or more Trade Unions may become amalgamated together as one Trade Union if in the case of each or every such Trade Union, on a ballot being taken, the votes of at least 50 per cent of the members entitled to vote thereat are recorded, and of the votes recorded those in favour of the proposal exceed by 20 per cent or more the votes against the proposal; and, accordingly, section 12 of the Trade Union Act Amendment Act, 1876, shall have effect as if the words 'by the consent of not less than two-thirds of the members of each or every such Trade Union' there were substituted the words 'if in the case of each or every such Trade Union, on a ballot being taken, the votes of at least 50 per cent of the members entitled to vote thereat are recorded, and of the votes recorded those in favour of the proposal exceed by 20 per cent or more the votes against the proposal'.

   (2) For removing doubts it is hereby declared that the said section 12 applies to the amalgamation of one or more registered Trade Unions with one or more unregistered Trade Unions.

2. This Act may be cited as the Trade Union (Amalgamation) Act, 1917, and the Trade Union Acts, 1871 to 1913, and this Act may be cited together as the Trade Union Acts, 1871 to 1917.

(26) *Labour Year Book* (1919)

Since the last issue of the Labour Year Book, a number of new schemes of closer union have come into force, of which the most interesting is the Iron and Steel Trades Confederation. This was formed in April, 1917, by the following Unions: British Steel Smelters' Association, Associated Iron and Steel Workers, National Steel Workers' Association, Engineering and Labour League, and superseded the old Iron and Steel Trades Federation. . . .

The new Federations can be more briefly summarised. The National Federation of General Workers was formed in May, 1917, by the following seven Unions: Workers' Union, National Union of General Workers, National Amalgamated Union of Labour, Gas, Municipal, and General Workers' Union, Dock, Wharf, Riverside, and General Workers' Union, National Union of Vehicle Workers, and the Navvies' Union. The National Amalgamated Union of Enginemen have since joined the Federation, which has superseded the General Labourers' National Council. Its objects are defined to be 'the provision of facilities for questions of common interest being dealt with from a common centre'. . . .

The Federation of Post Office Trade Unions was formed as a result of a Conference held in August, 1917, to consider the question of amalgamation or federation for Post Office Trade Unions. Forty-five societies of varying size were represented at this Conference, which decided against amalgamation. The scheme of federation finally adopted provides for three Federations, one of the manipulative, one of the supervisory, and one of the clerical grades, no definite line being laid down for the government of these Federations. . . .

The National Association of Unions in the Textile Trade was formed in July, 1917. With this Federation are connected 45 societies, mostly in the woollen trade (including the General Union of Textile Workers), but also including the Yorkshire Cotton Operatives, some Unions of hosiery workers and silk workers and calico block printers, and the National Union of General Workers. The Federation is a very loose one, the governing body being the quarterly joint meeting of the full Executive of all the affiliated societies.

The National Council of societies representing colliery workers, other than miners, was formed in February, 1917. Seventeen societies joined to form this Federation. These include the National Amalgamated Union of Enginemen, the National Federation of Colliery Enginemen, the National Federation of Colliery Surface Workers, the National Union of General Workers, the National Amalgamated Union of Labour, the Amalgamated Society of Vehicle Builders, and the National Federation of Colliery Enginemen and Boilermen. . . .

National Federation of Building Trades Operatives. This Federation was formed in April, 1917, and at present includes the following Unions: Amalgamated Society of Carpenters and Joiners, General Union of Carpenters and Joiners, Operative Stonemasons' Society, Operative Bricklayers' Society, National Amalgamated Society of Operative House and Ship Painters, Plumbers and Domestic Engineers, Amalgamated Slaters' and Tilers' Provident Society, Manchester Unity of Operative Bricklayers, National Association of Builders' Labourers, National Association of Operative Plasterers, Amalgamated Society of Woodcutting Machinists, and London Order of Bricklayers. . . .

Federation of Foundry Trades. This Federation was formed early in 1918, and includes the Friendly Society of Ironfounders, the London United Brass Workers, the National Union of Stove Grate Workers, the Central Ironmoulders' Association, the Associated Society of Moulders, the Amalgamated Moulders' Union, the Amalgamated Society of Coremakers, the Iron, Steel, and Metal Dressers' Society, the Associated Iron and Steel and Brass Dressers' of Scotland, the London Society of Amalgamated Brassworkers, the National Society of Brassworkers and Metal Mechanics, and the Associated Ironmoulders of Scotland, making a total of between 50,000 and 60,000 members. . . .

The Civil Service Alliance was formed in October, 1916, and comprises a number of organisations catering for clerical workers in the Civil Service, whose interests are closely allied. . . .

The Civil Service Federation (founded 1912) is a federation of various Civil

Service societies for co-ordinating purposes. Other Civil Service Federations not mentioned in the last edition of the Year Book are the Waterguard Federation and the Customs and Excise Federation.

The principal changes which have taken place in federation are as follows: –

The Amalgamated Association of Card and Blowing-Room Operatives have reaffiliated to the United Textile Factory Workers' Association. The Amalgamated Society of Engineers have left the Engineering and Shipbuilding Trades Federation. Two mining craft unions, the Northumberland Colliery Mechanics' Association and the Northumberland Enginemen's and Firemen's Association have affiliated to the Miners' Federation.

Among the amalgamations of the past two years the most important are the following: –

The Amalgamated Society of Carpenters and Joiners and the Amalgamated Union of Cabinet Makers formed in March, 1918, the Amalgamated Union of Carpenters, Cabinet Makers, and Joiners.

The United Garment Workers' Union was formed in November, 1915, by the fusion of the following Unions: The Waterproof Garment Makers, the Clothiers' Operatives, the London and Provincial Clothiers' Cutters, the London Society of Tailors and Tailoresses, and the Jewish Tailors and Tailoresses. Of these the Waterproof Garment Makers have since left the amalgamation.

In December, 1917, the Associated Blacksmiths and Ironworkers agreed to amalgamate with the United Kingdom Society of Smiths and Strikers.

The Amalgamated Society of Gas Workers, Brick Makers, and General Labourers in 1916 joined with the Birmingham and District Municipal Employees' Association to form the Gas, Municipal, and General Workers' Union.

In 1916 the Amalgamated Union of Machine and General Labourers joined the National Union of General Workers, which was also joined in 1917 by the British Labour Amalgamation.

During the past year the two most important amalgamations have been that of the Municipal Employees' Association with the Workers' Union, and that of the Amalgamated Union of Co-operative and Commercial Employees with the Warehouse and General Workers' Union.

In January, 1918, the Postmen's Federation decided to amalgamate with the Postal and Telegraph Clerks' Association.

At the end of 1916 the Amalgamated Society of Telephone Employees was dissolved; one section of the membership was transferred to the Postal and Telegraph Clerks' Association owing to the action of the Postmaster-General, while the rest joined the Engineering and Stores Association to form the Post Office Amalgamated Engineering and Stores Association.

(27) TGWU, *The Union, Its Work and Problems* (1939)

In 1920 two factors arose which led the executive Council of the Dock, Wharf,

Riverside and General Workers' Union to take the step of initiating amalgamation discussions. They were:

(1) The growth of national agreements and the handling of industrial problems
     on a wider basis meant that there must inevitably be a uniform direction of
     policy if progress was to be maintained. It became patent that where efficient
     management existed within a union the very best could be secured from the
     agreements. On the other hand, where slackness existed, local control or a
     lack of understanding of the main purpose behind the national movements,
     there was an indifferent observance of the agreements and disputes arose in
     consequence.

(2) By the sheer drive of the policy of the trade union, the employers had been
     forced to come together in association and federations, and it therefore
     became imperative that there should be efficient national organisation on
     the trade union side to deal with the situation.

FIRST STEPS. Conversations first took place with the National Union of Dock,
Riverside and General Workers (Liverpool). The two unions appointed a joint
sub-committee and after frankly facing the difficulties of amalgamation they
decided to send an invitation to the following unions associated with the dock
industry, who had previously co-operated together, to participate in amalgamation discussions:

Amalgamated Society of Watermen, Lightermen and Bargemen
Amalgamated Stevedores' Labour Protection League
Cardiff, Penarth and Barry Coal Trimmers' Union
Dock, Wharf, Riverside and General Workers' Union
Labour Protection League
Mersey Watermen
National Amalgamated Labourers' Union of Great Britain and Ireland
National Union of Dock, Riverside and General Workers
National Union of Docks, Wharves and Shipping Staffs
National Shipping Clerks' Guild
National Union of Ships' Clerks, Grain Weighers and Coalmeters
North of England Trimmers' and Teemers' Association
Scottish Union of Dock Labourers
Weaver Watermen's Association. . . .

During its deliberations, the amalgamation committee extended the scope of the
proposed amalgamation to include the unions catering for road transport
workers, and the executives of the following unions were accordingly invited to
participate in the discussions:

Amalgamated Association of Carters and Motormen
Liverpool and District Carters' and Motormen's Union
National Union of Vehicle Workers

North of Scotland Horse and Motormen's Association
Scottish Horse and Motormen's Union
United Vehicle Workers. . . .

GROUPING SYSTEM. The grouping system became the basis of the amalgamation discussions, for it soon became apparent that unity could not be secured unless a way could be found to allow each industry or group of industries to have its own committees to deal with trade problems. The grouping system, with a central executive authority, supplied this need, and gave a considerable confidence, inasmuch as the very nature of the system constituted a guarantee against any one section being dominated by others . . .

AMALGAMATION BALLOT. After months of examination and consultation the amalgamation committee completed its task and submitted the result of its deliberations to a conference of representatives of 19 unions held in London on December 1, 1920. The conference approved the scheme of amalgamation and arrangements were thereupon made for its submission to a ballot vote of the members. . . .

Actually, 14 unions came together as a result of the ballot, and at a conference of representatives of those unions held on May 11, 1921, it was determined that the new Union should commence to function on January 1, 1922.

The 14 unions were:–

Amalgamated Society of Watermen, Lightermen and Bargemen
Amalgamated Carters, Lorrymen and Motormen's Union
Amalgamated Association of Carters and Motormen
Associated Horsemen's Union
Dock, Wharf, Riverside and General Workers' Union
Labour Protection League
National Amalgamated Labourers' Union
National Union of Docks, Wharves and Shipping Staffs
National Union of Ships' Clerks, Grain Weighers and Coalmeters
National Union of Vehicle Workers
National Amalgamated Coal Workers' Union
North of England Trimmers' and Teemers' Association
North of Scotland Horse and Motormen's Association
United Vehicle Workers

(28) Labour Research Department, *Monthly Circular*, VI, no. 6 (1 June 1920)

The A. E. U. The A. S. E. and other well-known initials of engineering Unions will now give place to the A. E. U., the Amalgamated Engineering Union, whose rules have been finally adopted by its constituent bodies, and become operative on July 1. The new organisation will have a membership of over 460,000, and will absorb eleven craft Unions. The constitution gives the local district committees wide powers over local conditions. They are empowered to forbid any overtime being worked (subject to special breakdown and similar emergencies) while any member of the particular branch of a trade affected is in receipt of unemployment pay. Shop Stewards are given much fuller official recognition. They are to be made universal, and are to have much wider powers, including powers of workshop negotiation. Shop Committees and Councils of Shop Stewards are also recognised. And there is provision for workshop meetings and for regular consultation between the Stewards and the District Committees. The Stewards are also to appoint one representative to the District Committee for every 10,000 members or part thereof. District Committees elect two representatives to a Divisional Committee, who in turn elect two delegates to a National Committee, which includes also the Executive Council and the organising district delegates. The National Committee, which is to meet at least annually, has power to request the E. C. to call a national conference on any vital question, and will generally act in an advisory capacity to the Executive.

(29) *Labour Year Book* (1924)

The propaganda of the Guild Socialists has so far influenced Labour and Trade Union policy that many organisations have incorporated the demand for 'self-government' or 'workers' control' in their officially declared programme. The Labour Party itself, in 'Labour and the New Social Order' (1918), definitely proclaimed itself as standing for such an ideal. The Independent Labour Party much later revised its aims and programme to fit in with the same principle, and many of the most convinced supporters of the old nationalisation policy came round entirely or partially to the same view. The Miners' Federation dropped their old Nationalisation Bill in 1918, and put forward a new measure which incorporated joint control by miners and other interests.

The Post Office Workers were, however, the first Trade Union to use the term National Guild in their programme. They demand that the service shall ultimately be conducted as a National Guild managed by the workers in conjunction with the State.

The Railway Unions have also formulated a scheme for joint control. None of these proposals has as yet gone beyond the 'paper' stage. The nearest any of them came to realisation was that of the miners, when the Sankey Commission proposed a scheme, not indeed going as far as the one suggested by the Unions, but still a 'joint control' scheme.

While the Guild theories presupposed a complete change in the structure of society and industry, the Building Guild and other projects attempted to set up the distinctive features of workers' control here and now within the capitalist system. The Building Guild was first set up in Manchester in 1920 by the Building Trades Operatives. Others were later set up in various towns, the *modus operandi* being much the same in each case. The governing body was formed of the delegates from the local branches of the Building Trades Unions. The local authority was then approached with the offer to build houses, the Guild supplying the labour and, if necessary, the materials, the cost price only being charged. In the cost price was included an item for maintenance of all the workers at full standard rates for the duration of the work, irrespective of time lost owing to bad weather, etc. This principle of 'continuous pay' is one of the distinctive features of the Guild enterprise, and was hotly attacked by private employers. Arrangements were made with the Co-operative Insurance Society to cover the risk of costs exceeding estimates. The Ministry of Health was the next difficulty, because, although many local authorities were willing to hand work over to the Guilds, contracts had to be approved by the Ministry if Government grants were to be secured. Finally, the Ministry agreed to accept the Guild contract, provided the sum set aside for continuous pay did not exceed £40 per house. Under this form of contract ('basic sum contract') work to the value of nearly £1,500,000 was undertaken in various parts of the country.

In 1921 the numerous Guilds which had sprung up all over the country amalgamated, and became the National Building Guild, Regional Guild Councils being formed to link up local committees in each area. In addition new forms of contract were devised, the 'maximum sum contract' being the most important. In this case a sum is quoted which the cost is guaranteed not to exceed, this sum including a margin towards an insurance fund to cover risks of loss on such contracts. If the cost is below the maximum sum quoted the purchaser is charged a lower sum.

The other form of contract provides that the purchaser shall supply materials and, if desired, the plant, the Guild supplying only the labour. . . .

(30) Maurice B. Reckitt and C. E. Bechhover, *The Meaning of National Guilds* (1920 edn)

The fundamental basis, then, of all Trade Union reorganisation must be the adoption of a principle of structure which will enable Labour to spend its energies – and its funds – in the struggle with Capitalism and not in miserable demarcation squabbles within their own ranks, and which will, further, provide it with a framework whereby it can assume control as opportunity offers and as its own initiative decides. Industrial Unionism provides this principle and opens up these prospects; this is why it is the cardinal issue for Trade Unionists to-day. But though it may offer us the clue for which we are seeking to the maze of the modern Labour movement, there is much more upon which we have to make up our minds before we can feel assured that our plans for the future of that movement are well and truly laid. If the Industrial Unionist principle of structure be accepted, five main problems still lie before those who seek to build the new Trade Unionism: the creation of a central co-ordinating authority, the reproduction of a similar authority in the localities, the establishment of the Union securely upon the essential unit of the workshop, the amalgamation of the competing and overlapping unions, and the assignment to the general labour

Unions of a definite function in relation to the rest of the world of labour. . . .

But little is to be hoped for from the Trades Union Congress till it shakes itself free from the deadweight of officialism and the monstrosity of misrepresentation known as the block-vote. By means of this ridiculous device the whole weight of the Union's voting strength is cast for or against a measure, though opinion upon it within the Union may be almost equally divided. . . .

Nationalisation in itself will do nothing to raise the status of the worker or upset autocratic administration. It is to be hoped and expected that when the nationalisation of any industry is proposed by the State the Trade Unions associated with the industry will press urgently for large instalments of control. . . .

(31) G. D. H. Cole, *Guild Socialism Re-stated* (1920)

The element of identity between the mediaeval Gilds and the National Guilds proposed by the Guild Socialists to-day is thus far more of spirit than of organisation. A National Guild would be an association of all the workers by hand and brain concerned in the carrying on of a particular industry or service, and its function would be actually to carry on that industry or service on behalf of the whole community. Thus, the Railway Guild would include all the workers of every type – from general managers and technicians to porters and engine cleaners required for the conduct of the railways as a public service. This association would be entrusted by the community with the duty and re-sponsibility of administering the railways efficiently for public benefit, and would be left itself to make the internal arrangements for the running of trains and to choose its own officers, administrators, and methods of organisation.

I do not pretend to know or prophesy exactly how many Guilds there would be, or what would be the lines of demarcation between them. For example, railways and road transport might be organised by separate Guilds, or by a single Guild with internal sub-divisions. So might engineering and ship-building, and a host of other closely-related industries. This is a matter, not of principle, but of convenience; for there is no reason why the various Guilds should be of anything like uniform size. The general basis of the proposed Guild organisation is clear enough: it is industrial, and each National Guild will represent a distinct and coherent service or group of services.

It must not, however, be imagined that Guildsmen are advocating a highly centralised system, in which the whole of each industry will be placed under a rigid central control. The degree of centralisation will largely depend on the character of the service. Thus, the railway industry obviously demands a much higher degree of centralisation than the building industry, which serves mainly a local market. But, apart from this, Guildsmen are keen advocates of the greatest possible extension of local initiative and of autonomy for the small group, in which they see the best chance of keeping the whole organisation keen, fresh and adaptable, and of avoiding the tendency to rigidity and conservatism in the

wrong things, so characteristic of a large-scale organisation, and especially trusts
and combines under capitalism to-day. . . .

During 1920, as the cost of living continued to rise, a new militancy began to appear
among some non-manual workers (32,33) and, as the slump developed from the autumn
of 1920 protests grew and there was fear of a general onslaught on wages (34).
   Decontrol of the mines came on 31 March 1921, accompanied by wage cuts. The
miners struck and plans were laid for a sympathetic strike by their associates in the Triple
Alliance (35, 36). When the miners refused to resume negotiation the railwaymen
withdrew their support on 'Black Friday', 15 April 1921.

   (32) Labour Research Department, *Monthly Circular*, vi, no. 2 (1 Feb. 1920)

The adoption of the Burnham Committee Report by the Conference of the
National Union of Teachers has aroused a storm of protests from various sections
among the teachers. The National Federation of Women Teachers has
unanimously rejected the Report on the ground that the minima of £160 for men
and £150 for women are totally inadequate in view of the present cost of living.
They also take exception to different minima being fixed for men and women.
The London Schoolmasters' Association, which recently split off from the
London Teachers' Association, on account of the N. U. T. conference voting in
favour of equal pay, also refuses to endorse the Burnham Report, and has
reserved the right to draw up a salary scale of its own. A still more drastic step has
been taken by teachers in Canterbury, who have tendered strike notices as a
protest against the adoption of the Report locally, which will materially reduce
the salaries in many cases fixed by a scale which came into operation in October
last.

   (33) *The Times* (15 May 1920)

At the Postal Workers' Conference at Morecambe yesterday, the General
Secretary moved that a strike policy be instituted as a permanent plank in the
policy of the union, that a strike fund be created by a contribution of 6d per
member per week, and that arrangements for concerted action be made with
other trade unions which might be implicated.

   An amendment to delete the reference to a strike fund was rejected. Another
amendment providing that in the event of a strike, certain essential services
should be maintained was also rejected, the Secretary urging that they could not
afford to play at striking. The strike policy was afterwards endorsed
unanimously.

   (34) Labour Research Department, *Monthly Circular*, viii, no. 2 (1 Feb. 1921)

Reductions: The employers' campaign to reduce wages has begun to take effect in
a number of cases. South Wales copper workers have agreed to a 5 per cent

reduction in the wages. The Furness Miners' Union has accepted a reduction from 22s 8d a day to 19s 7d. In both instances the employers threatened to close the works. The effect of the sliding scale in Scottish steel works has reduced wages by 15 per cent. The Electrical Trades Union has received an application from the Employers' Association for a reduction of wages by 20 per cent in reply to the Union's claim for a general increase of 3d per hour. Glamorgan Farmers are also demanding a reduction from 50s to 46s. 6d. a week in reply to the workers' claim for an increase of 10s a week. An attempt is also being made by employers to reduce rates fixed by Trade Boards. Bristol employers have cut the rate fixed by the Flax Trade Board from £2 14s to £2 10s. The Midland Railway Company have adopted the method of degrading sections of their staff. They have asked a number of men of 18 to 23 years of age to sign a form stating that they voluntarily accept junior work with junior rates of pay and conditions, owing to adult work not being available. The National Union of Railwaymen has taken the matter up with the company and also with the Minister of Transport. An attack is also being made on the railwaymen's guaranteed week, and is being vigorously resisted by the Union.

(35) *The Times* (12 April 1921)

The following manifesto was issued by the Triple Industrial Alliance last night:–

The miners are locked-out by their employers. The National Union of Railwaymen and the Transport Workers' Federation have decided to yield them all the assistance in their power.

Unless an offer is made to the miners which their colleagues in the Triple Alliance can feel justified in recommending them to accept, a stoppage of Railwaymen and Transport Workers will begin. . . .

The lock-out of the miners is a crisis in the history of the Labour movement. The issues involved in it are of vital importance to every section of the working classes. Organized Labour, as it has repeatedly informed both employers and the Government, will allow no encroachment on the standard of life of the people, and will resist to the uttermost every attack upon the trade union organization by which that standard is defended. The proposals which the mine-owners, with the support of the Government, are seeking to enforce by the weapon of the lock-out are a menace to both.

ATTACK ON A LIVING WAGE. The unprecedented reduction in wages (described by a leading coalition journal as a 'staggering cut') which is demanded by the mine-owners would, by itself, condemn their proposals as provocative in spirit and impossible of acceptance. The Attorney-General, in arguing against the miners' claim for unemployment pay, stated that, if these demands took effect, the money wages of the miners would be 91 per cent above the pre-war standard. Prices are at present 141 per cent above it. . . .

Nor is this all. For generations the Trade Union movement has set the establishment of national wage agreements in the forefront of the programme. The miners, the railwaymen, and the transport workers, after prolonged effort, have secured them. Now the mine-owners have flung the principle on one side, insist that the miners shall be forced back to district agreements, and declare that a worker who hews coal in South Wales or Scotland or Durham shall have his economic status entirely severed from his fellow-worker, a member of the same organization and performing similar work, in Yorkshire, Lancashire, or the Midlands. The miners have secured what all trade unionists have long demanded, that they shall not be entirely deprived of payment when, through no fault of their own, they are unemployed. The owners now insist that that right shall be taken from them.

This arbitrary and unjust action threatens principles which are vital to trade unionism. It is designed to break up the unity of the Miners' Federation. The conditions which it is sought to-day to impose on the miners will, unless resisted, be imposed tomorrow on other classes of workers. The control of railways ends on August 31. The standardization of wages among all grades of railwaymen is in danger. The dockers' minimum of 16s a day, whether in Hull or Liverpool or any other port, and the uniform rates of the seamen, will be insecure if the miners are defeated. In supporting the miners the Triple Alliance is defending the interests both of its own members and of the whole body of organized labour. . . .

(36) NUR Central Strike Committee, Edinburgh District, *Strike Bulletin* (12 April 1921)

THE ISSUE

YOUR FELLOW-WORKER'S FIGHT IS YOUR FIGHT

The Ruling Class have decided that now is the time to reduce the Working Class to conditions worse than pre-war. They have attacked the Miners first – believing that the Miners hold the weakest sector of the working-class front. If they break the line they will easily defeat the rest of the Workers. Therefore, we railwaymen stand shoulder to shoulder with the Miners, exclaiming with one voice – 'If they go down we go down' . . . .

THE STRUGGLE. It is with feelings of relief that railwaymen to-day line-up with their fellow workers the miners.

For two reasons we have thrown ourselves into the fray. Primarily we recognise that the defeat of the miners now means sure and certain defeat for ourselves in August, when the railways are to be decontrolled. Secondly, we recognise that the lock-out of the miners is but the ringing-up of the curtain on the first act of a bitter drama – call it what you will – but a drama in which the whole forces of Capital are linked together in a desperate effort – let us hope a dying effort – to reduce the workers to a state of industrial slavery worse than was our lot in pre-war days, intolerable though our conditions were then.

All good dramas are preceded by an overture which sketches more or less the idea and development of the piece. The 'show' we are about to take part in is no exception. About the beginning of 1919 the Chairman of the F. B. I. stated that after two years of intense production to make good depleted stocks there would be a readjustment of prices and wages. That was the first note, and ever since, our Masters' Voice – the Press of the country – has been running up and down the scales, improvising on the general theme, 'Wages must come down', or 'production must be increased'. Here and there, notably by the lock-out of the ship-joiners, we could discern the germ of future action. Press, pulpit, platform, theatre and cinema – every agency of Capital – has worked hard to swell the strain, and incidentally to prepare a mental state in the worker which would render him readily receptive of the 'readjustment' in 'remuneration' – as the professors of alleged economics call it.

To-day we railwaymen have ceased work in order that we may line up with our fellow workers the miners, who have been brutally locked-out by the mine-owning section of the ruling-class.

9. *The Years of Crises*

As the 1920s progressed there was an increasing sense of confrontation between the two sides of industry, with both employers and workers united in 'giant' organisations (1, 2, 3, 4, 5). The TUC was reformed with the creation of the General Council (6) and there was a call for streamlining the movement (7), though sectional differences could still appear, as they did when ASLEF rejected an agreement worked out with the new railway managements in 1924 (8, 9).

(1) Labour Research Department, *The Workers' Register of Labour and Capital* (1923)

The Mining Association of Great Britain, which was among the earliest of employers' organisations, was founded in 1854, and is now a federation of twenty-four district associations. These include 700 undertakings, which are responsible for 95 per cent of the total coal output of the country.

The Engineering and National Employers' Federation, formed in 1896, now includes over 2,500 firms, whose combined capital was estimated in June, 1922, at £500,000,000.

The Shipbuilding Employers' Federation, with its membership of thirteen Associations, holds a similar position in the shipbuilding industry.

The National Federation of Building Trades Employers, which in 1913 included nine district associations, now covers nine districts and about 250 local associations.

The Federation of Master Cotton-Spinners includes a large number of district associations, representing the great majority of firms in the spinning branch of the trade. The Cotton-Spinners and Manufacturers' Association covers weaving. The British Wool Federation and the Woollen and Worsted Trades Federation represent employers in the wool trade; and the Allied Trades Association represents bleaching, dyeing, etc. The chief employers' organisations in the clothing trades are the Wholesale Clothing Manufacturers' Federation, the Master Tailors' Federation, and the Federated Associations of Boot and Shoe Manufacturers.

Newspaper owners are organised in two main bodies; the Newspaper Proprietors' Association, representing London employers, and the Newspaper

Society, in which all the important groups of provincial newspaper owners are now combined.

Employers in chemical trades are mainly in the Chemical Employers' Federation, and food industries are still in the position of being represented on the employers' side through a number of separate organisations in the various wholesale and manufacturing sections of the trade.

In the iron and steel trade the chief association is the National Federation of Iron and Steel Manufacturers, which claims to represent from 80 to 90 per cent of the trade; printers (other than newspaper printers) are organised in the Federation of Master Printers and Allied Trades; manufacturers of gas in the recently formed Federation of Gas Employers; and farmers in the National Farmers' Union, which grew considerably in strength during the war, and is a political association of some importance, though it adopts the attitude of 'no relations with Labour' nationally.

(2) Ibid.

The creation of the Federation of British Industries marked a new stage in capitalist organisation. It was not enough that employers should have powerful associations within each separate industry. It became evident that a federation covering the more powerful firms in all the leading industries would have a stronger influence in directing legislation and controlling the general economic policy of the country than could possibly be secured by employers in any single industry. Thus, in 1916, mainly through the initiative of the engineering employers, there came into being this vast Federation, which in 1920 claimed that it represented a combined capital of £4,000,000,000. The history of the F. B. I., with its kindred associations, is in itself the most significant record of the consolidation of British capitalist interests since the war. The Federation combines all the functions of separate employers' organisations on a national scale. Its objects include:

1. 'The promotion and encouragement of free and unrestricted communication and discussion between masters and workmen with a view to the establishment of amicable arrangements . . . and the avoidance and settlement of industrial warfare' (Rule 3(ii)).
2. 'The encouragement, promotion and protection of the interests of manufacturers of all kinds of goods and commodities and the organisation of industries of all kinds' (Rule 3 (iii)).
3. 'The promotion of improvements in the law' (Rule 3 (c)).

The Federation now consists of 167 associations and 1,739 firms, divided into twenty-two industrial groups, which cover all the important industries of the country . . . .

Through its parliamentary organisation the Federation took action on a large number of proposed measures, and the F. B. I. *Bulletin* contains a proud record of its successes. The Safeguarding of Industries Bill, introduced in 1921, was largely a result of the persistent campaign for the revival of import restrictions after the war which was carried on by the Federation; and the announcement that Excess Profits' Duty was to be abolished was reported under the heading, 'F. B. I. Victory against E. P. D.', as a result of the Federation's policy . . . .

(3) FBI, *Bulletin* (29 Nov. 1921): Presidential Address by Sir Peter Rylands

It cannot be denied that by far the greatest element in cost of production is the wage cost, since we must include in this not only the direct wage cost, but the wages involved in the production of fuel, power, materials and machinery, and in transport. We must, therefore, face the fact that to secure a substantial reduction in prices we must effect a substantial reduction in wage costs. This can be done in two ways: either by reducing the rates of wages or by the work-people giving a greater output for the wages which they receive. . . . If price reductions are to be made without impairing the standard of living, the workers must be prepared to give a higher output per head and even, where efficiency may make it desirable, to extend the existing working hours. This in itself would in many trades have a very considerable effect in reducing production costs, but it may be necessary to go further, and for the workers to be prepared to accept a money wage which may, until business revives, give them a lower standard of living than that which prevailed before the trade depression set in, or even than their pre-war standard.

(4) FBI, *Year Book and Register of British Manufactures* (1924)

The Federation of British Industries provides an epitome of the activities of the British Manufacturer and of a wide range of his products. Every important Manufacture in the United Kingdom is represented by firms holding direct membership. In addition, the Federation is truly National by reason of its Banking, Shipping and Insurance Members, as well as by affiliation with Trade Associations, whose individual membership embraces other thousands of producers and traders.

The course of recent events has fully proved the necessity for a National Federation to co-ordinate the efforts of every trade, exerted through its own Trade Association, in order that British Industry might speak and act in a manner commensurate with its real importance. . . .

The principal aims and objects of the Federation may be summarised as follows:–

To encourage and develop British Manufactures and to safeguard the interests of British Producers both at Home and Abroad.

To centralize and facilitate the interchange of views between Manufacturers and Government Departments, Public Bodies, Institutions and Associations in all matters affecting Industry, directly or indirectly.

To protect Industry as a whole from legislation which may affect it adversely and to promote improvements in administration.

To provide a central medium of information, advice and assistance, available for the use of its Members. . . .

In the seven years of its existence the Federation has succeeded in becoming almost completely representative of the industries of the country. It has enrolled as its members some 170 Trade Associations and 2,000 individual firms. Taking both classes of membership, it is in touch, directly or indirectly, with at least 20,000 manufacturing firms covering every industry in the country, with a capital of nearly £6,000,000,000 and giving employment to over 5,000,000 workers.

(5) TGWU, *Rules* (1923 edn): Rule 21 – Objects

1. – The principal objects of the Union are the regulation of the relations between workmen and employers, and between workmen and workmen, and also the provision of benefits for members.

2. – The objects of the Union shall further include –

(a) The organisation of all members and other persons qualified for membership, being employees in port, harbour, dock, warehouse, waterside, waterway, road, aerial, and other transport services, and such other workers as may be deemed eligible by the General Executive Council of the Union, and the obtaining and maintaining of just and proper hours, rates of wages, and to endeavour by all means in their power to control the industries in which the members are engaged.

(b) The settling and negotiating of differences and disputes between the members of the Union and employers, and other trade unions and persons, by collective bargaining or agreement, withdrawal of labour, or otherwise.

(c) Generally, the power to promote the welfare of the members of the Union in such manner as the General Executive Council from time to time shall deem expedient.

(d) The provision of benefits to members as follows:–

(i) Assistance to members, or particular classes of members, (1) when out of work or in distressed circumstances; (2) in cases of sickness, accident, and disablement; (3) in old age; (4) in trade disputes; (5) for funeral expenses; and such other forms of assistance as may from time to time be decided by the Union, or the General Executive Council.

(ii) Legal advice and legal assistance to the Union or its members where, in the opinion of the General Executive Council, it is necessary or expedient.

(iii) Grants and endowments, including scholarships, to members and to the colleges and institutions having among their objects the education of trade unionists.

(e) The furtherance of political objects of any kind.

(f) The transaction of insurance business, including insurance under the National Health Insurance and the Unemployment Insurance Acts.

(g) The extension of co-operative production and distribution.

(h) The establishment or carrying on, or participation, financial or otherwise, directly or indirectly, in, the business of printing or publishing of a general newspaper or newspapers, or of books, pamphlets, or publications, or of any other kind of undertaking, industrial or otherwise, in the interests of and with the main purpose of furthering the interests of the Union or of trade unionism generally, together with such subsidiary action and purposes as may be calculated to enhance the prosperity of the publications or the business generally, after submission to Delegate Conference or ballot of members.

(i) The furtherance of, or participation, financial or otherwise, directly or indirectly, in, the work or purpose of any association or federal body having for its objects the furthering of the interests of labour, trade unionism, or trade unionists, including the securing of a real measure of control in industry, and participation by the workers in the management, in the interests of labour and the general community.

(j) The furthering of any other action or purpose, or the participation, financial or otherwise, directly or indirectly, in any other purpose, so far as may be lawful, which is calculated, in the opinion of the Union or the General Executive Council, to further the interests of labour, trade unionism, or trade unionists.

(k) The provision of opportunities for social intercourse and promotion of sport and social events among the members.

(6) *Trade Unionism in Action. The General Council of the T. U. C.: Its Powers, Functions and Work* (1925)

The powers, functions and work of the General Council are, of course, far wider in their range than those of the old Parliamentary Committee which it has superseded. The steps by which the Parliamentary Committee developed its authority until the time came for the General Council to inherit that authority and to carry it still further, brought the Congress to a realisation of the fact that they were no longer members of a voluntary association merely, but units of a closely knit and strongly centralised organisation. Congress has itself assumed a more permanent form, in the sense that it continues to function from day to day through the General Council, which has ceased to be merely an administrative body carrying out a general policy framed by Congress; the General Council is now an actively functioning organ dealing systematically with the problems of Trade Unionism as they arise, and taking action upon its own initiative in regard to a wide range of questions with which Congress may not have been previously concerned, or in relation to which Congress has only laid down guiding principles for the General Council to observe.

There is thus a vital difference both of function and method between the old

Parliamentary Committee and the General Council. This difference is reflected in the composition of the two bodies. The old Parliamentary Committee was an undifferentiated general body, elected by ballot of Congress on the principle of the single transferable vote, and the only concession made to Unions in the matter of representation was the provision that societies with more than 500,000 members would be entitled to an additional representative, if elected by Congress, the Parliamentary Committee being increased in number accordingly. The General Council, on the other hand, is much more exactly representative of the balance of forces in Congress. This result followed the demand that arose after the railway stoppage of 1919 for a central co-ordinating body which would be fully representative of the Trade Union Movement, and be capable of dealing with the growing number of problems involving questions of policy and organisation which require a specialised knowledge to understand.

RISE OF THE GENERAL COUNCIL. The organic changes that took effect in the establishment of the General Council at the Cardiff Congress in 1921 arose out of the belief then current that the time had come to attempt to realise the idea of a Labour 'General Staff', equipped for the preparation of general plans, able to eliminate overlapping of Unions, and so organised as to establish and develop the closest possible relations with the different groups of industrial organisations operating in the various trades and industries of the country. These ideas took shape at the special Trades Union Congress held in December, 1919, at which the Trades Union Co-ordination Committee that had been considering the matter presented its conclusions in the form of a series of recommendations. These recommendations, so far as they affected the position and composition of the old Parliamentary Committee, raised two points: (1) an increase in the number of its members, and (2) a division of its members into sub-committees or groups corresponding to the accepted classification of the several industries and trades. For the first three decades of its history the old Parliamentary Committee's membership did not exceed twelve, with its secretary as an additional member. From 1906 down to the date when these changes took effect (1921) the membership of the Committee remained stationary at sixteen, with its secretary as ex-officio member, notwithstanding the fact that the affiliated membership of Congress rose from about $1\frac{1}{2}$ millions to over $2\frac{1}{4}$ millions within that period. There was general consent that the huge expansion of Trade Unionism justified an enlargement of its central co-ordinating authority. It was also recognised that reorganisation of the Committee on the principle of grouped trades must lead to an increase in the number of its members.

(7) TUC, *Trade Union Structure and Closer Unity. Interim Report* (1944): Resolution at Congress of 1924 in Hull

This Congress declares:–

(a) That the time has arrived when the number of Trade Unions should be

reduced to an absolute minimum.
(b) That the aim should be as far as possible organisation by industry, with every worker a member of the appropriate organisation.
(c) That it is essential that a united front be formed for improving the standard of life of the workers.
(d) And accordingly instructs the General Council to draw up –

(1) a scheme for organisation by industry, and
(2) a scheme which may secure unity of action, without the definite merging of existing Unions, by scientific linking up of same to present a united front.

(8) *Daily Herald* (19 Jan. 1924): 'Threatened Railway Strike. The Companies' Case'

The Railway Companies consider it desirable in the public interest to state briefly their position with reference to the present trouble with the Associated Society of Locomotive Engineers and Firemen.

In November last the National Wages Board were called upon to consider an application from the Railway Companies for a reduction of wages. The claim put in by the Railway Companies represented a reduction in their Wages Bill of £4,000,000 per annum. In December, the National Wages Board issued its decision, conceding reductions approximating to £500,000 per annum, to be brought into force as from the third full pay-week in January.

The National Wages Board includes representatives of the Railway Companies and of the Railway Trade Unions, together with outside representatives of employers, of the Trades Union Congress, and of the Co-operative Union, under the Chairmanship of Sir Wm. Mackenzie, President of the Industrial Court. The case was exhaustively considered, and the decision was signed by all members of the Board.

Decisions of the Board are not obligatory, but it is evident that if all parties signatory thereto are not prepared to carry them out, the whole machinery of negotiation, established under the Railways Act of 1921 at the joint instance of the men and the Companies, becomes unworkable. The Railway Companies had stated from the outset that they were prepared to abide by the decision, whatever it might be. The National Union of Railwaymen and the Railway Clerks' Association have accepted the decision. The Associated Society of Locomotive Engineers and Firemen refuse to accept it, although their representatives on the National Wages Board were signatories to it.

In these circumstances the Railway Companies have no alternative but to apply the decision from the date fixed. Any other course would be tantamount to an abandonment of the principle of settlement by the approved machinery, and would be fatal to the prospects of collective bargaining in the future. The Railway Companies have reason to believe that this view is strongly held by the Unions who have accepted the decision.

It has been alleged that the acceptance of the decision will lead to extensive degrading and dismissal of staff. There is nothing in the decision which in any way warrants this statement, and the suggestion is wholly without foundation.

It has further been stated that heavy reductions of wages will be involved in the case of Drivers at present working on what is known as the mileage basis, and that large numbers of these men will have their wages reduced by as much as 29s. 6d. a week. Such statements are misleading.

Out of 36,000 Drivers, only 2,400 receive payment on the mileage basis, and the average reduction of wages in the case of these men is 4s. 5d. a week. Only 48 Drivers will suffer the maximum reduction of 22s. 6d. a week, and the total earnings of these men will average £6. 12s. 5d. a week even after the reduction has taken effect.

It is always possible that the application of a decision affecting large numbers of men may involve cases of individual hardship. It is well-known to all railwaymen that the Companies are at all times prepared to look into such hard cases, and that machinery exists for bringing them before the management and getting them dealt with. The acceptance of the decision of the National Wages Board by the Associated Society of Locomotive Engineers and Firemen will not in any way prejudice the right of the men to bring forward any instances of hardship which they desire the Companies to consider.

(9) ASLEF, *Locomotive Journal* (Feb, 1924): 'Railway Strike of Locomotivemen'

9, Arkwright Road, Hampstead, N. W. 3
January 14th, 1924.

Fellow Members, – The official date and hour for the cessation of work by all members of the ASSOCIATED SOCIETY OF LOCOMOTIVE ENGINEMEN AND FIREMEN has been sent to all Branch Secretaries. Please make yourself acquainted with it so that the stoppage of work may be simultaneous throughout the country.

REMEMBER that if the suggestions of the National Wages Board are put into operation the Locomotivemen only will lose:–

1. Firemen on mileage trains, from 9s. to 18s. per week immediately.
   Drivers on mileage trains, from 11s. 3d. to 22s. 6d. per week immediately.
   NOTE. – This will also cause hundreds of men now engaged on disposal of mileage engines to become redundant, and their consequent reduction in grade and wages. Cleaners will be replaced by reduced firemen, and forced into unemployment, and the promotion of all will be stagnated.
2. Drivers who have not yet received their maximum, and who are not regularly employed on train working, will lose their advance to the maximum, 6s. per week on the bare week, without counting overtime or night duty.
3. Drivers and Firemen will lose their Guaranteed Day for Sunday Duty, and

only be sure of four hours' pay for a Sunday turn of duty, whilst the hours of a Sunday turn of duty after midnight will not be paid for at Sunday rate.

4. Cleaners will only have a guarantee of two hours for a Sunday turn of duty.

Out of nearly 700,000 railwaymen, the locomotivemen only will lose wages and conditions of service, others being only affected by the loss of Sunday Guaranteed Day.

Locomotivemen will – (1) Lose wages heavily.
                    (2) Suffer classification.
                    (3) Suffer reduction, redundancy and Dismissal.
                    (4) All Firemen will in future not be paid the quarter of an hour per day which they have so far received for booking off.

Despite the set-back of 'Black Friday', which, together with the trade depression, brought a lull in industrial unrest, militancy was kept alive by many former members of the shop-stewards' movement who found their way into the Communist Red International of Labour Unions (10, 11), which developed into the National Minority Movement seeking to offer an alternative to the existing moderate leadership of unions. Supporters of the movement in Fife formed a separate mineworkers' union (12).

Meanwhile, there was continuing Government intervention on behalf of the less well paid and less well organised (13, 14).

(10) **Harry Pollitt,** *Serving My Time* (1940): 'Manifesto of the Provisional International Council of Trade and Industrial Unions to the Organised Workers of Great Britain' (1921)

The World is now divided into two great divisions, and

WE MUST MAKE OUR CHOICE

as to which camp we belong to. On the one side is the capitalist class with its League of Nations, its Supreme Council, its remnants of the Second International, its 'yellow' Amsterdam International, its Léghiens and Jouhaux, its Hendersons and Braces and Thomases, its Gompers and Barnes – traitors all to the working class by their preaching of 'class peace'! On the other side is the Communist International and all that is loyal and true to the working class. Supported by millions of organised workers, it is led by comrades who realise the tremendous task history is thrusting upon the workers, who dare to tell the workers what they must fight for and who are unafraid to be with them in the struggle. To this side must come every man and woman who hates hypocrisy and cowardice. To this side we must rally our labour unions. There is no alternative for the workers who mean to win through to victory over capitalism.

(11) Ibid.: Document issued by the London Committee of the Red International of Labour Unions, 1922

It is the duty of every active worker of the R. I. L. U. to participate in every action and question concerning the trade unions. It is not enough to call for the revolution; we must relegate our principles and experiences to the every-day struggles of the trade unionist. The unions are experiencing a testing time that gives better opportunities for propaganda than we have ever had. These opportunities must be made use of . . . .

In your speeches, show how the employers, by the use of the Press and speeches, are preparing the ground for the introduction of a campaign to lengthen the working hours per week. Already, the railwaymen, textile workers and building trade workers are threatened. Lord Weir is conducting a campaign amongst the engineering and shipbuilding employers in support of a fifty-three-hour working week. There must be united resistance to this. Here also, the employed are sure of the support of the unemployed.

If the unions fail to act, then we must popularise the idea of getting our members to work the existing hours and then leave the factory. Remember, this tactic only wants a start and it would immediately catch on. *The unions would either have to support it or once again prove their inability to defend the conditions we have already got.*

TRADES COUNCILS. The London Committee urge that more attention should be given to the trades councils that now exist in every locality. . . . Every branch that is represented on a trades council should see that its delegate is a revolutionary who realises the potentialities of the council. Remember the part these councils would have had to play when the National Council of Action was formed or if the Triple Alliance Strike had materialised, and it is easy to see that in the very near future the trades councils will play an ever-increasing role in the class war. Therefore our slogan must be:

'Capture the trades councils!'

(12) *Manifesto to the Mineworkers of Fife, Kinross and Clackmannan* (March 1925)

The coalowners are again endeavouring to reduce our standard of living. They say that unless wages are reduced, or hours of labour increased the coal industry will perish owing to the keenness of foreign competition and of home restrictions. . . .

Since the termination of the lockout in 1921 to May, 1924, the beginning of the present agreement, the Scottish coalowners have secured an actual trading profit of nearly 8 million pounds (£7,712,473).

The coalowners' scribes, through their newspapers, tell us that they have been losing heavily since May, 1924, but the actual trading loss is only £260,531, and only amounts to 2½d. per ton.

If the employers had sold the coal at 3d. more per ton there would have been no loss. . . .

The more subservient we are, the worse our conditions become, the coalowners have no mercy, they only respect us when they fear us, and we cannot for a single moment forego our right to live as men should live.

Resist all attempts to reduce wages. The managers are taking advantage of our apparent weakness and are cutting rates and reducing wages almost everywhere, but their unscrupulous tactics can be overcome if we have only faith in ourselves, and in our fellow men.

One section successfully attacked one day by the manager leads to another being attacked; their policy is to divide us and thus conquer us all in turn.

An attack on one section is an attack on all, all the men therefore should fight on behalf of those attacked. Never accept a reduction without a vigorous protest being made. Interview the manager, let your deputation be 200 strong and the morning is the best time for the interview.

If unemployed join the nearest unemployment organisation and thus keep yourself in touch with kindred spirits.

Don't hesitate in applying for relief from the Parish Council and see to it that your children are properly fed and clad by the Education Authorities. . . .

By all means don't lose heart. The dawn may be breaking and we may march out of all this destitution and distress into a happier and brighter world, much sooner than we expect.

Desperate men, if determined, can prevent disaster and achieve success where more optimistic men would fail.

Get ready. Keep ready, resist and fight, and to the brave all things are possible.

> Signed on behalf of the Sub-Executive of the
> Mineworkers' Reform Union of Fife, Kinross,
> and Clackmannan
>
> PHILIP HODGE

(13) F. E. Gannett and B. F. Catherwood, *Industrial and Labour Relations in Great Britain* (1939): Extract from the evidence of Mr. W. E. Counsell (Trade Board Inspector in Charge of Special Enquiries) given to the Committee appointed to enquire into the working and effects of the Trade Boards Act (the Cave Committee) in Feb. 1922

Many employers frankly welcome the fixing and enforcing of minimum rates because they provide a basis for equitable competition by materially reducing, if not eliminating, that element of the trade which previously 'cut' market prices by 'trimming' the wages of its workers.

That the enforcement of these minimum rates has resulted in most employers acquiring a greater knowledge of the details of their business is beyond question, and may properly be attributed to one or more of the following factors:–

(a) Realisation of the possibilities of increasing industrial efficiency by improved methods of working, thus maintaining rates of wages while reducing costs of production.

(b) Sympathy with the Acts and anxiety to carry out their provisions.
(c) Knowledge that non-compliance might incur liability for proceedings.

While it is true to say that each advance in the minimum rates causes a large number of employers to look around with a view to improving the organisation and equipment of their establishments, it is equally true that it has been a constant source of surprise to officers in the past to find how high a proportion of businesses are run on a 'rule of thumb' principle. It is in respect of this class of case that the greatest difficulty is experienced in enforcing the rates laid down. If, for example, inspection in such an establishment discloses piece rates yielding, say, 20 per cent below the minimum, the employer, when informed of the deficiency would probably declare:–

(a) that his rates were as high or higher than those paid by his competitors on the class of work in question, and that the low output of his workers was due entirely to slacking on their part, and
(b) that to be compelled to increase his rates would result in closing down his business.

In such a case it would be the duty of the officer to explain –

(a) that piece rates must be valued according to the conditions existing in each establishment, and
(b) that it is not always necessary to increase rates in order to increase their value, i.e., that workers' earnings depend almost as much on factory organisation and equipment as upon the rates themselves.

It not infrequently happens, however, in cases where the employer appears to lack the initiative or ability to determine for himself the defects in his factory organisation that it is possible for the officer to do this for him.

(14) *Industrial Relations Handbook* (1944): Agricultural Wages (Regulation) Act, 1924 14 and 15 Geo. V, c. 37

Under the 1924 Act the Minister of Agriculture and Fisheries was required to set up in each county or group of counties an Agricultural Wages Committee consisting of representatives in equal numbers of employers and workers, together with two impartial members appointed by the Minister and a Chairman selected by the Committee. Such Committee was required to fix minimum rates of wages in the area, which as far as practicable must be such that an able-bodied man's earnings will be 'adequate to promote efficiency and to enable a man in an ordinary case to maintain himself and his family in accordance with such standard of comfort as may be reasonable in relation to the nature of his occupation'.

In 1925, with exports falling and the employers demanding wage reductions, relations in the colliery districts became increasingly bitter (15), though there was well established negotiating machinery (16). The Government and the TUC were inevitably involved (17, 18), though, as usual, the true facts of the industry's situation were both obscure and controversial (19).

Matters reached their climax with the General Strike of May 1926. Negotiations between the General Council and the Government broke down when NATSOPA members refused to print a *Daily Mail* article headed 'For King and Country' (20), but duplicated or brief newspapers – including Winston Churchill's official *British Gazette* and the TUC's *British Worker* reported events (21–32).

The General Council of the TUC with Arthur Pugh (1870–1955) as chairman and Walter Citrine (b. 1887) as acting general secretary directed operations (33) and on 12 May decided to call off the strike (34). The miners were left to continue their fight on their own and considerable bitterness remained (35).

(15) Mining Association, *The Mines for the Miners! What Nationalization Really Means* (1925)

Those who demand nationalization of the mines do not want it for the good of the nation.

What they want is to create a gigantic coal trust which would be controlled by the Miners' Federation and run solely in the interests of the miners.

Remember Mr. Smillie's appeal to the miners:–

'Organize, and the Industry will be yours.'

In order to obtain this control they introduced a Nationalization Bill into Parliament in May last.

Under this Bill the industry was to be controlled by a Mining Council on which the miners would have a predominating influence. This Council would have the power

To fix wages
To fix hours
To fix output
To fix prices
And Fleece the Public

All profits, if there were any, which is very doubtful, would go to the miners.
All Losses were to be made up by the Public

Nationalization of mines has been tried in other countries, but the Socialists do not mention it. Why?

Because it has been a gross and utter failure.

Germany tried it on a large scale. Russia has tried it, and Australia has tried it. What has been the result?

Germany has handed back her state mines to private enterprise. In Russia, where women have to be employed, the mines are in a state of chaos with reduced output and starvation wages. Australia and New Zealand have handed back most of the State mines to private enterprise. Of those that are left only two show a small profit. The others are run at a loss, which the taxpayer has to make up.

They have all failed for the same reasons.

> Output has decreased.
> Prices have gone up.
> Quality has declined.
> The men strike on the slightest pretext.

Slackness, indifference, wastefulness and general inefficiency are always the result of nationalization.

Before the war the British coal industry was the most efficient and flourishing in the world.

The constant inteference of politicians, the continued agitation and unrest produced among the men for political objects threaten to wreck it.

If the mines are nationalized other industries will follow. 'We are only beginning with the mines', says Mr. Smillie.

If that happens we shall witness the decline and fall of British industry, which has been built up on private enterprise.

Slow starvation, universal unemployment, and national decay would inevitably follow.

(16) Committee on Industry and Trade, *Survey of Industrial Relations* (1926): Negotiating machinery in coal-mining

Each District Association within the Federation has complete local autonomy in administrative and financial matters, and is free to act independently in regard to local strikes, and in making representations to Government Departments. But during the war the Federation was recognised by the Government as the spokesman of the miners throughout the country, and all necessary negotiations were conducted with it. In the same way the Federation has acted for the miners as a whole in making its demands (leading to the Sankey Commission) in 1919, and in negotiating with the colliery owners in 1921 and 1924.

The Federation represents approximately 1,000,000 men (over five-sixths of the whole number of colliery employees); and it puts forward candidates for Parliament in a number of constituencies, forty-one of whom were elected at the last general election.

The organisation of the employers is at present on the same lines as that of the miners, but differs in its origin in that the central body was formed first (1854), the District Associations not being definitely established till 20 years or more later, though informal associations of employers had existed at earlier dates for the purpose of negotiating with the workers. Originally, the Mining Association was open to individual owners as well as to organised District Associations, but since 1920 membership has been restricted to the latter. The original purpose of the Association was mainly to consider and take action on proposed legislation. Questions of wages and conditions of employment, except in so far as they formed the subject of legislative proposals, did not come within the purview of the Association, and the relations between employers and employed in each of the coalfields was dealt with by joint bodies or committees, consisting of representatives of the District organisations concerned. During the war, however, the Mining Association undertook the duty of acting as the central body for the owners in all questions of a national character, including questions of wages, and this is now its principal function. The present membership of the Association represents approximately 94 per cent of the total output of the country.

The machinery for negotiation and for dealing with disputes varies with the nature of the matter requiring settlement. Questions affecting an individual colliery are dealt with between the men or their representatives and the colliery management. There are no hard and fast rules of procedure common to all mines and all districts, but generally speaking, the men have always some recognised means of access to the management, e.g. through their local representative with a deputation. If no settlement results, the miners' agent for the district will usually be called in, and if agreement is still impossible, the general practice is that the dispute can be referred by either side to the District Conciliation Board. Conciliation Board agreements vary to some extent from district to district both in the precision of their terms and in the rules laid down. It can, however, be said that in all cases there is at least a moral obligation, in default of mutual agreement, on the one hand not to strike and on the other hand not to alter conditions of employment (apart from the matters of management), without seeking the intervention of the District Conciliation Board. These Boards consist of equal numbers of owners' and workmen's representatives. They usually appoint a small special Committee to investigate disputes and report. If settlement is not secured in this way, the matter in dispute is in some districts referable to an independent chairman; in other districts it is not. These conciliation agreements are influential in practically all districts, with the exception of Durham and perhaps Scotland (particularly Lanarkshire).

Disputes under the Minimum Wage Act are referable to a Statutory District body called the Joint District Minimum Wages Board, having an independent chairman appointed by the Board itself, or in default of agreement by the Board of Trade.

(17) *Daily Herald* (31 July 1925)

The Prime Minister met the mineowners and the miners separately again yesterday morning. He handed a statement to the miners summarising the position as he saw it.

No progress was made, and the parties left the Ministry of Labour with no arrangement to return.

Mr. Baldwin had failed to get a suspension of the lock-out notices. He had failed to get a withdrawal of the owners' terms.

And he had failed to understand the miners' position.

WHY PREMIER FAILED. Why he had failed to do so was revealed in an illuminating passage at yesterday morning's talk with the miners.

His written statement urged the miners to make a contribution 'towards meeting the difficult situation with which the industry is confronted'. This conversation ensued:–

Miners: But what you propose means a reduction of wages.
Prime Minister: Yes. All the workers of this country have got to face a reduction of wages.
Miners: Who do you mean?
Prime Minister: I mean all the workers of this country have got to take reductions in wages to help get industry on its feet.

In a flash this Premier, whose name is associated with one of the big coal and steel companies of Great Britain, thus revealed himself and threw down a challenge to the whole Labour Movement.

(18) *Daily Herald* (31 July 1925): Declaration of the Special Industrial Committee of the TUC

Never in the history of the modern working-class movement has the imagination of the workers been more roused and their resistance more stiffened than by the impending attack upon working-class standards threatened in several of the principal industries of this country to-day.

It is generally felt that if the miners are defeated in the present struggle, successive attacks will be launched in other industries. The textile industry is now in the throes of such a struggle.

The Committee is thoroughly satisfied that there can be no doubt of the moral support of the whole movement being undividedly behind the miners.

(19) RC on the Coal Industry, *Report*, Cmd 2600 (1925), 1: 'Cost and Proceeds' (shillings, quarter ended Dec. 1925)

	Wage costs	Other costs	Total cost	Proceeds without subvention	Actual profit or loss (4)-(3)	10% of wages cost as in Col. (1)	Profit or loss with wages reduced 10%
	(1)	(2)	(3)	(4)	(5)	(6)	(7)
			Per ton commercially disposable				
Scotland	11·60	4·64	16·24	14·40	−1·84	1·16	−0·68
Northumberland	10·98	4·99	15·97	12·98	−2·99	1·10	−1·89
Durham	11·54	5·56	17·10	14·16	−2·94	1·15	−1·79
South Wales and Monmouth	14·43	6·28	20·71	17·51	−3·20	1·44	−1·76
South Yorkshire	11·58	4·08	15·66	15·32	−0·34	1·16	+0·82
West Yorkshire	12·33	4·68	17·01	17·25	+0·24	1·23	+1·47
Notts and Derby	11·51	4·11	15·62	15·60	−0·02	1·15	+1·13
Leicester, Cannock Chase and Warwick	11·72	4·27	15·99	17·11	+1·12	1·17	+2·29
Eastern Division	*11·65*	*4·11*	*15·76*	*15·97*	*+0·21*	*1·17*	*+1·38*
Lancashire, Cheshire and North Staffs	14·99	5·36	20·35	19·41	−0·94	1·50	+0·56
Other districts	13·86	5·31	19·17	16·72	−2·45	1·39	−1·06
Great Britain	12·48	4·97	17·45	15·98	−1·47	1·25	−0·22

(20) TUC General Council, *Mining Dispute National Strike Report of the General Council to the Conference of Executives of Affiliated Unions, 25th June 1926:* Exchanges of Letters between General Council of TUC and the Prime Minister, 3 May 1926

(a) His Majesty's Government believe that no solution of the difficulties in the coal industry which is both practicable and honourable to all concerned can be reached except by sincere acceptance of the Report of the Commission. In the expression 'acceptance of the report' is included both the reorganisation of the industry which should be put in hand immediately, and pending the results of the reorganisation being attained such interim adjustment of wages or hours of work as will make it economically possible to carry on the industry meantime. If the miners or the Trade Union Committee on their behalf were prepared to say plainly that they accept this proposal the Government would have been ready to resume the negotiations and to continue the subsidy for a fortnight.

But since the discussions which have taken place between Ministers and members of the Trade Union Committee it has come to the knowledge of the

Government not only that specific instructions have been sent (under the authority of the Executives of the Trade Unions represented at the Conference convened by the General Council of the Trades Union Congress) directing their members in several of the most vital industries and services of the country to carry out a general strike on Tuesday next, but that overt acts have already taken place, including gross interference with the freedom of the Press. Such action involves a challenge tò the constitutional rights and freedom of the nation.

His Majesty's Government, therefore, before it can continue negotiations must require from the Trade Union Committee both the repudiation of the actions referred to that have already taken place, and an immediate and unconditional withdrawal of the instructions for a general strike.

(b) Dear Sir, – Your letter of the 3rd inst. announcing the Government's decision to terminate the discussions which had been resumed on Saturday night was received by the General Council with surprise and regret. The negotiations which have taken place between the Industrial Committee of the General Council and representatives of the Cabinet had been adjourned for a brief period in order to allow the Industrial Committee to confer with the full General Council and representatives of the Miners' Federation who were on your premises, in order to advance the efforts which the Industrial Committee had persistently been making to accomplish a speedy and honourable settlement of the mining dispute.

The Trade Union representatives were astounded to learn that without any warning the renewed conversation which it was hoped might pave the way to the opening up of full and unfettered negotiations had been abruptly terminated by the Government for the reasons stated in your communication. The first reason given is, that specific instructions have been sent under the authority of Trade Unions represented at the Conference convened by the General Council of the Trades Union Congress directing their members in several industries and services to cease work. We are directed to remind you that it is nothing unusual for workmen to cease work in defence of their interests as wage earners, and the specific reason for the decision in this case is to secure for the mineworkers the same right from the employers as is insisted upon by employers from workers – namely, that negotiations shall be conducted free from the atomosphere of strike or lock-out. This is a principle which Governments have held to be cardinal in the conduct of negotiations.

With regard to the second reason, that overt acts had already taken place, including gross interference with the freedom of the Press, it is regretted that no specific information is contained in your letter. The General Council had no knowledge of any such acts having occurred and the decisions taken by it definitely forbid any such independent and unauthorised action. The Council is not aware of the circumstances under which the alleged acts have taken place. It cannot accept any responsibility for them, and in taking prompt measures to prevent any acts of indiscipline, the Council regrets that it was not given an opportunity to investigate and deal with the alleged incidents before the Government made them an excuse for breaking off the peace discussions which were proceeding.

The public will judge the nature of the Government's intentions by its precipitate and calamitous decision in this matter, and will deplore with the General Council that the sincere work which the Council has been engaged in to obtain an honourable settlement has been wrecked by the Government's unprecedented ultimatum.

> Yours faithfully,
> Arthur Pugh (Chairman)
> Walter M. Citrine (Acting Secretary).

(21) *Daily Mail* (4 May 1926)

The miners after weeks of negotiation have declined the proposal made to them and the coal mines of Britain are idle.

The Council of Trades Union Congress, which represents all the other trade unions, has determined to support the miners by going to the extreme of ordering a general strike.

This determination alters the whole position. The coal industry, which might have been reorganised with good will on both sides, seeing that some 'give and take' is plainly needed to restore it to prosperity, has now become the subject of a great political struggle, which the nation has no choice but to face with the utmost coolness and the utmost firmness.

We do not wish to say anything hard about the miners themselves. As to their leaders, all we need say at this moment is that some of them are (and have openly declared themselves) under the influence of people who mean no good to this country.

A general strike is not an industrial dispute. It is a revolutionary movement intended to inflict suffering upon the great mass of innocent persons in the community and thereby to put forcible constraint upon the Government.

It is a movement which can only succeed by destroying the Government and subverting the rights and liberties of the people.

This being the case, it cannot be tolerated by any civilised Government and it must be dealt with by any resource at the disposal of the community.

A state of emergency and national danger has been proclaimed to resist the attack.

We call upon all law-abiding men and women to hold themselves at the service of King and country.

(22) *The Times* (5 May 1926)

A wide response was made yesterday throughout the country to the call of those Unions which had been ordered by the T. U. C. to bring out their members.

Railway workers stopped generally, though at Hull railway clerks are reported to have resumed duty, confining themselves to their ordinary work, and protested against the strike. Commercial road transport was only partially suspended. In London the Tramways and L. G. O. C. [London General Omnibus Company] services were stopped. The printing industry is practically at a standstill, but lithographers have not been withdrawn, and compositors in London have not received instructions to strike. Large numbers of building operatives, other than those working on housing, came out.

The situation in the engineering trades was confused; men in some districts stopped while in others they continued to work. There was no interference with new construction in the ship building yards, but in one or two districts some of the men engaged on repair work joined in the strike with the dockers.

(23) Ibid. (6 May 1926)

A general strike having been proclaimed, and being to some extent in force, the nation are called upon to support the constitutional Government which they themselves placed in power by huge majorities. The duty to obey the call is manifest, and there is already evidence that they will perform it with alacrity and with resolve. They will not patiently suffer any self-constituted authority, however well-organized, to supersede Parliament and to over-ride the will of the people. The pretension to do so is intolerable, as LORD OXFORD declared on Tuesday. No Government worthy of the name can give it the slightest countenance, or dream of abdicating into other hands duties and responsibilities entrusted to them – and to them only – by the Constitution and by the people. The people would have no pardon for such a breach of trust. 'England expects every man will do his duty', and the first duty of every man and of every woman in the country is to stand by their lawful Government.

(24) J. Simon, *Three Speeches on the General Strike* (1926): Speech by Sir John Simon delivered in the House of Commons, 6 May 1926

We speak of the present disaster as a 'general strike', and this general cessation of work is regarded by a great many people in the country as though it were merely a variety – no doubt more serious, widespread and threatening – of the strikes we have usually known. By referring to it as a 'general strike', there has grown in some quarters a belief that this situation is the same in character as previous strikes, though of course on a vastly greater scale. . . . But I wish to address this consideration to the House. When this disturbance is over, and when Parliament resumes its normal functions, it will be very necessary to appreciate that this so-called general strike is not a strike at all. It is something very different. I am not apportioning blame or praise; I am merely pointing out a most important fact. A strike, properly conducted, is perfectly lawful. The right to strike is the right of workmen in combination, by pre-arrangement, to give due notice to their employers to terminate their engagements, and to withhold their labour when these notices have expired. That is what the right to strike is. . . .

What I wish, however, to point out to the House, and if my voice can reach outside, I desire to point out wherever I can, is that the Resolution which was arrived at at the Memorial Hall last week, or, at any rate, the decision of the Council of the Trade Union Executive, to call out everybody, regardless of the contracts which those workmen had made, was not a lawful act at all. Every workman who was bound by a contract to give notice before he left work, and who, in view of that decision, had either chosen of his free will or has felt compelled to come out by leaving his employment without proper notice, has broken the law. . . . Let me point out another serious thing. Every Trade Union leader who has advised and promoted this course of action is liable to damages to the uttermost farthing of his personal possessions. . . . Negotiations must be resumed: who would not wish them to be promoted and to succeed? But, whatever the cause or the excuse, those who have called the general strike have this responsibility – that they have committed hundreds of thousands of decent labouring men to a crusade which must end in failure, and which is in danger of setting back the useful peaceful progress of the working classes of this country, it may be for a generation.

(25) *Daily Mirror* (7 May 1926)

The General Strike has been unaccompanied by any grave disorder. That is excellent. Everybody must keep their tempers under unrelaxing restraint. We deeply sympathise with the countless thousands of workers rendered idle by ukase of their so-called leaders. Mr. Thomas, Mr. McDonald and Mr. Clynes know full well, none better, that the General Strike is a crime against the community. Let these three men be worthy of their citizenship and their leadership by obtaining the cancellation of the strike. It is clearly Mr. McDonald's duty as an Ex-Premier to do this. He rightly holds the strike weapon in contempt. Why let the workers be fooled in the manner they are being fooled?

(26) *Sunday Pictorial* (9 May 1926)

The Archbishop of Canterbury, as representing the Churches, has suggested as a threefold basis, to be simultaneously accepted, for resumption of negotiations:

1. The calling off of the General Strike
2. Withdrawal by the mineowners of their proposed new wages schedule.
3. A Government subsidy to enable mine wages to continue at the April rate pending agreement on re-organisation of the industry.

(27) Fred Maddison (former editor of *Railway Review*, journal of the NUR) in *British Gazette* (10 May 1926)

First of all, they have broken their contracts with the companies by leaving their work without the required notice. What would railwaymen now be saying if they had been discharged without notice? They would have rightly denounced such illegal action and taken steps in the law courts to rectify it. What is wrong in the employers cannot be right in trade unionists. Sanctity of contract is of the essence of civilised society, whether in the national or international spheres, and its violation strikes at the very root of collective bargaining.

Then it seems to me that the Trades Disputes Act never contemplated such a position as has been created by the General Strike. This measure had my steady support in the House of Commons, because the Taff Vale judgement altered, to the prejudice of the unions, the practice of many years. But does anyone think that the Trades Disputes Bill would have passed if the strikes dealt with by it had been of the nature of the present one? Of course it would not, and certainly it would not have had my support.

It was not necessary for railwaymen to break their contracts and join the General Strike in order to help the miners. By doing so they have injured the workers far more than capitalists.

What is the attitude of a man like myself to be? I have a great respect for railwaymen, believe thoroughly in trade unionism, and, in spite of what has happened, I am prepared to defend every legitimate right of organised labour.

But when the unions abandon their fundamental principles, and seek to become dictators to the nation, then this or any other Government can only accept the challenge and defeat at any cost the attempt to usurp the sovereign function of the State. This is democracy; anything else is anarchy.

(28) *British Worker* (10 May 1926)

We are entering upon the second week of the general stoppage in support of the mine workers against the attack upon their standard of life by the coalowners.

Nothing could be more wonderful than the magnificent response of millions.

From every town and city in the country reports are pouring into the Central Council headquarters stating that all ranks are solid, that the working men and women are resolute in their determination to resist the unjust attack upon the mining community.

The General Council desire to express their keen appreciation of the loyalty of the Trade Union members to whom the call was issued and by whom such a splendid response has been made.

They are especially desirous of commending the workers on their strict obedience to the instruction to avoid all conflict and to conduct themselves in an orderly manner. Their behaviour during the first week of the stoppage is a great example to the whole world.

The General Council's message at the opening of the second week is 'Stand firm. Be loyal to instructions and Trust Your Leaders.'

(29) *Daily Express* (11 May 1926)

The Earl of Balfour, in an article in the 'British Gazette', says:–

'Neither in fact, nor, I believe in law, is the course adopted by the Trade Unions a strike in the proper sense of the term. It is an attempted revolution.

'Were it to succeed the community would thenceforth be ruled by a relatively small body of extremists who regard trades unions not as the machinery for collective bargaining but as a political instrument by which the industrial system itself may be utterly destroyed.'

Viscount Grey, broadcasting from 2LO, said:–

'The strike has let loose forces of disorder which are no part of the trade unionism of this country – hooligan forces which trade union leaders themselves in ordinary times would disown. Either the strike is revolutionary or it is not. If it is revolutionary there is nothing for it but to resist to the end with all the power of the community. If it is not revolutionary there is no reason for the strike.'

Cardinal Bourne states: 'There is no justification for a general strike of this character. It is, therefore, a sin against the obedience which we owe to God. All are bound to uphold and assist the Government.'

(30) *British Gazette* (12 May 1926)

The situation throughout the country shows a further improvement.

The distribution of food supplies gives no cause whatever for apprehension. . . .

The situation at the ports is entirely satisfactory. . . .

The distribution of petrol is proceeding more rapidly than at any previous period of the General Strike.

There has been no interruption of the power services, and traffic on the railways is continuously increasing. . . .

Order and quiet reign throughout the whole island, and practically no attempts at sabotage have been brought to the notice of the authorities. . . .

The recruitment of special constables proceeds apace. . . .

As regards the strike position generally, it can be said that the number of individuals returning to work is increasing, and in some cases considerable bodies of strikers have applied for reinstatement. On the other hand, there is as yet little sign of a general collapse of the strike, and the Trade Union Committee is believed to be making efforts to call out certain trades still at work.

It can be, however, definitely stated that there is a growing dissatisfaction among the strikers with the policy of a General Strike, and considerable uneasiness as to its ultimate results.

(31) *Daily Chronicle* (13 May 1926)

Everybody's first thought today must be one of profound satisfaction that the general strike is over. The British people have come with credit out of a severe ordeal. During an unprecedented struggle, extending over nine days, not a cartridge – not even a blank cartridge – has been fired by a soldier, and no single fatal collision has occurred between the strikers and the civil power. There has been no food shortage, no panic, and wonderfully little loss of temper on either side. In a fair trial of strength, which we hope may never be repeated, the nation has stood up to the general strike and overcome it.

Trade unionists, we believe, will agree that the calling of the general strike was a serious blunder. It placed their movement in a false position. . . .

(32) *Daily Graphic* (13 May 1926)

The General Strike has been called off. The community, both by the rightness of its cause and by the strength of its resources, has won a memorable triumph. The cost has been heavy, but the cost is light compared with the completeness with which the nation, against all the forces of illegality, intimidation, and recklessness, has vindicated the principle that there is going to be in this land only one Government, and that Government the Government elected by the people.

The mass of the nation, the women no less than the men, has been splendid. It never doubted that victory would come. Under a bludgeoning, cruel and continuous, it has stood firm as a rock. We salute every man and woman who, by iron endurance and good humour, has made possible the triumph we celebrate today.

What of the future? If in the gruelling days we have passed through one thing more than another has bitten deep into the mind of the nation, it is that never again shall any body of men, whoever they be, have the means or the opportunity to inflict another such outrage on the community.

So far as the General Strike is concerned, the national demand is, 'Never again!' The common people of this land, who have stood the racket, look today to the Government to give effect, immediate and beyond a quibble, to this demand.

(33) *Labour Year Book* (1927): 'Proposals for Co-ordinated Action of Trade Unions'

(It should be understood that memoranda giving detailed instructions will be issued as required)

1. SCOPE

The Trades Union Congress General Council and the Miners' Federation of Great Britain having been unable to obtain a satisfactory settlement of the matters in dispute in the coalmining industry, and the Government and the mineowners having forced a lockout, the General Council, in view of the need for co-ordinated action on the part of affiliated unions in defence of the policy laid down by the General Council of the Trades Union Congress, directs as follows:–

TRADES AND UNDERTAKINGS TO CEASE WORK. Except as hereinafter provided, the following trades and undertakings shall cease work as and when required by the General Council:–

Transport, including all affiliated unions connected with Transport, i.e., railways, sea transport, docks, wharves, harbours, canals, road transport, railway repair shops and contractors for railways, and all unions connected with the maintenance of, or equipment, manufacturing, repairs, and groundsmen employed in connection with air transport.

Printing Trades, including the Press.

Protective Industries. (a) *Iron and Steel*. (b) *Metal and Heavy Chemicals Group*.– Including all metal workers and other workers who are engaged, or may be engaged, in installing alternative plant to take the place of coal.

Building Trade. – All workers engaged on building, except such as are employed definitely on housing and hospital work, together with all workers engaged in the supply of equipment to the building industry, shall cease work.

Electricity and Gas.– The General Council recommend that the Trade Unions connected with the supply of electricity and gas shall co-operate with the object of ceasing to supply power. The Council request that the Executives of the Trade Unions concerned shall meet at once with a view to formulating common policy.

Sanitary Services.– The General Council direct that sanitary services be continued.

Health and Food Services.– The General Council recommend that there should be no interference in regard to these, and that the Trade Unions concerned should do everything in their power to organise the distribution of milk and food to the whole of the population.

With regard to hospitals, clinics, convalescent homes, nursing homes, schools, the General Council direct that affiliated unions take every opportunity to ensure that food, milk, medical and surgical supplies shall be efficiently provided.

(34) TUC General Council, *Mining Dispute National Strike, Report of the General Council to the Conference of Executives of Affiliated Unions, 25 June 1926*

The same evening (Monday, 10th May), a meeting between the General Council and the Miners' Executive was held, when the following formula from Sir Herbert Samuel was discussed:–

1. The T.U.C. are of opinion that the negotiations on the conditions of the coal industry, which in their judgment ought never to have been broken off, should be resumed forthwith.
2. They are of opinion that any negotiations are likely to be unsuccessful unless they provide for some measure of settling disputes in the industry

other than conferences between the mineowners and the miners alone. They, therefore, favour the establishment of a Mines National Board, which should include representatives of the miners and mineowners with a neutral element and an independent chairman.

3. They are of opinion that there should be no revision of the previous wage rates unless there are sufficient assurances that the measures of re-organisation will be actually put into effect. It should be one of the functions of the Mines National Board to ensure that the necessary steps will in fact be taken within the industry. A committee, including representatives of the miners, should be appointed to co-operate in preparing the measures of legislation and administration that are necessary.

4. After these points have been agreed the Mines National Board should proceed to the preparation of a wage agreement which should:–

   (a) if possible be on simpler lines than those hitherto favoured;
   (b) should not affect in any way the wages of the lower paid men;
   (c) should fix reasonable figures below which the wage of no class of labour should be reduced in any circumstances.

5. Negotiations cannot in any case be begun until the lock-out notices at the mines are withdrawn.

SECOND PROPOSALS ACCEPTED BY GENERAL COUNCIL BUT REJECTED BY MINERS.

In the joint discussion the Council informed the miners that they regarded the Memorandum as representing a satisfactory basis for drawing up proposals for the purpose of reopening negotiations in the mining industry.

The Miners' Executive retired at 10 p.m. (Monday, May 10th) to consider the Memorandum. After three hours' adjournment they intimated that they could only accept the Memorandum subject to the deletion of paragraph 4, which included:–

(a) A simplified wages agreement;
(b) Protection for the lower paid men;
(c) Fixing of an irreducible minimum.

The Miners' Executive also proposed to alter the first part of paragraph 3 to read as follows:–

They are of opinion that there should be no revision of the previous wage rates or conditions, because if the measures for reorganisation are actually put into effect such revision would be unnecessary.

In view of the attitude of the miners' representatives with regard to the Council's efforts, they were told that there was no obligation upon them to submit alternative constructive proposals.

WHY DECISION TO TERMINATE THE STRIKE WAS REACHED. The fact was, however, borne upon the Council from the attitude of the Miners' Executive that no matter what provision might be made to obtain a basis for reopening negotiations and enabling a settlement to be reached, they were not prepared to agree to consider, as part of such negotiations, anything which indicated possible wage adjustments for any section or grade of mine workers in any district.

Having regard to the impossibility of excluding the wages question from consideration in dealing with the Commission's Report, and the enormous responsibility involved in carrying on the strike, the Council felt the position was too grave to justify their being tied to a mere slogan. From all the facts known to them, the Council decided that if in accordance with the instructions given them by the Conference of Trade Union Executives the strike was to be terminated with a maximum of advantage both to the miners and to the other unions, a decision must be reached while the unions remained both strong and disciplined. They felt the objects of the strike would be achieved and a practical basis for re-opening negotiations on the lines of the Royal Commission's Report would be secured if the miners joined with the General Council in submitting reasoned and constructive proposals. As the miners did not appear disposed to assist either in advancing constructive proposals on their own account, or in regard to proposals formulated through the Council, the Council had to face its responsibility to the great Trade Union movement which had sacrificed so much to secure a fair settlement. . . .

The Council were satisfied that, however long they continued the strike, they would still be in the same position so far as the attitude of the Miners' Executive was concerned, and consequently the Council were not justified in permitting the unions to continue the sacrifice for another day.

(35) *Statement of the Miners' Federation of Great Britain on the Occasion of the Conference of Trade Union Executive Committees Held to Receive the Report of the General Council of the Trades Union Congress on the Work Entrusted to Them in the General Strike of May, 1926* (1927)

III If we were deserted and forced to fight a lone fight, it was not by the workers that we were abandoned. Their hearts beat true to the end. From the workers of our country, and of the world, and especially from the Trade Unionists of Russia, we obtained unstinted aid. For the help given, whether from union funds or from individual workers, we convey the gratitude of the miners' wives and children.

10. *Consolidation Despite Economic Difficulties*

The collapse of the general strike brought some victimisation, much recrimination within the ranks of the trade-union movement and an Act intended to prevent the recurrence of such a strike (1).

However, attempts to create a new atmosphere were also made at discussions between leading unionists and employers. The main figure on the employers' side was Sir Alfred Mond, 1st Lord Melchett (1868–1930), the chairman of ICI, while Ben Turner (1863 1942) led the deputation from the General Council of the TUC (2, 3).

The Mond–Turner discussions set a pattern for future moderation in industrial relations. A number of meetings was held on questions of industrial reorganisation (4), and, although the policy of discussion was backed by the TUC, it was scathingly attacked by such figures of the extreme left as A. J. Cook (5, 6). None the less, such meetings became the pattern (7) and the National Minority Movement found it difficult to make much progress against entrenched leaderships (8).

(1) *Labour Year Book* (1928)

The principal changes which are to be found in the Trade Disputes and Trade Unions Act, 1927, may, therefore, be summarised as follows;

(1) Sympathetic strike action (whether on a national or local scale) if designed or calculated to coerce the Government, either directly or by inflicting hardship upon the community, is illegal, provided it is not within the trade or industry in which the original dispute arose. (Section 1 (1).)
No final interpretation of the above Section with all its ambiguities, can be attempted until it has been interpreted judically. In its present form, however, it may fairly be said that it will render the law so uncertain as to make any and every form of sympathetic strike action very liable to be declared illegal, and those responsible liable to criminal prosecution.

(2) Lock-outs are also similarly illegal.

(3) All primary strikes not connected with disputes over hours, wages, or other conditions of employment are illegal, if they are designed or calculated to coerce the Government either directly or by inflicting hardship upon the community, e.g., a national coal strike to secure a statutory minimum wage. (Section 1 (1).)

(4) Any strike declared to be illegal by the Act will be none the less illegal, even though the workmen may have lawfully terminated their contracts of employment by due notice. (Section 1 (1).)

(5) A criminal liability is imposed on all union officials, which would include branch officials, shop stewards, members of strike committees, whether national, district, or branch and all other persons (excepting the workmen themselves) who in any way take part in or act in furtherance of any strike which is made illegal by the Act, even though they may be unaware of the facts or circumstances which render the strike illegal. Moreover, the individual workman who, in addition to ceasing work, acts as a strike picket or in any other way renders active support will be criminally liable (Section 1 (2).)

(6) In the case of strikes made illegal by the Act, the liability of union funds in respect of damages which may be awarded to employers and others, as imposed in the Taff Vale case, is restored. (Section 1 (4).)

(7) In the case of strikes made illegal by the Act, members expelled by their trade Unions for breach of rule, e.g., members who remain at work after a strike has been called in accordance with the rules of the union, are given the right to claim damages, which will be payable out of the union funds. This right is made retrospective so as to cover the 1926 general strike. (Section 2.)

(8) The right of picketing is curtailed and restricted, and the border line between what is permissible and what is prohibited is so vague as to render almost all forms of picketing dangerous and the pickets liable to prosecution. (Section 3.)

(9) The statutory rights of Trade Unions to use their funds for political purposes is to be taken away, and the Act gives Trade Unions little in return which they do not possess under the present law, namely, the right which any group of individuals enjoys voluntarily to subscribe to a common fund. The 1927 Act, therefore, takes away the substantive legal rights conferred on Trade Unions by the 1913 Act, and accordingly, is more than a mere change of machinery from 'contracting-out' to 'contracting-in'. (Section 4.)

(10) Civil Servants are prohibited from joining any Trade Union which is not confined to employees of the Crown, or which has political objects, or which is affiliated to any outside industrial or political organisation, e.g., the Trades Union Congress, or the Labour Party. Any Civil Servant who fails to observe the above provision is liable to be dismissed from his employment, together with the loss of his pension. (Section 5.)

(11) Liability of municipal employees, or employees of any public authority, e.g., Port Of London Authority, for breaches of their contracts of employment, to be a criminal as well as civil liability, and so renders them liable to criminal prosecution, as well as the civil liability to pay damages. (Section 6.)

(12) The Attorney-General is given the right to interfere in union affairs by means of an application to the court to restrain the expenditure of union funds in support of strike action, declared illegal under Section 1 of the Act. In this connection it should be noted that, under the present law, costs cannot always be obtained against the Crown, even when it loses the action. (Section 7.)

(2) TUC General Council, Industrial Committee, *Report to the Executives of Affiliated Unions on the Discussions with the Employers' Group* (1928): 'Origin of the Conference'

Ever since the war and the economic dislocation which, in the absence of constructive measures on the part of the Government was an inevitable consequence, it has been clear that Britain's industrial position is a very serious one.

The severe and widespread unemployment, the decline in the standard of living of certain sections of the working class, the situation of the coal industry, and the grave position of the iron and steel, shipbuilding and engineering, cotton, and other industries, are all factors in the experience of the past seven years that must be of great concern to the Trade Union Movement.

Whatever beliefs may be held as to the immediate tactics or wider policy of the movement, all those whose duty it is to promote the interests of the workers must regard the situation with grave anxiety and with the earnest desire to examine the problems relating to these distressing conditions with a view to finding immediate relief. The Council is fully convinced that any elected body which at such a time failed to explore any and every means which has for its object the improvement of the conditions of those it represents would be unworthy to hold office.

(3) Sir Ben Turner, *About Myself* (1930)

What criticism we got! What vulgar cartoons were issued about us! What opposition and jeers we had to face! It was no pleasant job, but it was a right one.

Our first programme was altered and amended, and ultimately jointly agreed upon by the employers' seven and our seven, and put to our General Council and the Employers' group separately and accepted. This programme was and is as follows:–

I. THE ORGANISATION OF INDUSTRIAL RELATIONS.
    (a) Trade Union Recognition.
    (b) Collective Bargaining.
    (c) SECURITY AND STATUS. – The formulation of means for increasing security of employment and for raising the status of the industrial worker, including the new standing wage scheme.
    (d) Victimisation of Employees by Employers.

(e) Legal regulation of hours of labour.

(f) Management and Labour.

(g) Works Councils.

(h) INFORMATION. The provision of information on the facts of industry to all those concerned in industry.

(i) PRELIMINARY INVESTIGATION. The application of preliminary investigation into potential causes of industrial disputes before their actual declaration.

(j) The extension of the function of Industrial Courts.

(k) Factory legislation.

(l) Health and Unemployment Insurance (National and Industrial).

(m) Provision of machinery for suggestion and constructive criticism.

(n) Maintenance of personal relationship.

II. UNEMPLOYMENT.

III. THE DISTRIBUTION OF THE PROCEEDS OF COMMODITIES AND SERVICES.

(a) High Wage Policy.

(b) The consideration of plans for the participation by all concerned in industry in the prosperity of their industry and in the benefits of increased production, including shareholding, profit and cost sharing.

(c) Payment by results.

(d) Minimum Wage Principles.

IV. THE ORGANISATION, TECHNIQUE, AND CONTROL OF INDUSTRY.

(a) RATIONALISATION. The advantages to be gained by the scientific organisation of industries. . . . The effects upon Labour. . . . Interchangeability or flexibility. . . .

(b) The effect of unnecessary internal competition.

(c) Sheltered and unsheltered industries.

(d) Distribution.

V. FINANCE.

(a) Monetary technique. Banking and credit systems and policy.

(b) Industrial Finance.

(c) Taxation and Local Rates.

VI. CONSTITUTIONAL.

(a) National Industrial Council. . . .

(b) The co-ordination of the present and if necessary the provision of further machinery for continuous investigation into industrial conditions.

VII. INTERNATIONAL.

(a) Competition of countries with lower labour standards.

    (b) International Agreements and Conventions

    (c) International Economic Conference.

VIII. GENERAL.

    (a) Housing.

    (b) Health problems.

    (c) Education. . . .

    (d) Technical education (including apprenticeship).

    (e) Research.

(4) *The Times* (5 July 1928)

The object of the Conference to discuss the entire field of industrial re-organization and industrial relations is to assist in the solution of the greatest problem confronting the country at the present time, namely the restoration of industrial prosperity, and with it the progressive improvement in the standard of living of the population. It is, however, understood that the parties do not intend to interfere with the functions of the existing joint machinery of employers and trade unions, nor with the right to withdraw and dispense labour. It is also recognized that the present position of industry is not necessarily final, but that it is only a phase in its evolutionary development.

It is realized that industrial reconstruction can best be undertaken in conjunction with, and with the cooperation of, those entitled and empowered to speak for organized labour. Every effort will therefore be made to further the cooperation of all those who participate in production, and to secure the objective that all those who participate in production should also participate in the prosperity of industry. It is agreed that the most effective cooperation in industry can be obtained by deliberation and negotiation with the accredited representatives of affiliated trade unions. . . .

When entering upon the discussion of proposals for new conciliation machinery both sides readily agreed from the outset . . . that nothing in the nature of compulsory arbitration could be considered, and that any new machinery created should be at liberty to discuss and consider in relation to industrial disputes all questions of any character relating to the industry under consideration. It was agreed that any scheme adopted for new conciliation machinery should be an integral part of a scheme for a National Industrial Council consisting of the whole of the members of the General Council of the Trade Union Congress and an equal number of representatives of the recognized employers' organizations. . . .

It is recognized that industry in this country in the last generation has benefited by the progressive increase in the volume of negotiations which have taken place between employers and representatives of trade unions and by an enormous growth of joint machinery for such negotiated in varying forms – namely, industrial councils, conciliation boards, Conferences, etc. It may be stated that it is now the usual practice of employers to negotiate on all questions of working conditions, including wages, with the executives and officials of the appropriate affiliated unions or of other *bona-fide* trade unions as already defined.

This practice and method of procedure have, in our experience, proved to be so beneficial that, in our view, they should be encouraged and extended. . . .

It is recognized that misunderstanding exists upon consequences which it is claimed followed the great dispute of 1926. Without expressing any views upon the events of 1926 and their consequences we consider, on account of the vital importance of improved industrial relations, that where workmen are being penalized for any part they played in those events, whether justified or not, such action is to be deprecated. For the sake of a better understanding in the future in the industrial world we hope efforts will be made to restore the pre-1926 position. . . .

The tendency towards a rational organization of industry and trade, including the grouping of individual units within an industry into larger units, is recognized, and this tendency should be welcomed and encouraged in so far as it leads to improvements in the efficiency of industrial production, services, and distribution and to the raising of the standard of living of the people. . . .

It is recognized that a certain measure of rationalization may tend to displace labour or to modify in undesirable ways the conditions of work, and that safeguards are therefore necessary to ensure that the interests of the workers do not suffer by the adoption of such measures. It is therefore agreed that schemes for providing such safeguards should be considered as part of the general question of the displacement of labour.

Recognizing the necessity for adaptability and elasticity in industry it is suggested that the trade unions and employers concerned should consider the advisability of making provisions for testing variations from existing practices or rules on agreed experimental bases with proper safeguards against an extension of such conditions being claimed by, or imposed upon, the industry beyond the agreed limits.

(5) A. J. Cook, *Mond's Manacles. The Destruction of Trade Unionism* (1928): Speech at Conference on Industrial Organisation, 4 July 1928

The conception running through these memoranda [on Rationalisation and on the National Industrial Council] is that the interests of the working class will best be served by striving for a régime of industrial peace on the basis of rationalised capitalism. Making capitalism more effective by rationalisation will not abolish the workers' subject position in relation to the owners of industry, his low standard of life and opportunity as compared with theirs, his servile status in the workshop and his insecurity due to recurring periods of unemployment. . . .

The only rational organisation of industry which I recognise is the social organisation of industry to serve social ends. The capitalist organisation of industry cannot be rational from the workers' standpoint. The formation of larger productive units, the speeding-up of the workers, the application of science (when profitable) to industry, can only intensify the competitive chaos when the control of industry is in the hands of groups of capitalists whose driving force is (and will always remain) the search for the highest possible profit. . . .

I do not believe in the sincerity of the employers in respect to their talk about 'safeguarding' the workers during rationalisation. The best 'sfeguard' of the workers at all times is a strong trade union movement. *I believe that it is power that counts*; our power lies in our right to withhold our labour, and you ask us in effect in this project to give this right up. . . . The National Industrial Council is not . . . a step to workers' control of industry. It is merely a fig-leaf upon the naked capitalist autocracy in industry.

The so-called conciliation machinery of this scheme is worthless. I deny the initial assumption of this scheme that good relations are possible under capitalism. The relation of the employers and employed must from its very nature be one of domination and exploitation when viewed from standpoint of the worker. By good relations are meant amicable relations between employers and employed. I assert that it is not the object of the Labour Movement to secure good – amicable – relations between employers and employed, but to abolish the relation between employer and employed altogether. . . .

(6) Ibid.: Speech in St Andrew's Hall, Glasgow, 8 July 1928

I am further opposed to Mondism because I regard Mond as a Fascist. I regard the present scheme agreed to at the Mond Conference as largely the foundations for Fascist trade unionism in this country. I do not say it is the whole building, but undoubtedly it is the foundations of Fascism. There are close analogies between the Mond scheme and the system of compulsory trade unionism now operating in Italy. Both the Mond scheme and the scheme of Fascist unions were introduced after the defeat of the working class. . . .

To save the soul and the body of the Labour Movement we must kill Mondism. . . .

Our policy is to continue to develop the Trade Union Movement as an instrument not merely for defending the standards of the working-class but for assisting in the achievement of the overthrow of capitalism and the attainment of Socialism at the earliest possible moment. Because Mondism cuts across this aim we declare war to the death against Mondism.

(7) *Labour Year Book* (1931): 'Relations with Employers' Organisations'

During the year a further development took place in connection with the discussions between the General Council, the National Confederation of Employers' Organisations and the Federation of British Industries. As a result of the preliminary conversations reported to the 1929 Congress and described in the last Year Book, a definite scheme of consultation and co-operation between the three bodies has been agreed upon. The scheme provides for discussions covering a wide area of subjects connected with the welfare of British industry, and thus establishes a medium for the joint consideration of problems and difficulties common to the whole of industry.

The scheme . . . was adopted by Congress.

(8) National Union of Scottish Mineworkers, *To the Members* . . . (1928)

TRADE UNIONISM V. COMMUNISM. The paramount reason is the subversive actions of the Communist and Minority Movements in our respective District Organisations. More especially in Lanarkshire, and Fife, Clackmannan and Kinross. The actings of this Section in matters recently before the National Organisation, raises the important and far reaching issue of Constitutional Trade Unionism and Labour Party principles, methods and objects versus Communism.

These men make no secret of their attitude to Trade Unionism and all it stands for. They belong to a Party affiliated to the Communist International. They are bound by the following conditions of admission to that body, passed at the Second Congress in August, 1920:–

> All parties belonging to the Communist International, must carry on systematic and persistent Communist work in Trade Unions, Co-operative Societies and other class Organisations of the workers. It is necessary to form Communist groups *within* these Organisations in order, by persistent and lasting work, to win them over to Communism. These groups must be completely subordinated to the party as a whole. They are bound to conduct a relentless struggle against the Amsterdam International of Trade Unions. They must propagate insistently amongst the organised workers the necessity of breaking with the Amsterdam International and joining up with the Red International of Trade Unions adhering to the Communist International.

NOTE: Subsequent Congress of the Communist International have in no way altered or modified these instructions.

MINORITY MOVEMENT. This so called movement, while outwardly proclaiming their desire to further the interests of Trade Unionism, is in reality part and parcel of, and the willing tools of their parent, the Communist Party who brought them into being. Their obedience and subservience to their Masters, the Executive of the Red International, is only surpassed by their desire to be elected to the positions of these Officials, whom they have systematically traduced, misrepresented and abused.

OUR POSITION. We refuse to take our instructions from this alien and Hybrid Junta. We ask you to do your part in purging your Organisation of this evil, disruptive influence.

Communism seeks to displace Constitutional Trade Unionism by unconstitutional means. These two forces cannot, in the nature of the case, exist together in one Organisation.

The Communists have, and are endeavouring to capture the Executive Authority of the National Union of Scottish Mine Workers, with the settled intention of using the machinery and prestige of your National Union to further their own sinister purpose. You cannot, in your own interests, allow them to succeed.

UNDER WHICH BANNER? The question we must put to you is – 'Under which banner are you prepared to fight for justice and fair play to yourselves and your families?'

By the end of the 1920s the amalgamation movement in trade unionism had largely run its course (9), but the General Council continued to press for at least co-operation and co-ordination between unions (10). However, a more serious problem was the decline in union membership from a peak of 8,334,000 in 1920 to 4,839,000 in 1930, following the rise of unemployment – which caused further social problems for TUC and Government alike (11).

(9) *Labour Year Book* (1931)

(a) Federations

Joint working is brought about chiefly, though not entirely, by means of federation of groups of unions, and we have now a number of Federations doing excellent work in various branches of industry.

The Miners' Federation of Great Britain, in spite of the difficulties following the stoppage in 1926, continues its enormous task of co-ordinating the District Miners' Associations in the country. Its representative standing and character have been recognised under the Coal Mines Act, 1930, as a result of which the power and influence of the Federation have been increased.

The Cotton Industry provides a unique form of very close federation within other Federations. Local associations of Spinners, those of weavers and those of Card Room Operatives are linked up within their respective 'Amalgamated Association', which in turn are federated with other Cotton Unions in the National Association of Unions in the Textile Trades, the work of this Association being that of promoting closer unity and conducting negotiations. In addition there is the United Textile Factory Workers' Association, which deals mainly with matters of a legislative and political character.

The Engineering and Shipbuilding Trades Federation has had, in the last few years, one of the hardest tasks which could fall to the lot of any association. The trade slump has affected no body of workers more than those engaged in the engineering trades, and this has naturally had an effect on the Unions and through them on the Federation. However, in spite of the disadvantages under which it is operating, the Federation has done much good work and is still a force in the industries which it covers.

The National Federation of Building Trade Operatives and the Printing Trades Federation are typical examples of virile Federations and perform invaluable work in their various spheres.

The National Transport Workers' Federation and the General Labourers' National Council have ceased to exist. They served a most useful purpose in their day, but large scale amalgamations rendered their existence unnecessary.

OTHER METHODS OF JOINT WORKING. Other groups of trade unions, though not actually federated in the accepted sense of the term, operate jointly in negotiations affecting the industry. The three railway Unions, the N. U. R., the R. C. A. and the A. S. L. E. F., deal with questions of wages through the medium of a Central Wages Board, consisting of representatives of the Unions and the Companies, whilst in the event of disagreement, the cases of the Unions and the Companies are dealt with by a National Wages Board, representative of the Unions and the Companies, together with four representatives of outside interests.

The wages and conditions of Seamen and kindred workers are also dealt with in the main by one body known as the Maritime Board.

(b) Amalgamations

The early years of the period were marked by the formation, by amalgamation, of several large unions.

The Amalgamated Engineering Union was formed in 1920 from 10 Unions in the engineering trades including the Amalgamated Society of Engineers, and had at the time of amalgamation a membership of 407,000.

The Transport and General Workers' Union was formed in 1921–22, from 17 Unions catering chiefly for workers in and about dockyards, but including general workers of all kinds. In 1922, the membership of this Union was given at 300,000. A further accession of strength to this Union came in 1929, when amalgamation with the Workers' Union became effective, the membership at the time of the 1930 Congress being about 389,000.

The National Union of Sheet Metal Workers and Braziers also came into being in 1921, as a result of amalgamation of 10 Unions, most of them local in character.

The National Union of General and Municipal Workers took its present name in 1924, on amalgamation with the Municipal Employees' Association.

Other amalgamations during this period include the Amalgamated Union of Building Trade Workers formed in 1921 from two unions catering for bricklayers and masons; the National Union of Distributive and Allied Workers, which, in 1920, incorporated the Amalgamated Union of Co-operative and Commercial Employees and Allied Workers, and the National Warehouse and General Workers' Union; the Amalgamated Society of Woodworkers formed in 1920 from two unions catering for carpenters and joiners; the National Amalgamated

Society of Operative House and Ship Painters and Decorators, in 1920, incorporated a local union catering for these workers in the Liverpool district; the National Union of Vehicle Builders amalgamated in 1920 with a union catering for coachmakers, and in 1926 with one catering for wheelwrights and smiths; in 1921 the United Operative Plumbers and Domestic Engineers' Association incorporated the Plumbers' Association of Scotland, and the Musicians' Union amalgamated with two other unions catering for musicians.

In 1922 the National Union of Foundry Workers amalgamated with three other unions catering for workers in the various branches of the industry; the Amalgamated Society of the Boot and Shoe Makers and Repairers incorporated a union catering for workers in the hand-sewn section of the trade and the National Union of Textile Workers was formed from three unions catering for workers in the woollen textile industry.

In 1924 the Walsall and District Amalgamated Leather Trades Union incorporated two unions, one catering for women in the trade, and the Altogether Builders' Labourers and Constructional Workers were joined by another union catering for labourers.

The United Road Transport Workers Association of England incorporated a union catering for motor drivers, and the Amalgamated Society of Dyers, Bleachers, Finishers and Kindred Trades amalgamated with two unions catering for workers in stuff and woollen warehouses.

In 1928 the National Union of Leather Workers was formed from three Unions organising the different grades of workers in the industry.

(10) TUC, *Trade Union Structure and Closer Unity. Interim Report* (1944): Summary of 1927 report on organisation of unions

1. The General Council considers that in pursuing the Hull resolution Congress placed upon it an impossible task on account of the following facts:–

    (a) The resolution, which is composite in character, was based upon resolutions and amendments containing opposing principles and was merely a compromise in wording which left a wide divergence in policy.

    (b) The varying structure and method of working of unions, the differing circumstances in the various trades and industries, and the impossibility of defining boundaries make the general application of any particular scheme impracticable.

AMALGAMATION AND JOINT WORKING

2. (a) The General Council is of opinion that greater co-ordination in the forces of the movement is essential: that changes which have taken place and which are constantly developing in industry make it necessary for the Trade Union Movement to adopt the greatest possible measure of co-ordination; and that the most effective way is by Unions with closely related trade interests to seek amalgamation.

(b) The General Council considers the task of submitting any general scheme for amalgamation to be impracticable on account of the fact that the problems confronting the various organisations differ in character. In the foregoing report, however, suggestions are offered as to methods of overcoming some of the difficulties which usually arise.

(c) The advisability of grouping affiliated unions to provide a basis for amalgamation has been considered, but the course was found to be impracticable owing to the difficulty in defining industrial boundaries. Further, it was felt that amalgamation is more likely to be achieved where the driving force comes from within a group of unions rather than by any theoretical grouping.

(d) Pending amalgamation, the General Council considers that unions with closely related industrial interests should enter into joint working arrangements on all industrial matters with a view to joint negotiations on questions of rates of pay and working conditions, and also the elimination of competition for members and consequent overlapping.

The General Council, therefore, recommends that each affiliated union should consider its attitude towards greater consolidation and declare to the General Council in writing:–

(i) Whether it is prepared to participate in amalgamation negotiations with other unions.

(ii) The extent to which it is prepared to agree to joint working arrangements with other unions.

(iii) With which unions, in its opinion, is there the greatest possibility of progress being made in negotiations on either or both of the above questions?

CONTRIBUTIONS AND BENEFITS

3. Upon the question of contributions and benefits, the General Council is of opinion that more uniform rates of contribution are necessary, and that such contributions should be on a basis which will assure the establishment of adequate funds for all purposes and the speedy recovery of a union's financial position after a prolonged dispute. It is further of the opinion that the Trade Union Movement should adequately cater for provident benefits, to the mutual advantage of the member and the organisation.

CO-ORDINATION ON GENERAL QUESTIONS

4. The extent to which the Confederation of Employers' Organisations controls questions of general policy, in the opinion of the General Council points to the necessity for centralised negotiations to deal with general questions for the whole movement.

The General Council, therefore, recommends that this necessary co-ordination should be in the hands of the Trades Union Congress through the medium of the General Council.

(11) TUC General Council, *Pauperising the Unemployed. The T. U. C. Case against the Means Test* (1932)

1. The views of the General Council of the Trades Union Congress regarding the method of providing for the unemployed are fully set forth in their evidence to the Royal Commission on Unemployment Insurance, of which the following paragraph may be quoted:–

Unemployment is a national and international problem resulting from the industrial system under which we live. The workers are not the authors of the system but the victims of it, and unless the community so organises its resources as to provide work for every willing worker, the unemployed, as the reserves of industry, are entitled to maintenance.

2. The present Government have not only increased contributions to the unemployed fund and reduced the already inadequate benefit, but have in addition put an arbitrary limit on the number of weeks' benefit which may be drawn after which unemployed persons, irrespective of every other consideration, have to subject themselves to a means test if they desire further assistance.

3. There is no justification from an insurance point of view for the limit of benefit to 26 weeks in a year; it is simply an expedient. An applicant who may have paid regularly to the fund for the best part of 20 years and goes on to benefit for the first time can only get 26 weeks in the same way as an applicant who has only paid to the fund for a few years.

4. A person who has once drawn 156 days benefit in his benefit year has to undergo a means test for further assistance, no matter how many contributions remain to his credit, whilst a person who has drawn anything less than 156 days in his benefit year may go on to a further 156 days without a means test, so long as he can show that he has 30 contributions in the preceding two years.

5. These instances serve to show that it is a travesty to talk of unemployment benefit being based on insurance. The amount of benefit and the period for which it is paid are fixed in an arbitrary way and founded on nothing more than expediency.

6. The General Council of the Trades Union Congress have always been opposed to the imposition of a means test, believing as they do that it would never work effectively, and is bound to result in the penalisation of decent people. The means test applied by the present Government is the worst possible form in which it could be imposed. Hundreds of local authorities with their numerous subcommittees are left to deal with the matter in their own way.

7. Whatever justification there might be for allowing a local authority to impose tests and make allowances according to its own discretion when dealing with local rates, there is no justification whatever for allowing this procedure in the

case of unemployment benefit which is provided by the general taxpayer through the Exchequer.

8. The method adopted has resulted, as was inevitable, in the penalisation of people whose only crime is that they are unemployed through the mismanagement of the world's affairs by those who are in control. It has resulted not only in depriving people of amounts to which they were properly entitled, but has also resulted in different amounts being paid to persons whose circumstances are the same.

9. As shown in the attached examples, local authorities in the same area have adopted different methods of dealing with people whose industrial and economic circumstances are the same; relief scales differ for no apparent reason, except the fact that they are drawn up by different authorities, and these scales are taken into consideration inevitably in dealing with transitional benefit cases.

10. The allowances and deductions to be made in arriving at income figures on which to base assessments are left entirely in the hands of local authorities, so that in some cases all income is taken into account, whilst in others various amounts – reaching as high as 25s. per person in one case – are disregarded as income. In some cases the interest on investments is taken into account, whilst in others the applicants are refused benefit until they have spent their meagre savings. People are thus being compelled to withdraw small amounts which they have painfully accumulated in the cooperative stores or the Post Office Savings Bank, and they are in effect being penalised for their thrift. It is even alleged in some places that people are being forced to realise articles of value which they may possess.

11. The great majority of the people who are being subjected to this treatment are people who have not been in touch with the Poor Law before. Their affairs are pried into by investigating officers, who do not hesitate to visit relatives and employers in order to find out every possible halfpenny the applicant may be getting. Many complaints have been received that those officials assume the right to enter people's houses and make observations regarding the furniture. Applicants for transitional benefit are in fact treated as if they were liars and malingerers whose word cannot be accepted, and in respect of whom a rigorous inquiry must take place before they can be trusted with a few shillings.

12. Trade Unionists who are in receipt of unemployment benefit from their unions, for which they have paid, are finding that so far from this being an advantage to them it is used by many authorities to reduce the amount assessed for transitional benefit. Seven shillings and sixpence of National Health Insurance Benefit and 5s. from friendly societies sickness benefit is statutorily excluded from consideration by Public Assistance authorities. There is an equally strong case for the exemption of Trade Union unemployment benefit, which is one result of the thrift and foresight of the individuals concerned.

13. Trade Unions are compelled by law to pay benefit from their own funds if they desire to administer State Unemployment Benefit. This amount which the Government compels the Trade Unions to pay on the one hand is being used on the other hand by Public assistance authorities to cut down the amount of transitional benefit to which an applicant would otherwise be entitled.

14. In a recent circular issued by the Ministry of Labour it is suggested that whilst unions need not pay more in benefit than the amount required by the Unemployment Insurance Acts, the continued payment of additional sums would enable members 'in whole or in part to refrain from seeking State assistance outside the insurance scheme'. The unions were asked to give consideration to that aspect of the matter before altering rules with a view to limiting benefit to the amount required by the Acts. In effect the Trade Unions are asked to continue to find money from their members with which to pay benefit, which in turn will be used to cut down the benefit of their fellow members in the interests of the Exchequer, whilst at the same time Trade Unionists as taxpayers are also to contribute their share of taxation.

15. This is not dealing fairly with the matter and we suggest that the Minister should seek immediately power either to prevent Public Assistance Authorities from taking Trade Union benefit into consideration or to waive the requirements of the Unemployment Insurance Acts as regards additional benefit.

16. Many Trade Unions have endeavoured to secure the right to help their members in dealing with Public Assistance Committees, but they have been refused any facilities, and in one case indeed a Public Assistance official refused to hold any communication with a Trade Union secretary simply because he was a Trade Union official. . . .

21. The General Council of the Trades Union Congress are confident that they are expressing the view of the majority of the country when they say that the public never intended and would not tolerate for an instant the harassing and persecution of the unfortunate unemployed which is entirely unjustifiable and not worthy of our country.

22. We therefore demand the abolition of this vicious and inequitable means test. Those who are fortunate enough to be employed or to have an adequate income, have not failed to rise to their responsibilities and we are perfectly certain that they would welcome the opportunity of doing anything that was required of them rather than that, in their name, the poorest and most helpless of their fellow citizens should be harassed and badgered.

As the Government became increasingly involved in attempts to mitigate the consequences of large-scale unemployment in the former 'staple' industries by means of rationalisation and regulation, it also extended its interest in industrial relations (12, 13, 14, 15). Union amalgamation and growth continued simultaneously after 1933 (16), sometimes provoking inter-union clashes (17), with which the TUC attempted to deal by means of the 'Bridlington Agreement' of 1939 (18). Meanwhile, unions maintained their traditional interest in education and self-improvement, notably through the Workers' Educational Association of 1903 (19).

(12) Committees on Industry and Trade, *Survey of Industrial Relations* (1926): Negotiating Machinery in the Cotton Industry.

The cotton industry of Lancashire and adjacent countries is well organised for the treatment of matters affecting industrial relations. The majority of the employers in the spinning section of the trade are represented by the Federation of Master Cotton Spinners' Associations, Ltd., while the employers in the weaving section are organised in the Cotton Spinners' and Manufacturers' Association. These two bodies, each of which comprises a number of district associations cover most of the employers in the industry.

On the Trade Union side the outstanding bodies are in the spinning section, the Amalgamated Association of Operative Cotton Spinners and Twiners, and the Amalgamated Association of Card and Blowing Room Operatives; and, in the manufacturing section, the Amalgamated Weavers' Association with other Unions in the Northern Counties Textile Trades' Federation.

Arrangements based on the effective organisation of both parties have been entered into for the systematic consideration of differences arising in the industry, and these have proved of great value in maintaining satisfactory relations between employers and operatives. In the spinning section of the trade these arrangements arose out of the 'Brooklands Agreement' which terminated the great spinning trade dispute of 1892–3, and which provided, *inter alia*, that no local Employers' Association or Trade Union should countenance, encourage or support any lock-out or strike until the matter had been submitted to and considered by a local Joint Committee of the Federated Association of Employers and the Operatives' Trade Unions. The 'Brooklands Agreement', which was largely based on the joint arrangements already existing in the weaving section of the trade, was terminated in 1913, but agreements now exist providing that notices shall not be tendered until the matter in dispute has been considered by local and central Joint Committees of the Employers' and Operatives' Organisations.

While these standing arrangements for dealing with local and district differences are operating constantly to remove friction and avoid disputes, the largest issues, such as changes in wages or matters of importance affecting the whole industry (or the spinning or weaving section as a whole), are negotiated direct between the central authorities of the organisations concerned. There are no standing arrangements for arbitration in case of breakdown of such negotiations, and it is well understood by the parties that failure to arrive at a settlement may involve a general stoppage. But by the nature of the case differences of this order arise more rarely than local and district troubles; and the fact that the issues rest with the most responsible leaders on both sides, and the realisation of the serious consequences of failure to agree, are, of course, potent factors making for peace on such occasions.

(13) *Industrial Relations Handbook* (1944): Cotton Manufacturing Industry (Temporary Provisions) Act, 1934, 24 and 25 Geo. V, c. 32

Under the Act, an organisation of employers and an organisation of workpeople both of which must be representative of the Industry, or the grades of the Industry concerned, may make joint application to the Minister of Labour and National Service for the making of an Order in respect of any agreement reached by such organisation, as to the rate of wages to be paid to persons employed in the Industry.

Unless the Minister is satisfied that the organisations making the application are not representative of the Industry or of the grades of the Industry concerned, he is required to appoint a Board consisting of a Chairman and two other members unconnected with the Industry to consider the application. Each of the parties to the application may appoint six of its members as assessors to the Board.

If the Board makes a unanimous recommendation to that effect, the Minister may make an Order setting out the rates of wages embodied in the agreement, which are thereafter considered as a term of contract of every employed person concerned. Employers are required to keep records showing compliance with the Order, and any employer paying less than the prescribed rate is liable to a monetary fine. Action to secure enforcement of such Orders is a matter for the Industry.

(14) Ibid.: Road and Rail Traffic Act, 1933, 23 and 24 Geo. V, c. 53

As a result of consideration of the reports of the Royal Commission on Transport and of the Salter Conference, the Government reached the conclusion that, for the regulation of road traffic, a licensing scheme was necessary, and that a fair basis of competition could not be established without removing unfair competition based on unfair wages. It also considered that a 'fair wage' requirement was necessary,

(1) in the interests of those hauliers who were struggling to maintain satisfactory wage rates,
(2) in justice to the workers, and
(3) as a contribution to ensuring safety on the roads.

Accordingly, under the Road and Rail Traffic Act, 1933, provision was made for all motor vehicles used for the carriage of goods on the road to be licensed according to the following classes:

(1) an 'A Licence' or public carrier's licence, which entitles the holder to use the authorised vehicles for the carriage of goods for hire or reward;

(2) a 'B Licence' or limited carrier's licence, which entitles the holder to use the authorised vehicles for the carriage of goods either for hire or reward or in connection with any trade or business carried on by him; or

(3) a 'C Licence' or private carrier's licence, which entitles the holder to use the authorised vehicles for the carriage of goods only in connection with any trade or business carried on by him.

All licences were made conditional on the vehicles being maintained in fit condition; and on driving hours being limited in the interests of public safety.

The payment of fair wages was made a condition of A and B Licences. Provision was made for complaints about the payment of unfair wages by A or B Licence holders to be submitted to the Traffic Commissioners for the area, and for any dispute not otherwise disposed of to be referred by the Minister of Labour to the Industrial Court for settlement. . . .

(15) MFGB, *Proceedings* (1936)

In an admirable statement issued by our Secretary in March, 1934, entitled 'Coal Trade Policy', there was set out the adverse effects of multiple ownership in the following words; –

> Several Royal Commissions and other statutory bodies have inquired into the industry and have made their reports. The Sankey Commission and the Samuel Commission both made exhaustive inquiries, and, later, the Lewis Committee made a special investigation into the marketing side of the industry. All these bodies confirmed a view which has long been held by miners and others closely associated with the industry; they found that the industry had failed, both in the production and in the marketing of coal, to take advantage of the benefits to be derived from co-operative effort, and that the existing practice, whereby thousands of separate colliery concerns were given complete freedom to produce and compete one with the other, seriously lowered the economic position of the industry.

In that same statement which was widely circulated and generally appreciated, the policy of the Federation was set out with the utmost clarity in the following terms;–

> The Federation has always realised the harmful effect on wages of artificially keeping old and out-of-date collieries in production, but has always emphatically refuted the view that these should be eliminated by the free play of economic forces. The problem here was gradually to close down the least efficient concerns (having regard to the social problems involved) while retaining for the industry the great benefits of regulated sale and production. The provision for the sale and purchase of quotas should not have been included in the Act which should have compelled the adoption of schemes for the gradual elimination of the old collieries.

Our reasons for advocating the unification of colliery ownerships were also enumerated in the report of our representatives at the Sankey Commission under the following heads: –

1. Prevention of competition.
2. Control of freights.
3. Economy of administration.
4. Provision of capital allowing of quicker and more extensive development of backward mines.
5. More advantageous purchase of materials.
6. Reduction of colliery consumption.
7. More harmonious relations between the workmen and the operators due to steadier work and adequate remuneration of workmen.
8. Obliterations to a great extent of vested interests and middle-men.
9. Unification of the best knowledge and skill leading to greater interchange of ideas and comparison of methods.

(16) TGWU, *The Union, Its Work and Problems* (1939): 'List of Amalgamated Unions'

	Year of Amalgamation
Amalgamated Society of Watermen, Lightermen and Bargemen	1922
Amalgamated Carters, Lorrymen and Motormen's Union	
Amalgamated Association of Carters and Motormen	
Associated Horsemen's Union	
Dock, Wharf, Riverside and General Workers' Union	
Labour Protection League	
National Amalgamated Labourers' Union	
National Union of Docks, Wharves and Shipping Staffs	
National Union of Ships' Clerks, Grain Weighers and Coalmeters	
National Union of Vehicle Workers	
National Amalgamated Coal Workers' Union	
National Union of Dock, Riverside and General Workers	
National Union of British Fishermen	
North of England Trimmers' and Teemers' Association	
North of Scotland Horse and Motormen's Association	
United Vehicle Workers	
Belfast Breadservers' Association	
Greenock Sugar Porters' Association	
Dundee Flax and Flax Stowers' Association	1923
North Wales Craftsmen and General Workers' Union	
North Wales Quarrymen's Union	
Scottish Union of Dock Labourers	
United Order of General Labourers	1924
Association of Coastwise Masters, Mates and Engineers	1925

	Year of Amalgamation
Weaver Watermen's Association Irish Mental Hospital Workers' Union National Amalgamated Union of Enginemen, Firemen, Motormen, Mechanics and Electrical Workers	1926
Cumberland Enginemen, Boilermen and Electrical Workers' Union	1928
Workers' Union	1929
Belfast Operative Bakers' Union Northern Ireland Textile Workers' Union	1930
London Co-operative Mutuality Club Collectors' Association National Union of Co-operative Insurance Society Employees Portadown Textile Workers' Union Scottish Farm Servants' Union	1933
'Altogether' Builders' Labourers and Constructional Workers' Society Scottish Busmen's Union	1934
National Winding and General Engineers' Society	1935
Electricity Supply Staff Association (Dublin) Halifax and District Carters' and Motormen's Association	1936
Power Loom Tenters' Trade Union of Ireland Belfast Journeymen Butchers' Association Scottish Seafishers' Union	1937
Humber Amalgamated Steam Trawlers' Engineers and Firemen's Union Port of London Deal Porters' Union.	1938

(17) NUPE, *Five Years' Review. Address of the General Secretary, Bryn Roberts to the Conference of Organisers held at Anderton's Hotel, Fleet Street, London January 7th and 8th, 1939*

It was at the Weymouth, 1934, T.U.C. that I attended as General Secretary for the first time. On that occasion I moved the resolution (directed against Nalgo) expressing concern at the growth of non-Political associations in Local Government. You will no doubt remember that it was referred back to the General Council for Report. It led to Nalgo writing monthly Editorial attacks upon us. Most of you followed this up by referring to Nalgo in your own Journal articles. I did likewise in my Editorial. Nalgo organisers, in turn, produced thousands of articles and leaflets denouncing us. I at once realised that this powerful organisation (and Nalgo is that), in denouncing us, was conferring upon us a status of importance out of all proportion to our then size and power. Nalgo's intention was to do us harm, yet every time they fired at us we became more and more widely known.

In the light of this experience, it became my settled policy to continue a sustained attack upon the Nalgo organisation. At the following Margate, 1935, T. U. C. I attacked the General Council for entertaining the idea of forming an alliance with Nalgo. Nalgo's Journal returned the usual compliments. Result: N. U. P. E.'s fame was further extended. Our policy was sustained at the 1936 Plymouth Congress, when I again launched an attack upon the General Council for taking a further step towards Nalgo. Again Nalgo, in leaflets and Journal, decried us. Our importance grew accordingly.

At the 1937 Norwich Congress, I again pursued this proven profitable trail of attacking Nalgo, by the indirect process of moving back the portion of the General Council's Report which proposed to establish the Joint Advisory Committee for the Local Government Service. The issue was now widening because N. U. P. E drew upon itself the intense wrath of Sir Walter Citrine and that of the Transport Workers' Union and the General and Municipal Workers Union. But this time, every delegate to Congress, every affiliated Union knew what N. U. P. E. stood for and that it had, for five successive years, followed a consistent and persistent line. At the 1938 Blackpool Congress, we 'stuck to our guns' and once again charged this profitable Nalgo enemy.

I am not overlooking that this constant attacking has cost us the good will of a local Government Officer here and there, but it is my deep conviction that this policy of using the annual gathering of the T. U. C. to throw verbal bricks at Nalgo has been, on balance, a sound investment, and I sometimes feel benevolently disposed towards them for the 'harmful' good they have done us by affording us such fine advertisement.

But whatever advantages may have been derived in the attack itself, it must also be remembered that our anti-Nalgo attitude has been fully justified upon these Trade Union principles. N. U. P. E., by its logical condemnation of Nalgoism and its non-political form of organisation, has rendered no mean service to the General Labour Movement. That this fact will be, in due course, acknowledged I have not the slightest doubt.

(18) TUC, *Trade Union Structure and Closer Unity. Interim Report* (1944): Rules of 'Good Trade Union Practice'

(a) Unions should consider the possibility of joint working agreements with unions with whom they are in frequent contact in regard to –

(i) Spheres of Influence;
(ii) Recognition of cards;
(iii) Machinery for composing difficulties;
(iv) Conditions of transfer of members.

(b) No member of another Union should be accepted without inquiry from that Union.

(c) No member of another Union should be accepted where inquiry shows that the member is –

   (i) Under discipline;
  (ii) Engaged in a trade dispute;
 (iii) In arrears with contribution.

(d) No Union should commence organising activities at any establishment or undertaking in respect of any grade or grades of worker in which another Union has the majority of workers employed and negotiates wages and conditions, unless by arrangement with that Union.

(e) Each Union should include in its membership form questions on the lines of the T. U. C. Model Form in regard to past and present membership of another Union.

Summary.

1. – Basic alteration of Trade Union structure is impracticable. Schemes of amalgamation, federation and joint working should be developed wherever possible. Unions themselves must strive for closer unity, probably making sacrifices to achieve it. In a changing world, the Trade Union Movement cannot retain its pre-war conception of organisation if it is to be fully efficient.

As in 1927, the General Council are still of opinion that greater co-ordination in the forces of the Movement is essential; that changes which have taken place and which are constantly developing in industry make it necessary for the Trade Union Movement to adopt the greatest possible measure of co-ordination; and that the most effective way is by Unions with closely related trade interests to seek amalgamation.

For cases where complete amalgamation is not yet possible, the General Council have formulated several proposals which they feel can serve as an intermediate objective and which would result in a highly developed form of Federation closely related with Congress machinery. These proposals suggest that:

(a) Administrative functions of Unions remain within the full autonomy of Unions, but Unions should now consider how far their internal machinery has attained maximum efficiency. Special attention is directed to the need for fullest provision for Trade Union Technical Education and the most comprehensive general service possible for members.

(b) Individual Unions should extend as far as possible the principle of mutual recognition of cards, not merely as a war-time measure, but as a principle which can at all times contribute towards the removal of inter-Union competition. The maintenance of membership is a prime function of the Union, and the way could be prepared for the development whereby Federations themselves could be responsible for the main work of recruitment within an industry by:

    (i) Strict observance of the 1939 (Bridlington) proposals
   (ii) Joint working arrangements

    (iii) Determination of spheres of influence
    (iv) Recognition of cards
    (v) Inter-Union machinery for composing differences.

(c) The Federal body in an industry would be primarily responsible for dealing with the "Economic" questions outlined in this report in addition to the proposals concerning recruitment.

II. – The closest possible relations between the Federations and the T. U. C. should be developed.

III. – The machinery of the T. U. C. should be developed to provide for: –

(a) The Congress system of Advisory Committees to be developed to cover each industry, service, or related group.
(b) The Federal body in an industry or service to be associated with such an Advisory Committee along with representatives of the General Council.
(c) Additional research facilities to cover all general research for all industries, and the whole of the research and other facilities of Congress to be made available to Federations.
(d) Extended educational facilities.

The above proposals are an acceleration of the developments which have taken place in the light of the Movement's capacity for adaptation. For the future, Unions cannot afford to maintain the rate of evolution of the last twenty years.

(19) Sir A. Pugh, *The WEA and the Trade Union Movement* (1936)

It is one of the tributes which can be paid to the WEA that it has laid the ground for the development of adult educational work, which requires only increasing support from the trade unions to ensure its progress and success.

The need and purpose of workers' education call for rather closer examination.

When we speak of such education in its application to members of trade unions, we are not thinking of any form of narrow doctrine, but of healthy study in those subjects which will enable our members to get a closer understanding of the history, practice and problems of the Movement to which they belong, which will give them the reasoning, mental and moral equipment and inspire disinterested service to the Labour Movement.

The view was admirably expressed some fifteen years ago in the Report of the University Joint Committee, which consisted of representatives of Oxford University, the T. U. C., the Co-operative Union, the Club and Institute Union, the WEA, and the Friendly Societies.

Dealing with the question of the after-careers of working-class students, the Committee asserted the aim of working-class education to be – 'to enable workmen to fulfil with greater efficiency their duties which they owe to their own class and, as members of their class, to the whole nation'.

11. *The Second World War and After*

The Second World War brought major changes in industrial relations. In 1940 Ernest Bevin became Minister of Labour and dealt brilliantly with short and long-term problems (1). Order 1305 substituted compulsory arbitration for strikes and lockouts (2, 3), though it was not always effective (4); and unions continued to seek ways of avoiding inter-union disputes (5) and to modify some traditional practices (6). In addition to attempting to avoid industrial disputes, Winston Churchill's Government sought to hold back inflation (7). The TUC, under Walter Citrine, held meetings on this matter with Ministers from 1939 and, while rejecting statutory control of incomes, agreed that increases should be moderate (8). Such counsels did not appeal to members of the Left, such as Arthur Horner of the MFGB (9).

(1) *The Trade Unions and the War. Address of the Rt. Hon. Ernest Bevin, Minister of Labour and National Service, to the Trades Union Congress, Cambridge Hall, Southport* (1940)

RISING MASS OF LABOUR. One thing I am at liberty to say. There has been established – I think for the first time – a very close liaison between the Ministry of Labour and the Foreign Office. The object of that liaison is, in future to get the whole of the Diplomatic Service to move and have their being in a new environment; to recognise that the limited Court Circular Society of the Chancelleries will never return; that if there is to be a reconstruction of the world, then that reconstruction has to be brought about by harnessing and utilising the rising mass of labour to whom the future really belongs, and who must be the dominant factor in a new democratic world. There must be an absolute broadening of the curriculum, and of the right of entry into the Diplomatic Service. If the boys from the secondary schools can save us in the Spitfires, the same brains can be turned to produce the new world. . . .

EDUCATE THE MANAGEMENT. I beg of you to do that in all your works with your Management. If your Management is rather stand-offish we will give them a bit of advice in order that their education may be improved. On the whole the Works Managers are not bad. They are like Trade Union Officials – something to love and something to swear at (Laughter). Whatever you may say about them you are still pals with many of your Managers, your technicians, and your metallurgists. I want to see a great combination between the Trade Union representatives and the man who is actively managing the show, who has got to get the job done with you and others.

Management is becoming every day more of a profession and I ask you to try and show to them that they are your future allies in these new methods and not in the old. . . .

The Army has to be increased, more man-power has to be mobilised, and that great reserve of human power, the women, will have to be called upon more and more, with others, for other industries.

PROBLEMS OF TRANSFER. This raises an enormous problem. This winter needs the thought and attention of every one of us. Thousands of women and men have been moved from their domestic circles, and more will be moved into billets, and there is another enemy to be fought besides Hitler. That enemy is epidemic disease, cold, influenza. Now there are things that can be done to check it. You people who deal with management, have a look at the canteens. Are they as efficient as they ought to be? . . . What is more vital, we shall be calling upon more and more married women.

(2) *Industrial Relations Handbook* (1944): Recommendations of the Joint Consultative Committee of the Minister of Labour and National Service, 1940

(1) In this period of national emergency it is imperative that there should be no stoppage of work owing to trade disputes. In these circumstances the Consultative Committee representing the British Employers' Confederation and the Trades Union Congress have agreed to recommend to the Minister of Labour and National Service the arrangements set out in the following paragraphs.

(2) The machinery of negotiation existing in any trade or industry for dealing with questions concerning wages and conditions of employment shall continue to operate.

Matters in dispute which cannot be settled by means of such machinery shall be referred to arbitration for a decision which will be binding on all parties and no strikes or lock-outs shall take place. In cases where the machinery of negotiation does not at present provide for reference to such arbitration the parties shall have the option of making provision for such arbitration, failing which the matters in dispute shall be referred for decision to a National Arbitration Tribunal to be appointed by the Minister of Labour and National Service. The Minister shall take power to secure that the wages and conditions of employment settled by the machinery of negotiation or by arbitration shall be made binding on all employers and workers in the trade or industry concerned.

(3) In any case not covered by the provisions of paragraph (2), any dispute concerning wages or conditions of employment shall be brought to the notice of

the Minister of Labour and National Service, by whom, if the matter is not otherwise disposed of, it shall be referred within a definite time limit to the National Arbitration Tribunal for decision, and no strike or lock-out shall take place.

(4) The foregoing arrangements shall be subject to review on or after 31st December, 1940.

(3) Ibid.: Conditions of Employment and National Arbitration Orders, 1940–2

. . . the main purpose of the Order made in 1940 was to prevent work being interrupted during the war by trade disputes. At the same time the principle underlying all its provisions was in line with earlier policy. Thus, the Order provides that existing joint machinery in any trade or industry should continue to operate and reported disputes are only to be taken to compulsory arbitration where the matter cannot be settled by negotiation between the parties or by an agreed reference to voluntary arbitration. It was recognised, however, that to achieve the full purpose of the Order, it was necessary not only to supplement existing machinery for the settlement of differences by providing an ultimate resort to arbitration, but also to require recognised wages and working conditions to be observed and so to minimise causes of disputes. Consequently, while Part I of the Order provides for the settlement of disputes by negotiation and if necessary by arbitration, Part III makes it obligatory upon employers in every district to observe terms and conditions which have been settled by collective agreement or by arbitration for the trade concerned in that district. Part II of the Order prohibits lock-outs and strikes unless the difference has been reported to the Minister and has not been referred by the Minister for settlement within three weeks from the date on which the difference was reported to him. Part IV of the Order provides for the recording of departures from trade practices during the war, with a view to facilitating the operation of legislation for the restoration of those practices after the war.

(4) RC on Trade Unions and Employers' Associations, *Report*, Cmnd 3623 (1968)

The evidence which we have received shows that it was not effective: it did not succeed in reducing the incidence of unofficial strikes at that time. Indeed from 1941 until the Order was revoked in 1951 strikes were considerably more frequent that in any of the preceding twenty years. In December 1941 an attempt was made to enforce penalties against a number of miners who had struck work in the Kent coalfield. This attempt did not succeed. The evidence which we have had from Sir Harold Emmerson [Chief Industrial Commissioner, 1942–4], which is reproduced in Appendix 6, shows the fruitlessness of the use of penal sanctions for the purpose of enforcing industrial peace.

(5) National Union of Furniture Trade Operatives, *Statement on a Trades Union Congress 'Relations Between Unions' 1940 Award* (1953)

At a conference held on February 7th, 1940, between representatives of the National Amalgamated Furnishing Trades' Association and the Amalgamated Society of Woodworkers, convened by the General Council of the Trades Union Congress under the chairmanship of Mr G. A. Isaacs, M. P., the following draft Agreement was arrived at for submission to the respective Executives. . . .

(1) As from this date the National Amalgamated Furnishing Trades' Association agrees that the Amalgamated Society of Woodworkers had the right to enrol woodworkers employed in the building industry, and the A. S. W. accepts that the N. A. F. T. A. has the prior right to organise cabinetmakers in the furnishing industry.

(2) That as there is a mutual recognition of cards in shops and on jobs where the furnishing trade rates of wages and conditions of labour are applicable, the A. S. W. agree to recognise the card of the cabinetmaking section of the N. A. F. T. A. in the building industry on the definite understanding that such members observe building trade conditions of employment. Members of the cabinetmaking section of the N. A. F. T. A. who obtain work in the building industry must, within two weeks of securing employment therein, obtain from their Head Office a certificate showing that they were actually admitted into that section, failing which they may be removed from their place of employment at the discretion of the A. S. W.

(3) In case of doubt of any member of the N. A. F. T. A. who was employed in the building industry prior to the date of this Agreement, he must obtain a certificate as stated above from his head office.

(4) Any member of the N. A. F. T. A. who has been or may be employed in the building industry for a period of not less than three months, desiring to pay up and resign from his present Society to join the A. S. W. as a new member, may do so provided no pressure with this object in view is used by any member or official of the N. A. F. T. A. to prevent a member of the N. A. F. T. A. joining the A. S. W. under these conditions. Any member of the A. S. W. who has been or may be employed in the cabinetmaking industry for a period of not less than three months desiring to pay up and resign from his present Society to join the N. A. F. T. A. as a new member, may do so provided no pressure with this object in view is used by any member or official of the N. A. F. T. A., and no pressure must be used by any member or official of the A. S. W. to prevent a member of the A. S. W. joining the N. A. F. T. A. under these conditions.

(5) N. A. F. T. A. and the A. S. W. agree that if respective members' arrears exceed 26 weeks' contributions, such persons shall be classified as non-unionists and must apply for readmission to the previous Society, and each

Society agreed not to accept into membership ex-members excluded for violation of the respective general rules without consultation with the branch or branches on whose books they were enrolled when excluded.

(6) P. Inman, *Labour in the Munitions' Industry* (1957): Memorandum of Agreement between Engineering and Allied Employers' National Federation and AEU, 28 Aug. 1939

Temporary Relaxation of Existing Customs as to Employment of Skilled Men Members of the A. E. U. to provide for Peace-time Emergency Conditions

It is hereby mutually agreed:

1. In order to supplement skilled manpower in the Industry, where it can be shown that skilled men are not available and production is prejudiced, it is agreed that an alternative class of worker may be employed on jobs hitherto done by such skilled men under reservations to be mutually agreed.
2. Supplementary to this, semi-skilled labour may be utilised for the purposes of working with skilled men or under their direction, or performing such duties as may supplement the work of skilled men.
3. In the case of machining, the employer shall be allowed to put men of a semi-skilled character on to machines previously operated by skilled men under reservations previously referred to.
4. These reservations shall include that a register of standard type shall be kept of changes made under this agreement and an undertaking given by the Company that as and when skilled labour becomes available restoration to the pre-agreement practice shall be made.
5. The procedure for operating agreements shall be as follows:

   (a) An application for a change of practice shall be referred to a local joint Committee representative of the local Employers' Association and local representatives of the A. E. U., whose agreement shall be subject to confirmation by the executive bodies.
   (b) Failing agreement by the local joint Committee, or confirmation by either executive, the matter shall be referred for consideration by the executive bodies, i.e. representatives of the Federation and the Executive Council of the A. E. U.
   (c) Changes made under this agreement shall be registered by the employer on a standard form and a copy of such registration supplied to the worker or workers affected and to the local representatives of the Union and the Executive Council of the A. E. U. . . .

(7) *Price Stabilisation and Industrial Policy*, Cmd 6294 (July 1941)

The Government believe that all parties in industry are alive to the dangers of inflation. It is incumbent on employers and trade unions, with all the help the Government can give them, to do their best to prevent the costs of production from rising, from whatever cause. A special responsibility falls upon managements to eliminate waste and to see that the organisation of work is such as to make the most effective and economic use of plant capacity. By the concessions in regard to the Excess Profits Tax, the Government have endeavoured in the most effective way to provide an incentive to maximum development of productive capacity, and the urgent needs of the country make it a duty to increase efficiency of production to the utmost. The Government will take such steps as are possible to secure efficiency in establishments engaged in war production and the most effective use of labour resources.

It is regarded as the duty of both sides in industry to consider together all possible means of preventing the rise of costs of production and so to obviate rise of prices which is the initial step in the inflationary process. The use of the experience and knowledge of the workpeople is not less necessary than the application of managerial training and experience and the maintenance of wages and employers' remuneration at a reasonable level should be achieved as far as possible by improvement in the efficiency of production by the joint efforts of employers and workpeople. At the same time there may, consistently with these considerations, be proper ground for adjustment of wages in certain cases, particularly among comparatively low paid grades and categories of workers, or for adjustment owing to changes in the form, method or volume of production. . . .

Since the outbreak of war, the existing joint voluntary machinery for wage negotiation has operated successfully. Increases in wage-rates have been reasonable; the authority of the unions in the day to day adjustment of wages and conditions has been maintained; the freedom of opportunity to make claims and to have them discussed has enabled industrial peace to be maintained.

The policy of the Government, therefore, is to avoid modification of the machinery for wage negotiations and to continue to leave the various voluntary organisations and wage tribunals free to reach their decisions in accordance with their estimate of the relevant facts. These will no doubt pay due regard to cases where there are special grounds for adjustment such as those referred to in paragraph 8. If there were to be further increases in the cost of living this would need to be taken properly into account; but it is the object of the policy of price stabilisation to prevent such increases from arising, or at least to keep them within small dimensions, and the success of this policy will be dependent on the extent to which it achieves this object. It will therefore be necessary to bear in mind, particularly when dealing with general wage applications, that the policy of price stabilisation will be made impossible and increases of wage rates will defeat their own object unless such increases are regulated in a manner that makes it possible to keep prices and inflationary tendencies under control.

(8) TUC, *The Trade Unions and Wage Policy in War-Time* (1941): Memorandum to the Minister of Labour, July 1941

(1) The statements made by the Chancellor of the Exchequer, Sir Kingsley Wood, and the Minister of Labour, Mr Bevin, do not differ in any essential respect from that made by Lord Simon to the National Joint Advisory Council to the Ministry of Labour on December 6, 1939, as the then Chancellor of the Exchequer (Lord Simon) covered much the same ground and put forward the same broad reasons as those now presented. In effect he suggested 'that an increase in the cost of living should not be made the ground for an increase in wages. Wages should be increased only as a consequence of harder work. He, however, made it clear that he was not implying that an alteration of prices was no ground for reconsidering the rates of salaries and wages at all, as that would be going too far. What he asked was that there should be a slowing down of the tempo.

(2) In the statement of the present Chancellor and Minister of Labour it was stated that, 'since the outbreak of war, the existing joint voluntary machinery for wage negotiations has operated successfully. Increases in wage-rates have been reasonable; the authority of the Unions in the day to day adjustment of wages and conditions has been maintained; the freedom of opportunity to make claims and to have them discussed has enabled industrial peace to be maintained.' This statement supports the contention of the General Council that any attempt to control movements for the increases of wages is impracticable and undesirable. It is also a welcome recognition of the fact that no attempt has been made by the trade unions to exploit the war situation in the interests of their own members.

(3) It would appear, however, that despite this testimony to the manner in which wage negotiations have operated since the war, the statement does envisage an attempt to control the movement of wages. The General Council understand that it is the desire of the Ministers concerned to make a public statement, which would include a passage to the effect, 'that the purchasing value of existing and future wage rates depends largely on the maintenance of the policy of price stabilisation and that efforts to increase wage-rates will defeat their own object unless they are regulated in such a manner as to make it possible to keep prices under control and to avoid inflation'.

(4) The effect of such a statement would in the judgment of the General Council be such as to induce employers to refuse to grant advances of wages, and to remit these to arbitration. Arbitrators, and particularly such bodies as the National Arbitration Tribunal and the Industrial Court, would be bound to take note of such a pronouncement. Having regard to the passage in the proposed statement that, 'the maintenance of wages and employers' remuneration at a reasonable level should be achieved as far as possible by improvement in the efficiency of production by the joint efforts of employers and work-people', arbitration

proceedings would be seriously prejudiced, applicants would be required to show that output had actually increased, or that commensurably greater output would result from an increase in wages.

(5) Nowhere in the suggested statement is it made clear that provision would be made for comparatively low paid grades and categories of workers to have their earnings improved. Indeed by implication it would appear that only in exceptional cases affecting individuals or small groups of workers would an upward adjustment be permitted. . . .

(8) The economic arguments presented by Sir Kingsley Wood and Mr Bevin are not dissimilar from those submitted to the Council on behalf of the Government in December, 1939. The General Council, in considering those arguments, expressed the emphatic view that any attempt to control movements for increases in wages is impracticable and undesirable. That view was endorsed by the Trades Union Congress at Southport in October last year. The Council just as emphatically affirms that conviction to-day.

(9) When considering Lord Simon's statement, the Council agreed that the dangers arising from inflation would aggravate the financial problems of the Government, and supported the general policy of checking rises in the cost of living through controlling the selling prices of essential commodities, by rationing these articles so as to ensure equality of distribution, and by the Exchequer bearing the increased cost at the source, and urged that such measures should be further developed.

(10) The General Council further supported the policy of controlling profits arising through the war. At the same time it stressed the necessity for all members of the community to make all possible savings, and to lend these to the Government. The General Council welcomes the developments which have taken place in these matters, and believes that by their extension and fuller application the dangers of inflation can be avoided without the necessity for interfering with the adjustment of wages, which, on the Ministers' own showing, has worked admirably during the present war. Any attempt to interfere with that system would undoubtedly cause undesirable repercussions, and would seriously impair national unity and the prosecution of the war effort.

(9) MFGB, *Report of Special Conference . . . London . . . 25th and 26th November, 1943* (1943): Speech of Arthur Horner (South Wales)

This is not a simple wage demand, as many people seem to think it is. There appears to be an impression amongst the delegates to this Conference that nothing is important in the demands of the M. F. G. B. except the wage demand. That is not the view of the Executive Council. We are trying something much bigger than that. We are endeavouring to claim for the mineworkers of this country a new position, a new standing, in relation to other workers in this country. We are declaring that the industry is not efficiently organised. At this particular moment we find ourselves in the position that Government intervention in coal production has been accompanied by a serious decline in the amount of coal produced. In other words, judged in a post-war period, private enterprise has proved to be more efficient than the kind of control we have had up to the present time. Therefore it is vital for us to bring into being as rapidly as possible an effective form of control to prevent a reversion to the kind of operation which we had by private enterprise before this war. It is a very important thing that we should not be called upon at the end of the war to confront the nation with the fact that output per manshift is down 4 cwts. as compared with what it was before the war. We must force a situation in respect of control that will entitle us with better justification than we have at the present time to claim a development of Government Control rather than the automatic reversion to private enterprise, which will be the case if the facts at the end of the war are as they are at present.

The other thing we are trying to do is to claim, not on the basis of any agreement we have got, that miners' wages should be brought into accord with the average of the higher-paid industrial workers in the country. We are throwing on one side our District Agreements, our system of Ascertainments – throwing on one side our Cost-of-Living Agreement, the Attendance Bonus Award, the Greene Wage – we are saying, 'Forget that we said at the beginning of this war that if we have an automatic adjustment of wages to meet the increase in the cost-of-living we will be satisfied until six months after the war.' We are saying to the Government, 'Forget that; we are declaring that the miners of this country have the hardest work to do, the most dangerous work to do, and they should be paid as high a wage as any other industrial worker in the country.'

This is a revolutionary attitude. In respect of the other things we have found from the Districts what is really the trouble with our people? What are they complaining about? Why are they dissatisfied? And we have told the Government, first, give us more men; secondly, instal a system of organisation in the industry that will be efficient; thirdly, satisfy the reasonable demands of the men you expect to get the coal. And we are saying something else: We are concerned about after this war – is it to be the same as after the last war? We want guarantees from the Government, and we think there is no difficulty in giving the guarantees, that the miners shall be assured of a certain position at the end of the war.

As the war progressed, patriotic exhortations failed to restrain 'unofficial' strikes among miners, transport workers, engineering apprentices, gasworkers and others, and in April 1944 Bevin urgently discussed the matter with the TUC, which supported Regulation 1AA against such strikes (10). There was concern among unionists about the entry into old industries of new 'directed' conscripts, like the 'Bevin Boys' in the mines (11), who did not invariably share fellow-workers' attitudes (12). And from 1944 the TUC began to consider post-war problems in some detail (13, 14, 15). In preparation for the post-war world the miners at last organised a National Union in 1945 (16).

(10) TUC, *Statement on Regulation 1AA* (31 May 1944)

Obviously, we cannot traverse here the precise difficulties which Mr Bevin reported were being experienced, but it can be said that he gave a detailed review of the existing legislation and stated that he was not concerned with any additional provision against participation in strikes, but that, as matters then stood, there was no suitable legislation dealing specifically with incitement to strike.

Members of the General Council emphasised that it was difficult sometimes to ascertain the exact cause of a strike, and that there were undoubtedly occasions where these were provoked by the precipitate and autocratic action of employers. They felt that some protection should be afforded to Trade Unionists against vexatious prosecutions and against the possibility of miscarriage of justice. Finally, however, the Council agreed without a dissentient voice that, in view of all the circumstances of the immediate position and of the events which were expected to take place at an early date, they would support the Minister in taking steps to provide penalties against persons inciting men to come out on unofficial strike. . . .

It will be remembered that the Defence Regulations of 1939 were formulated prior to the outbreak of war and that in Regulation 1A of those Regulations, acts calculated to prevent or interfere with the carrying on of work by persons engaged in the performance of essential services were offences under the Regulation. As the right to strike was at that time perfectly lawful, the General Council persuaded the Minister to insert the following safeguard: –

> Provided that a person shall not be guilty of an offence against this Regulation by reason only of his taking part in, or peacefully persuading any other person to take part in, a strike.

In May, 1940, however, at the request of the Government, on the occasion of the collapse of France, the General Council entered into an undertaking that no resort would be had to strikes and lock-outs. In consultation with the TUC and the British Employers' Confederation the Conditions of Employment and National Arbitration Order (No. 1305) was then drawn up making strikes and lock-outs illegal. The question of instigating strikes was not then dealt with and the anomalous position remained that a person could be penalised for taking part in a strike or lock-out but not for instigating or persuading others to take part in the same. The amending Regulation 1AA removes this anomaly and stipulates that:–

> No person shall declare, instigate or incite any other persons to take part in, or shall otherwise act in furtherance of, any strike among persons engaged in the performance of essential services, or any lock-out of persons so engaged.

(11) MFGB, *The National Reference Tribunal under the Conciliation Scheme in the Coalmining Industry* (1944): Evidence of Enoch Edwards

My next point is that there is no comparison between our industry as it is today and as it was in 1942. That is the important fact; that is the point which I desire to emphasise. At that time it was true that the Essential Work Order was operating to retain in the industry those who were already in the industry; but the position to-day is quite different, because to-day people who have never been in our industry, are being directed to go into our industry. It is to-day the only industry in the country that cannot be manned by voluntary labour. When they have to choose, men choose the battlefield to working in the bowels of the earth; and you have an indication of their feeling on this matter when you find that out of thousands and thousands of persons in this country who have been asked to choose, only about three thousand have accepted mining as an alternative.

I want to emphasise this point to show the distinction between the circumstances in 1942 and the circumstances of to-day. This direction of labour has lifted the mining problem from the isolated valley and village, and made it a problem of the general community. I think nothing has taken place which has affected labour power so much as this definite State direction within a recent period, which has brought about a substantial change in the conditions and circumstances of the industry as between 1942 and the present time. This system, by which men are forced to work in the mines, has revolutionised the industry. We all know – and I am sure the other side will agree with me in this at any rate – that we are now in the hour of preparation for delivering the final blow to the enemy. We are now in a serious and critical position from the national point of view, and at this time, if there were a shortage of coal, it would not merely give a headache to the Government representatives, but would also give a headache to the two sides of the industry at this crucial moment. Really a psychological revolution is going on in the coalmines at present, and this smothers all phrases about 'substantial change', and makes them meaningless jargon; and it is because we want the workers of this industry to be in a situation in which we shall be able to meet that changed psychological position within the coalfield that we have tabled our demands.

(12) Bullcroft NUM, *A Final Appeal* (1946) – duplicated notice

A Branch meeting resolution has been unanimously passed instructing me to give final warning to non-union workmen, and unfinancial members that unless they become members of the N. U. M. action will be taken against them.

I therefore appeal to you to join at once and save any unpleasantness that may arise from you ignoring this resolution.

Do you realise that the benefits that YOU are in receipt of have been dearly fought for and won by the N. U. M.?

Ask yourself in all fairness, if you are playing the game with your financial workmates in participating in these benefits, whilst you sit back and shirk YOUR responsibilities.

So come into the fold and help us at Bullcroft to once again attain our 100% unionism.

Call and see me at the Union Cabin any day, any time, and I am sure you will not regret it.

TOM COWAN

SECRETARY.

(13) TUC, *Interim Report on Post-War Reconstruction* (1944)

The attitude of the Trades Union Congress towards the *Public Control and Regulation of Industry and Trade* was broadly defined in the report issued under that title submitted to Congress in 1932. The report opened by calling attention to the fact that:

> Labour policy . . . is tending to emphasise the transitional form of public control and the immediate steps to be taken rather than the more ideal programme of complete socialisation with the entire elimination of private enterprise. As a practical policy this would appear to be inevitable, given present conditions and the existing psychology of the British people. We may therefore expect that the change from undiluted private enterprise in many industries and services will be by way of general governmental regulation leading to operation by public corporations.

This conception of a gradual transition of the economic system involves more than a charge in the organisation of separate industries. There are certain minimum objectives of Trade Unionism which coincide with the general public interest and whose fulfilment ought not to wait upon the complete realisation of any long-term policy. The abolition of unemployment, the provision of an adequate number of good houses, reduced hours of labour, better working conditions and progressive improvements in the standard of living generally, for example, are objectives which must be achieved in the post-war world even if private ownership continues in a substantial section of the economic system. The achievement of such objectives, moreover, prepares the ground for further developments in the scope and form of public ownership; and all forms of public control and regulation can be examined according to the contribution which they can make to that development.

The 1932 report defined three categories into which industries and services fell: —

(a) Those immediately ripe for socialisation.
(b) Those less important or less unified but needing some measure of regulation in the public interest.

(c) Those of minor importance which can be left for the time being under completely private enterprise.

The report did not consider it possible to say 'with any exactness and finality' into which of those categories the various industries and services fell but that amongst the criteria of fitness of an industry or service for socialisation or public control were: –

(a) The importance of the industry to the life and safety of the community.
(b) The existence of monopoly or unification in an industry serving a wide demand.
(c) The importance of an industry as a source of demand for new investment.

(14) Ibid.: Composite resolution passed unanimously at the Southport TUC, 1943

This Congress registers its deep concern lest the end of the war shall not find the nation any better prepared for the tasks of peace than it was for those of war and urges upon the Government the pressing need for making clear to the nation and to the people of the subjugated countries its policy in relation to post-war social and economic affairs.

Recognising that Trade Unions constitute an integral part of the industrial and social life of the nation and that the industries of this country will require considerable reconstruction if a progressive standard of industrial and social security is to be attained, Congress authorises the General Council to prepare and to circulate a general plan for the post-war reconstruction of the industries of this country.

The plan to have specific regard to the maintenance of full employment; the degree of national ownership or control to which each industry shall be subjected; the extent to which the supply of raw materials, the output of finished goods, prices, standards of quality, etc., shall be subjected to public control and direction; and the place and responsibility of Trade Unions and the Trades Union Congress in such a plan. The plan to be so formulated as to allow for its adaptation by Trade Unions to the industries with which they are associated.

Congress recognises that the cost of additional staff necessary for the preparation and the publicising of the proposed reconstruction programme will be considerable, and in order to meet this cost the affiliated Unions shall, if required, contribute to a special Social Ownership and Reconstruction Fund the sum of one half-penny per member per annum in addition to their present affiliation fee.

Congress believes that unless this positive course is purused the country will be confused and deceived by the propaganda of the reactionary elements and the hopes and aspirations of the people for a new and better world after the war will be defeated.

(15) Ibid.

The extension of public control must mean an increasing democratisation of economic life. It will be essential for the Trade Union Movement to participate in the determination of all questions affecting the conduct of an industry.

Central machinery will be required to ensure that detailed industrial experience including that of work-people, is drawn upon in the formulation and administration of the Government's economic policy. For this purpose a National Industrial Council should be set up representative of all responsible for economic and industrial development, including the trade unions.

In publicly-owned industries the right of the organisations of work-people to be represented on the governing bodies should be recognised by statute. This could be secured by the selection of a number of the board's members from nominations submitted on behalf of the appropriate trade unions by the T.U.C. In addition there would be consultative councils at national, regional and sectional levels to advise the governing bodies and their responsible officials on the formulation and administration of policy, and on these the trade unions would be directly represented by persons appointed by and responsible to them.

In private industry there should be equal representation of the employers and the trade unions on industrial boards or other organisations established for the regulation of industry. . . .

Full employment as defined by Sir William Beveridge, namely a situation in which 'though on any one day there may be some men unemployed there are always more vacant jobs than there are unemployed men, so that every man whose present job comes to an end for any reason can find fresh employment without delay', is a general objective to which the Trade Union Movement subscribes. This does not imply, however, that the Trade Unions would approve *any* policy which might be likely to achieve this objective, or that they could commit themselves in advance to the details of any particular scheme for maintaining full employment without full and careful examination of all its implications for work-people. They could not, for example, accept a scheme which implied that workers could be compelled to work at wages less than established Trade Union rates.

Whilst we recognise that a disciplined observance of collective agreements and a high degree of mobility of labour between occupations are necessary to the permanent maintenance of a condition of full employment, we do not consider that compulsory arbitration or direction of labour are required or are in any way desirable. . . .

The main features of an adequate employment policy are now clearly established. Such a policy must include action by the Government to maintain the demand for the products of industry at a level sufficient to employ the whole of the population available for work; to direct the location of industry with proper regard to the supply and availability of labour; to ensure that industry is properly organised so that the demand for its products becomes effective in the provision of opportunities for employment; to regulate the total and character of our needs for imports and the character of our industries; and to train work-people and re-train them, when, for any reason, they become redundant to their existing industry or occupation.

Fluctuation in employment, however, as instability in the general level of prices, is attributable in the first place to the violent swings in private expenditure on industrial equipment. Success in the attainment of full employment will therefore be dependent ultimately on the extent to which private enterprise gives place to public ownership or is subject to public control.

(16) NUM, *Annual Conference, 1945. Report of the National Executive Committee* (1945)

Great changes have taken place in the form of our organisation since the Annual Conference held in 1943. It will be remembered that the Executive Committee having been instructed in 1942 to draft proposals for a change in the form of our Miners' Organisation, presented a scheme to the Annual Conference of 1943 and draft Rules which would form the basis of the new organisation.

These draft Rules were referred to the Districts and after they had had an opportunity of submitting amendments thereto, the proposals of the Executive Committee together with the amendments of the Districts were submitted to a Conference specially convened for the purpose of altering the Rules of the organisation.

That Special Conference held in Nottingham in August, 1944, was, in fact, a really historic event. Whereas at the commencement of their deliberations the delegates represented a number of wholly autonomous trade union organisations, the decisions arrived at by the delegates during the three day Conference were responsible for the establishment of one of the largest national industrial organisations in this country.

The National Union of Mineworkers, born as it was at Nottingham, could not have been expected to function immediately. In the first place, the Executive Committee had decided, a decision endorsed by the Special Conference itself, to seek the approval of the members as to the decisions taken by the delegates at Nottingham. The ballot vote of the members who were asked 'Are you in favour of approving and consenting to the decisions of the Special Conference held at Nottingham on August 16th–18th, 1944, whereby it was resolved that the name of the trade union heretofore known as the Mineworkers' Federation of Great Britain be changed to The National Union of Mineworkers and new Rules were adopted based on the principle of establishing a single trade union composed of workers employed in or connected with the coalmining industry of Great Britain to be registered under the Trade Union Acts, 1871 to 1927?' took place in October. When the result was declared it was found that the members of every District Association had overwhelmingly decided to support the proposed change. The national figures were 430,630 against 39,666, a majority of 390,964 in favour of endorsing the decisions of the Conference.

Having obtained the strongest possible authorisation to proceed, the National Executive Committee then had to deal with the great changes which were required from an administrative point of view. Head Office had to be re-organised and we had to ensure that there would be the closest possible co-ordination between the Area offices and Head Office.

Whilst the Rules adopted at Nottingham came into force when they were adopted on August 18th, it was obviously quite impossible to operate them until such time as the members had given their consent to the decisions of the Special Conference and until certain preparatory work had been put in hand on the administrative side: it was decided, therefore, that the 'One Union' should operate as from January 1st, 1945.

During the war, union membership rose substantially from 6,244,000 in 1939 to 7,803,000 in 1945 (of whom 4,867,000 and 6,671,000, respectively, belonged to organisations affiliated to the TUC). The election of Clement Attlee's Labour Government in 1945 was undoubtedly assisted by many unionists – who were rewarded by the repeal of the 1927 Act in 1946 (17). But post-war problems permitted no relaxation on income restraint, and in January 1947 Sir Stafford Cripps warned of the dangers of inflation (18), adding in February 1948 a classic statement on the necessity of an 'incomes policy' (19). For a time the TUC was willing to accept restraint (20), though the voting became increasingly narrow, as the 'Right', under such men as Arthur Deakin (1890–1955) of the TGWU and Lincoln Evans (1889–1970) of the ISKTC, (21, 22) argued for moderation against the 'Left' under such men as James Mortimer (b. 1921) of the Association of Engineering and Shipbuilding Draughtsmen and Arthur Horner (1894–1968) of the NUM (23, 24). The great argument over State intervention on incomes had begun. In general such 'plans' appealed to theorists of the 'Left', though they were accepted by the predominantly 'Right-wing' leadership of the TUC, and were hotly opposed by left-wing union leaders. On the face of the matter, the practical 'Right' agreed with the intellectual 'Left', to protect a Labour Government; but it had long suspected 'intellectual' plans (25), although many unions continued to advocate a socialist commonwealth (26).

(17) An Act to Repeal the Trade Disputes and Trade Unions Act, 1927, 9 and 10 Geo. VI, c. 52
Be it enacted. . . .

1. The Trade Disputes and Trade Unions Act, 1927 . . . is hereby repealed, and subject to the transitional provisions set out in the Schedule to this Act, every enactment and rule of law amended or otherwise affected by that Act shall, as from the commencement of this Act, have effect as if the Act of 1927 had not been passed.

(18) *Statement on the Economic Considerations Affecting Relations between Employers and Workers*, Cmd 7018 (Jan. 1947)

The object of all our economic policy and the prime purpose of all our industrial activity is to improve the standard of living of the people. This depends upon the output and efficiency of all our industries and essential services. The Government has maintained a substantial measure of control over the movement of prices. This has been achieved at a very heavy cost of subsidies and no guarantee can be given that some rise of prices may not be necessary to mitigate the burden on the Exchequer and the taxpayer. But the Government will maintain control and ensure that no unregulated increase in prices of essential goods and services occurs.

The keynote of all our industrial activities during the immediate period must be to steady the costs of production, to man up the essential undermanned industries and above all to step up production, until we have struck a balance between total demand and total supply. A great responsibility rests on both sides of industry to play their full part in rousing the nation to an appreciation of the country's very serious economic position and in ensuring that there is such a large and sustained increase in production as will enable us to have sufficient goods to pay for our essential imports and to meet the urgent needs of the people at home.

(19) *Statement on Personal Incomes, Costs and Prices*, Cmd 7321 (Feb. 1948)

The nation's economic welfare depends largely upon our ability to make and sell the exports necessary to buy the imports we need to feed and keep our industry going. Our costs of production are of vital importance and they depend to a considerable extent on the amount which industry has to pay in profits, salaries and wages. These in turn on the form of individual incomes affect the total value of money available in relation to the quantity of goods. . . .

The danger of inflation is ever present and will be accentuated by the drive to achieve a balance of payments, which will reduce the total volume of goods available on the home market. . . .

It is essential, therefore, that there should be no further general increases in the level of personal incomes without at least a corresponding increase in the volume of production. Unless we are prepared to check any such tendency we shall find ourselves unable to fulfil our export task owing to the rise in costs, which will also be reflected in rising prices on the home market. . . .

The Government accordingly feel bound to set out the following general considerations as a guide to all those deliberations and actions contributing to the settlement of incomes, from whatever source.

(a) It is not desirable for the Government to interfere directly with the income of individuals otherwise than by taxation. . . .

(b) In the view of the Government it is essential that there should be the strictest adherence to the terms of collective agreements. . . .

(c) In present conditions, and until more goods and services are available for the home market, there is no justification for any *general* increase of individual money incomes. . . .

(d) It does not follow that it would be right to stabilise all incomes as they stand

today. There may well be cases in which increases in wages or salaries would
be justified from a national point of view. . . .

(20) TUC, *Trade Unions and Wages Policy* (1950): Report of the TUC General
Council to the executives of affiliated unions

In March, 1948, following the publication of the White Paper on 'Personal
Incomes, Costs and Prices', the Trade Union Movement at a Conference of
Executives adopted a policy of restraint in wage demands as a contribution to a
national policy of full employment and the economic recovery of the country.

This trade union policy of wage restraint within the framework of collective
bargaining and free negotiation was adopted as part of a wide co-operative effort
involving all sections of the community. Voluntary limitation of dividends was
introduced at the same time. Manufacturing industry and commerce were called
upon to participate and to reduce prices voluntarily wherever possible. The
Government tightened price control and proclaimed its intention to do its
utmost to keep down domestic prices to the lowest practicable level. Trade union
participation was itself made conditional on the Government pursuing 'vigorously and firmly a policy designed not only to stabilise but to reduce profits
and prices'.

The policy of restraint was reaffirmed at the 1948 Margate Trades Union
Congress and the 1949 Bridlington Trades Union Congress at which it was
agreed that the joint endeavour had been reasonably successful, although
criticism could be directed at some of its aspects. Throughout this period
economic conditions remained difficult and in a Supplementary Report 'Trade
Union Policy and the Economic Situation', adopted by the 1949 Congress, the
General Council stated that they 'would be failing in their duty if they did not
make it unmistakably clear that there is no possibility of securing any widespread
and sweeping price reductions as long as the economic situation remains what it
is in the world at large'. Prices on the home market were, however, then being
held, and it was an implied condition of the continuation of the policy that the
price level should continue to be held approximately stable.

On September 18, 1949, the Government announced the alteration of the
dollar–pound exchange rate. Insofar as devaluation meant that we would have
to pay considerably higher prices for imports (the prices of which in recent
months had shown a tendency to decline) a new situation was created, and the
General Council met immediately to consider the impact of these changed
economic conditions on wages policy. . . .

Thus, while the General Council are satisfied that the policy which they
recommend to affiliated members is in the best interests of trade unionists
throughout the country, they are not yet satisfied that the requisite degree of
equality of sacrifice has been secured. They have noted increases of higher
salaries in industry, in the professions, and in the academic world. They view
with disapproval extravagant payments to directors in the motor-car manufac-

turing industry. The General Council will, therefore, take such steps as seem appropriate to secure a more equal sharing of burdens. . . .

The conclusions and recommendations of the General Council, which were circulated for the information and guidance of affiliated unions on November 23, 1949, are as follows –

(a) The General Council consider they should once again stress the gravity of the present economic situation, and emphasise the fact that devaluation has been adopted as an alternative to deflation. The dangerous inflationary tendencies which devaluation inevitably intensifies must be counteracted by vigorous restraints upon all increases of wages, salaries and dividends.

(b) The General Council insist that the existing machinery of voluntary negotiation must be preserved, as the only method – and one which has proved successful – of governing the adjustment of wages and working conditions and maintaining the authority of Unions in the day-to-day settlement of industrial problems.

(c) The General Council are emphatic that, whilst it is the responsibility of Unions themselves to operate the wages policy, Unions nevertheless must pay regard to the realities of the economic situation in framing their policy and act loyally in conformity with the policy now recommended by the General Council.

(d) The General Council recognise that the problem of the standard of living of low-paid workers may call for consideration in certain cases but nevertheless urge that in consideration of even such cases regard be had to the general economic problems necessitating rigorous restraint; and that special regard be given to the possibility of assisting lower-paid workers by the establishment of incentive schemes.

(e) The General Council recommend Unions to reconsider existing wage claims and sliding-scale arrangements with a view to holding agreed wage rates stable whilst the Interim Index of Retail Prices remains between upper and lower limits of 118 and 106; on the express condition that if and when the Index figure reaches either the upper or lower limit, both sides of any industry would be entitled to resume the normal consideration of wages questions in accordance with the provisions of their agreements, and that cost-of-living agreements would again operate. Should neither of these limits be reached before January 1, 1951, the above arrangements shall continue until that date and be reviewed in the light of the then existing facts.

(f) The General Council will intensify their campaign for increased productivity and more efficiency in industry and urge that the utmost publicity be given in each industry to all constructive suggestions to this end, not excluding overtime working.

(g) The General Council recommend that a review should be made within each industry with a view to extending systems of payment by results over the widest possible range, relating wages to output.

(h) The General Council intend to maintain a constant review of the operations of this policy and will report their conclusions periodically to affiliated Unions. . . .

(21) Ibid.: speech of Arthur Deakin

We have known since 1945 that this problem was with us and that it was increasing in intensity. I suggest we have been grappling as effectively as anyone possibly could with an issue of that character. What is the alternative suggestion? – let us have 'a free for all'. Mr Horner says: 'We are going on with a claim to which we think we are entitled involving an additional cost to the industry of £25 million.' I want to remind this Conference that in 1948 the surplus of the Coal Board amounted merely to £1,650,000. For the first three quarters of last year the surplus of the Coal Board amounted to £8,500,000. What does that mean? Where is the difference between £8,500,000 and £25,000,000 to come from? (Cries of 'Compensation'.) By increasing the price of coal to the consumer. . . .

(22) Ibid.: speech of Lincoln Evans

The thing that strikes me as curious is this, that the people who are most vociferous for a planned society are the most opposed to the idea of any voluntary plan for wages. You cannot have a planned society, you cannot have a controlled economic system, unless some control, voluntary or compulsory, is going to be exercised on wages. We might as well make up our minds to that, whatever our opinions are, because they are sheer hard economic facts. We can get that control by two methods, by the compulsions of the State or by the action of responsible bodies that are free, voluntary and independent like our own Trade Union Movement. Unless we exercise that responsibility and free control of our own volition, economic events will do it for us.

(23) Ibid.: Speech of Jim Mortimer

My executive recognise fully the need to pay regard to wider economic objectives in the formulation of a wages policy, and in particular to the avoidance of inflation and the maintenance of full employment. But the fulfilment of these objectives requires a comprehensive policy covering not only wages but prices and profits. It was this matter that was uppermost in the minds of the delegates to the conference of Trade Union Executives held in this hall in March, 1948. In the terms used in the General Council's recommendations at that time the principles of the White Paper were acceptable to the Trade Union Movement on condition that a firm and vigorous policy was pursued not only to stabilise, but to reduce prices and profits. The same thought was expressed by the General Council spokesman on that occasion. He said: 'We cannot be expected to restrain wage movements if the present general level of profits is allowed to continue.'

What has happened since that time? It is that which gives cause for concern to the Draughtmen's Executive. Prices have risen by moderate proportions but profits have risen by extravagent proportions. Profits have not been reduced; they have not even been stabilised; they have gone up substantially.

(24) Ibid.: Speech of Arthur Horner

It is now well known that the miners by an overwhelming majority have rejected the wages policy of the Trade Union Congress even though it was recommended for acceptance by the National Executive Committee and by a national conference. We are faced then with the fact that Demos has spoken and spoken in no uncertain terms. For after all, it is not in the main the persons who are present in this Conference this morning who are going to be affected by the acceptance of this wages policy: it is, in the main, the workers in industry who will feel the draught of any decision at which we might arrive. Every influence has been used in the discussions in the minefields to persuade the miners to a different point of view. Discussions have taken place in the atmosphere of an imminent General Election, and no one can accuse the miners of being lacking in political consciousness. Nowhere in this country is there such a terrible hatred of the Tories and all that the Tories stand for. Nowhere is there such a unanimous determination to install another Labour Government at the General Election of February 23. So it will be a waste of time, and a waste of breath to argue these temporary factors as reasons why the miners should change their point of view. Time and again the miners have saved the Labour Movement when all has seemed to be lost. In spite of all this the miners have, as I say, replied in definite terms that they are opposing this carefully thought out policy of the Trades Union Congress.

(25) ISKTC: *Man and Metal* (April 1944)

Professor Harold Laski, who is now Vice Chairman of the National Executive Committee of the Labour Party, thinks, according to a newspaper report, that the time had come when the trade unions should give second place to what he called 'bread and butter' questions. To put it bluntly, we should spend less time on wages and conditions and give first place, presumably, to advocating Laski's theories on how the world should be organised and governed, though we must confess it is sometimes beyond the wit of ordinary mortals to know exactly what these are. We suggest that such a piece of advice could only come from one in whose life a bread and butter problem never existed, and where the chief anxiety was about cake.

(26) NUR, *Rules* (Jan. 1942)

The objects of the Union shall be to secure the complete organisation of all workers employed on or in connection with any railway or transport undertaking in which any railway company has a financial interest in the United Kingdom or Irish Free State; to improve the conditions and protect the interests of its members; to obtain and maintain reasonable hours of duty, rates of wages, adequate retiring allowances, and other conditions of labour. To settle disputes between its members and their employers, and to regulate the relations between them by the collective withholding of labour or otherwise. To further, if and when and so far as the same shall be or become a lawful object of a Trade Union, the interests of members by representation in Parliament and on local governing bodies, and to employ the Political Fund of the Union in procuring such representation. To work for the supersession of the capitalist system by a Socialist order of society. To regulate the relations between the Union and its members. . . . To provide temporary assistance to members when out of employment. . . . To provide legal or other assistance when necessary. . . . To make grants to and share in the management and control of the Labour College or any College or institution having for its object to educate and train Trade Unionists in social science, in, and to take part in, the political and industrial life of the Labour Movement. To provide donations to any institutions from which members may derive benefit. . . .

The 'Left' continued to assert its voice against Government and TUC policies after 1945. The Communist Party of Great Britain attacked any form of 'incomes policy' (27) and tried to control some unions, particularly the ETU, whose rules were consistently violated by a small Communist group, which secured control of the union (28). The TUC strongly opposed such developments (29) and Deakin strictly applied TGWU rules of 1949 against Communist or Fascist officials (30), while many ETU members bravely fought against Frank Foulkes's control (31) and at last proved allegations of ballot-rigging.

(27) Harry Pollitt, *Trade Unionists – What Next?* (1948)

But perhaps the most serious and dangerous statement of all was that made by Mr Harold Wilson, President of the Board of Trade, who stated at Southport on 5 October: 'Last year and this year the amount we could export had been determined by what we could produce and screw out of the home market. From now on what we could export depended on the cost at which we could produce.'

That is exactly the same type of statement, on the eve of a general offensive against the workers' conditions, that has been made by open representatives of a monopoly capitalism in the past, and it has always been followed by a drive for lower wages, longer hours and speeding up of every worker on the job. But always this policy in the past has met with the sharpest resistance from the workers, and there are many signs to prove it will do so again.

There is often a tendency to see the main issue today as the prospect of a slump. But this is not the immediate issue. The immediate issue is the organisation of the workers to fight against the offensive of the Labour Government and the Federation of British Industries, who are out for lower real wages, speed-up and longer hours. . . .

We note that the speeches of Sir Stafford Cripps and General Council leaders always express opposition to any idea of asking the workers to work harder – *but*; they are not asking for longer hours – *but*; they are not asking for wage freezing – *but*.

And behind all these *'buts'* the ground is being prepared for an actual attempt to secure increased exploitation, lower wages, and longer hours. That is what lies behind Mr Wilson's speech. . . . That is what lies behind the statements of Sir R. Weeks and Mr E. H. Browne.

All the talk of Mr Tewson and Mr Lawther about the 'new status and responsibilities of the trade union' is only meant to cover the real policy, which is (1) to prepare the trade unions passively to accept the policy of the Labour Government and big business; (2) to stand for the complete dependency of Britain on the U. S. A., which in reality means dependence on capitalism, the age-old policy of right-wing Social Democracy. It is the responsibility of the working class to find another solution – a Socialist one.

(28) Woodrow Wyatt, *The Peril in our Midst* (1956)

I am convinced that the great majority of the 216,000 rank and file members of the E. T. U. do not wish their union to be run by Communists. But under present conditions they are helpless. I will prove it.

In December, 1947, there was an election for the post of general secretary. A Mr Byrne, an official from the E. T. U. in Scotland, opposed the Communist nominee, the late Mr W. C. Stevens.

In his election address he pointed out that he was a member of the Labour Party. He suggested that the time had come to end Communist domination of the union since nearly all its members supported the Labour Party and not the Communist Party.

He didn't win. But the size of his vote startled the Communists. At once the Communist-dominated executive council of the union passed a resolution that, in future, no candidate for a full-time national office should be allowed to mention his politics.

Not only that, another resolution was passed that 'candidates be instructed to submit their election addresses to the Head Office of the Union' before they were sent out.

Despite this precaution, another shock came for the Communists when an election took place in June, 1948, for the post of assistant general secretary. There was three candidates: Mr Byrne; Mr Haxell, a Communist; and a Mr Lowden.

Although Mr Byrne had been muzzled and was no longer able to state his political beliefs in his election address and warn the members against the dangers of continuing Communist domination, he topped the poll. He got 27,587 votes; Mr Haxell just over 25,000 votes.

But the third candidate, Mr Lowden, got just enough votes to make the total of his own and Mr Haxell's votes exceed those of Mr Byrne by 229. Consequently,

Mr Byrne had narrowly failed to win over both his opponents together.

As a result – and this is correct trade union practice – a second ballot was called for between Mr Byrne and Mr Haxell as they were the two at the top of the poll. In the second ballot, held in September, 1948, Mr Haxell got 33,399 votes and Mr Byrne got 28,732.

How was it done? By some of the Communist-influenced branches falsifying the returns.

Before the Communists secured control of the union not more than around ten per cent of the membership of the E. T. U. used to vote in elections for national officers. In the ballot that re-elected the Communist general secretary in December, 1947, the voting recorded was nineteen per cent of the membership.

By the time of the second ballot for the assistant general secretaryship in September, 1948, when a Communist was officially returned as the winner, the voting had mysteriously increased to thirty-four per cent of the total membership.

The system of voting for national officers in the E. T. U. is that ballot papers are sent to the secretaries of local branches. They, in turn, post them to the members of their branches, enclosing an envelope in which the ballot paper is supposed to be returned to the branch.

The method of returning the ballot paper is either by putting a 2½d. stamp on the enclosed envelope and sending it through the post, by handing it to a shop steward, or by handing it in personally at a branch meeting.

During the present state of apathy in trade unions, it is unlikely that even as many as nineteen per cent of the membership of any union would bother to go through this procedure.

In fact, many branches in the E. T. U., not dominated by the Communists or their friends, often do not trouble to hold a vote at all.

The votes are counted in the branches by two rank-and-file scrutineers in the presence of the branch president and secretary. Counting is at the branch, but can begin an hour before the meeting.

All that then has to be done is to fill in a form saying how many votes each candidate got. The number of those who voted should be declared at the end of the meeting (but often is not) and entered in the branch minutes.

Many rank-and-file members of the E. T. U. do not even know or care when an election is taking place. And many Communists and fellow-travelling branch secretaries know how to take advantage of this apathy.

They do not stop at failing to urge the laggards to vote. Frequently they send out only fifty to sixty ballot papers out of several hundreds, to those members who, they have found, take an interest in trade union proceedings. They bank on the rest never hearing about the election. This makes the falsification of returns less troublesome.

If anyone has not received a ballot paper for an election and wants to know why he has been left out the answer is pat: 'It must have been lost in the post', or: 'It was a clerical error. I ticked you off as having been sent one.'

The return showing how the branch has voted is sent to head office. There the total votes are added up.

And that is the end of the matter unless someone in a branch demands to know how its votes were cast. This has hardly ever been known to happen.

It is easy for an official who is a Communist or fellow traveller to fill in the votes in any way he likes – and no questions asked – provided he has access to the forms. Once the branch meeting has started the President and Secretary are concerned with conducting that and may not be able to watch closely the counting of the votes. Consequently not even the connivance or complaisance of all the officials concerned is required to falsify the returns.

(29) TUC, *The Tactics of Disruption – Communist Methods Exposed* (1949)

. . . once inside the Communist Party, contact is maintained not by means of open meetings but mainly by means of factions and group meetings in obscure places without publicity, at which decisions are taken and tactics determined whereby Communist policy can be projected inside the organisations with which they are individually connected. . . .

Lines of policy, and methods of securing its adoption, are thus determined not only outside the machinery of the trade union, but also outside of its membership. Decisions are taken by these Communist factions, who may be advised in advance by Communists and 'fellow-travellers' who hold official positions in the branch or on the trades council not only of the items on the agenda of the meeting, but also of the nature of the items. . . .

Similarly, decisions are taken outside of trade union machinery to regulate nominations of Communists for elections in trade unions and trades councils, and frequently strong pressure is brought to bear by Communists to secure the withdrawal of certain Communist nominees in order to ensure that only the same number of Communists are nominated as there are vacancies to fill.

Having ensured that only the same number of Communists have been nominated as there are vacancies to fill, the Communist Party underground gets to work appropriately. . . .

(30) *Daily Mail* (11 July 1951)

Appeals by eight former full-time officials of the Transport and General Workers' Union, dismissed because they failed to declare themselves non-Communists, were turned down by the union yesterday.

The union, meeting in annual conference at Whitley Bay, Northumberland, went into secret session to hear the appeals.

Later, a delegate said: 'The appeals were a flop. We did not even bother to count the votes. It was overwhelming.'

The men, dismissed in January 1951 by the general executive council, are: Mr S. Henderson, former national secretary of the Passenger Services Group; Mr D.

J. Lewis, Mr W. J. Warren, and Mr C. A. Jordan, all of London; Mr C. H. Player, East Anglia; Mr G. McKay, Glasgow; Mr A. E. Scarr, Wolverhampton; and Mr H. Windle, Huddersfield.

Action against them was taken following acceptance by the 1949 conference of a rule that no Communists or Fascists would be eligible for office in the union.

Since then all candidates for election to national or local office have been required to sign an undertaking, and failure to do so had rendered the nomination invalid.

Mr Henderson said later: 'The executive council had acted more ruthlessly than any private employer. It has refused to adopt the historical and traditional role of the union as a protector and advocate against the intimidation and political discrimination of the workers.'

(31) *Daily Telegraph* (22 Jan. 1954)

A move to oust Mr Frank Foulkes from the presidency of the Electrical Trades Union is planned by some of Scunthorpe's 'rebel' electricians. They have accused Mr Foulkes, a Communist, of 'undemocratic conduct'.

He completes his first three-year term as president this year. He has been bitterly criticised for overruling the Scunthorpe men, when they decided, by 243 votes to 17, not to join in the union's guerrilla strikes last week.

He ordered the men to strike under threat of severe disciplinary action. His conduct was denounced by some members as 'dictatorship with the lid off' and 'intidimation of the worst sort'.

Within the next few months the union will call for nominations for the presidency. Many of the electricians' mates say that the national ballot for the post will give them 'an opportunity to show Mr Foulkes that Moscow methods will never be tolerated by Britons'.

One of them said to me last night: 'Many non-craftsmen will not vote for Mr Foulkes. We hope to nominate someone who will appeal to the majority of members, whether they are craftsmen or only labourers. Above all, he must not be a Communist.'

12. *The Fifties*

While in 1941 the TUC favoured the extension of Order 1305, from 1946 the ETU, in 1947 the AEU, in 1948 the Bakers' Union and from 1949 the NUJ advocated its abolition. The TUC of 1950 by a two-to-one majority favoured retention, but in February 1951 the General Council demanded 'revocation' and 'the removal of all restrictions on strikes and lockouts', in the new situation of inflation and prosecutions. The consequent substitution of Order 1376 (the Industrial Disputes Order), retaining a measure of compulsory arbitration, did not please all unionists (1). Bryn Roberts's NUPE, composed of low-paid workers, inevitably favoured 'a national wage policy' (2, 3), as did others (4), but Frank Foulkes's ETU was bitterly hostile (5, 6). Skirmishing over incomes restraint thus continued. Other politically oriented arguments also continued. After considerable trouble with some 'left-wing' trades councils (especially in London), the TUC issued a warning to the councils (7). Regular dock strikes, despite the attempts of the Dock Labour Board of 1947 to decasualise labour, raised much public protest (8) and led to attacks on Deakin's vast TGWU.

(1) **NUPE**, *Public Employees' Journal* (March–April 1951): Speech of Bryn Roberts, General Secretary, to the Haldane Society

This beats everything that has so far emerged from King Street. The Communists only want arbitration abolished; they are discreetly silent about strikes and lock-outs. But the General Council goes the whole hog!

As information from Transport House only comes to affiliated Unions in driblets there is no information available to account for this sudden and unexpected decision of the General Council. . . .

Instead of devising a bold, industrial programme designed to remove the causes that generate strikes, the General Council, with what seems to be a gesture of fatalistic resignation, slides back to its traditional pre-war role.

Which is more preferable – full employment and a planned economy or unfettered liberty to strike? We cannot have both. . . .

Nor can socialist planning proceed without compulsory arbitration, and its proposed abolition is a retrograde step in industrial relations. Without compulsory arbitration large masses of workers will be deprived of a valuable negotiating instrument.

. . . I hope . . . that the National Arbitration Tribunal as at present constituted will be preserved.

In spite of what I have said, I would not renounce the strike weapon in all and every circumstance. In a democracy there is no need to renounce it. Only in the Police State is the strike weapon a museum piece.

If, at some future date, a Tory Government proceeded to transfer the nationalised industries back to private enterprise, or if our rights and freedom were to be threatened, this great movement would be fully justified in resorting to direct action, as it would be in resisting aggression from abroad.

(2) Ibid., (Jan.–Feb. 1951): Paper by Bryn Roberts

I can never understand why so many of my trade union colleagues who claim to be good socialists, should oppose a national wage policy and do everything possible to prevent its realisation.

(3) Ibid., (March–April 1951): Article by A. W. Fisher

At the 1950 T. U. C. our Union [NUPE] tabled two addenda to resolutions submitted by the General Council. The first sought to cut out the competition between Unions in the Nationalised Industries, and the second to bring about a revision of the present Trade Union structure so that it might be planned to play a fuller part in meeting the needs of a planned economy. Clearly, both would have a material contribution to make to the production battle, but, unfortunately, with lack of vision and blocked by vested interests, they were defeated. . . .

Bro. Bryn Roberts has advocated the setting up of a Central Wages Authority vested with power to allocate the available income to the competing sections of industry and the public services.

(4) IRSF, *Taxes*, (June 1951)

Conference also re-affirmed its belief in a National Wages Board and decided that efforts to convert the Trades Union Congress on this matter should continue.

(5) *Daily Telegraph* (27 May 1952): ETU conference

Of wages, Mr Foulkes said: 'The trade unions should fight with all their industrial might against any attempt by any political party to introduce a wage freeze, particularly during a period of rising prices.'

(6) Ibid. (12 May 1953): ETU conference, speech by F. Foulkes

Negotiations alone will not be sufficient to persuade the employers of the needs of our members. In conjunction with the negotiations it will be essential for the workers themselves to give expression to their desires.

The employers must be informed through workshop organisation, through the shop stewards, that the workers are determined to obtain for their families sufficient to enable them to live in comfort and decency.

There will be no fundamental difference in the answer of the nationalised industries and the private employers to our claims; the mood of the workers will decide the answer. Our members must be in the forefront of the struggle.

(7) TUC, *Trades Councils, 1949. Report to the Annual Conference of Trades Councils* (1949)

In addition to giving services to affiliated branches, Trades Councils are registered in order to support and publicise, and where appropriate to administer, national policy decided by the elected delegations of union at Congress. One of the functions of Trades Councils, as local agents, is to nominate representatives to put the trade union point of view on local committees. It follows that if the T. U. C. decide to support particular aspects of public endeavour and nominate a trade unionist to represent the Movement nationally on a particular committee, that Trades Councils should accept similar responsibilities in their localities. Most Councils, of course, fully understand the position, and their affiliated branches readily accept that there can be only one policy-making body for the Movement as a whole. A minority of Councils, however, misinterpret their responsibility of administering policy made nationally and wish only to carry out certain aspects of Congress policy and to nominate representatives only on certain committees. . . .

Since the General Council did not recognize two agents in one locality, in such cases considerations would have to be given to withdrawing recognition from a Trades Council which had shown itself unable to act as an agent.

Branches which do not agree with decisions made by one Congress are at liberty to seek to change the policy of their own union and thereby to influence the decisions taken by all unions at the next Congress. Until policy is changed, however, it is the duty of Trades Councils to administer it in their localities.

(8) *The Spectator* (26 Nov. 1951)

The popular impression that there is always trouble with dockers, especially London dockers, and that nothing is ever done about the root causes of it, is not far from the truth. The current quarrel between a firm of master stevedores and its employees at Tilbury, over a proposal to make a small number of men permanent members of the firm's staff instead of casual workers, is only the latest manifestation of an old problem which has exercised dock employers and workers for many years and last led to a major strike in London as recently as April, 1950. The apparently innocuous desire to give certain men – usually the most reliable and vigorous – permanent employment is always interpreted by some dockers as a device for pushing the weaker men to the wall. It is attacked, in other words, because it does not share the work out equally among good and bad, weak and strong, energetic and lazy. The arguments that the good docker deserves his reward, that there is no virtue in levelling down, and that the man who cannot get enough work at the docks can find plenty elsewhere have little weight with the aggrieved dockers. They cling to the casual labour system. . . .

Representing, as they did, the 'Right', the big unions regularly infuriated both Communists and 'Bevanite' supporters of the Labour Party by casting doubt on 'orthodoxies' of the 'Left', such as wider nationalisation of industry (9, 10). 'Political' strikes were condemned by the National Council of Labour (composed of members of the TUC, Labour Party, Parliamentary Labour Party and Co-operative Movement) on 26 February 1952 (11), to the anger of the 'Left' (12). Another cause of friction was the decision of Lincoln Evans, the ironworkers' leader, to join the Steel Board: the 'Left' strongly disapproved, but Evans hotly defended his decision (13) and other leaders condemned the notorious 'unofficial' strikes of the period (14) – as did Aidan Crawley, successively a Labour and a Conservative MP (15).

(9) Iron and Steel Trades' Confederation, *Man and Metal* (Feb. 1950) Paper by Lincoln Evans, General Secretary

One of the strongest arguments for nationalisation had been that the workers will be inspired by entirely different motives when working for the good of the nation rather than private shareholders. So far there has been no marked evidence that this is the case.

(10) *Daily Express* (12 July 1951): Report by Trevor Evans on speech by Arthur Deakin, TGWU conference

'If in October the Government appeals to the country and there is any considerable extension of proposals to nationalise industry, we shall get the biggest whacking we've ever had.

'Don't let us fool ourselves. We have not got the capacity at this time to bite off more than we can chew.'

To those who want more state-owned industries, he said: 'We must accept a greater measure of responsibility than we have up to now. We have got to justify further nationalisation by making present nationalisation work.'

He pointed to the possible nationalisation of the building industry, whose workers are in Mr Bevan's camp: 'The building industry has been a fruitful field for development by local authorities, but we haven't made the outstanding job there that we might have.

'Again it comes back to the responses of the people in industry.'

(11) *Daily Telegraph* (27 Feb. 1952): National Council of Labour

The Council unanimously decided to express 'in strongest terms its condemnation of the attempts now being made by irresponsible elements to persuade trade unionists to take industrial action in order to achieve political ends.

'Such action, in addition to threatening the economy of the nation, is in itself a direct challenge to the supremacy of our established democratic institutions.

'The campaign which is being organised under the pretext of protesting against the action of the present reactionary Government is in fact part and parcel of a world conspiracy to undermine the industrial power of the nation and to weaken its resistance to totalitarianism.'

(12) *Daily Telegraph* (27 May 1952): F. Foulkes to ETU conference

It has been suggested that industrial action should not be used for political objectives. Experience has shown, however, that there is no line of demarcation between an industrial objective and a political objective.

We cannot afford to wait until a Tory premier decides the time is opportune to consult the electorate. The living standards of the workers must be defended at all times by industrial and political action.

If it is correct to support a government well disposed to the working classes, it must logically be correct to oppose a government well disposed towards the employing class. This union will never hesitate to give maximum support to its members who take action to defend themselves against exploitation or victimisation, or to safeguard their living standards.

(13) *Daily Mail* (10 June 1953)

Sir Lincoln Evans yesterday hit back at the Bevanites by accusing them of 'McCarthyism in reverse'.

He asserted that they had deliberately whipped up the controversy over the Steel Board appointments as part of the cold war they have been conducting in the movement.

Sir Lincoln launched his counter-attack in his union journal, *Man and Metal*, and aimed what was clearly intended as a direct hit at Mr Harold Wilson, the Bevanite who was President of the Board of Trade in the Socialist Government.

'These loyalty tests', Sir Lincoln Evans declared, 'produce strange results. When ex-Ministers and others associated with the Left group are employed as advisers to private firms their loyalty is never questioned'.

Sir Lincoln states that when his executive approved his acceptance of the Steel Board post they took into account the declared policy of the T. U. C. to work amicably with any Government where trade union interests are involved in the industrial sphere.

He declares: 'The doctrine that trade unions, for political reasons, should not help private industry to become more efficient is too silly for words, and to be charged with disloyalty if one does not accept this view is sillier still.'

(14) NUGMW, *Journal* (June 1955): Article by Tom Williamson, General Secretary

Never in its history has the Trade Union Movement been faced with a more serious situation than during the past few months.

Irresponsible stoppages of work in certain sections of British industry have threatened the employment of thousands of other workers and caused injury to the economic stability of the nation.

This is naturally creating an impression that the organized labour force is acting irresponsibly and becoming out of hand.

The fact is, however, that never were there so many at work (over 22 millions), whilst only a small proportion of this vast labour force has been directly involved in these serious stoppages of work.

But whilst only comparatively few workers are involved in these stoppages, the effects can be serious, and there are suggestions in some quarters for remedial action – legal action, if necessary.

The right to strike is a fundamental principle of democratic trade unionism, and any attempt to interfere with the right of a workman or workmen to withdraw his or their labour, subject to authority of proper notice in accordance with contract or agreement, would be met with the fierce opposition such a move would deserve.

But there are some who do not know, or seem to forget, that the rights of democratic trade unionism, which do not exist in some parts of the world, carry with them certain responsibilities, and that in the long run we cannot have the rights without having the responsibilities.

And the sooner this elementary precept is understood and accepted, the better for us all. . . .

If we, as a Trade Union Movement, want to commit suicide, there is no surer way than by allowing the creeping paralysis of undisciplined industrial action to grow within our ranks.

Indeed, if anything is likely in the long run to prejudice the right to strike, it is the unjustified abuse of it, often in breach of contract, and in spite of provisions for negotiation and conciliation. These flagrant breaches of constitutions and rules bring trade union organization into disrepute and warrant the strongest condemnation. . . .

(15) Aidan Crawley, *Signpost to Success* (1957); repr. from the *Sunday Times* (6–27 Jan. 1957)

In other words *the general standard of living of trade unionists in this country is much lower than it should be. This is a measure of the trade unions' failure.*

Yet what is stopping the trade-union leaders from raising the standard of living of their members is not too much power but too little. There is no lack of clear-sightedness among the leaders themselves. With a few notable exceptions they have made it abundantly clear that they understand the change that has taken place in Britain's trading position in the world. They have stated over and over again that it is no longer a question of winning for labour a larger share of the wealth that is going, but of steadily increasing wealth as a whole and of seeing that labour gets an increasing share. But the leaders have failed to get their message across.

If the only strikes which the country had to fear were the strikes deliberately called by union leaders there would be very few stoppages in industry. If the only restrictive practices in operation were those which union leaders thought necessary for the protection of their members, productivity would be enormously increased. If the only wage claims submitted were those which the union leaders themselves believed could be granted without raising the cost of living, the inflationary spiral would at once be reduced, but none of these conditions is fulfilled.

The truth is that the leaders are no longer their own masters. There has been an enormous shift of power within the trade-union movement from the centre to the factory floor.

However vigorously the leaders themselves deny this, the evidence is too strong to be contradicted. For example, since the war the vast majority of strikes have been not official but unofficial. They have been called not by the union leaders but against their wishes. The most significant thing about the inter-union dock strike of 1955 was not that it rendered the ports of the country idle but that the leaders of the union representing the vast majority of dockers were opposed to it and were unable to persuade the men to return.

And for every strike on a nation-wide scale there have been hundreds confined to particular industries and particular factories about which nothing has been heard. The most glaring example is in the coal mines, where unofficial stoppages have cost us more than half the coal we are having to import every year. The occasions of the stoppages are infinitely varied. . . .

Few employers stood out against their employees engaging in trade unionism, but D. C. Thomson and Co., the Dundee-based publisher of a wide range of Scottish newspapers, such as the *Sunday Post*, and of comics, such as *Dandy* and *Beano*, staunchly insisted on non-unionism (16, 17). More commonly, however, it was union efforts to establish a closed shop that came to public notice (18), and the 'Bonsor Affair' raised the issue of the individual's relations with his union (19). During the same year, the issue of enforcing union membership against the wishes of certain workers was tested in the case of *Spring* v. *NASDS* (20).

(16) *Report of a Court of Inquiry into a Dispute between D. C. Thomson and Company Limited and Certain Workpeople, Members of the National Society of Operative Printers and Assistants*, Cmd 8607 (1952)

Mr Harold Thomson in his evidence gives a two-fold reason for the introduction of the non-union policy in 1926, namely, that 'it is a safeguard to the management that everyone who is employed does know the real conditions of the house, that it is a non-union house. That is, that they can feel that they will not have a man in the next seat who is an exponent of unionism'.

Mr D. C. Thomson who was 'very, very vexed' at the course taken by the unions at the time of the General Strike, which he then described as having 'seriously damaged this publishing industry' and as being 'the culmination of a long growing series of tyrannical attacks on the control of the industry which had really reached the stranglehold in which neither managers nor men could call their souls their own', has more recently asserted that the object of the non-union policy is to protect the workers from the 'hell' they had when prior to the General Strike the Company recognised the Unions.

The non-union policy, it is claimed, has resulted since 1926 in peace in the Company's establishments.

(17) *Yorkshire Post* (9 May 1952)

The [Printing and Kindred Trades' Federation] regret that the firm of D. C. Thomson and Co. still refuse to make any proposals on the reinstatement of strikers or to agree to the question being referred to arbitration. The detailed terms on which the two unions principally concerned in the dispute and on which the Federation Executive are prepared to make a settlement have been communicated to the firm through the Ministry of Labour.

The terms include an undertaking to withdraw immediately action against the firm and assurances that the unions would not exert pressure on Thomson employees to join a union, nor would they seek to impose an obligation on the firm only to employ trade unionists.

They feel that they have gone a long way to meet D. C. Thomson and to give him safeguards which he considered necessary. They are, however, entirely unable to give way on the important principle of reinstatement, and in this they have the support of the T. U. C.

An unsuccessful appeal has been made to Sir Walter Monckton, Minister of Labour, to use his influence to try to persuade D. C. Thomson to refer the reinstatement question to arbitration.

The printing trade unions have tried to reach a settlement on the dispute in accordance with the letter and spirit of the report of the Court of Inquiry.

The unions consider, however, that no such conciliatory attitude is displayed by the firm.

(18) *Daily Telegraph* (27 May 1952)

Mr Richard W. Briginshaw . . . said that the object of the strike at Thomson's was 'to obtain for members the right to belong to a trade union without the fear of dismissal for so doing'.

He had no personal ill-will or ill-motive towards Mr Thomson. Natsopa had received immediate support from the trade union movement.

About a fortnight after the dispute began he had a chance conversation with

Sir William Lawther and Mr Arthur Horner, leaders of the National Union of Mineworkers, 'in our local pub, where we all have our lunch'. The conversation took place before a writ was issued by Thomson's.

The N. U. M. had contributed £1,000 towards the Natsopa strike and 'probably hundreds of other unions' had signified their support either general or financial. Natsopa were paying strikers about £800 a week.

Asked by Mr Gilbert Beyfus, Q. C. for D. C. Thomson and Co., if it was not a principle of trades unionism to try and get a closed shop, Mr Briginshaw said: 'It is a principle to try to get 100 per cent membership.'

He agreed that a London bus driver could not get employment unless he belonged to the Transport and General Workers Union.

He also accepted counsel's statement that a smaller union to which some London bus drivers had belonged had been smashed by the Transport and General Workers Union and the London Passenger Transport Board. He would not say that his union sought by strikes to secure 100 per cent membership.

Mr Beyfus: The policy of your union can be described in three words – infiltration, penetration and domination – I accept the first two but not the third.

I do not mean domination of the whole of the industrial policy of a company. I mean 100 per cent T. U. membership? – A 100 per cent T. U. membership, yes.

That may include strike action? – Most of the actions of the trade unions may at sometime include strike action.

Mr Briginshaw denied that Natsopa had tried to coerce Messrs Waterlow's into applying a 'closed shop' policy. There was an aspect that union members declined to work with non-union men.

Mr Beyfus: You are going to deny a man the right to abstain from joining a trade union by having a strike? – Not necessarily by strike.

Why do you pretend you are in favour of freedom of choice when quite obviously you are not? – Those who try to contract out pretend it is a matter of conscience when usually it is not so.

Mr Beyfus read a union circular which he claimed stated that Thomson's premises should be permanently picketed, and that drivers who delivered goods should be told of the dispute. The circular added: 'If the driver is non-co-operative it will be necessary to have the haulier's name.'

Mr Beyfus: When you went to Glasgow on a Saturday night did you genuinely believe that within half an hour the policy of 26 years could be reversed? – Yes.

You chose a Saturday night for a lightning strike because it would be the most effective time for Thomson's who print the Sunday Post? – Quite honestly, certainly.

Mr Briginshaw said that strikers had been paid their full wage, and 'we can go on paying them that for a long time'.

Mr Beyfus repeatedly asked whether Natsopa had not tried to stop Thomson's supplies of new materials.

When Mr Briginshaw answered: 'We have not done that', counsel said: 'If you pursue that line, I have to suggest that not a word of your evidence is to be believed.'

(19) *Bonsor* v. *Musicians' Union*, House of Lords [1956] AC 104

Lord Keith: My Lords, I think that the decisions of this House show that, in a sense, a registered trade union is a legal entity distinguishable at any moment of time from the members of which it is at that time composed. It remains a voluntary association of individuals but it is capable of suing and being sued in its registered name; it holds property, through trustees, against which a creditor holding a decree against it could levy execution; it acts by agents; and it has other rights and is subject to other liabilities set out in the Trade Union Acts.

In the result, then, my view is that Mr Bonsor's contract of membership was a contract between himself and the other members of the union. On the view I have endeavoured to express it may be regarded also as a contract with the trade union, for the trade union, in its registered capacity, is representative of all the members. So long as this is kept in view it is convenient to talk of a member's contract of membership as a contract with his trade union. . . .

If the expulsion takes place on the initiative of the union officials it appears to me that it reduces the position to an absurdity to say that the officials were acting as the expelled member's agents in the matter of the expulsion. They are no more his agents in the matter complained of than would be a majority who expelled him in a general meeting.

(20) *Spring* v. *NASDS*, [1956] 1 WLR 585

After a dispute between the defendant union and another union affiliated to the T. U. C., the T. U. C. Disputes Committee made an award deciding that the defendant union should exclude from membership all the members recruited at certain ports after a certain date. These members included the plaintiff. The union purported to exclude the plaintiff from membership. When sued, the union argued, *inter alia*, that it was an implied term of the plaintiff's contract of membership that he could be expelled if this was required by the T. U. C. Disputes Committee under the Bridlington Agreement. The contention was rejected.

A national railway strike in May-June 1955 pushed the British Transport Commission into re-examining its industrial relations policy. It committed itself to joint consultation (21, 22) and many other firms sought to improve their negotiating procedures (23, 24.)

(21) British Transport Commission, *Making Joint Consultation Work* (1956)

Very simply, joint consultation is a means by which representatives of all who work on British Railways can get together round a table and exchange ideas on the working of our industry and on the best and most satisfactory ways to get things done. . . .

Joint consultation is not just a device to enable representatives of staff and management to argue with each other. That is certainly not the aim. Discussion should be around the table and not across it. True, it happens to be convenient that the same representatives sit round the same table for joint consultation as for negotiation – the negotiation about rates of pay and conditions of service which has been a feature of the railway industry almost as long as any present-day railwaymen can remember. But there the resemblance ends – finally.

Joint consultation is co-operation in practice. It is based on two ideas. First, that in a large concern such as British Railways no one, however good at his job or whatever position he holds, can have thought of and provided for every possibility, every snag, every problem that is likely to arise in the detailed working out of a new scheme. Second, that even in the case of work which has been going on in much the same way for years there is always scope for improvement, if only everyone concerned in it has the chance to discuss it fully and frankly with his colleagues. That is why it is so important that joint consultation should really work. It is without doubt the best way of ensuring that through the consultative committees all matters concerning any particular place of work can be discussed quickly, and on the spot, by people with local knowledge.

(22) Ibid.

What is Joint Consultation?
It is management and staff co-operating to get the best results. This co-operation can cover any aspect of railway working.

Where should it take place?
At every level throughout the railways. The procedure provides for consultation meetings:

(a) of Local Committees.
(b) of Sectional Councils.
(c) at Headquarters level.

Of these, the *local* meetings are of vital importance for the success of joint consultation as a whole. This is where detailed discussion of the job can help more than anywhere else towards making improvements in service and methods. . . . .

Who says what is to be discussed?
Subjects for discussion may be put forward by staff or management representatives. . . .

At what stage are staff representatives consulted about contemplated lines of action initiated by the management?

The procedure says 'as early as possible'. . . .

What happens when a subject is too big to be discussed by one Local Committee?
It can be arranged for representatives of several local committees (or Sectional Councils) – either from different departments or from different areas – to meet together. . . .

What sort of subjects may be discussed?
Anything to do with the working of the railways, except matters already covered by the machinery of negotiation – that is, rates of pay and conditions of service . . . .

What happens if staff and management representatives cannot reach agreement at a consultative meeting?
If both sides are satisfied that their point of view has been fairly heard, and there is still no agreement, then it is the responsibility of local management to make a decision on the matter at issue. . . .

Who is responsible for getting Joint Consultation going?
The Commission and the Unions have jointly made it clear that they are very anxious to see joint consultation working successfully. . . .

Where the views of the staff have affected the decision – as may often be the case – the purpose of joint consultation has been fully achieved. In cases where it has not been found possible to adopt suggestions made by the staff at joint consultation meetings, the management is under an obligation to explain why this is so. Here too joint consultation will have achieved its purpose, since management know the views of the staff and the staff know *why* the decision is what it is, which in itself removes a source of misunderstanding and frustration.

(23) ICI, *Memorandum on Labour Relations*, 5th edn (July 1959)

It was as far back as January 1918 that Brunner, Mond and Co. Ltd first instituted a General Works Committee, which may be said to have been the parent of the subsequent Works Councils. This was, as far as is known, the first committee of its kind in the country. There was recognition from the outset that the committee could only function with the co-operation and good will of the trade unions, although its functions would be in the domestic field only and outside their strict sphere of interest. . . .

Upon the formation of I. C. I. the same principles . . . were extended throughout the whole Company, the present Works Council Scheme dating from 1929. The Councils are made up of equal numbers of management and workpeople, the latter being freely elected by ballot among their fellow workers. . . . The Works Councils are at the factory level, but there are also Division Councils comprising representatives from the Works Councils. . . .

Finally, from the Division Councils there are representatives to the General

Council, which is representative of all works in the Company. . . . There is thus a link provided between the workers and the Board of Directors. . . .

(24) National Coal Board, *Guide to Consultation in the Coalmining Industry*, 2nd edn (1963)

Why Consultation?
Every worker in the mining industry has a stake in its well-being. Everybody has the right to say how he thinks the work of the National Coal Board can be improved. Management wants to hear ideas, suggestions and constructive criticisms. This can be done most effectively through the machinery of consultation. When management and mineworkers meet to discuss problems and policies many good ideas will emerge. Consultation mobilises the collective commonsense of everyone – provides a means to put it to good use. For these reasons there are Consultative Councils at all levels of the industry: National, Divisional, Area and Colliery. . . .

What can be discussed at the Committees and Councils?
Questions relating to safety, health and welfare and the organisation and conduct of the industry; and other matters of mutual interest to employees and the Board.

While the traditional art of negotiation was maintained (25, 26) and education schemes were continued (26, 27) new notions of 'comparability' on wages were also developed (28).

(25) Ben Smith, 'The Art of Negotiation', *Public Service* (June 1956)

N.A.L.G.O's main purpose as a trade union is to negotiate satisfactory salaries and service conditions for its members, and to obtain improvements in negotiated agreements as circumstances from time to time demand. For the most part, these negotiations are conducted through the medium of national and district Whitley Councils, on which N. A. L. G. O. is represented by elected members and its full-time officers.

To negotiate is to confer with others, with an object in mind. A negotiator is one who is seeking, either for himself or for others, something which he thinks should be granted because it is reasonable.

The first elementary condition for success is that the negotiators should know precisely what they want and what will be its effect if conceded. In preparing a claim for a new salary structure, for example, the staff side negotiations must be able to see clearly, before joint discussions begin, how the proposal would operate and what special provisions should be made to prevent anomalies arising. Nobody, of course, can foresee all the effects of introducing new conditions, but some forethought is necessary if a far-reaching claim of this kind is to stand the test of examination and argument by another – and by no means sympathetic – party.

(26) *The Workers' Educational Trade Union Committee, 31st Annual Report* (1951)

The W.E.T.U.C. exists to stimulate workers to take part in serious long-term studies. One-day, week-end and summer schools are used as means to create the desire for putting forth greater personal efforts for educational advancement in W.E.A. classes. When short courses of study succeed in guiding students to tutorial classes, a main aim of W. E. A. and W. E. T. U. C. policy is achieved.

	Year Ended May 31st, 1950	Year Ended May 31st, 1951	Increase or Decrease
Number of classes	6,354	6,217	−137
Number of students	107,454	102,739	−4,715
Three-year tutorial classes	876	903	+27
Advanced tutorial classes	18	16	−2
Classes not less than one year	1,643	1,660	+17
Classes not less than ten meetings	2,384	2,185	−199
Shorter Courses	1,433	1,063	−370

Having stressed the importance of the high standard work we must not rest content with the present position. Every effort must be made to arrest the downward movement in the total number of classes and students.

(27) *Sunday Times* (10 May 1953)

The Electrical Trades Union which, under acknowledged and aggressive Communist leadership, has had a spectacular rise during the war and post-war years, now breaks new ground with the establishment at Esher Place of its own residential college.

It will be the first trade union to own and operate such a college of its own. Opening ceremonies have been set for June 4, but union officials deny any effort at counter attraction to another collegiate occasion on that day.

Purchased for £20,000 and calculated to cost £14,000 or more a year to run, the new college will provide one-week courses for 1,200 to 1,500 shop stewards and branch officials each year. If E. T. U. literature and policies are a guide, it will probably become the most potent Communist-line indoctrination centre in the country. The union has 203,000 members in all the major industries, with 670 branches and more than 30 full-time officials.

Of its top executives, the general president, Frank Foulkes, the general secretary, Walter C. Stevens, the assistant general secretary, Frank Haxell, and three of the four national officers are all Communists. These seven, with the Warden, Mr J. O. N. Vickers, will be responsible for the instruction at the new college. The officials all stress that they are responsible to the executive council, whose members are by no means all Communists, but this has had little apparent effect on the union's persistent Communist-line activities.

The opening of the college will mark another milestone in the career of Walter C. Stevens, who is the main-spring of the union's drive to wider power. He first achieved national prominence at the 1950 Trades Union Congress, when he led the successful revolt against the General Council's resolution favouring continued wage restraint. . . .

(28) Special Joint Committee on Machinery of Negotiation for Railway Staff, *Report of Railway Pay Committee of Inquiry* (2 March 1960).

We conclude, therefore, *that if all other factors are excluded,* the rates of pay of salaried and manual jobs in the Railways for which we have been able to discover comparable occupations in other industries are, in general, approximately 10% below the rates for those of comparable occupations. We further suggest that it would be reasonable to assume that this difference between the value placed on labour by the Railways, and by other industries, applies also to those railway jobs for which we could discover no comparisons, except for [some] grades. . . .

On the basis of the work of our investigation officers and of our Secretaries, we have reached agreement as to which jobs could be regarded as comparable with railway work; and in the case of those jobs which we have decided to be comparable, we compare the rates of pay with the corresponding railway rates.

Wherever possible we have compared the rate for an individual railway job with the median of a group of rates paid for comparable work in other industries. We have also made overall comparisons with outside industry, of rates of pay for salaried staff as a whole, and for conciliation grades as a whole.

These comparisons had led us to the conclusion that with certain exceptions, both the salaries and wages of railway workers are below those of workers, doing comparable jobs, by a margin of the order of ten per cent.

13. *The Sixties*

During the early years of the 1960s there was a substantial agreement on the weaknesses of British trade-union structure (1). Traditional patterns of organisation into craft (2), general (3), industrial (4) and white collar unions (5, 6) were not satisfactory amid the complexity of modern industry. Many unionists pressed for a union structure based on industry (7), though not all agreed that this was the solution (8).

The rationale behind the amalgamation of some unions in the 1960s was not always clear, but one of the most important of such was the amalgamation of the Amalgamated Engineering Union and the Amalgamated Union of Foundry Workers into the AUEFW (9).

(1) Political and Economic Planning, *The Structure and Organisation of British Trade Unions* (1963)

Descriptions of the structure of the trade union movement in Britain generally divide unions into four categories: craft unions, general unions, industrial unions and white-collar unions. This conventional picture arises out of the historical growth of union organisation, which followed a horizontal rather than a vertical pattern, cutting across industrial boundaries and not coinciding with them. . . .

This typology had a comforting clarity, and it still contains a good deal of truth in that it indicates the original recruiting area and philosophy of a particular union. However, each year it becomes less and less accurate since it fails to take into account the changing situation in the unions and in industry. To begin with, many craft unions are no longer exclusive in their membership. Several large unions which are often known as 'craft', for instance, the Engineers, the Electricians, the Printing, Bookbinding and Paper Workers, the Vehicle Builders, the Building Trade Workers, and the Foundry Workers, have widened their membership to include supervisory and technical staffs, semi-skilled and unskilled workers and women, working in the same industries as the craftsmen. Non-craftsmen now make up more than one-third of the membership of the half-dozen unions mentioned above, though their full-time officers are usually craftsmen and there are often different rates of contribution and voting rights for the different kinds of member. The general unions have also broadened their recruiting fields and now take craftsmen and technical, clerical and professional workers into their ranks. Moreover, the traditional definition of skill in terms of apprentice training has been blurred as new skills have arisen and old crafts have declined or been mechanised. Many workers without an apprentice training are as skilled in the work they do as the traditional craftsmen. Thus, even the craft unions which have not diluted their membership may in certain cases have lost some of that distinction and superiority to the general unions which was based on an exclusive control of superior skills.

Although these changes have occurred, fracturing the old horizontal divisions between unions, the result has not been to produce a more rational union structure. Indeed, the changes have tended to make the problem of multiplicity of union representation more acute, without as yet removing the restrictive practices associated with the original craft unionism. . . . An extreme example of this proliferation of union representation is the situation at Ford's of Dagenham, where nearly two dozen unions operate.

(2) *General Rules for the Government of the National Union of Printing, Bookbinding and Paper Workers* (1960)

The objects for which this Union is established are to obtain 100 per cent organisation, provide funds for the protection of the trade, the rights and privileges of its members, the safeguarding of their interests in respect to hours of labour, the settlement of disputes by any lawful means, to maintain the Trade Union wage of the district, to provide assistance to its members in search of work, to provide legal aid and to assist members in distress, to provide them with a pension in old age, and the payment at death of a free member, or his wife, or her husband, of the amount provided by these rules, and to promote the general welfare of members. . . .

The Union shall consist of members employed as paper makers, paper-mill workers, bookbinders, loose-leaf workers, paper bag and paper box workers, machine rulers, gilders, show-card window ticket and gold blockers, printers, printers' warehousemen, clerks, stationers, relief stampers, cutters, letterpress feeders, box cutters, fixture-box makers, paper-tube makers, creasers, packers, envelope cutters, leather workers, pattern card makers, rolling and folding machine minders, publishers, assistant publishers, travellers, despatchers, newsagents' employees, outdoor distributors, all machine assistants, and motor drivers employed in any industry covered by the categories in this Rule, and all females engaged in the paper making, paper-tube making, paper box and paper bag making, die stamp printers, printing, stationery, bookbinding, machine ruling, relief stamping, publishing and newspaper trades, and all workers, engaged in the production, coating, cold milling, linen facing, enamelling, staining and distribution of paper, millboard, parchment, vellum, leatherette, asbestos, paper towels, perforated paper toilet requisites, polythene and plastic books, and other like material.

(3) NUGMW, *This is Your Union* (1964)

But the Union has made clear beyond doubt that a 'general' union is one that makes the benefits of trade union organisation and skill in collective bargaining available to a general – and genuine – cross-section of the nation's workers. The gas-worker, the man in the shipyard, and the women in the factory are still important members of the NUGMW as they were in the beginning. So is the air hostess who acts as stewardess to the Queen on her flights or, for that matter, the Leader of the Labour Party, Mr. Harold Wilson.

The nation's gas and electricity and water come largely through the work of the Union's members. The hospitals would come to a halt without them. They man the civic services of the local authorities. You will find many NUGMW members white-coated beside the reactors of the Atomic Energy Authority or shirt-sleeved amongst the cameras of the TV studios. The NUGMW is active in the old, traditional industries and in the new pioneering industries.

(4) John Hughes, 'Trade Union Structure and Government', in RC on Trade Unions and Employers' Associations, *Research Paper* no. 5 (1967), pt 1

The N. U. M. has come closest to the realisation of 'industrial' unionism, since virtually all manual workers in the coal industry are members of unions that are 'constituent associations'. But beyond this occupational field, it shares with other unions representation of clerical workers. Supervisory workers are mainly members of a separate occupational–industrial union [The National Association of Colliery Oversmen, Deputies and Shotfirers], and managerial personnel are organised in other associations. As in manual employment in the coal industry there is effectively 100 per cent unionism. N. U. M. membership is largely a function of the number of wage earners on colliery books. As a result, N. U. M. membership in 1966 is a quarter of a million less than a decade ago, and by 1970 can be expected to fall to about a third of a million (or less than half of the membership of the mid 1950s).

(5) Guild of Insurance Officials, *Membership Card* (1942 edn)

Membership. – The following are eligible for membership of the Guild:– Employees (both male and female), permanent or temporary, of any insurance Office in Great Britain, Northern Ireland and the Irish Free State, or having a recognised Branch Office in such territory; or otherwise coming within the scope of the Insurance Unemployment Board and the Irish Free State Unemployment Board, but excluding collectors engaged in outdoor Industrial Life Assurance work and household and cleaning staffs.

(6) IRSF, *Constitution and Rules* (1950 edn)

3. The objects of the Federation shall be:

(a) To protect and promote the interests of its members, to regulate the conditions of their employment and the relations between them and their employers, and to provide and maintain such services for the benefit of members as may be approved by the Annual Conference from time to time.

(b) To provide through such Funds as the Annual Delegate Conference may from time to time decide, financial and other assistance to members in need, former members retired from the public service and dependent relatives of deceased members in necessitous circumstances.

(c) To maintain and administer funds for these purposes. . . .

9. The management of the Federation shall be vested in the Conference, the Executive Committee and the Officers. . . .

15. The Executive Committee, subject to the over-riding authority of the Conference, shall be the immediate governing and managing body of the Federation. . . .

41. The basic unit of organisation will be the 'office'. . . .

(7) NUPE, *The Challenge of New Unionism* (Leicester, 1963)

In their multiple task of winning immediate benefits for members, providing protection for members and acting as a spur for social change, unions are faced with a set of conditions which demand an end to those old patterns of organisation which were originally fashioned to meet an entirely different set of historical conditions. Craft unions, general unions and vocational unions – however valuable they may have been in the past – have now slipped back from the peak point of their impact. The conditions which brought these types of unions into being have now been replaced by new conditions which require new forms of trade unionism.

The present pattern, with many unions of varying types, creates wasteful duplication of effort, it perpetuates antiquated sectional interests, it creates conflicting policies and it provokes unnecessary competition for memberhsip. All the evidence points to the need for deliberate efforts to develop industrial unionism – a form of organisation in which all workers within an industry or service are members of a single union. The single union is linked in turn with other industrial unions through a centralised body which is able to represent the widest interest of workers in a responsible and authoritative fashion.

(8) NUGMW, *Evidence to the Royal Commission on Trade Unions and Employers' Associations* (1966)

The comparative merits of different forms of trade union structure have been extensively analysed elsewhere. We merely comment that there are no conclusive merits in one form or another which warrants the universal adoption of any particular form of organisational principle. Advocacy of industrial unionism rests on the basic assumption that the industry is the primary interest of any group of workers. When the assumption is tested against the views of the workers themselves and their determination in many cases to retain their occupational unions, its general validity is more than doubtful. It can be counter-claimed that the occupational principle, upon which our own horizontal form of structure is based, has equal if not stronger validity. Horizontal organisation in many ways conforms more to the realities of the structure of British industry and with the increased likelihood of the further growth in the size and number of large multi-industry forms, it is also likely that horizontal organisation will increasingly fit industrial circumstances better than exclusively industrial organisation. We consider that general unionism can provide a framework within which a variety of circumstances can be accommodated and the industrial and occupational interests of workers can be efficiently safeguarded and promoted.

(9) AEU, *Journal* (Nov. 1966): 'A Joint Statement by the Amalgamated Engineering Union and the Amalgamated Union of Foundry Workers'

The membership of the AUEFW shall consist of members of the constituent unions, i.e., the AEU and AUFW, and shall, for the purpose of administration, be organised into appropriate trade groups, i.e., Engineering Group and Foundry Workers Group.

The registered General Office of the AUEFW, unless otherwise decided, shall be situated at 110, Peckham Road, London, SE15.

The objects of the Amalgamated Union shall be:

(a) The control of industry in the interests of the community;
(b) The organisation of workers qualified for membership; the development of fraternal relations with other unions in the industry; and the maintenance of just and proper working hours, rates of wages, conditions of labour;
(c) The negotiation and settlement of differences and disputes between members of the amalgamated union and employers by collective bargaining and agreement, withdrawal of labour, or otherwise;
(d) To promote the welfare of the members of the amalgamated union;
(e) The provision of benefits to members as provided by the Rules;
(f) The furtherance of political objects as provided by the Rules;
(g) To co-operate with other trade unions and with federations of unions and to subscribe to their funds;
(h) To promote schemes and provide facilities for the educational achievement of the members.

And shall include the whole of the objects of the unions party to the amalgamation.

A crucial figure that came to the fore in the 1960s in the industrial relations system was the shop steward. His role was often vague and ill-defined in union rule books (10), and his activities very often different from the popular image presented in the press (11). But stewards' importance steadily increased (12) and the Donovan Commission devoted considerable attention to their position (13).

(10) TGWU, *Shop Stewards Handbook* (1964): 'Joint Consultation – Your Responsibilities'

THE FIELD COVERED BY JOINT CONSULTATION. Joint Consultation is historically an after-thought. The employers hold firmly to their rights of management and the trade unions have won, and firmly hold, the right to negotiate wages and conditions with them. Joint consultation between the employers and workers in a particular place of work ranges in between these two sets of rights. The employers will allow (and if they are sensible they will encourage) the workers to discuss production efficiency and to make suggestions; indeed, they will normally permit consultation on the whole range of working problems. They may even divulge and ask for advice upon future production and manpower problems.

Where relationships with the union are good, and the joint machinery is firmly established and intelligently used, the employers will consult their workers before decisions are taken, not merely inform them afterwards. But they will not normally discuss pricing and marketing policy or the appointment of managerial staff. Nor will they relax their control over the ultimate decisions of production policy. They will not usually – though this should not prevent workers' representatives from asking them to – reveal statistical information about costs and pricing, nor do they often supply any other financial information than they have to. Under the Companies Act of 1948, they have, in all normal cases, to publish an annual balance sheet and statement of accounts. On the other hand, Joint Consultative Committees must not trench upon the field of industrial negotiation. The Trade Unions have established their authority in this field and strongly resent any interference.

(11) Garfield Clack, *Industrial Relations in a British Car Factory*, University of Cambridge Department of Applied Economics, Occasional Paper 9 (1967)

The strikes could not be attributed to the activities of a tightly-controlled or militant shop steward organisation – either at the factory or drawing support or inspiration from steward or trade union organisation external to the factory. Departmental stewards sometimes recommended strike action; they also sometimes did their best to prevent their members from taking such action. They were generally concerned about the 'constitutionality' of their conduct, and, on balance, seemed more concerned to prevent strikes occuring, to limit such actions where they could not prevent them, and to induce strikers to return to work. This attitude could be attributed to a number of factors: for example, to the practical and sometimes tactical need to assess the priorities amongst a number of current issues, to the fact that stewards were subject to managerial sanctions of various kinds, to an awareness of the loss of earnings by strikers and others laid-off in consequence, and sometimes, to what might be described as a seeming preference for a quiet life. Many stewards – when asked – said that they had taken the job unwillingly, and often only because there had been nobody else in the department who would accept the task. . . .

In the case of the conveners, the position was more clear-cut. While they might individually induce or support a demonstration by their own members, such activity was almost incidental to their avowed and collective policy of keeping as many men at work as possible (for at least a normal working week). This policy was not pious but was put into practice (although with varying degrees of success). . . . In short, the conveners and shop stewards organisation at the factory did not appear as a driving force behind labour unrest, but could more validly be regarded as 'shock absorbers' of the industrial relations machinery. The suggestions that trade unions should prevent unofficial action by their members by 'disciplining' their shop stewards in some way would be inappropriate to situations of this kind.

(12) NUPE, *Public Employee* (Oct. 1970)

It is no coincidence that the past few years should have witnessed the development of a strong tendency towards the growth of union stewards within NUPE. All of the objective factors necessary for such a development exist.

In the first place there has been an opening up of opportunities for local bargaining. Traditionally – since the establishment of centralised wage bargaining machinery like National Joint Councils and Whitley Councils – much of NUPE's negotiating has been conducted at national level. The main job locally has been to police national agreements and to take up individual grievances.

The increasing use of modern management techniques, particularly work-study based incentive schemes and productivity bargains, has introduced a new dimension into the Union's work. While the broad frames of reference for such agreements can be established at national level the critical task of fitting them into particular circumstances can only be done at the workplace, and with a high degree of involvement by workers on the job. . . .

The second factor prompting the development of Union Stewards is the development of services in which NUPE members are employed. In size, structure and scope, the local government and health services are growth industries. . . .

The practical results are well known to every NUPE member. The time lag in between raising an issue and getting an answer becomes longer. Real managers – those with the power to make decisions – become increasingly remote from the work force. Frustration becomes a common feature of life for the ordinary worker.

In response to this situation, Union members at the workplace push management harder in an effort to break down the communications barrier. This is a spontaneous reaction which encourages the growth of confidence in local work groups and promotes the emergence of articulate spokesmen who argue the workers' case with management: instant stewards, in fact.

Another important factor in promoting the development of stewards within NUPE is the growth of the Union itself. For thirty-five years, NUPE has continually expanded its membership: with more than 315,000 men and women in its ranks it is now twenty-five times the size it was when Bryn Roberts embarked on an expansionist policy on becoming General Secretary in the mid '30s.

This growth in size has meant that the Union has grown in influence: increased representation on national and local negotiating bodies, a voice on the TUC General Council and a firm foothold in all the places where power resides in the trade union movement.

At the same time, however, the sheer size of the Union poses the need to develop organisational forms which preserve and extend the democratic character of the Union. Just as a worker can become isolated and frustrated by the communication blocks which exist in a large employing authority, he can experience the same problem when his union becomes a large and complex organisation.

Recognising this, successive National Conferences have carried through measures – such as the reshaping of Conference itself and the creation of National Committees – designed to open up the lines of communication and improve the decision making process. The development of a system of Union Stewards is a natural extension of these efforts....

(13) **RC on Trade Unions etc,** *Report* (1968) *PP* 1967–8, xxxii, Cmnd 3623

In most factories in which trade unions are strong their members in each workshop choose one of their number to speak for them. If there is more than one union, each usually has its own representative, although in some instances one representative speaks for two or more unions. He or she may go under a number of titles, but the most common is 'shop steward'.

. . . tasks include recruiting new members and seeing that existing members do not lapse. . . . In many instances shop stewards are also responsible for collecting union subscriptions. . . . In addition shop stewards have a responsibility for communications between unions and members; and with average attendance at branch meetings well below ten per cent, this is the main link between unions and their members.

These are important services. Without shop stewards, trade unions would lack for members, for money, and for means of keeping in touch with their members. Even so none of them is the most important of the British shop steward's tasks. That is the service which he performs by helping to regulate workers' pay and working conditions and by representing them in dealings with management. . . .

First of all it must be emphasised that there is no uniformity. A minority of stewards do not negotiate with managers at all, whereas some of them negotiate over a wide range of issues. But over half of them regularly deal with managers over some aspect of pay, and about half of them deal regularly with some question relating to hours of work, the most common being the level and distribution of overtime. About a third of them regularly handle disciplinary issues on behalf of their members, and other matters which some of them settle include the distribution of work, the pace of work, the manning of machines, transfers from one job to another, the introduction of new machinery and new jobs, taking on new labour and redundancy. Since there are probably about 175,000 stewards in the country, compared with perhaps 3,000 full-time trade union officers, this suggests that shop stewards must be handling many times the volume of business conducted by their full-time officers.

Firmly established restrictive labour practices proved a major obstacle to reorganisation of work methods in many industries. Those in the national newspaper offices were merely the most notorious of many (14). Productivity bargaining was one method of trying to overcome such practices (15). A pioneer in such bargaining was the Esso Petroleum Company at its Fawley oil refinery, where a famous productivity agreement was adopted in 1960 (16).

(14) RC on the Press, Cmnd 1811, *PP* 1961–2 xxi, appendix xii, annex 8: 'Restrictive Practices'

The practices recorded below are a representative selection of the many Restrictive Practices which were observed during the course of the investigation. . . .

(a) *Composing Room*

   (i) No pieceworker will start work at the beginning of the shift until copy is available to enable every operative present to be issued with the equivalent of 12 lines of setting. Twenty or thirty operatives may thus have to wait while copy is made available for the last one.

  (ii) Special operatives are employed in some offices to distribute the matrices after Ludlow set lines have been cast, although the Case Hands, who set and cast the lines, have considerable waiting time.

 (iii) Case and Stone Hands, although members of the same Trade Union, do not interchange duties in spite of the fact that the Case Section is relatively under-occupied at the time of peak activity on the Stone.

 (iv) Block adjustments are not carried out in the Composing Room and blocks requiring adjustment are returned to the Stereotyping Department. This practice results in delay in the completion of page make-up on the Stone.

(b) *Foundry*

   (i) There is a very restricted amount of interchange of staff between moulding, packing, casting and bench work in almost all offices.

  (ii) All foundry work, whether skilled, semi-skilled or unskilled, is performed
       by craftsmen or skilled apprentices. This includes drossing, counting and
       recording plates, and floor sweeping.

(c) *Machine Room*

  (i) Machine Running Speeds have been negotiated at levels substantially
       below those of which the equipment is capable and in many cases the
       actual running speeds are lower than the negotiated speeds.
  (ii) Although the Machine Minder is in charge of the machine the Brake
       Hand, who is a member of another Trade Union, is physically responsible
       for starting and stopping it; the former, therefore, gives the signal and the
       latter presses the button. This demarcation dispute had resulted in
       disputes and stoppages.
 (iii) Machine Assistants are promoted through the grades, Fly Hand, Reel
       Hand, Oiler, Magazine Hand and Brake Hand, and will not undertake
       duties outside the grade to which they have been allocated.
 (iv) In one office the Oilers will not fit plates to a cylinder until a complete set
       of plates is available.

(d) *Publishing Room*

  (i) An agreement exists whereby paper sizes, and hence staffing arrange-
       ments, will not be changed without giving 48 hours notice, other than in
       exceptional circumstances. Interpretation of the words 'exceptional
       circumstances' has led to disputes.
  (ii) The newspaper delivery points, when delivery is by Igranic conveyor, are
       considered to be an extension of the Machine Room and are manned by
       Machine Assistants. Transfer of the papers from the delivery points,
       however, must be carried out by Publishing Hands, who are members of
       another Trade Union, and duplication of staffing results.

    (15) RC on Trade Unions etc., *Research Paper* no. 4

Productivity bargaining may be described as a type of wage–work bargaining.
The term 'productivity bargain' lacks precision, but broadly it may be described
as an agreement on which advantages of one kind or another, such as higher
wages or increased leisure, are given to workers in return for agreement on their
part to accept changes in working practice or in methods of work which will lead
to more efficient working. The changes in the interests of efficiency are seen as an
integral part of the bargain and as a necessary contribution to meeting the cost of
the advantages conceded to the workers.

    The concessions on the workers' part must, if the agreement is to be a
'productivity agreement' in the generally accepted sense, be in concrete terms.

(16) Allan Flanders, 'The Fawley Blue Book. An Initiative in Labour Relations', *Esso Magazine*, xII, no. 3 (1963)

What has become known as the 'Blue Book' at the Esso refinery, near Southampton, was an elaborate series of proposals put forward by management for negotiation with the unions in February 1960. In the course of the negotiations, one or two of the proposals fell by the wayside and others were modified and extended, but the greater part of the programme did become the subject of two agreements signed in July 1960. The one with the Transport and General Workers' Union, which organises the non-craft hourly paid employees at the refinery, and the other with a body known as the Crafts Union Committee, which, as far as Esso is concerned, consists of seven unions representing craftsmen in its employment at Fawley.

These agreements had two prominent features which are, I believe, without precedent in the history of collective bargaining in this country. The first was that they represented a quite specific productivity package deal. The Company offered large increases in wage rates for all its employees of the order of 40 per cent. – 2/6 an hour in the case of craftsmen – in return for the men's and their unions' consent to certain defined changes in their existing working practices. There have been other agreements where the unions gave vague promises about reviewing restrictive practices, as in the engineering settlement of 1957. This is the first agreement in which the relaxing of practices which management experiences as restrictive was spelled out unambiguously. . . .

Having given the background to the Blue Book I want to answer the question: 'What lessons has the Fawley experiment to offer the rest of British industry?' Let me say at once that in my view it offers pre-eminently lessons for management. Some of these I shall state rather dogmatically, but they are the convictions I acquired in the course of sifting the evidence.

The first one is this. *Systematic overtime is symptomatic of managerial irresponsibility.* I have chosen my words carefully. Systematic overtime as opposed to occasional overtime is an inefficient method of work, but it is far more than that. The condition of management of which it is a symptom is that of allowing things to drift, and that is precisely what the word 'irresponsibility' implies. . . .

That brings me to my second lesson: *The changing of restrictive union practices is a managerial responsibility.* What was rather unique about Fawley was management's departure from the general pattern of employer behaviour towards union restrictive practices in post-war Britain. That pattern may, at the risk of over-simplification, be summarized thus: encouraging vague but negative criticism of these practices in public, and collaborating with the union to uphold them in private. . . .

My third lesson may at first glance sound trite, almost tautological, but it is the most important one of all. *Management learns to manage by being forced to accept the full responsibilities of management.* . . .

In 1964 trade-union branch officials found their position to be a highly risky one, as a result of the House of Lords' judgement in the case of *Rookes* v. *Barnard and others* (17) and immediately there was a demand for a reform of the law to restore the protection previously believed to have been given by the Trade Disputes Act of 1906 (18, 19). One of the first measures of the new Labour Government of that year was to do just that (20).

(17) *The Times*, (22 Jan. 1964)

Lord Reid said that the appellant was employed by B. O. A. C. as a skilled draughtsman in their drawing office at London Airport. He was a member of the Association of Engineering and Shipbuilding Draughtsmen, a trade union to which all who were employed in that drawing office belonged. He became dissatisfied with the conduct of the union and resigned from it. The union, anxious to preserve the position that no non-member should be employed in that office, took energetic steps to get the appellant to re-join. He refused. As a result of steps taken by the union and its members, B. O. A. C. were induced, first, to suspend the appellant and, then, to terminate his employment, after giving him due notice. The appellant had no remedy against B. O. A. C. They neither broke their contract with him nor committed any tort against him.

In the present action the appellant sought a remedy against two members and an official of the union on the ground that they wrongfully induced B. O. A. C. to act as they did. . . .

The case, therefore, raised the question whether it was a tort to conspire to threaten an employer that his men would break their contracts with him unless he dismissed the plaintiff, with the result that he was thereby induced to dismiss the plaintiff and cause him loss. . . .

In considering whether the respondents were absolved from liability by section 1 of the Trade Disputes Act, 1906, the only difficulty was to discover what was meant by 'unless the act, if done without any such agreement or combination, would be actionable'. In the present case the precise act complained of could not have been done without previous agreement. The section could not reasonably be held to mean that no action could be brought unless the precise act complained of could have been done by an individual without previous agreement or combination. In his Lordship's view, the section required one to find the nearest equivalent act which could have been so done and see whether it would be actionable. In the present case suppose one of the respondents said to B. O. A. C.: 'I am acting alone but I think I can and intend to induce the men to break their contracts and strike if you do not get rid of Mr Rookes.' If his Lordship was right, that would have been actionable if B. O. A. C. had succumbed to that threat and got rid of the appellant in the way they did. So section 1 did not help the respondents.

Section 3 dealt with two classes of acts done by individuals, and, by virtue of section 1, the immunity given by section 3 to individuals had also to extend to combinations or conspiracies. The classes of acts permitted (if done in contemplation or furtherance of a trade dispute) were (1) inducing a breach of contract of employment, and (2) interfering with a person's trade, business or employment or right to dispose of his capital or labour as he willed. The facts in the present case fell within the second class: if B. O. A. C. had to safeguard themselves by giving notice to the appellant but had dismissed him summarily the case would have come within the first class.

His Lordship considered section 3 and the authorities, and concluded that, in his judgment, it was clear that section 3 did not protect inducement of breach of contract where that was brought about by intimidation or other illegal means, and the section had to be given a similar construction with regard to interference with trade, business or employment. So, in his Lordship's opinion, the section did not apply to the present case because the interference here was brought upon by unlawful intimidation. His Lordship would therefore allow the appeal.

(18) DATA, *The Draughtsman* (March 1964)

In the Rookes versus Barnard case it was accepted by all the lawyers who participated that the agreement setting out the procedure of negotiations forms part of the individual contract of service of the Association's members employed by B. O. A. C. A threat to break a 'no-strike' clause was regarded as an individual breach of contract, actionable at law.

This contention that the terms of a negotiating procedure agreement form part of the contract of service of each individual trade union member will certainly come as a surprise to the great majority of trade union officials. Hitherto, it has been generally assumed that a negotiating procedure agreement is a voluntary arrangement for resolving problems that arise in industrial relations. Its implementation and supervision, it has usually been held, depend on the good faith of the parties, and the procedure cannot be enforced by action at law.

The legal arguments employed in the Rookes versus Barnard case, and the judgment of the House of Lords, seem to suggest that this understanding is wrong. If so, there is a possibility of many legal actions in industrial disputes.

In every negotiating procedure agreement it is either explicit or implicit that there shall be no strike or lockout until the agreed procedure has been exhausted. There is now a real danger that trade unionists will find themselves sued for damages if they participate in a strike, or a threat of strike, in immediate response, say to the victimisation of a shop steward or office representative. Active trade unionists, however, are well aware that the threat of strike action is the only really effective answer to victimisation. It is not an issue to be taken through protracted negotiations.

(19) *Sunday Telegraph* (1 March 1964): 'Trade Unionists under the Law', George Doughty, General Secretary of DATA

I suggest that completely fresh legislation should be introduced as soon as possible to reinstate the legal immunity of the trade unions which Parliament wished to ensure when it passed the 1906 Act. The new law should lay down clearly that agreements and understandings between unionists and employers on procedures for solving problems in industry do not form part of the individual contract of service between a company and its workers.

Three vital civil rights must also be affirmed in the new Act. All three are embodied in the [International Labour Organisation] conventions. They are:

The right of workers and employers to organise for the furtherance of their mutual interest; to exercise their rights of membership and to be protected against interference by each other or each other's agents in the function of their organisations.

The right of workers and employers to bargain collectively, and the duty of the State to encourage, but not to impose, means for the settling of disputes through the machinery of collective bargaining.

The right of workers and employers to engage in trade disputes, including strikes, and lockouts.

The enforcement of these rights must be kept away from the normal courts of law.

(20) The Trade Disputes Act, 1965

1. *Certain acts not actionable in tort or as delicts.*

(1) An Act done after the passing of this Act by a person in contemplation or furtherance of a trade dispute (within the meaning of the Trade Disputes Act, 1906) shall not be actionable in tort on the ground only that it consists in his threatening (a) that a contract of employment (whether one to which he is party or not) will be broken, or (b) that he will induce another to break a contract of employment to which the other is a party; or be capable of giving rise to an action of reparation on the ground only that it so consists.

(2) An act done as aforesaid by a person before the passing of this Act shall not be actionable in tort as mentioned in the foregoing subsection unless proceedings in respect thereof have been instituted either before or within the period of six months beginning with the date of the passing of this Act or be capable of giving rise to an action or reparation as so mentioned unless proceedings in respect thereof have been so instituted.

Since the Second World War there had been numerous attempts by governments to work out an agreed policy on wages, though the trade unions were resistant to what they regarded as wage restraint. In the 1960s the search for an 'Incomes Policy' continued (21, 22, 23) and the National Incomes Commission sought to lay down guidelines (24). One major difficulty that immediately arose was that an attempt by the Government to impose a policy on wages affected its position as an employer and brought problems in the nationalised and other industries (25). None the less, Governments of both major parties continued to see such a policy as essential for the solution of Britain's economic difficulties (26, 27, 28, 29).

(21) *Incomes Policy: The Next Step*, Cmnd 1626 (1962)

The Government's policy is to promote a faster rate of economic growth and a more vigorous development of our export trade. This depends on maintaining the strength of the pound and our competitive efficiency, which in turn depend on our ability to keep costs and prices stable. In pursuing this policy the Government are expecting to receive valuable assistance from the National Economic Development Council. But the policy will be put in jeopardy if money incomes rise faster than the volume of national production, as has been the persistent tendency since the end of the war. . . .

In the debate in the House of Commons on 18th December, 1961, the Chancellor of the Exchequer said that it was the Government's intention to try to work out with both sides of industry a policy to keep increases in money incomes in line with the long-term rate of increase in national production.

. . . the Chancellor emphasised that it would be a negation of policy to bring the first phase, the pay pause, to an end and to put nothing in its place. Accordingly, on 10th January, he invited the Trades Union Congress to collaborate with the Government and with representatives of the employers' organisations in working out a restraining influence on the levels of incomes during the next phase, pending the evolution of a long-term incomes policy. . . .

The objective must be to keep the rate of increase of incomes within the long-term rate of growth of national production. The Government aim to secure a soundly-based increase in the rate of growth, so that real incomes will rise more rapidly than hitherto. For the moment, however, we must deal with things as they are. In recent years national production per head has risen by about 2 to $2^1/_2$ per cent a year. We ought to be able to do better than this but on present trends it seems likely to increase at about this rate in 1962. It is accordingly necessary that the increase of wages and salaries, as of other incomes, should be kept within this figure during the next phase. . . .

It is not possible to lay down hard and fast rules by which any given proposal for a wage or salary increase should be judged in the period immediately ahead. But some arguments which have in the past been widely used to justify higher wages and salaries, certainly ought not to be given the same weight as hitherto. For example, arguments derived from the increased cost of living, or from the trends of profits or productivity in a particular industry, cannot in present circumstances be regarded as providing of themselves a sound basis for an increase. . . . A shortage of labour within a particular industry or firm would not of itself warrant an increase in pay. . . . In the past comparisons with levels or trends of income in other employments have played a large part in discussions leading to wage and salary increases and have been accepted as guiding criteria, especially in the public services. These comparisons will still have a part to play.

But at any rate in the immediate future more regard will have to be given to the general economic considerations set out in this paper. The Government will emphasize the need for this in their negotiations with their own employees.

(22) *T. U. C. Statement on Economic Policy and the N. E. D. C.* (24 Jan. 1962)

The letter which the Chancellor of the Exchequer sent the T. U. C. on January 10th is based on the assumption that increases in incomes, and above all wages, are the critical cause of Britain's economic difficulties. Accordingly, he proposes that the pay pause should be followed by a transitional period of slightly less rigid restraint and eventually by a permanent national incomes policy. The Chancellor insists that the alternative to what he describes as an incomes policy, but what is in practice wage restraint, is further restriction of demand with loss of economic growth and higher levels of unemployment. . . .

There is no clear evidence for the Chancellor's claim that the pay pause as such has materially contributed to a growing feeling that Britain is becoming more competitive. What is clear is that since the pay pause has been operating production and productivity have fallen sharply and that, with more men and machines standing idle, unit costs have tended to rise.

That is why the T. U. C. proposed that action should be taken to reverse the decline in economic activity. . . .

It is possible that a concerted move to a higher level of economic activity could generate an increase in personal incomes which could not be matched immediately by an increase in the resources available for personal consumption. In such circumstances, pressure might have to be relieved not only by higher taxation, but even by temporarily limiting increases in incomes or preventing part of those increases for a time from being spent.

This is not, however, the challenge which the Chancellor is offering to the community. He is asking for wage restraint as a means of avoiding doing other things which should have priority in the efforts to improve the balance of payments in 1962. What is more, he is asking trade unions to accept wage restraint – that is, a greater measure of restraint than is imposed naturally by the process of collective bargaining – in circumstances when they would be least likely to be able to secure the assent of their members. In a democracy wage restraint is difficult to apply in any circumstances.

Without the willing co-operation of work-people, any agreement on the part of executives or of the General Council themselves would be worth little. The climate of opinion has been vitiated by the Government's arbitrary introduction and dogmatic maintenance of the pay pause. Moreover, one of the results of the pay pause will be an accumulation of claims requiring settlement in the coming months.

(23) *National Incomes Commission*, Cmnd 1844 (1962): Terms of reference

(i) The parties immediately concerned may refer to the Commission for enquiry any current claim or specific question relating to pay or other conditions of service or employment. . . .

(ii) The Government may refer to the Commission for review any matters relating to pay or other conditions of service or employment where the cost is met in whole or in part from the Exchequer. . . .

(iii) The Government may refer to the Commission for retrospective examination any particular settlement relating to pay or other conditions of service or employment (other than an award at arbitration). . . .

In considering any such reference the Commission is also required to have regard both to the circumstances of the case concerned and to the national interest, including in particular:–

(a) the desirability of keeping the rate of increase of the aggregate of monetary incomes within the long-term rate of increase of national production:

(b) the desirability of paying a fair reward for the work concerned;

(c) the manpower needs of the service, industry or employment concerned, taking into account any regional or local differences in such needs, and the importance of securing the most efficient deployment and use of national resources including manpower;

(d) the policies and practices in the service, industry or employment concerned in such matters (where appropriate) as pricing, profit margins, dividends, efficient use of manpower and equipment, and organisation;

(e) the repercussions which a particular settlement in the case concerned might have in other employments.

(24) National Incomes Commission, *Remuneration of Academic Staff in Universities and Colleges of Advanced Technology* (1964), *PP* 1963–4, xvii, Cmnd 2317

In paragraph 16 of our first Report we stated that the fundamental principle of an incomes policy is to keep the rate of increase in money incomes within the long-term rate of increase of national production. . . .

In order, however, to carry the discussion a stage further we may point out that underlying this statement there are two assumptions which have to be made if any incomes policy is to be successfully initiated and is to become a practical feature of the nation's economic life. An incomes policy must start somewhere and its first preoccupation must be with short-term considerations. The assumptions to which we refer reflect these necessities.

The first of them is that, in general, changes in rates of pay designed without any long-term justification, to alter relativities in remuneration will not succeed in their object except perhaps for a very brief period of time. Every attempt on the part of one section of the community simply to go ahead of or to catch up with the general level of increases in income will supply momentum for the acquisition of parallel increases by other sections and will in consequence be rapidly defeated. What is gained will be almost immediately lost and the overall result will be nothing but the familiar cost inflation, the continued alteration of 'stop' and 'go' in the national economy and a slowing down in the growth of real income which is a loss to all.

The second assumption is that existing relativities in remuneration are satisfactory. Inability to alter differentials except temporarily and at the ultimate price of inflation leads to their perpetuation. Both these assumptions have to be made when an incomes policy is first formulated. They are justifiable as the starting point for such a policy based on immediate and short-term considerations. . . .

It is neither possible nor desirable to attempt to categorise the exceptional circumstances in which a departure from the normal standard of increases in incomes may be justified. It seems to us, however, to be clear that two possible situations of a general nature may arise in which such a departure is required in the national interest.

The first situation is where the circumstances are such that a long-term change in the relativities of remuneration is desirable on economic grounds. These circumstances must be of a kind which can be shown and be seen to be outstanding, unusual, and the subject of a necessary change. . . .

The second situation is where, although in the short run there can be no case for trying to increase the remuneration of one of the lowest paid groups relative to that of others, there is nevertheless a long-term justification on social grounds for amending a pattern of differences created by historical factors which have ceased to apply to modern conditions.

(25) *Court of Inquiry into the Electricity Supply Industry. Trade Unions' Statement* (1964), *PP* 1963–4, xv Cmnd 2361

As stated in this submission, since its inception in 1919 until 1961, the industry enjoyed peaceful and harmonious relationships at all levels. The dispute under inquiry was the occasion of the first official industrial action since the present negotiating machinery was established and this is sufficient evidence of the responsibility of the Trade Unions and the manual workers of the Industry. We have at no time exploited our strength in a vulnerable industry and the balance of interest struck between our members as producers and the consumers of the industry has, if anything, been persistently tilted in favour of the latter.

We are of the opinion that this dispute raises fundamental issues far beyond the questions raised by the inconveniences and hardships inevitably caused by any industrial action taken by the trade unions. We reiterate our belief that the changed policies and attitudes of the Electricity Council have their source in the desire to conform as far as possible to the policies of the Government in the field of wages and that this is fundamentally responsible for the industrial relations problems now confronting the industry. We have acknowledged that those responsible for labour relations in nationalised industries, and the ultimate responsibility must rest with the Chairman, cannot ignore the Government. It is again a question of the balance to be struck between the interests of the Government and the interests of the workers in the industry. Since 1961 the balance struck has been highly unfavourable to the workers and in this situation serious problems for the industry and its collective bargaining machinery are bound to ensue.

(26) *Working for Prosperity. The National Plan in Brief* (1964)

To make the policy work, industry will have to break out of the bad old habit of passing on higher costs to the public. Much greater efforts can and should be made to offset increases by greater efficiency. And the customer should get out of the habit of accepting higher prices without question. Where costs can be brought down, prices should fall as well.

In addition, the growth of wages and salaries must be kept in line with the growth of output. That is why a 'norm' of $3-3^1/_2$ per cent a year has been fixed as a national standard for increases in income per head. Obviously there will be exceptional cases where a bigger increase can be justified, but these exceptions must be kept to a minimum.

(27) *Joint Statement of Intent on Productivity, Prices and Incomes* (16 Dec. 1964)

THE GOVERNMENT

(f) The Government will prepare and implement a general plan for economic development, in consultation with both sides of industry through the National Economic Development Council. This will provide for higher investment; for improving our industrial skills; for modernisation of industry; for balanced regional development; for higher exports; and for the largest possible sustained expansion of production and real incomes.

(g) Much greater emphasis will be given to increasing productivity. The Government will encourage and develop policies designed to promote technological advance in industry, and to get rid of restrictive practices and prevent abuses of monopoly power, and so improve efficiency, cut out waste, and reduce excessive prices. More vigorous policies will be pursued designed to facilitate mobility of labour and generally to make more effective use of scarce manpower resources, and to give workers a greater sense of security in the face of economic change. The Government also intend to introduce essential social improvements such as a system of earnings-related benefits, in addition to the improvements in national insurance benefits already announced.

(h) The Government will set up machinery to keep a continuous watch on the general movement of prices and of money incomes of all kinds and to carry out the other functions described in paragraph (j) below. They will also use their fiscal powers or other appropriate means to correct any excessive growth in aggregate profits as compared with the growth of wages and salaries, after allowing for short-term fluctuations.

MANAGEMENT AND UNIONS

(i) We, the representatives of the Trades Union Congress, the Federation of British Industries, the British Employers' Confederation, the National Association of British Manufacturers, the Association of British Chambers of Commerce accept that major objectives of national policy must be: to ensure that British industry is dynamic and that its prices are competitive; to raise productivity and efficiency so that real national output can increase, and to keep increases in wages, salaries and other forms of incomes in line with this increase; to keep the general level of prices stable.

(j) We therefore undertake on behalf of our members: to encourage and lead a sustained attack on the obstacles to efficiency, whether on the part of management or of the workers, and to strive for the adoption of more rigorous standards of performance at all levels; to co-operate with the Government in endeavouring, in the face of practical problems, to give effective shape to the machinery that the Government intend to establish for the following purposes:

(i) to keep under review the general movement of prices and of money incomes of all kinds;
(ii) to examine particular cases in order to advise whether or not the behaviour of prices or of wages, salaries or other money incomes is in the national interest as defined by the Government after consultation with management and unions.

(k) We stress that close attention must be paid to easing the difficulties of those affected by changed circumstances in their employment. We therefore support, in principle, the Government's proposals for earnings-related benefits and will examine sympathetically proposals for severance payments.

(l) We – Government, management and unions – are confident that by co-operating in a spirit of mutual confidence to give effect to the principles and policies described above, we and those whom we represent will be able to achieve a faster growth of real incomes and generally to promote the economic and social well-being of the country.

(28) *Machinery of Prices and Incomes Policy*, Cmnd 2577 (1965)

The Government have discussed with Management and Unions the practical problems involved in establishing machinery to investigate particular cases of price and income behaviour and with their agreement now propose the setting up under Royal Warrant of a National Board for Prices and Incomes working in two separate Divisions and the Incomes Review Division respectively.

The Government have been encouraged by the Statement of Intent and in subsequent discussion to believe that all parties concerned will give the Board their voluntary co-operation in its investigations of particular cases. The Government would have to consider giving the Board statutory authority, however, if experience showed this was necessary.

(29) *Prices and Incomes Policy*, Cmnd 2639 (1965)
'Employment Incomes',

12. Wages and salaries are determined by many factors, including changes in the supply and demand for different kinds of labour, trends in productivity and profits, comparisons with levels or trends of incomes in other employments and changes in the cost of living. The weight given to these different factors varies with circumstances. They are also influenced by the policies which the Government pursue in relation to the distribution of incomes. The Government in the Joint Statement of Intent on Productivity, Prices and Incomes have affirmed that their social objective is to ensure that the benefits of faster growth are distributed in a way that satisfies the claims of social need and justice. It is in that context that the following considerations are set out for the guidance of all those concerned with the determination of wages and salaries.

13. If wages and salaries per head are to keep in step with the long-term rate of increase in national productivity, less weight than hitherto will be given to the factors mentioned in paragraph 12 and more weight will have to be given to the incomes norm. Moreover, in applying the norm to wages and salaries, it will be necessary to take into account not only increases in wage and salary rates, but also increases in costs resulting from reductions in working hours without loss of pay, from higher rates of pay for overtime or shift work and from improvements in fringe benefits.

14. It would be impracticable and undesirable to lay down detailed rules so as to provide an indication of what changes in wages and salaries were warranted case by case. Nor would it be desirable to inhibit the structural changes necessary in the interests of faster growth. However, experience has shown that in conditions of full employment the normal processes of collective bargaining both at national and local level can result in pay increases which are inflationary in effect. It is accordingly important to ensure that increases in wages and salaries above the norm should be confined to cases in which exceptional treatment can be shown to be required in the national interest. These exceptional increases should be kept to a minimum, bearing in mind that they will need to be balanced by lower than average increases to other groups if the increase in wages and salaries over the economy as a whole is to be kept within the norm.

15. Exceptional pay increases should be confined to the following circumstances:

   (i) where the employees concerned, for example by accepting more exacting work or a major change in working practices, make a direct contribution towards increasing productivity in the particular firm or industry. Even in such cases some of the benefit should accrue to the community as a whole in the form of lower prices;

  (ii) where it is essential in the national interest to secure a change in the distribution of manpower (or to prevent a change which would otherwise take place) and a pay increase would be both necessary and effective for this purpose;

 (iii) where there is a general recognition that existing wage and salary levels are too low to maintain a reasonable standard of living;

  (iv) where there is widespread recognition that the pay of a certain group of workers has fallen seriously out of line with the level of remuneration for similar work and needs in the national interest to be improved.

Many unionists and others looked to Sweden's system of industrial relations as a model which Britain might usefully follow (30, 31), and the emergence of the powerful Confederation of British Industry in 1965 (32) brought greater centralisation on the employers' side. On the critical issue of incomes policy, however, trade unions remained badly divided: the NUGMW favoured such a policy (33, 34), while craft unions were often hostile (35). The TUC, under George Woodcock, tried to operate an 'early warning' system on forthcoming claims (36) and pressed for co-operation with the Government (37).

   (30) Jack Cooper, *Industrial Relations: Sweden Shows the Way*, Fabian Research Series no. 235 (1963)

The main characteristics of the Swedish system of industrial relations can be summarised thus:

(a) Rational, centralised, 'pyramidical' structure of both trade unions and employers' organizations, demanding high quality leadership at all levels.

(b) Centralised wage-bargaining, presenting the negotiators with the opportunity to survey the entire wage and salary picture, rather than isolated segments, and to attempt to implement a rational wages policy.

(c) Positive attempts on the part of the trade union movement to make its own contribution to an equitable wages policy.

(d) Legalisation of collective agreements, with the concomitant prohibition of strikes and lockouts over the terms of an agreement during its currency.

(e) A Basic Agreement stipulating a procedure for negotiation, a number of 'hostile' acts that are forbidden, the treatment of disputes that may endanger the public interest, and the procedure to be followed in laying off and dismissing workers.

(f) A framework of Central Agreements on Workers' Protection, Vocational Training, Works Councils, Time and Motion Study, and Women's Questions.

(g) A permanent body (the Labour Market Committee) for the discussion of major issues.

The development and operation of this system has taken place within the context of these factors:

(a) For the past thirty years, the Social Democratic Party has played the dominant role in Swedish government, implying a wide measure of acceptance of the self-discipline implicit in social democracy.

(b) Positive efforts are continuously made, through the machinery of the National Labour Market Board, to create and maintain full employment.

(c) The Swedish system of social security aims at preventing a substantial fall in living standards as a consequence of sickness, accident, unemployment, retirement, etc.

(d) Over the years, it has become the socially acceptable thing to belong to the appropriate trade union.

(e) Equally, over the years, employers have developed a positive attitude towards trade unionism.

(f) Both trade unionists and employers are motivated by determination to avoid government intervention in industrial relations.

(g) Both trade unions and employers' associations make strenuous efforts in the field of education. . . .

. . . the 'system of self-imposed restraints' was the response of Swedish employers and unions to the challenge which confronted them in the mid-1930s when they were offered the choice between voluntary self-discipline or restraints imposed by the State in the public interest. . . .

The choice between self-discipline and imposed restraints confronts us in Britain today.

(31) TUC, *Sweden – Its Unions and Industrial Relations* (May 1963)

It is a common mistake to base comparisons between Swedish and British trade unionism on the view that it is centralisation of structure that differentiates them. The real difference lies in the sense of collective purpose that pervades the Swedish movement: in this sense there is no British trade union movement but only a collection of trade unions. It is this shared sense of purpose, rather than the centralised machinery, that, for example, enables the LO [*Landsorganisationen*] leaders to persuade discontented groups of trade unionists not to carry their dissatisfaction to the point of breaking up the system.

The Swedish unions adopted a centralised structure because it suited their purpose, and if it ceased to do so they would scrap it. The justification of centralisation has in fact changed.

Conceived initially as a means of collective defence against employers' attacks, it has in some measure, and to some extent initially under Government pressure, come to be used as a method of unifying policy and of persuading trade unionists to accept the leaders' views of the needs of the national economic situation. Not that trade union needs are made subservient to the broader needs of the nation.

Swedish unions have to justify themselves by securing higher living standards for their members, and in this way they have been very successful.

It is highly probably that the comparative absence of industrial disputes in Sweden is the result, rather than the cause, of the higher living standards that have been made possible by more rapid economic expansion.

The imposition by law of a warning period and the legal enforceability of agreements obviously have something to do with the maintenance of industrial peace, but the provisions of agreements can only be enforced legally if there is a general willingness on the part of the trade union community to accept enforcement and if the agreements themselves are flexible enough to allow generous interpretations by employers. Perhaps part of the price paid for industrial peace can be seen in wage-drift.

Yet the fact of peace remains, and even if on average the margin between Sweden and Britain is only two hours lost per worker per year, the benefits may be seen more clearly in a generally better climate of relations between employers and workers and in the more liberal attitude that Swedish trade unionists take towards labour mobility. One factor in a union's bargaining strength is its ability to limit entry into the job: the banning of the closed shop (as distinct from the union shop) and the acceptance and indeed promotion of active labour market policies obviously reduce this source of strength.

The reasons for the willingness of Swedish trade unionists to modify their traditional attitudes and policies are to be found in part in anxiety to avoid Government intervention in the regulation of industrial relations, and in part in recognition of the repercussions on employment and on trade unionists of national economic difficulties.

Certainly the LO sees its relationships with the Government in terms of rights and obligations. It expects the Government not only to provide specific advantages for workpeople in legislative form but also to create an economic climate in which trade unions can operate effectively to secure their objectives. Equally it recognises the need to make its own actions conform to the achievement of those objectives, and accepts that, if the trade union movement by its actions disturbs the equilibrium of the economy, it will leave the Government no alternative to adopting policies which are necessary to redress the balance, even if they are distasteful to trade unions.

(32) CBI, *Spokesman for British Industry* (n.d.)

At home and abroad the Confederation of British Industry is the acknowledged spokesman and representative of the management side of industry for the United

Kingdom. Founded on July 30 1965 and incorporated by Royal Charter, it combines in a single democratic and voluntary association the roles previously played by the long-established British Employers' Confederation, the Federation of British Industries, the National Association of British Manufactures and also the Industrial Association of Wales and Monmouthshire.

The prime aim is to promote the prosperity of British industry and those elements of British business which are closely associated with it. Through its highly representative membership and regional structure the CBI is able to observe the whole economic pattern from a national viewpoint and to act as a central point of reference for those who seek the view and reactions of industry and business. It is the officially recognised spokesman of British employers in the work of the International Labour Organisation.

Although it maintains strict political neutrality, the CBI sees it as part of its job to advise, consult and where necessary take issue with the British Government on all aspects of its policies which are likely to affect either directly or indirectly the interests of British business both now and in the future. In addition to formulating policies through the whole field of economic activity and dealing with general problems which concern more than one particular sector of its membership, the Confederation also helps its members in a variety of ways with their individual day-to-day problems.

(33) NUGMW, *Why An Incomes Policy?* (Esher, n.d. [1964?])

Some attempts to secure an incomes policy have been made before. They failed largely because it was not sufficiently recognised that at the bottom success required the co-operation of everybody and guarantees that nobody would selfishly exploit the situation for their own advantages. Now there is a greater recognition that co-operation and a willingness to pull in the same direction are needed if we are to overcome our economic problems and avoid falling behind countries like Germany, France, Sweden, Italy, in economic achievement and increases in living standards. The right climate for an incomes policy is being created.

An incomes policy offers great opportunities and a great challenge. The challenge is our ability to change our attitudes and ways of doing things. It is a challenge which applies to everyone, Government, employers, and unions, at all levels of activity. Nowhere will the challenge be greater than in individual work-places. In a democracy, whether it be a country or a union, on important decisions the consent and co-operation of those who will be affected by the decisions must be obtained. It is hoped that this pamphlet will have shown our members that it is in the best interests of themselves and their families that their consent and co-operation should be given to an incomes policy.

(34) NUGMW, *Productivity, Prices and Incomes* (Esher, 1966)

A productivity, prices and incomes policy is vital for continuous economic expansion, the preservation of full employment and higher increases in real wages and living standards. Our basic purpose as a trade union of maximising the living standards and job security of our members can best be pursued through co-operation in the implementation of a productivity, prices and incomes policy.

We must retain the ultimate right to determine wages of members within a framework of free collective bargaining. The exercise of this right, however, should be related to the objectives of the productivity, prices and incomes policy.

The Prices and Incomes Bill does not violate any of the essentials of free collective bargaining. At present, however, the voluntary 'early warning' system of the TUC should be the method through which the wages policy of individual unions and groups of unions should be assessed in the light of productivity, prices and incomes policy. The TUC system should be given time to develop and succeed.

(35) Peter Jenkins *et al.*, *The Trades Union Congress 1965* from the *Guardian* (Manchester, 1965)

Mr Danny McGarvey (secretary Boilermakers' Society) proposing the motion calling on Congress to reject the Government's present productivity, prices and incomes policy said: 'If you give up the right of collective bargaining in a free and democratic society to any Government you are giving up the right of a free people to ask, to demand, what belongs to them. When you take the first step to giving authority to a Government which takes away that basic principle of democracy, democracy no longer exists.'

Congress replied with a throaty murmur of agreement, a murmur which melted to laughter as McGarvey added: 'Even if, at the beginning, the syrup is very sweet, at the end of the deal the syrup will turn into cascara.'

Mr McGarvey, his face shiny with sweat, began by saying he was beginning to think the General Council was becoming like some politicians – 'professional confusionists'. He challenged Mr Woodcock and delegates to deny that the principles in his motion had been rejected by previous congresses. The boilermakers were opposed to the incomes policy because it had to be an 'in for a penny, in for a pound' policy. The declaration of intent had been only a first step. 'If anyone thought it was going to be left there, they were living in a fool's paradise.'

The trade union movement had played its part in returning the Labour Party to power, but the democratic Socialist movement, of which Congress was a part, was not entitled to follow 'willy nilly politicians who are not prepared to carry out policies benefitting the members we represent'. Democratic Socialists would always insist that a Government chosen by a free society listened to the people and to bodies as the TUC and the Labour Party conference.

The boilermakers believed in planning. 'But we believe in Socialist planning.' The boilermakers thought the present Government had more or less adopted policies similar to those of the last Government. 'We understand that the (Labour) Government may have some difficulties, but we expect them to understand that we have a function to perform in relation to our members. Our members pay us our wages to see they get decent wages and better conditions and a better standard of living. They don't pay trade unionists to postpone increases.'

Collective bargaining was something the trade union movement had always cherished. The boilermakers would concede it to nobody. He then made his remarks about the threat to democracy of giving a Government authority over trade unions.

'I know that most unions have taken the decision. But there are uncommitted unions. If this document (the General Council's recommendations) is carried, and if you accept the right of any Government to throw into the dustbin your constitutions, your members will slaughter you when you return to say what you have done.'

Mr George Doughty (secretary, Draughtsmen's and Allied Technicians' Association), seconding, said his union believed in economic planning. He assured Mr Woodcock that the union did not take its responsibilities to its members lightly. The reason it supported the boilermakers' motion was that it did not believe the General Council's recommendations were in its members' interests. He did not want to expose his members to what would arise from a decision to control incomes without imposing the same control on other aspects of economic life.

He was sorry to have to say that the Government's plans for dealing with economic problems were following well known, orthodox and traditional lines – following the policy termed by Congress some years ago as 'stop–go.' The Government was apparently using only persuasion to get businesses to limit their profits. Recent figures had shown that the wages of workers in Britain, including the value of social services, were lower than corresponding wages in Germany, Italy, France and Belgium.

(36) TUC, *Incomes Policy. Speech by George Woodcock, TUC General Secretary at a Conference of Executive Committees of Affiliated Organisations . . . London . . . March 2 1967* (1967)

What we propose to do . . . is to continue to operate the notification system that we adopted in 1965. We propose that it shall be a moral obligation upon all unions affiliated to the TUC to notify the TUC as early as possible of their intentions in respect of wage adjustments or adjustments in their industrial agreements affecting costs. We intend that these notifications shall be examined by a committee of the General Council of the TUC and that we shall make our comments upon them sometimes in writing, sometimes in discussions with the unions before the committee, sometimes perhaps in discussions between the union representatives and myself. This is the policy, this is the procedure we adopted in 1965. If there is a difference it lies in this, that having had experience in the past of operating this system, having gained as I think we have gained, the confidence that we are dealing with this sensibly as trade unions with trade unionists, we can now improve or tighten or toughen – I do not care what you call it – the procedure. The form will be the same. But we may be able to be more persuasive, more argumentative, more pressing upon unions to accept or take into account the views of the General Council. The form is the same, but we hope, we expect, that, having gained the confidence of unions what happens in discussion will be somewhat tougher.

In order to operate this system, in order to toughen, in order to make this policy actually what I have just claimed it to be in intention – not a device for dodging the problems of incomes policy, not a clever dodge to bluff the Government – in order to operate our system we need when we are in that committee the genuine authority of the trade union Movement, and that is what this conference is really about. For you to give to us by your approval to-day, not in votes alone (because votes matter nothing in this trade union Movement) but in showing that you understand what we are about, and that you approve what we are about, the right to say, 'This is part of trade unionism, this is part of the duty of the TUC, and the TUC has authority in this field.' That is what we want. Because in this procedure we cannot operate without genuine authority. We cannot operate without the belief that what we are doing is understood and approved by trade unionists as the right thing to do. . . .

There are two questions that arise. On what terms do we co-operate with Government, or to what extent does the Government interfere? Where do the Government's interests in the field of wages stop? They have a right to a view, they have a right to point out how wage movements affect their ability to deal with these problems which we insist they shall undertake. The question is where do they stop. Apart from the question of where they stop there is the further question: on what terms do they seek our cooperation? We are not going to be told by Governments just what we should do, and then do nothing but say, 'Yes, sir, we will do it.' We will not be made the agents of Government. . . .

We have to work with them and we want to work with them. We are not seeking to fight the Government. Let us make this absolutely clear. We have been disputing with Governments, I think quite unnecessarily, the merits of our scheme as against their scheme. Their scheme involves sanctions. I think this is a pity . . . . I do not believe, to begin with, that at this stage, at any rate, whatever may happen as the years go by and things develop, legal penalties have any place in an incomes scheme when your are dealing with these problems of industrial relationships.

(37) TUC, *Economic Review and Report of a Conference of Executive Committees of Affiliated Organisations* (1968)

A sharp rise in costs and prices could effectively put a halt to expansion and it is therefore necessary to examine the contribution that incomes policy can make to stabilising and reducing costs. Incomes policy can help to promote changes in the structure and practice of collective bargaining which will assist the improvement of productivity, and thus keep down costs. It can also help to create the circumstances in which the economy as a whole can be allowed to expand more rapidly without running into inflation.

The reason for having an incomes policy at all is not to hold down real wages but, on the contrary, to help provide conditions in which unions can secure for their members bigger and more regular improvements in real wages and conditions. Unless trade unionists are willing to play their part they have no real right to expect the Government to pursue the growth policies advocated in this review. Equally, trade unions will only be able to persuade their members to abandon the methods which in the past they have adopted for the defence of their standards and jobs, provided that the Government is prepared to reshape its own economic strategy. The General Council recognise that precipitate expansion at any cost would lead rapidly to serious labour shortages and to inflationary pressure. They believe that it is realistic to set the target for expansion at about 5 per cent a year averaged over the next four years, taking account of the prospective labour supply, provided that both sides of industry are willing to adopt methods which will enable the labour available to be used to its best effect.

Almost exactly a century after the first Royal Commission on Trade Unions and Employers' Associations, another Royal Commission was set up in April 1965, under Lord Donovan. The 'Donovan Commission's' comments on such matters as 'formal' and 'informal' bargaining (38), restrictive labour practices (39), the craft system (40), the extent of disputes (41) and unofficial disputes (42) were generally familiar. The virtue of the *Report* was, perhaps, that it brought together a *corpus* of researched material in a single volume. In its broad examination of the situation in the mid-1960s it is a modern classic, albeit a sometimes controversial one. There was, however, no consensus among the Commissioners as to the solutions required for the problems which they had discussed – particularly over the role of the law (43, 44).

(38) RC on Trade Unions and Employers' Associations, *Report*, Cmnd 3623 (1968)

Britain has two systems of industrial relations. The one is the formal system embodied in the official institutions. The other is the informal system created by the actual behaviour of trade unions and employers' associations, of managers, shop stewards and workers. . . .

Workplace bargaining is informal because of the predominance of unwritten understandings and of custom and practice. Informality applies not only to arrangements concerning pay and conditions of work at the factory, but also to the procedure under which these arrangements are reached. Most industry-wide agreements give only sketchy guidance about the procedure to be followed within the factory. There is, for example, rarely any provision for compensating shop stewards for any loss of earnings due to their work as stewards. Usually nothing is said about stewards holding meetings with their constituents on the employers' premises, inside or outside working hours. . . . Joint committees of stewards and managers to discuss and settle problems are also normal, but if they are mentioned in industry-wide procedure agreements there may be little guidance on their powers and conduct of business. Some managements draw up their own procedures in agreement with their shop stewards or district union officers, but it is more common to rely on precedent. Even where written procedures are established they often come to be 'short-circuited' in the interests of speedy settlements. . . .

The formal and informal systems are in conflict. The informal system undermines the regulative effect of industry-wide agreements. The gap between industry-wide agreed rates and actual earnings continues to grow. Procedure agreements fail to cope adequately with disputes arising within factories. Nevertheless, the assumptions of the formal system still exert a powerful influence over men's minds and prevent the informal system from developing into an effective and orderly method of regulation. The assumption that industry-wide agreements control industrial relations leads many companies to neglect their responsibility for their own personnel policies. Factory bargaining remains informal and fragmented, with many issues left to custom and practice. The unreality of industry-wide pay agreements leads to the use of incentive schemes and overtime payments for purposes quite different from those they were designed to serve.

(39) Ibid.

Restrictive labour practices may be defined as 'rules or customs which unduly hinder the efficient use of labour'. It is necessary to limit the definition to cases where efficiency is 'unduly' hindered, because there are many provisions in safety legislation and in collective agreements, for example, which limit employers' freedom in the use of manpower but which can unhesitatingly be accepted as justified. Indeed all restrictive labour practices have or once had some justification. The justifications should not be ignored, but judged against the loss which the practices entail.

Most of the practices which result in serious waste of manpower can be understood only in relation to particular circumstances in particular undertakings or plants. For example, there is no standard practice as regards the use of craftsmen's mates. Practice varies from company to company, and even within companies from plant to plant. The use of mates may not be inefficient at all; on the other hand the high priority given in many productivity agreements to the redeployment of mates, and the improvements in productivity gained as a result, show that they are often seriously under-employed. Again each company has its own levels of overtime; and although the use of habitual overtime may be very extensive the problems it presents are complex and vary a great deal from one factory or workshop to the next.

Where practices of this kind exist, insistence on retaining them usually comes from the workers themselves, acting as groups which have certain interests in common which they try as best they can to further rather than from trade unions as such.

(40) Ibid.

The crafts system is deeply rooted in much of British industry. The broad assumptions underlying its observance are that ranges of skilled work can be identified, the right to perform which should belong exclusively to a particular kind of craftsman; and that the normal way of becoming a craftsman should be the serving of an apprenticeship of a specified length of time before the age of 20 or 21.

In its origins the craft system reflects the need for specialisation in any but the most rudimentary economy. Workers can be trained in the special skills necessary for the performance of identifiable types of task. The craft conception has fostered pride in skill and high standards of workmanship. It is true that a craft union pursues a sectional interest, as do all trade unions and employers' associations; but a craft union also stands as a witness to its members' pride in their special skill, which they believe makes a valuable contribution to the well-being of society.

Against the merits must be set the disadvantages. In practice precise and rigid boundaries between crafts or between a craft and semi-skilled grades of labour can be settled only on an arbitrary basis. The boundaries are therefore a fruitful source of dispute especially where new work is introduced which does not conform to established limits. Yet the knowledge that they have virtually committed themselves to a craft for life makes men alert to guard what they consider to be their own preserve, and to oppose relaxations in practices which, however desirable and even essential for efficiency, may seem to constitute a threat to their whole way of life. The most highly skilled are less endangered because the difficulty of acquiring their expertise protects them. Where a craft is less skilled its boundaries must be fixed on largely artificial lines which may nevertheless be stubbornly defended. . . .

In the context of technological change the drawbacks of the craft system become even more marked. It is unreal to assume that the demand for any particular range of skill will be constant. If the only normal method of entry into the craft is via an apprenticeship, supply will respond slowly and inadequately to demand. Where expansion is required it will be delayed. Where technological innovation reduces the demand for a given craft then there will be waste and suffering among the men whose livelihoods and expectations for the future are bound up with its continuing existence.

(41) Ibid.: 'Official, Unofficial and other Stoppages of Work due to Industrial Disputes. Average Annual Figures for Stoppages in the Period 1964–66'[1]

Type of stoppage	Number of stoppages	Number of workers involved[2]	Number of Working days lost
Official strikes	74	101,100	733,000
Partly-official strikes[3]	2	600	7,000
Unofficial strikes	2,171	653,400	1,697,000
Others, e.g. lock-outs or strikes by unorganised workers unclassified	25	2,700	15,000
ALL	2,272	757,800	2,452,000

Source: Ministry of Labour

(1) The figures relate to stoppages *beginning* in the years covered and the total number of working days lost due to them.
(2) Including workers thrown out of work at establishments where stoppages occurred, although not themselves parties to the dispute.
(3) I.e., a strike involving more than one union and recognised as official by at least one but not all the unions concerned.

(42) Ibid.

To summarise, it is apparent that the causes of unofficial strikes in the motor industry are complex, and that employers and unions both bear a considerable responsibility for them. Insofar as fluctuations in demand have been caused by fiscal measures which fall with particular force on the motor industry, Governments too must take some responsibility, since these fluctuations have led to insecurity of employment and of earnings. Employers have failed to develop adequate management policies, and in particular have not tackled effectively the problem of devising rational wage structures. Trade unions have been handicapped by their multiplicity and consequent rivalry, and have failed to bring an effective influence to bear at workplace level.

Above all, employers and trade unions have failed to develop adequate institutions in changing circumstances.

(43) Ibid.

The British system of industrial relations is based on voluntarily agreed rules which, as a matter of principle, are not enforced by law. This is an outstanding characteristic which distinguishes it from the systems of many comparable countries. . . .

The evidence which we have received shows a wide measure of agreement that this non-intervention should continue to be the normal policy. Most of us arrive at the same conclusion. In the preceding chapters of this report we recommended a number of important legislative measures concerning collective bargaining and agreements, trade unions and employers' associations, and the rights and remedies of individual employers and employees. We do so, however, only where we are convinced that new institutions need to be created in order to strengthen and to improve the enforcement of individual rights; or where a clear enunciation of legal principles is required in the public interest; or where some machinery has to be set up for imposing legal sanctions in circumstances in which voluntary action is likely to be insufficient for the solution of urgent social and economic problems.

(44) Ibid: Note of Reservation by Mr Andrew Shonfield

It seems inconceivable in the long run that in a society which is increasingly closely knit, where the provision of services to meet the elementary needs of a civilised daily life depends more and more on the punctual performance of interrelated work tasks of a collective character, trade unions will be treated as if they had the right to be exempt from all but the most rudimentary legal obligations. This is the traditional view, which has bitten deep into the British system of industrial relations. . . .

I start from the proposition that the deliberate abstention of the law from the activities of mighty subjects tends to diminish the liberty of the ordinary citizen and to place his welfare at risk. If organisations are powerful enough to bully then very special grounds are necessary to justify the decision not to subject their behaviour to legal rules. . . .

One of the reasons why collective agreements have lacked precision is that they have not been treated as enforceable contracts. As the Report makes clear, the typical agreement at present in operation is of a kind that could not be made legally enforceable. However, the same disability would not attach to a new kind of collective agreement which, it is hoped, will emerge as the reforms proposed in the Report take effect.

The arguments that are commonly advanced for the contention that the contractual form is an appropriate one for collective agreements are not persuasive. They are regarded as having binding force in other countries, and no special difficulties arise from that fact. Of course it should be open to the two parties to a collective agreement to avoid making promises to one another about fulfilment if they specifically state, at the time that the agreement is signed, that neither side regards it as being a contractual obligation. But otherwise it should have the character of a normal undertaking, in which each party has a claim for redress if it suffers loss because the other fails to keep its side of the bargain. . . . At the very least the proposed reform would induce trade unions which were offered more advantageous terms, on condition that they were prepared to treat their side of the bargain as a genuine promise, to consider their own attitudes more closely and critically. At the moment the inducement to promise anything seriously is weak; it should be strengthened. . . .

It is the long-run consequences of the habit of entering into binding agreements which are the main objectives of the proposed reform. The probability is that those unions which are able to promise reliably to perform their part of a collective agreement will obtain better bargains from employers for their members than weaker or less determined unions. The assumption underlying this proposal is that there are dynamic employers in British industry who would be inclined to innovate more rapidly, if the orderly introduction of new methods had the active support of strong trade unions carrying out contractual obligations which they had freely undertaken. After a time binding agreements would be seen to confer benefits on members of trade unions which had accepted them. Their chief benefit would be that of a wider range of management decisions would be subject to negotiation with the workpeople affected by them. Management would be induced to enlarge the scope of the collective bargain, if the reward for doing so were to allow it to plan for more rapid change in a climate of security.

14. *The Search for a Solution*

Even before Lord Donovan's seminal report appeared, politicians of all parties had considered the causes of and remedies for industrial strife. The Conservatives issued their proposals in 1968 (1), and in the following year the Labour Government published its policy (2). Such was the trade-union opposition to any legal interference with free collective bargaining, that the Government withdrew its proposed measure.

(1) Conservative Political Centre, *Fair Deal At Work. The Conservative Approach to Modern Industrial Relations* (April 1968)

Industrial efficiency is the key to Britain's future prosperity. Since the war, enormous efforts and huge sums of money have been devoted to re-equipment, technical training, research, and the introduction of modern systems and techniques in production, marketing and administration. No one questions the need for this: but Britain will never release her full productive potential while, over a wide area of industry, the working relationships between management and men are embittered by fears, suspicion and self-destroying conflict. Unless, as a nation, we can get more harmony, positive co-operation and unity of purpose into our industrial life, our struggles for higher productivity, expanding exports and higher standards of living can make only marginal progress.

Our first conclusion is that if, since the war, government and industry had given industrial relations – in its widest sense – a top-priority label, the world would not be looking on Britain today as a nation of Humpty-Dumpties, poised on the remnants of a fast-crumbling wall. People remain today, as always, the most important element in any enterprise, and high morale is the first essential for its success. This applies as much to the nation as to its smallest factory.

Our second conclusion is that no government action can, in itself, create good industrial relations. No Act of Parliament will make people like each other or understand each other.

Laws cannot create qualities of leadership; and it is the right sort of leadership – particularly in management – which, above all else, determines the quality of human relations and morale in any establishment.

But acceptance of this does not mean that government can therefore do little to

347

influence the situation; that it should just sit on the sidelines. . . . The concept of freedom under the law is fundamental, but if that freedom is abused by irresponsible elements to the detriment of the nation or of the basic rights of individuals, government has a duty to step in.

This leads to our third conclusion, which is based largely on our studies of legislation in other countries and the extent to which it has influenced industrial relations and efficiency. This is that a fair, relevant and sensible framework of law, while providing no panaceas, can exert stabilising pressures and help to raise general standards in the way men do business together. And we believe that the piecemeal, anomalous – and, in some respects, unjust – provisions of our own trade union law tend to handicap, rather than help, industry in tackling the human problems which inevitably stem from industrial change. It is sometimes overlooked that the Trade Union Acts of the nineteenth and early twentieth centuries have profoundly influenced not just the structure and attitudes of the trade union movement, but the outlook and efficiency of our industrial society as a whole. And Britain, as the world's oldest industrial nation, has most to unlearn in order to modernise.

We agree that success or failure in this field depends principally on human behaviour, not the law. And in the rapidly changing conditions of industry there is particular need for greater communication and consultation between management and employees, management and unions, and between unions and their own members. This is essential not only to avoid disputes and gain acceptance of new methods; it is also essential in creating a greater sense of 'participation' among employees and in stimulating job-satisfaction. Good industrial relations are important for social, as well as economic, reasons.

But it is easy to theorise and deliver exhortations on how things would improve if only people and institutions would change their methods, attitudes and behaviour. We have seen our main task as being to concentrate on those problems which we believe can be alleviated by direct government action through legislation and other means. They fall into four categories:

(1) Industrial disputes.
(2) Restrictive labour practices.
(3) Excessive, unfair or harmful authority exercised by organisations or 'pressure groups', whether of employers or workpeople.
(4) The misuse of economic power for the furtherance of sectional objectives.

Our recommendations involve three separate forms of government action:

First, the introduction of a comprehensive Industrial Relations Act – something which Britain has never had in her history.
Second, the reconstitution of the National Board for Prices and Incomes into a Productivity Board whose main task would be to help rid industry of restrictive practices and promote the most effective use of manpower.
Third, new responsibilities for the Ministry of Labour.

We recognise the immense influence of broad economic factors on the climate of industrial relations but regard these as outside the scope of this report. It is concerned primarily with the relationships between people and the organisations which represent them.

(2) *In Place of Strife. A Policy for Industrial Relations*, Cmnd 3888 (1969)

Our present system of industrial relations has substantial achievements to its credit, but it also has serious defects. It has failed to prevent injustice, disruption of work and inefficient use of manpower. It perpetuates the existence of groups of employees who, as the result of the weakness of their bargaining position, fall behind in the struggle to obtain their full share of the benefits of an advanced industrial economy. In other cases management and employees are able unfairly to exploit the consumer and endanger economic prosperity. It has produced a growing number of lightning strikes and contributed little to increasing efficiency. There are still areas of industry without any machinery for collective bargaining at all. Radical changes are needed in our system of industrial relations to meet the needs of a period of rapid technical and industrial change. . . .

The Government intends, after further consultations, to introduce an Industrial Relations Bill, including provisions:

(1) To put a Commission on Industrial Relations on a statutory basis. . . .

(2) To require employers to register certain collective agreements and arrangements with the Department of Employment and Productivity. . . .

(3) To modify section 4(4) of the Trade Union Act 1871, to facilitate the direct legal enforcement, where the parties wish, of agreements between trade unions and employers' associations, and to provide that agreements should only be legally binding if they include an express written provision to that effect. . . .

(4) To give trade unions the right to have certain sorts of information from employers, subject to safeguards for confidential commercial information. . . .

(5) If necessary, to facilitate the appointment of workers' representatives to boards of undertakings. . . .

(6) To establish the principle that no employer has the right to prevent or obstruct an employee from belonging to a trade union. . . .

(7) To stop Friendly Societies from having rules debarring trade unionists from membership. . . .

(8) To empower the Commission on Industrial Relations to look into recognition disputes, and to arrange a secret ballot if it thinks this desirable. . . .

(9) To enable the Secretary of State, where the Commission on Industrial Relations recommends that an employer shall recognise a union (or that he shall negotiate with it) but there is continuing difficulty,

(a) to make an Order requiring the employer to recognise and negotiate with the Union and, in default, giving the union the right to take the employer to arbitration at the Industrial Court. . . .

(b) to make an Order giving the union a similar right against an employer who is refusing negotiating rights . . . and

(c) if necessary to make an Order excluding one or more unions from recognition, with penalties for breach of the Order by either the employer or a union. . . .

(10) To establish an Industrial Board to hear certain types of case against employers, trade unions and individual employees. . . .

(11) To amend the law relating to Wages Councils and section 8 of the Terms and Conditions of Employment Act 1959. . . .

(12) To provide for the Commission on Industrial Relations to make grants and loans for trade union development. . . .

(13) To enable the Secretary of State by Order to require those involved to desist for up to 28 days from a strike or lock-out which is unconstitutional or in which for other reasons adequate joint discussions have not taken place, and to require the employer meanwhile to observe specified terms or conditions. . . .

(14) To enpower the Secretary of State, where an official strike is threatened, by Order to require a ballot. . . .

(15) To protect inducement of breach of contract other than a contract of employment, in the circumstances of a trade dispute. . . .

(16) To introduce safeguards against unfair dismissal. . . .

(17) To amend the Contracts of Employment Act. . . .

(18) To extend the jurisdiction of Industrial Tribunals. . . .

(19) To require trade unions and employers' associations to have rules on certain subjects and to register. . . .

(20) To create a new Registrar of Trade Unions and Employers' Associations – the post to be combined for the present with that of the Registrar of Friendly Societies. . . .

(21) To provide new legal definitions of 'trade union' and 'employers' association'. . . .

(22) To require all but the smallest unions to have professional auditors, and to make new provisions regarding superannuation funds for members. . . .

(23) To enable a union to be sued in tort, except in the circumstances of a trade dispute. . . .

(24) To make any necessary amendment to the definition of a trade dispute. . . .

(25) To enable the Industrial Board to hear complaints by individuals of unfair or arbitrary action by trade unions. . . .

On being elected in 1970 the Conservative Government proceeded to implement its proposals (3) and the Industrial Relations Bill was passed in 1971 (4). Again the unions forcefully expressed their opposition (5), although parts of the Act (particularly the clauses concerning unfair dismissals) were extensively used (6).

(3) Conservative Central Office, *Industrial Relations Reform: The Bill in Brief!* (1971)

NEW LEGAL FRAMEWORK: One clear, modern new framework of law will replace the antiquated hotch-potch of unrelated Acts that stretch back into the 19th century.

'UNFAIR INDUSTRIAL PRACTICES': A new concept of specifying practices which fair-minded people would consider to be wrong or unjust. This list will help unions, employers and individuals to know exactly how they stand.

CODE OF PRACTICE: Additional to the Bill, this will set standards which unions and management should observe in their dealings with each other and with individual men and women. Not directly enforceable, it will operate largely as a code of good practice somewhat like much of the Highway Code.

INDIVIDUAL RIGHTS: More effective safeguards will protect individual rights. For the first time, everyone will have a clear legal right to join a union – or not to join a union. Again for the first time, everyone will have a clearly defined right to strike – or not to strike. There will be better contracts of employment, longer notice of dismissal, protection against unfair dismissal, and many employees will have a new right to information about their company's affairs.

COLLECTIVE BARGAINING: Agreements – including procedural agreements – will be made legally binding *unless* the agreement itself contains a clear statement to the contrary.

UNION RECOGNITION: Should an employer refuse to recognise a union, or where bargaining is serious fragmented by too many unions, an aggrieved union or employer will have channels of redress. Recognition claims will be probed by the Commission on Industrial Relations, whose recommendations could later be enforced if a majority of employees involved favoured them in a secret ballot.

'CLOSED SHOP' AND 'AGENCY SHOP': The 'pre-entry closed shop' is ruled out as a matter of principle – but so are 'free-riders'. Instead, unions and employers can agree to establish an 'agency shop' – in which individuals will have to join the union, *or* pay appropriate contributions to it, *or* pay to an agreed charity.

REGISTRATION: Only registered unions and employers' associations will enjoy the main rights set out in the Bill. A Registrar will ensure that their rules are in line with the standards laid down, and he will also have power to initiate investigations.

'COOLING-OFF' AND STRIKE BALLOTS: Before a major strike which might seriously threaten the essentials of life, national health, or the economy, the Secretary of State could apply for a 'cooling-off' period of up to 60 days, during which there would be an obligation on all parties to try to reach a settlement. In similar instances a secret ballot could be ordered to see if a majority of workers support a strike.

NEW SYSTEM OF COURTS: The National Industrial Relations Court will consist of presiding judges and lay industrial members. It will hear complaints about certain unfair industrial practices and procedures. Appeals from the NIRC – on points of law only – will be to the Court of Appeal. At the lower level will be the Industrial Tribunals – the principal role of which will be to consider cases on the rights and obligations of individuals. Appeals from the Tribunals will go to the NIRC.

ASSESSMENT OF COMPENSATION: Awards – if any – will be assessed by the NIRC or an [industrial tribunal]. In unfair dismissal cases, the maximum award will be two years' pay up to just over £4,000. For registered trade unions, compensation awards will be related to size of membership – less than 5,000 members, up to £5,000; 5,000 to 25,000 members, up to £100,000. In cases involving an official of a registered organisation, awards will be made against the organisation – not the official.

COMMISSION ON INDUSTRIAL RELATIONS: This will be put on a statutory basis, with powers to make enquiries, call and examine witnesses, etc. Industrial relations matters needing investigation could be referred to the Commission by the Secretary of State for Employment or the NIRC.

ARBITRATION AND CONCILIATION: The Secretary of State will retain his existing powers to arrange for conciliation, refer matters to arbitration, and to set up enquiries.

(4) Industrial Relations Bill, 1970: Introductory

1. – (1)   The provisions of this Act shall have effect for the purpose of promoting good industrial relations in accordance with the following general principles, that is to say, –

(a) the principle of collective bargaining freely and responsibly conducted;
(b) the principle of developing and maintaining orderly procedures in industry for the peaceful settlement of disputes by negotiation, conciliation or arbitration, with due regard to the general interests of the community;
(c) the principle of free association of workers in independent trade unions, and of employers in employers' associations, so organised as to be representative, responsible and effective bodies for regulating relations between employers and workers; and

(d) the principle of freedom and security for workers, protected by adequate safeguards against unfair industrial practices, whether on the part of employers or others.

(2) With a view to fulfilling that purpose those principles shall be regarded as guiding principles –

(a) by the Secretary of State, the Commission on Industrial Relations, and the Chief Registrar of Trade Unions and Employers' Associations, and assistant registrars, to be appointed under this Act, and
(b) by the National Industrial Relations Court to be established under this Act, and by Industrial tribunals, in the exercise of the jurisdiction conferred by or under this Act on that Court and on those tribunals.

2. – (1) It shall be the duty of the Secretary of State, before the end of the period of one year beginning with the passing of this Act, to prepare in draft a code of practice, containing such practical guidance as in the opinion of the Secretary of State would be helpful for the purpose specified in section 1 (1) of this Act.
(2) In preparing that code the Secretary of State shall in particular have regard to the need for providing practical guidance with respect to disclosure of information by employers, and with respect to the establishment and maintenance of effective means of information and communication at all levels between those who manage undertakings and the workers employed in them. . . .

4. A failure on the part of any person to observe any provision of a code of practice which is for the time being in force under this part of this Act shall not of itself render him liable to any proceedings: but in any proceedings before the Industrial Court or an industrial tribunal under this Act –

(a) any such code of practice shall be admissable in evidence, and
(b) any provision of such a code of practice which appears to the Court or tribunal to be relevant to any question arising in the proceedings shall be taken into account by the Court or tribunal in determining that question.

(5) TUC, *Report* (1971): Speech of Victor Feather, General Secretary

Congress made its attitude to the Industrial Relations Act abundantly clear at Croydon in March when it endorsed the General Council's seven Recommendations. . . .

The seven decisions add up to an attempt to ensure that the Act will be ineffective. Not because the trade union Movement is above or outside the law. But because we have the democratic right not to cooperate with the machinery of an Act which is abhorrent to all of us.

Congress has never been opposed to registration as such. Most unions are voluntarily registered under the 1871 Act. The Special Congress made it clear, however, that the trade union Movement is opposed to the kind of registration in the 1971 Act. I want to remind you why Congress took up this position.

It was because British trade unions are not prepared to hand themselves over to become a collection of state-licensed organisations subject to Government control.

Once a union is registered, it will become subject to the detailed and wide ranging powers of surveillance given to the Registrar. Such scrutiny is virtually without end: unions will be placed on the full register provided they are 'eligible' to be there, and only after that will changes be demanded in the rule book.

Changes might not be demanded by the Registrar for a considerable time after full registration. The Registrar has power, despite anything in the rule book, to override the customary provisions for rules revisions conferences. It cannot be forseen what the demands of the Registrar may be. Initially – and I have no doubt about this – they may be modest, but do not forget that the Act has political objectives. . . .

When this Bill was introduced we all knew that it was an attempt to weaken the trade union Movement. One of the most obvious things about registration is that it is a device to divide the Movement. To set one union against another. To make one union suspicious of what other unions are going to do.

(6) *P. J. O'Connor* (applicant) v. *Macpherson Bros (Wales) Ltd* (respondents), [1974] IRLR 306

The claimant is a young man of 22 years of age and has worked for the respondents, the company owning four supermarkets in this area, except for a break of some 12 months from 31. 7. 67. Clearly he was considered to be a young man of considerable ability and application because by May 1972 he was made the manager of one of the four stores. . . . Dissatisfaction with his conduct first became apparent in July 1973 when he returned from holiday and was found to be sporting – if that is the expression – a beard; albeit a beard it would seem of limited density. This and the fact he allowed his hair to grow below collar length excited the wrath of Mr Macpherson who for reasons which I have no doubt appeared sound to him was reluctant to allow his employees (the male employees I mean) to grow their hair to anything other that what might be called a strictly fashionable length; that is not below the collar. Mr Macpherson taxed him with the position, if not at that time; certainly quite soon afterwards. Mr O'Connor refused to shave off his beard or to shorten his hair, except as was put by Mr Macpherson in a 'token manner'. . . .

Ultimately he was given one month's notice of termination of his employment. . . .

Now hirsute appendages, although not everyone's idea of what is attractive, can hardly be a reason for dismissing a person from his livelihood in this day and age, unless of course, the safety of employees is imperilled and there can of course be no question of that in the present case. . . .

If all young men who indulge in this harmless conceit were dismissed for so doing the level of unemployment in this country would rise to astronomical heights. . . .

In those circumstances we cannot find that the respondents have discharged the undoubtedly onerous burden of proof which is placed upon them under s. 24 of the Act. Accordingly we propose to find for the claimant. . . .

We award the claimant the sum of £146 compensation for unfair dismissal. This sum is made up as follows:

1. Loss of earnings of one week. . . .
2. Notional loss of redundancy rights at the date of his dismissal. . . .
3. Estimated loss of earnings. . . .
4. Finally, once again as in the case of loss of redundancy rights, somewhat oddly, but this is established by authority, he has by reason of his dismissal sustained a notional loss in respect of a claim for unfair dismissal until two years have elapsed. . . .

Following the election of a Labour Government in 1974, the Industrial Relations Act was repealed. In its place an emasculated Trade Union and Labour Relations Act was passed (7), supported by a 'social contract' between Government and the TUC. Again, many unions still regarded this as an unwanted interference with free bargaining (8), and the miners and other unions quickly claimed to be 'special cases' (9).

(7) G. R. Rubin, 'The Pendulum Swings Again. The Trade Union and Labour Relations Act, 1974', *Journal of the Law Society of Scotland* (Dec. 1974)

By s 1(1) of the new Act, the Industrial Relations Act, 1971, is repealed. There are saving provisions in Schedule 1 to the 1974 Act . . . but the main thrust of the legislation is to dismantle the apparatus of the Industrial Relations Act and nearly all of its appurtenances. Thus, there are no longer registered trade unions or 'unregistered organisations of workers', although a particular body such as the Royal College of Nursing may be a 'special register body' (s 2(1)). There is no statutory provision for agency shop agreements, post-entry closed shop agreements, sole bargaining agents, emergency procedures, nor a presumption of legally enforceable collective agreements. The Commission on Industrial Relations and the Registry of Trade Unions and Employers' Associations have been wound up. Most significant, however, is that the National Industrial Relations Court is no more. . . .

Those elements of the 1971 Act retained in 1974 broadly fall into two categories. They are the Code of Industrial Relations Practice and the unfair dismissal provisions.

(8) AUEW (Engineering Section), *Journal* (Sept. 1974): Editorial by Hugh Scanlon

It was generally considered by the AUEW delegates that the General Council's report 'Collective Bargaining and the Social Contract' was really another name for wage restraint. Our Union has consistently opposed such restraint, whether voluntary or statutory, and it was thoroughly consistent with our National Conference policy that we could not vote in favour of the Social Contract. The present Labour Government was elected on a platform – among other things – of scrapping statutory wages policy and restoring free collective bargaining and it cannot honestly be said that the Social Contract is consistent with free negotiations. It was not a reversal of an election pledge but it was a variation with which our own Union's policy would not permit us to go along. . . .

In between the vote of the AUEW delegation opposing the Social Contract and the commencement of the Congress, some very unorthodox pressure was used to pressurise the Union into changing its position. . . .

The Social Contract is not really a contract at all. It is an assurance which the General Council has secured from Unions to restrict the size of their future claim to the increase in the cost of living since the previous settlement. There is no guarantee that employers will meet even this demand. . . .

Inflation must be solved, but this will never be achieved by wage restraint. All past attempts to do this have failed and the only result has been a cutting-back in the living standards of working people with an accompanying increase in profit levels and a further fall-off in investment. . . .

It was because the Social Contract outlined to the Congress said little or nothing about the paramount need to invest that the AUEW felt unable to vote for its acceptance. . . .

We very much regretted that the debate on the Social Contract should have taken place at all. It would have been far better had we waited until after the coming election when at least the political situation would have been resolved. . . . In view of all the present economic uncertainties we abstained on the TUC vote and, in doing so, we prevented those hostile to Labour from exploiting our genuine reservations on a matter of crucial significance to all working people.

If our decision not to vote against the Social Contract and to abide by the TUC decision helps the return of a Labour Government in any way whatsoever, then I think the AUEW has served the interests of the whole Labour Movement. . . .

If the Social Contract produces the electoral support Labour needs to carry out its promised fundamental changes in society, then the 1974 TUC will have earned a rightful place in history.

(9) Electrical, Electronic and Plumbing Trade Union, *Contact* (Feb. 1974): Article by Charles Lovell

Without a proper and thorough examination in depth of all trades, jobs and professions, I cannot agree that we can determine the place in any structure for one section of the work force.

There are many who claim equal if not greater right to a high place in such a structure. For instance, there are those who brave the elements to bring food to our shores . . . there are steel erectors, glaziers, window fixers and roofing fetters who work at terrifying heights . . . there are doctors, nurses and hospital workers who daily face the risks of disease. And what of those who have no means of drawing attention to their plight, such as the old age pensioners, the sick and infirm and others who can no longer do a job of any kind?

Meanwhile age-old problems still remained. Argument continued over the merits and hazards of the 'closed shop' (10) and there was a rising groundswell of interest in trade-union participation in management (11) and in workers' control (12). Studies continued to underline the need for new perspectives in modern industrial relations (13), and trade unions, while decreasing in number, continued to grow in membership (14, 15, 16).

(10) *Financial Times* (27 Nov. 1974): Closed shops

To understand this, one needs to go back to the years prior to the 1971 [Industrial Relations] Act, when closed shops were perfectly legal and flourished in a number of forms, many of them informal without any written agreement underpinning them, covering all or just part of an industry, company or factory. Basically, they divided into two main types – the pre-entry closed shop, where a man must have a union card before he can get a job, and the post-entry shop (sometimes called the union shop or 100 per cent trade unionism) where a worker has to join the union after he has been taken on. . . .

Formal post-entry closed shops were agreed during this period [1968–71] by three nationalised industries. In almost every case the closed shop followed management initiative rather than union pressure. This underlines the fact that managements like closed shops – although they may think differently now they are spreading to the higher white-collar ranks – because they help to stabilise labour relationships, help to avoid inter-union friction, and make it easier to operate and ease the 'check-off' system under which union dues are deducted from workers' wage packets. . . .

Where managements do resist closed shops, it is hardly ever on grounds of individual liberty or rights of choice. As happened quite often under the I. R. Act, managements would frequently rather send a man home on full pay or switch him around a factory rather than face upsetting closed shop conditions.

Generally, however, companies – along with most other interested parties – do not like pre-entry closed shops, although it has sometimes been argued that this system, where a union has to issue a union card *prior* to employment, can give the union a useful labour-market controlling role.

(11) Ron Smith, 'The Future of Employee Directors', *British Steel* (April 1972)

The employee director's role is to ensure that divisional boards are aware of the ideas and beliefs held by work-people and that the decisions taken following board discussions are informed by a knowledge and understanding of these ideas. At the same time, he will learn from the professional manager of the commercial, operational and other factors which influence decisions – and can thus contribute these points of view to shop floor.

. . . throughout industry there is taking place what I have seen best described as an 'explosion of men's expectations'. This is finding expression in many ways, including an increasing interest amongst workpeople in the running of the enterprise in which they 'invest' their labour – often for a lifetime. . . . The reasons for the trend are not hard to find: the economic uncertainty, mergers, and pace of change give sound cause for all employees to question their livelihoods, and the increasing level of education – both in the formal sense of schooling and the extra-mural information conveyed by mass-media – provide tools which are new to industry for questioning managers' behaviour. . . .

No system of employee directors is going to satisfy that 'explosion of men's expectations'. We have to recognise that these expectations are changing, that increasing education and knowledge are making men more capable of undertaking greater responsibility. . . .

The vital need in a healthy corporation is for men's expectations to be known and understood on the one hand, and for the external influences on the corporation to be understood by its workpeople.

(12) K. Coates and T. Topham, *The New Unionism. The Case for Workers' Control* (1972).

The term 'workers' control' has the advantage of being clear-cut when compared with 'participation'. 'Workers' control' emphasizes that the purpose of the policy and strategy should be to establish control, by workers over the hitherto unfettered decisions of the ruling party in industry, namely the employers and their managers. In this sense (which is not to be confused with the full industrial democracy possible in a socialized society, where 'self management' is the more appropriate term) the germs of workers' control exist, in greater or lesser degree, wherever strong independent trade-union and shop-floor powers act to restrain employers in the exercise of their so-called 'prerogatives'. When shop stewards operate their own overtime roster, or when they regulate, however informally, the speed of work, or when shop-floor strength and action prevent the carrying out of an arbitrary dismissal, there workers' control is being exercised. In this sense workers' control always exists in a conflict situation. . . . Seen in this light, workers' control is not something which is either established or not: it varies in degree and scope according to the circumstances of particular times and places, industries and occupations.

(13) Alan Fox, *Industrial Sociology and Industrial Relations*, RC on Trade Unions and Employers' Associations, Research Paper no. 3 (1966)

Much public discussion focuses wholly upon the role of unions in relation to the periodic fixing of wages, and a good deal of effort goes into trying to establish that collective bargaining has not significantly increased the share of the national income going to wages and salaries, and that wage rates in given industries would have risen by the same amount even had the labour markets remained unregulated.

A pluralistic frame of reference recognises that this is quite inadequate. The legitimacy and justification of trade unions in our society rests not upon their protective function in labour markets or upon their success, real or supposed, in raising the share enjoyed by their members, but on social values which recognise the right of interest groups to combine and have an effective voice in their own destiny. This means having a voice in decision-making. Now clearly decisions about wage rates are of great importance to wage-earners. But the public's preoccupation with the union's economic role in labour markets has meant that an even more important role has been neglected and insufficiently understood. This is the role of union organisation within the workplace itself in regulating *managerial* relations, i.e. the exercise of management authority in deploying, organising, and disciplining the labour force after it has been hired. The value of the pluralistic reference is that it both focuses our attention upon this crucial union role and illuminates the ground upon which union legitimacy rests – its character as a representative institution which participates with management in a process of joint decision-making in issues of day-to-day management. It is the *method* that is valued here, not necessarily the *results*. This point is important, for if it could be proved that management would make the same decisions in the absence of organized labour then a justification which rests on results would be nullified and trade unionism would be proved superfluous.

(14) *Department of Employment Gazette* (Nov. 1974): 'Membership of Trade Unions at End–1973'

Number of members	Number of unions	Total membership*	Percentage of Total number of all unions	Percentage of Total membership of all unions
Under 100	80	4,000	16·2	0·0
100–499	124	31,000	25·1	0·3
500–999	49	35,000	9·9	0·3
1,000–2,499	75	115,000	15·2	1·0
2,500–4,999	47	160,000	9·5	1·4
5,000–9,999	35	232,000	7·1	2·0
10,000–14,999	11	129,000	2·2	1·1
15,000–24,999	18	335,000	3·6	2·9
25,000–49,999	18	624,000	3·6	5·4
50,000–99,999	14	997,000	2·8	8·7
100,000–249,999	13	1,810,000	2·6	15·7
250,000 and above	11	7,035,000	2·2	61·2
Total	495	11,507,000	100	100

* Figures rounded to nearest thousand.

(15) TUC *Report 1972*: Affiliated societies.

Name of society	Number of delegates	Number of members
GROUP 1. MINING AND QUARRYING		
1. Colliery Oversmen, Deputies and Shotfirers, National Association of	5	22,663
2. Mineworkers, National Union of	56	271,089
GROUP 2. RAILWAYS		
1. Locomotive Engineers and Firemen, Associated Society of	6	28,834
2. Railwaymen, National Union of	18	193,924
3. Transport Salaried Staffs' Association	16	75,163
GROUP 3. TRANSPORT (OTHER THAN RAILWAYS)		
1. British Air Line Pilots' Association	1	4,178
2. Engineers' and Firemen's Union, Grimsby Steam and Diesel Fishing Vessels	–	200
3. Merchant Navy and Air Line officers' Association	5	21,000
4. Radio and Electronic Officers' Union	1	3,214
5. Seamen, National Union of	7	50,000
6. Transport and General Workers' Union	74	1,643,134
7. Transport Union, the United Road	5	20,475
GROUP 4. SHIPBUILDING		
1. Boilermakers, Shipwrights, Blacksmiths and Structural Workers, Amalgamated Society of	12	123;248
2. Iron, Steel and Wood Barge Builders' and Helpers' Association	1	446

Name of society	Number of delegates	Number of members
GROUP 5. ENGINEERING, FOUNDING AND VEHICLE BUILDING		
1. Domestic Appliance and General Metal Workers, National Union of	2	6,025
2. Engineering Workers, Amalgamated Union of, Engineering Section	35	1,194,628
Construction Section	5	27,435
Foundry Section	13	62,318
3. Metal Mechanics, National Society of	7	45,215
4. Metalworkers' Society, Associated	1	5,560
5. Military and Orchestral Musical Instrument Makers' Trade Society	–	145
6. Patternmakers and Allied Craftsmen, Association of	3	11,771
7. Scalemakers, National Union of	1	2,300
8. Screw, Nut, Bolt and Rivet Trade Society	1	2,524
9. Sheet Metal Workers, Coppersmiths, Heating and Domestic Engineers, National Union of	12	77,376
10. Sheet Metal Workers' Society, Birmingham and Midland	2	8,678
11. Shuttlemakers, Society of	–	160
12. Vehicle Builders, National Union of	14	79,687
GROUP 6. TECHNICAL ENGINEERING AND SCIENTIFIC		
1. Building Technicians, Association of	1	2,125
2. Electrical Power Engineers' Association	4	30,069
3. Engineer Surveyors' Association	1	2,201
4. Engineering Workers, Amalgamated Union of Technical and Supervisory Section	18	101,346
5. Scientific, Technical and Managerial Staffs, Association of	20	252,100
GROUP 7. ELECTRICITY		
1. Electrical, Electronic and Plumbing Union	33	419,646
GROUP 8. IRON AND STEEL AND MINOR METAL TRADES		
1. Blastfurnacemen, Ore Miners, Coke Workers and Kindred Trades, The National Union of	4	17,281
2. Chain Makers and Strikers' Association	–	238
3. Gold, Silver and Allied Trades, National Union of	1	3,539
4. Iron and Steel Trades Confederation	22	108,071
5. Laminated and Coil Spring Workers' Union	1	240
6. Lock and Metal Workers, National Union of	2	5,475
7. Roll Turners' Trade Society, British	1	984
8. Sawmakers' Protection Society	–	300
9. Spring Trapmakers' Society	1	90
10. Wire Drawers and Kindred Workers, The Amalgamated Society of	3	12,268
11. Wool, Shear Workers' Trade Union, Sheffield	–	20
GROUP 9. BUILDING, WOODWORKING AND FURNISHING		
1. Asphalt Workers, The Amalgamated Union of	1	2,924
2. Basket, Cane, Wicker & Fibre Furniture Makers of Great Britain and Ireland, The National Union of	–	48
3. Construction, Allied Trades & Technicians, Union of	36	260,490
4. Coopers' Federation of Great Britain	–	1,700
5. Funeral Service Operatives, National Union of	1	1,065
6. Furniture, Timber & Allied Trades Union	12	83,894
7. Sign and Display Trades Union	1	4,157

Name of society	Number of delegates	Number of members
GROUP 10. PRINTING AND PAPER		
1. Graphical and Allied Trades, Society of	22	183,276
2. Graphical Association, National	–	102,868
3. Journalists, National Union of	5	26,792
4. Lithographic Artists, Designers, Engravers and Process Workers, Society of	4	16,541
5. Printers, Graphical and Media Personnel, National Society of Operative	10	50,587
6. Typographical Association, Scottish	2	50,587
7. Wall Paper Workers' Union	1	4,010
GROUP 11. TEXTILES		
1. Beamers, Twisters and Drawers (Hand and Machine), Amalgamated Association of	1	1,534
2. Card Setting Machine Tenters' Society	1	168
3. Carpet Trade Union, Northern	1	2,154
4. Cloth Pressers' Society	1	120
5. Dyers, Bleachers and Textile Workers, National Union of	11	51,991
6. Engravers, United Society of	1	478
7. Healders and Twisters' Trade and Friendly Society, Huddersfield	1	240
8. Jute, Flax and Kindred Textile Operatives, Union of	1	3,380
9. Loom Overlookers, The General Union of Associations of	1	3,588
10. Machine Calico Printers, Trade Society of	–	430
11. Managers and Overlookers' Society	1	1,843
12. Pattern Weavers' Society	1	200
13. Power Loom Carpet Weavers and Textile Workers' Association	1	4,875
14. Powerloom Overlookers, Scottish Union of	1	340
15. Power Loom Overlookers, Yorkshire Association of	–	1,808
16. Spinners and Twiners, The Amalgamated Association of Operative Cotton	1	1,174
17. Textile and Allied Workers, National Union of	5	24,110
18. Textile Craftsmen, Yorkshire Society of	1	1,006
19. Textile Warehousemen, Amalgamated	1	4,026
20. Textile Workers and Kindred Trades, Amalgamated Society of	2	6,674
21. Warpdressers, Twisters and Kindred Trades Associations, Leeds and District	–	121
22. Weavers' Association, Amalgamated	6	27,852
23. Weavers and Woollen Textile Workers' Association, Saddleworth and District	1	1,333
24. Wool Sorters' Society, National	1	1,076
GROUP 12. CLOTHING, LEATHER AND BOOT AND SHOE		
1. Boot, Shoe and Slipper Operatives, Rossendale Union of	2	5,837
2. Felt Hatters & Allied Workers, Amalgamated Society of Journeymen	–	840
3. Felt Hat Trimmers & Wool Formers, Amalgamated Association	–	752
4. Footwear, Leather & Allied Trades, National Union of	16	78,176
5. Hosiery & Knitwear Workers, National Union of	10	64,372
6. Tailors and Garment Workers, National Union of	16	113,615
GROUP 13. GLASS, CERAMICS, CHEMICALS, FOOD, DRINK, TOBACCO, BRUSHMAKING AND DISTRIBUTION		
1. Bakers' Union, The	10	46,471
2. Bakers and Allied Workers, Scottish Union of	3	1,163
3. Blind and Disabled, The National League of	1	4,000
4. Brushmakers, National Society of	–	2,575

Name of society	Number of delegates	Number of members
5. Ceramic and Allied Trades Union	8	35,815
6. Cigarette Machine Operators' Society	1	390
7. Co-operative Officials, National Association of	–	6,241
8. Retail Book, Stationery and Allied Trades Employees' Association, The	1	3,580
9. Shop, Distributive and Allied Workers, Union of	37	319,372
10. Tobacco Workers' Union, The	4	19,897

GROUP 14. AGRICULTURE

1. Agriculture and Allied Workers, National Union of	16	90,000

GROUP 15. PUBLIC EMPLOYEES

1. Fire Brigades' Union, The	6	30,000
2. Greater London Council Staff Association	4	15,190
3. Health Service Employees, Confederation of	8	102,554
4. Health Visitors' Association	2	5,995
5. Medical Practitioners' Union	2	5,502
6. National and Local Government Officers' Association	41	463,798
7. Public Employees, National Union of	25	397,085
8. Schoolmasters, National Association of	10	67,964
9. Teachers, National Union of	29	277,176
10. Teachers in Technical Institutions, Association of	6	36,550

GROUP 16. CIVIL SERVICE

1. Civil and Public Services Association	30	188,085
2. Civil Service Union	7	38,418
3. Court Officers' Association	2	5,213
4. Government Supervisors and Radio Officers, Association of	3	10,495
5. Inland Revenue Staff Federation	9	50,175
6. Ministry of Labour Staff Association	4	17,307
7. Post Office Engineering Union	15	119,855
8. Post Office Executives, Association of	4	15,108
9. Post Office Management Staffs Association	4	16,142
10. Post Office Workers, Union of	15	192,255
11. Prison Officers' Association	3	14,782

GROUP 17. PROFESSIONAL, CLERICAL AND ENTERTAINMENT

1. Actors' Equity Association, British incorporating The Variety Artistes' Federation	3	19,495
2. Bank Employees, National Union of	5	92,603
3. Broadcasting Staff, Association of	3	11,401
4. Cinematograph, Television and Allied Technicians, The Association of	4	70,183
5. Film Artistes Association, The	–	1,961
6. Insurance Workers, National Union of	8	35,022
7. Musicians' Union	7	32,958
8. Professional, Executive, Clerical and Computer Staff, Association of	13	118,388
9. Professional Footballers, and Trainers Association	–	2,160
10. Theatrical, Television and Kine Employees, The National Association of	4	16,811
11. Writers' Guild of Great Britain	–	1,692

GROUP 18. GENERAL WORKERS

1. General and Municipal Workers, National Union of	65	841,524
2. Rubber Plastic and Allied Workers	1	4,392

(16) Membership of trade unions 1892–1972, HMSO, *British Labour Statistics Historical Abstract 1886–1968* (1971); *British Labour Statistics: Year Book 1975* (1977); *Dept of Employment Gazette* (November 1977)

	Number of trade unions at end of year	Membership at end of year (thousands)		
		Males	Females	Total
1892	1233	–	–	1576
1893	1279	–	–	1559
1894	1314	–	–	1530
1895	1340	–	–	1504
1896	1358	1466	142	1608 000
1897	1353	1584	147	1731
1898	1326	1608	144	1752
1899	1325	1761	150	1911
1900	1323	1868	154	2022
1901	1322	1873	152	2025
1902	1297	1857	156	2013
1903	1285	1838	156	1994
1904	1256	1802	165	1967
1905	1244	1817	180	1997
1906	1282	1999	211	2210
1907	1283	2263	250	2513
1908	1268	2230	255	2485
1909	1260	2214	263	2477
1910	1269	2287	278	2565
1911	1290	2804	335	3139
1912	1252	3026	390	3416
1913	1269	3702	433	4135
1914	1260	3708	437	4145
1915	1229	3868	491	4359
1916	1225	4018	626	4644
1917	1241	4621	878	5499
1918	1264	5324	1209	6533
1919	1360	6600	1326	7926
1920	1384	7006	1342	8348
1921	1275	5628	1005	6633
1922	1232	4753	872	5625
1923	1192	4607	822	5429
1924	1194	4730	814	5544
1925	1176	4671	835	5506
1926	1164	4407	812	5219
1927	1159	4125	794	4919
1928	1142	4011	795	4806
1929	1133	4056	802	4858
1930	1121	4049	793	4842
1931	1108	3859	765	4624
1932	1081	3698	746	4444
1933	1081	3661	731	4392
1934	1063	3854	736	4590
1935	1049	4106	761	4867
1936	1036	4405	800	5295
1937	1032	4947	895	5842
1938	1024	5127	926	6053

	Number of trade unions at end of year	Membership at end of year (thousands)		
		Males	Females	Total
1939	1019	5288	1010	6298
1940	1004	5494	1119	6613
1941	996	5753	1412	7165
1942	991	6151	1716	7867
1943	987	6258	1916	8174
1944	963	6239	1848	8087
1945	781	6237	1638	7875
1946	757	7186	1617	8803
1947	734	7483	1662	9145
1948	749	7677	1685	9362
1949	742	7644	1674	9318
1950	732	7605	1684	9289
1951	735	7745	1790	9535
1952	723	7797	1792	9588
1953	720	7749	1778	9527
1954	711	7756	1810	9566
1955	704	7874	1867	9741
1956	685	7871	1907	9778
1957	685	7935	1894	9829
1958	675	7789	1850	9639
1959	668	7756	1868	9623
1960	664	7884	1951	9835
1961	655	7911	2005	9916
1962	649	7960	2054	10,014
1963	643	7963	2104	10,067
1964	641	8043	2174	10,218
1965	630	8084	2241	10,325
1966	622	8006	2256	10,261
1967	603	7905	2285	10,190
1968	584	7831	2361	10,193
1969	563	7968	2504	10,472
1970	540	8440	2740	11,179
1971	523	8378	2750	11,128
1972	503	8449	2904	11,353
1973	513	8446	3003	11,449
1974	498	8582	3174	11,756
1975	488	8508	3442	11,950
1976	462	8816	3560	12,376

Index